The Revels Plays
COMPANION
LIBRARY

E. A. J. HONIGMANN former editor
J. R. MULRYNE, R. L. SMALLWOOD and PETER CORBIN general editors

For over thirty years *The Revels Plays* have offered the most authoritative editions of Elizabethan and Jacobean plays by authors other than Shakespeare. The *Companion Library* provides a fuller background to the main series by publishing worthwhile dramatic and non-dramatic material that will be essential for the serious student of the period.

Drama of the English Republic, 1649–60

MANCHESTER
UNIVERSITY PRESS

THE REVELS PLAYS COMPANION LIBRARY

Drama of the English Republic, 1649–60

Janet Clare

Manchester University Press

Manchester and New York

distributed exclusively in the USA by Palgrave

Published by Manchester University Press
Oxford Road, Manchester M13 9NR, UK
and Room 400, 175 Fifth Avenue, New York, NY 10010, USA
www.manchesteruniversitypress.co.uk

Distributed exclusively in the USA by
Palgrave, 175 Fifth Avenue, New York,
NY 10010, USA

Distributed exclusively in Canada by
UBC Press, University of British Columbia, 2029 West Mall,
Vancouver, BC, Canada V6T 1Z2

British Library Cataloguing-in-Publication Data
A catalogue record for this book is available from the British Library

Library of Congress Cataloging-in-Publication Data applied for

ISBN 0 7190 4482 0 *hardback*

First published 2002

10 09 08 07 06 05 04 03 02   10 9 8 7 6 5 4 3 2 1

Typeset in Sabon by
SNP Best-set Typesetter Ltd., Hong Kong

Printed in Great Britain
by Bookcraft (Bath) Ltd. Midsomer Norton

For John, Timothy and Robin

CONTENTS

ILLUSTRATIONS

GENERAL EDITORS' PREFACE

Since the late 1950s the series known as The Revels Plays has provided for students of the English Renaissance drama carefully edited texts of the major Elizabethan and Jacobean plays. The series includes some of the best-known drama of the period and has continued to expand, both within its original field and, to a lesser extent, beyond it, to include some important plays from the earlier Tudor and from the Restoration periods. The Revels Plays Companion Library is intended to further this expansion and to allow for new developments.

The aim of the Companion Library is to provide students of the Elizabethan and Jacobean drama with a fuller sense of its background and context. The series includes volumes of a variety of kinds. Small collections of plays, by a single author or concerned with a single theme and edited in accordance with the principles of textual modernisation of The Revels Plays, offer a wider range of drama than the main series can include. Together with editions of masques, pageants and the non-dramatic work of Elizabethan and Jacobean playwrights, these volumes make it possible, within the overall Revels enterprise, to examine the achievements of the major dramatists from a broader perspective. Other volumes provide a fuller context for the plays of the period by offering new collections of documentary evidence on Elizabethan theatrical conditions and on the performance of plays during that period and later. A third aim of the series is to offer modern critical interpretation, in the form of collections of essays or of monographs, of the dramatic achievement of the English Renaissance.

So wide a range of material necessarily precludes the standard format and uniform general editorial control which is possible in the original series of Revels Plays. To a considerable extent, therefore, treatment and approach is determined by the needs and intentions of individual volume editors. Within this rather ampler area, however, we hope that the Companion Library maintains the standards of scholarship that have for so long characterised The Revels Plays, and that it offers a useful enlargement of the work of the series in preserving, illuminating and celebrating the drama of Elizabethan and Jacobean England.

J. R. MULRYNE
R. L. SMALLWOOD
PETER CORBIN

PREFACE

This book focuses on drama and its production during the period when England was nominally a commonwealth or republic. While recent studies of dramatic activity through the civil wars and their settlement have revised the familiar view that with the closure of the theatres in 1642 the drama was dead, few of the dramatic texts which were written, and in some instances performed, during the 1650s exist in modern editions. One aim of this edition is to make accessible those works which were authorized for performance and which negotiate ideological preoccupations of the English Republic. In the anonymous *The Tragedy of that Famous Roman Orator Marcus Tullius Cicero*, the classical history play for the first time exemplifies republican values. James Shirley in *Cupid and Death* detaches the masque from its accustomed court setting while Davenant in *The Siege of Rhodes*, *The Cruelty of the Spaniards in Peru* and *The History of Sir Francis Drake* produces an innovatory and hybrid drama for distinct nationalistic purposes. In keeping with the general aims of the Revels Plays Companion Library, and to some extent departing from the more ideological premises of other studies of the drama of the Commonwealth, I have attempted to keep in focus the theatrical dimension not only of the edited texts but also of those plays discussed in the General Introduction. The Introduction offers an overview both of censorship and performance and of the genres, intertextualities and dynamics of dramatic writing during the period when it was forced into opposition.

This study is much indebted to earlier work on the subject of civil war and Commonwealth drama by Lois Potter, Susan Wiseman, Dale Randall and Nigel Smith. Lois Potter's excellent chapter on the plays and playwrights of the period 1642–60 in volume four of the *Revels History of Drama in English* is an essential starting point for any appreciation of the scope of dramatic writing during these years. In preparing this book, particularly in the final stages, I have incurred many debts. It soon became apparent that in editing *The Tragedy of that Famous Roman Orator Marcus Tullius Cicero* more specialist knowledge was required. I am most grateful to Llewelyn Morgan, Tutor in Classics, Brasenose College, Oxford, who acted as co-editor of the play. I would like to thank Cate Knowles, whose early assistance with the transcriptions of the texts was invaluable. Without the technical and editorial skills of Emer McManus the final text could not have been produced. Martin Butler, Declan Kiberd, Alan Marshall and Alan Fletcher read sections of the book and offered much helpful and encouraging comment. Susan Wiseman generously shared her ideas and knowledge of the period. Anthony Miller kindly passed on research on sixteenth-century editions of *Cicero*. Jim Binns assisted with Latin translation. Andrew Gurr, John Jowett and Declan Downey helpfully responded to my queries.

I am very grateful to the General Editor, Peter Corbin, for the care and goodwill with which he has read and commented on more than one version of the typescript. Matthew Frost at Manchester University Press has shown great forbearance and good humour in dealing with the delays in this project.

I am indebted to John Banks, who has been an exemplary copy-editor. I would like to acknowledge the help I have received from the librarians of University College Dublin, from Robin Adams of Trinity College Dublin, from Peter Day, Keeper of Collections at the Chatsworth Settlement, and from the librarians and staff of the Reading Room of Early Printed Books and Music of the British Library. I am grateful to Keith Wakefield of Stainer and Bell for allowing me to reproduce in Appendix 1 a song from *Cupid and Death*. Janet Birkett of the Theatre Museum, Covent Garden, kindly assisted in locating reviews of the performance of *Cupid and Death*. Part of the Introduction to *The Cruelty of the Spaniards in Peru* first appeared in *Modern Language Review* (89:4), 1994, 832–41. I am grateful to the editor, Dr Nicola Bradbury, for allowing me to republish this material.

It is with heartfelt thanks that I acknowledge the support and advice of family and friends. My mother, as always, gave more than generously with her time. Emer McManus offered much moral support as well as invaluable assistance with research. To the late Douglas Jefferson, friend and mentor, I will always be indebted. John Gallagher helped to sustain this project when it faltered. To him and our two sons this book is dedicated.

REFERENCES AND ABBREVIATIONS

Few of the plays discussed in the Introduction exist in modern editions. For the pamphlet plays included in the collection of publications compiled from 1641 to 1661 by the London bookseller George Thomason, held in the British Library, I have given in the notes British Library pressmarks (beginning with E) and numbers from Donald Wing's *Short-Title Catalogue, 1641–1700*. Both collections are available on microfilm. References to Shakespeare's plays are to Alexander's *Complete Works* and those to other Renaissance dramatists are to the Revels editions where available. Classical references are taken from Loeb editions. Unless otherwise stated (see p. 270 n. 15), I have modernized spelling, including the titles of dramatic and non-dramatic works. Old-style dates have been altered to conform with the modern calendar year.

In the commentary and textual collation the following abbreviations have been used.

EDITIONS

Cicero   Anon, *The Tragedy of that Famous Roman Orator Marcus Tullius Cicero* (1651).
Cupid and Death   James Shirley, *Cupid and Death* (1653).
Drake   William Davenant, *The History of Sir Francis Drake* (1659).
Harris   *Cupid and Death*, edited by Bernard Harris, *A Book of Masques* edited by T. J. B. Spencer and S. W. Wells (Cambridge, 1967).
Hedbäck   *1 and 2 Siege of Rhodes*, edited by Ann-Mari Hedbäck (Studia Anglistica Upsaliensia, 14, Uppsala, 1973).
Peru   William Davenant, *The Cruelty of the Spaniards in Peru* (1658).
Rhodes   William Davenant, *The Siege of Rhodes* (1656).

GENERAL

Actors' Remonstrance   *The Actors' Remonstrance or Complaint for the Silencing of their Profession and Banishment from their Several Playhouses* (1644).
Chew   Samuel C. Chew, *The Crescent and the Rose: Islam and England During the Renaissance* (New York, 1937).
CSPD   Calendar of State Papers, Domestic Series.
Feinberg   Anat Feinberg, 'Like Demie Gods the Apes Began to Move', *Cahiers Elizabethains*, 5:35 (1989), 1–13.
First Day's Entertainment   William Davenant, *The First Day's Entertainment at Rutland House* (1656).
Harbage and Schoenbaum   Alfred Harbage and S. Schoenbaum, *Annals of English Drama 975–1700*, third edition, revised by Sylvia Stoler Wagonheim (London and New York, 1989).

Knolles   Richard Knolles, *The General History of the Turks*, fourth edition, 1631.

Las Casas   Bartolomé de las Casas, *The Devastation of the Indies: A Brief Account*, trans. Herma Briffault with an introduction by Bill M. Donovan (Baltimore and London, 1992).

Love's Dominion   Richard Flecknoe, *Love's Dominion: A Dramatic Piece full of Excellent Morality Written as a Pattern for the Reformed Stage* (1654).

McKerrow   *The Works of Thomas Nash*, edited by R. B. McKerrow, 5 vols (Oxford, 1966).

Nichols   Philip Nichols, *Sir Francis Drake Revived* (London, 1628) in I. A. Wright, *Documents Concerning English Voyages to the Spanish Main 1569–1580*, Hakluyt Society (Liechtenstein, 1967).

OED   *Oxford English Dictionary*.

Orrell   John Orrell, *The Theatres of Inigo Jones and John Webb* (Cambridge, 1985).

Pepys   *The Diary of Samuel Pepys*, edited by Robert Latham and William Matthews, 11 vols (1970–83).

Potter   Lois Potter, 'The Plays and the Playwrights 1642–60' in *The Revels History of Drama in English, vol. IV, 1613–1660*, edited by Philip Edwards, Gerald Eades Bentley, Kathleen McLuskie and Lois Potter (London and New York, 1981).

Purchas   Samuel Purchas, *Purchas His Pilgrims* (London, 1625).

Tilley   M. P. Tilley, *A Dictionary of the Proverbs in England in the Sixteenth and Seventeenth Centuries* (1950).

Wind   Edgar Wind, *Pagan Mysteries in the Renaissance* (London, 1958).

Wing   Donald Wing, *Short-Title Catalogue of Books Printed in England, Scotland, Ireland, Wales, and British America and of English Books printed in Other Countries 1641–1700*, second edition, 3 vols (New York, 1972–94).

Winn   James Anderson Winn, *John Dryden and his World* (New Haven, 1987).

Wiseman   Susan Wiseman, *Drama and Politics in the English Civil War* (Cambridge, 1998).

GENERAL
INTRODUCTION
The theatre and cultural revolution

And it is Counsel now to fight the times,
Not in pitcht Prose, but Verse, and flying rhymes.
'Tis safe too: for the Poet (as men say)
Can forfeit nothing but some woods of Bay.[1]

The parliamentary prohibition of playing in 1642 has served as a useful boundary for studies of Renaissance drama. In the revolutionary context of events, this particular periodization would seem to have greater legitimacy than most such literary/historical delimitations. Renaissance theatre practice, with its indoor and outdoor theatre producing a regular repertoire of new and revived plays and employing well-established dramatic conventions, would seem to have terminated with the closure of the playhouses. The drama which had begun with the output of Kyd, Marlowe and Shakespeare, amongst others, was, when revived at the Restoration, of an altogether different character. Yet, we know that anti-theatrical measures imposed during the 1640s and continued during the 1650s were not as absolute as they may have appeared.[2] Plays were performed surreptitiously as part of an oppositional culture in a variety of venues.[3] Moreover, dramatic works produced between the two 'monoliths' of Renaissance and Restoration represent far more than the survival of drama in attenuated form. The novel and curious phenomenon of a royalist culture in opposition produced both a striking adaptability in the theatrical organism, able to contain current events, folk celebrations and pamphleteers, and the negotiation of innovatory theatrical aesthetics and techniques designed to appeal to the ethos of the Republic. Such developments will be addressed in this book.

In the texts included in this volume, the focus is on those works performed during the 1650s which tended in various ways to mediate the ideologies of the Commonwealth or which, in the case of the anonymous *Tragedy of that Famous Roman Orator Marcus Tullius Cicero*, promoted or reinforced republican values. *The Siege of Rhodes*, *The Cruelty of the Spaniards in Peru* and *The History of Sir Francis Drake*, all composed by William Davenant, and *Cupid and Death* by James Shirley demonstrate how former court dramatists were striving to work within the cultural and aesthetic parameters of the newly modelled godly Commonwealth led by Oliver Cromwell. The works of Davenant and Shirley were exceptional in that they were performed not illicitly, but with official sanction. The performance of *Cupid and Death* before the Portugese ambassador in 1653 marked a significant shift away from the anti-theatrical mentality of the Republic. In *The Siege of Rhodes* (1656), Davenant initiated a theatrical revival which was at the same time innovatory in technique. While evincing a continued experimentation in dramatic form, *The Cruelty of the Spaniards in Peru* and *The History of Sir Francis Drake* endorsed the imperial expansionist policy of the Protectorate. Yet these productions cannot be treated in isolation. The resistance of playwrights, players, patrons and audiences to the suppression of drama during the previous decade, as well as a continuing fascination with the forbidden on the part of those who outlawed it, ensured that theatre never disappeared from view and undoubtedly facilitated its limited revival in the 1650s. The proliferation of pamphlet plays engaged with contemporary events, the shaping of closet dramas as interventions in the cause of the Stuarts and the composition of ideologically nuanced tragicomedies meant the continuation of drama as a significant political medium. Within the scope of this introduction it would not be possible to allude to every play written during the 1650s. I have attempted to locate the diverse forms of dramatic writing and to discuss those texts which most evidently illustrate a theme of this book: the interaction of politics and dramatic aesthetics.

Theatre, of all public forums, would seem to have been singled out for repression by the Parliamentarians. The reasons for this are not hard to surmise. Theatrical production from its beginnings had associations with monarchs, courts and aristocratic patronage. On the other hand, public playhouses had always been warily regarded as places of mass gathering and of potential riot and disturbance. Then, there was the prejudice of Puritan reformers against theatrical practice, which had its roots in the anti-theatre polemic of the 1580s. In contrast, as the work of literary historians has shown, the period saw an unprecedented expansion of print culture. The age of the newspaper was born, parliamentary speeches were published and circulated, tracts and treatises on government were read by members of all parties. The writing and reading of poetry became much more of an intense political act.[4] Many old plays were published for the first time, including a number of plays contained in the handsome folio edition of the plays of Beaumont and Fletcher in 1647. It is through the ready availability of newspapers, political skits circulating in cheap pamphlet form, sermons, collections of plays and treatises on the stage that we can attempt a partial reconstruction of dramatic and theatrical activities during the English civil wars and Republic and an exploration of how the political helped to define the aesthetic.

THE PERFORMANCE OF PLAYS

It might reasonably be assumed that the outbreak of civil war in 1642 followed by the subsequent establishment of a commonwealth or republic in 1649 resulted in a virtual hiatus in dramatic activity. On 2 September 1642, just nine days after Charles I had raised his standard at Nottingham, it was decreed that public sports and playgoing should be for the moment suspended:

> Whereas the distressed estate of Ireland, steeped in her own blood, and the distracted estate of England, threatened with a cloud of blood by a civil war, call for all possible means to appease and avert the wrath of God, appearing in these judgements ... and whereas public sports do not well agree with public calamities, nor public stage-plays with the seasons of humiliation, this being an exercise of sad and pious solemnity, and the other being spectacles of pleasure, too commonly expressing lascivious mirth and levity. It is therefore thought fit, and ordained, by the Lords and Commons in this Parliament assembled, that while these sad causes and set times of humiliation do continue, public stage plays shall cease and be forborne.[5]

In its attempt to eradicate ungodly leisure pursuits, the Order seems to represent the triumph of the Puritan anti-theatrical view which throughout the decades since the establishment of professional theatre had been articulated in the writings of Stephen Gosson, Philip Stubbes, William Rackin and William Prynne and others.[6] Indeed, the wording of the Order recalls briefly the familiar negative associations of theatricality, as do later ordinances against the theatre. Nevertheless, the prohibition is not as absolute as it may appear. It contains no reference to actual closure of theatres, and the qualification 'while these sad causes and set times of humiliation do continue' implies that the measures are temporary. The injunction is less an expression of anti-theatrical polemic than a pragmatic expedient, impelled by the exigencies of a country at war. Given the nature of the political crisis in 1642, the decision to prohibit public theatre performance would seem unremarkable.

The context for all dramatic production during the ensuing years is that of theatre censorship enshrined in the acts and ordinances of the Commonwealth. But the defiance of Puritan social reform which is manifest in maypole dancing and the preservation of traditional sports and festivals[7] was also represented in the continuation of illicit theatre performance in which actors and audiences colluded. Following the close of the first civil war in 1646, groups of actors began to resume performance in overt challenge to the 1642 Order. Despite frequent raids by parliamentary troops, plays were performed surreptitiously at the private indoor theatres, Salisbury Court and the Cockpit in Drury Lane, and the outdoor public theatres, the Fortune and the Red Bull. The newsbook *Perfect Occurrences*, for instance, reports on 6 October 1647 that bills were put up advertising a performance at Salisbury Court of Beaumont and Fletcher's *A King and No King*.[8] The performance was to be interrupted by the sheriffs of London, who found 'a great number of people, some young lords and other eminent persons'. Notices of subsequent performances were circulated by other means. *Perfect Occurrences* again records that on 3 February 1648 bills were thrown into gentlemen's coaches, advertising a production of Fletcher's *Wit without Money* at the Red Bull. On 5 February 1648, the diarist John Evelyn records seeing an unnamed tragicomedy at the Cockpit.[9]

That such illicit playing continued was acknowledged in an ordinance of 11 February 1648 'for the utter suppression and abolishing of all stage-plays and interludes, within the penalties to be inflicted on the actors and spectators therein expressed'. In its terms, this order, which is considerably more expansive than the abrupt injunction of 1642, has resonances of Elizabethan regulation of players. The language of anti-theatre prejudice is now expressed in legislation. In terms reminiscent of earlier punitive injunctions, stage players and players of interludes are deemed rogues and are to be punished as such. The draconian sanctions of earlier legislation are reflected in the measures to be taken against the theatres. All playhouse galleries, seats and boxes are to be demolished; players who defy the ordinance are to be whipped and spectators fined five shillings. As with other social and cultural manifestations of the post-civil-war period, there is a reversion to Elizabethan attitudes: in the legislative evocation of the actor's marginalized social status, there is a reprise of Elizabethan ideology whereby players without aristocratic patent were condemned as rogues, vagabonds and sturdy beggars.[10] None the less there is a double-edged aspect to the legislation which seems to be acknowledged in a commentary in *Mercurius Anti-pragmaticus* of the previous year: 'They [the actors] are not only silenced, but branded with a name of infamy, rogues; but this word perhaps doth the less distaste them, on consideration that a famous Queen bestowed upon them the same epithet.'[11] Despite such censorship, occasional advertisements for theatrical entertainments continued to appear in royalist newspapers or 'mercuries'. A notice for rope dancing at the Red Bull in June 1653 concludes as follows: 'There will also appear a merry conceited fellow which hath formerly given content. And you may come and return with safety.'[12] The emphasis on rope dancing (on other occasions it was sword dancing) rather than performance betokens the circumspect advertisement of plays. Moreover, the supposition that the audience could attend without fear of arrest may indicate a degree of acquiescence towards performance on the part of the local authorities.

The actors were never completely silenced. Several who had been affiliated to the King's Company, Prince Charles's players and Beeston's Boys, based at the Cockpit, continued to act in improvised companies. During the first civil war, players, including William Cooke and William Hall, who had formerly belonged to Prince Charles's players, performed for the royal court in exile, first at The Hague and then, probably, in Paris. But by the close of 1648, a number of the players had returned to London and helped to constitute three companies of shifting personnel which played intermittently at the surviving theatres. In James Wright's account of the interruption in the winter of 1648/49 of a performance at the Cockpit of Fletcher and Massinger's *Rollo or the Bloody Brother*, the cast included such celebrated Caroline actors as John Lowin and Charles Hart.[13] Lowin had acted with the King's Company as early as 1604 and Hart, who, according to Wright, had entered the profession acting women's parts at Blackfriars, resumed his career at the Restoration as a member of the King's Men, now led by Thomas Killigrew. Indeed, as can be deduced from pension claims later made by William Hall, another veteran of the company, and Richard Baxter, the King's Men, or at least fragments of them, never entirely ceased playing throughout the Commonwealth.[14]

Crucial to the survival of theatre was the availability or the adaptation of theatrical space, since the ordinances of the Commonwealth sought to suppress theatre simply by the destruction of its buildings. Although the King's Company had been deprived of its outdoor venue in 1644 when the Globe had been dismantled and replaced by tenements, there were attempts to revive playing at what had been their indoor house at Blackfriars. It was reported in the parliamentary newsbook *The Perfect Weekly Account* that attempted restorations had begun in October 1647;[15] subsequently, complaints were registered in the Commons that 'stage-players were playing at public houses in the City'.[16] Such overt defiance of the earlier prohibition no doubt prompted the passing of an ordinance later in the month for 'the better suppressing of stage plays', empowering the Lord Mayor and City of London and justices of the peace 'to enter into all houses, and other places . . . where stage plays, interludes, or other common plays are, or shall be acted or played' and to call offending actors before the Sessions of the Peace, where they were to be punished as rogues.[17] The active suppression of the stage, however, seems to have been more zealously undertaken by soldiers, in the form of raids on the playhouses, than by the 'presbyterian' city leaders, opposed as they were to the power of the army and particularly its occupation of London in 1647. The most comprehensive raid on record is that which took place simultaneously at three theatres on 1 January 1649; the date suggests that the theatres were playing as part of traditional seasonal festivities. *The Kingdom's Weekly Intelligencer* reports a sweeping assault on those theatres still in operation:

> The soldiers seized on the players on their stages at Drury Lane, and at Salisbury Court. They went also to the Fortune in Golden Lane, but they found none there, but John Pudding dancing on the ropes, whom they took with them. In the meantime the players at the Red Bull, who had notice of it, made haste away, and were all gone before they came, and took away all their acting clothes with them. But at Salisbury Court they were taken on the stage, the play being almost ended, and with many links and lighted torches they were carried to Whitehall with their players' clothes upon their backs. In the way they oftentimes took the crown from his head who acted the king, and in sport would oftentimes put it on again. Abraham

had a black satin gown on, and before he came into the dirt, he was very neat in his white laced pumps. The people, not expecting such a pageant, looked and laughed at all the rest, and, not knowing who he was, they asked, what had the Lady done? They made some resistance at the Cockpit in Drury Lane, which was the occasion that they were bereaved of their apparel, and were not so well used as those in Salisbury Court, who were more patient, and therefore at their releasement they had their clothes returned to them without the least diminution. After two days' confinement, they were ordered to put in bail, and to appear before the Lord Mayor to answer for what they have done according unto Law.[18]

This account is corroborated by a shorter item in *Perfect Occurrences*, which also includes an interesting detail about the composition of the audience at the Salisbury Court playhouse. The journal recounts that amongst the spectators were members who had been purged from Parliament in December 1648 by forces under Colonel Pride for their willingness to negotiate with the King.[19] As Margot Heinemann argued for the early Stuart period, the play going Parliamentarian is, thus, not a misnomer.[20] The parliamentary journal also clears up an ambiguity in the observation that it was the soldiers (and not the actors, as might be inferred from the account above) who participated in the derisive act of crowning and uncrowning the King. Here, in January 1649, the month of the regicide, the mock street pageant of deposition, in which the actors from Salisbury Court playhouse were forced to participate, presages the worst royalist fears. Kingship is exposed as an act. In a period when events and individuals' experience of living through them were repeatedly theatricalized as tragedy and tragicomedy, street onlookers were confused as to the nature of the spectacle they were watching, mistaking the actor of female roles, Abraham Ivory, both for his part and the nature of his transgression.

Shortly after this invasion of the London theatres, the ordinance against theatrical activity dating from the previous year was ruthlessly enforced and the interiors of the Cockpit, Fortune and Salisbury Court were dismantled. On 6 August 1655, the Blackfriars was demolished and, as had happened with the Globe, replaced by tenements. The players now had only the stage of the Red Bull on which to perform. That some kind of theatrical activity continued at this venue throughout the period is attested to by records of the Middlesex Sessions of the Peace in May 1659, when the Restoration actor Edward Shatterell, together with Anthony Turner, was bound over for 'the unlawful maintaining of stage plays and interludes at the Red Bull'. The actors had apparently collaborated with the parishioners of Clerkenwell by paying them not only the substantial sum of twenty shillings a day for the hire of the Red Bull but also money towards the relief of the poor and the repair of highways.[21]

Theatre, like other prohibited pastimes, went underground, as improvised stages were set up in private spaces. James Wright recalls, during 'Oliver's time', private performances in 'noblemen's houses', in particular, Holland House in Kensington, the home of the Earl of Holland, Henry Rich.[22] William Davenant was eventually to inaugurate a theatrical revival by mounting theatrical production in his own home, Rutland House, which was sanctioned by the Council of State. But before this, private performance remained covert. *Mercurius Democritus* reports, in March 1653, preparation for a performance of Thomas Killigrew's *Claricilla* at Charles Gibbon's tennis court in Vere Street, Clare Market, which was betrayed to the army by one of the players. The journal castigates the unnamed actor, while also revealing that he had himself undertaken the production of a number of plays in his own home: 'An ill beast or rather bird (because the rest denied him a share of their profits) beshit his own nest, causing the poor actors to be routed by the soldiery, though he himself hath since the prohibition of plays had divers tragedies and comedies acted in his own home.' Outside London plays continued to be performed in country houses, inns and fairs.[23] The Cavendish sisters, daughters of the Duke of Newcastle and authors of *The Concealed Fancies*, may have acted in a performance at the family home of Welbeck Abbey before it was surrendered to parliamentary forces in November 1645.[24] A manuscript collection of plays written by Cosmo Manuche, several dating from the 1650s and dedicated to James Compton, the third Earl of Northampton, discovered in archives at Northampton's home, Castle Ashby,[25] may have been performed there before house guests. Dorothy Osborne certainly refers to such an occasion at Knowlton in Kent. Writing to William Temple in July 1654, Osborne tells him that she is in a house 'the most filled of any since the Ark', where she is to play— somewhat unwillingly—the title role in William Berkeley's *The Lost Lady*: 'They [the house guests] will have me act my part in a play, the Lost Lady it is, and I am she.'[26] How common such private performances were is difficult to know, but, as royalist gentry withdrew from London to those estates which had not been sequestrated, it is highly probable that play production comprised part of their entertainment: a pastime which reaffirmed royalist culture while expressing opposition to the order of the Commonwealth.

Theatrical space could be created—as it long had been—within other buildings, especially in places which had earlier theatrical associations. There is an arresting account of an amateur performance of *Mucedorus* at an inn in the town of Witney in Oxfordshire in 1653 which had a disastrous outcome, in that overcrowding caused the collapse of the floor. The narrative appears as part of the prefatory material to three sermons published by a local preacher, John Rowe. The long preface, as with earlier anti-theatrical polemic, combines a theatrical and retributive idiom, registered in the title, *Tragi-Comedia Being a Brief Relation of the Strange and Wonderful Hand of God Discovered at Witney*. Rowe addresses the town's inhabitants, admonishing them not to contest 'the Almighty for setting you up as the public theatre whereon he would manifest his holiness, justice, and other attributes to the world'. As the language suggests, Rowe interpreted the event as a manifestation of divine disapproval of the abomination of stage playing. That the event occurred during a production of *Mucedorus* was not, in Rowe's providential interpretation, a coincidence, for this was a play which contained mocking references to Puritanism. He reminds his reader that, on the same day as the accident occurred, the townspeople and scholars of Oxford were keeping a fast. Implying the current anachronism of the term 'puritan', Rowe comments: 'How remarkable was this that some of them that were called Puritans in the days of old, had spent that very day in Oxford in fasting and prayer; and that the Lord by so eminent an hand should testify against such who were not only scoffers at Godly persons, but at religion itself.' Triumphantly, he concludes that 'the hand of God hath remarkably appeared against the actors and frequenters of stage plays'.

Despite Rowe's dissociation from 'puritans in the days of old', the following sermon rehearses all the anti-theatrical arguments associated with fundamental Puritanism so brilliantly personified by Jonson forty years earlier in Zeal of the Land Busy in *Bartholomew Fair*. Stage plays are opposed to the word of God, which forbids idle conversation, jesting and unchaste looks, apparel and gestures. They are 'stuffed with scurrilous, filthy, unbecoming speeches, passages and gestures' and they defy the Deuteronomic injunction not to dress in women's attire. The entire piece resembles a parody of old anti-theatrical polemic. In its idiom the work recalls, and indeed cites from, *Theatre of God's Judgment* (1597), in which Thomas Beard had inveighed against the sins of dancing, singing and playing and warned of the retribution which befell those who pursued such dissolute activities. While attesting to the sustained popularity of provincial drama, Rowe's texts also reveal little change in the language and style of puritan hostility to dramatic practice.

THE PAMPHLET PLAY

Concomitant with attempted suppression of theatre was an effective deregulation of press censorship. With the collapse in 1641 of the Star Chamber and consequently its powers over the regulation of printing, together with the diminished role of the Stationers' Company,[27] there followed a lapse in pre-publication licensing. This facilitated the circulation of pamphlet plays which offered an alternative outlet for the dramatic imagination. Drama and journalism overlapped in an unprecedented manner, producing a novel form of intertextuality. Subject to erratic controls by parliamentary licensers, printed drama nevertheless became an effective medium for news, deploying the same sensational rumours, personal attacks, innuendo and exaggeration as the popular press. Even when the Treason Act of 14 May 1649 made writing against the government and army a capital offence, anti-parliamentarian journals and plays continued to be published, if less frequently. As government press control became more effective in the early 1650s[28] political satire was strategically replaced in pamphlet playlets by social and sexual satire.

The displacement of the theatre by the pamphlet play is referred to in the Actors' Remonstrance of January 1644, which includes amongst its catalogue of grievances the plight of dramatists: 'some of our ablest ordinary poets, instead of their annual stipends and beneficial second days,[29] being for mere necessity compelled to get a living by writing contemptible penny pamphlets'. In producing such works, playwrights are no longer using any 'attribute of their profession'. Instead they are reduced to 'faining miraculous stories and relations of unheard of battles' to the extent that soon, it is alleged, they will be enticed into the writing of ballads. The writing of news dramas was thus seen as akin to the oral culture of ballads, a vulgar alternative to the composition of drama proper, but compelled by financial necessity. Most of the playlets were, of course, published anonymously, and those authors who can be identified, such as Samuel Sheppard and John Crouch, were editors of royalist weeklies. These 'contemptible penny pamphlets', as they are termed in the Actors' Remonstrance, were written as political polemic, exploiting characters constructed on Jonsonian 'humours' and employing familiar stage motifs. They appeal to a theatrically literate, metropolitan audience familiar with the contents of the newsbooks. Whether or not they were performed is open to question. Some evidence of performance is provided by the presentation of a play within a play: Cosmo Manuche's *Loyal Lovers* (1652) contains an episode in which two 'loyal comrades'—thinly disguised Royalists—while away time before drinking by watching a play (2.1). The preparation for and performance of the play suggests something of the nature of informal playing during the Commonwealth. Parts are taken by a third 'comrade', Symphronio, and by Mettle, a servant. Mettle, playing the role of Fly-blow, a butcher, has already learnt his lines while Symphronio, as the priest, Phanaticus, announces that he will perform extempore. The playlet is performed in costume and with some stage properties and, in the use of hangings and curtains, there is improvised staging. In its satirical exposure of Phanaticus, one of the Puritan 'elect', the play is in the vein of the pamphlet play. That the performance takes place in a private room of a tavern is some indication of one venue for the acting of political satire.

It is possible that occasional public performances took place at the Red Bull, and that others would have been performed as street theatre, in taverns or as entertainment at fairs. Certainly, as might be expected, amateur theatre production did take place. On 13 November 1650, for example, Charles Cutts, a barber, was called before the General Sessions of the Peace for the City and Liberty of Westminster 'for being taken ready dressed in clothes and going to act a stage-play'.[30] The type of play in which Cutts was to act is open to question, but the short pamphlet play with its readily available script lends itself to a makeshift and illicit production. Conjectures that the pamphlet drama was acted at various venues arise from textual evidence. Many of the playlets show clear signs of having been conceived with performance in mind. The nature of the texts—notably in their detailed, often comic or farcical, stage directions, visual comedy and some quick-fire dialogue—are self-evidently theatrical in appeal. Indeed, the texts contain several oblique allusions to their performance. In *A Bartholomew Fairing*[31] Mrs Tryall, the wife of a committee man, makes an unconsciously ironic comment on the suppression of theatre: 'Deer was the tyrant's game; but bulls is ours / Bishops and plays were in a day put down / I well remember' (p. 14). In performance the complacent remark would have produced a good in-house joke. A number of pamphlet plays begin with a prologue which would have served to announce a performance in the tavern or fair and thus command an audience. A covert allusion to performance, for example, is made in the prologue to the sequel of a pamphlet play of 1648, *The Second Part of Crafty Cromwell or Oliver in his Glory as King*. After anticipating the audience's pleasure and applause at the representation of the army grandees and their rapid rise to power, the prologue urges caution:

> Hear then with candour; but be ruled by me,
> Speak not a word, what ere you hear or see,
> For this author, bid me to you say,
> He'd live, to see this played another day.

(p. 2)

The 'address to the readers of my former piece' sustains the idea or the illusion of the play's secret performance. With mock hyperbole, the author claims that he will dare the threats of Parliament in order to castigate 'justly on the stage' the crimes of the age. Obliquely, he states that the offences of Cromwell and the army grandees should be made a public laughing stock: 'a scorn / To those plebeians have their burdens borne'. It might be inferred from the author's comment that the pamphlet is to be read by those that can read it and afford it and performed for the benefit of the illiterate.

Texts of other pamphlet plays contain strong hints of performance. *The Disease of the House* is a short prose drama with a verse prologue and epilogue. The former, designated 'His Prologue on the Stage', is spoken by John Capon. Capon is mentioned specifically in an advertisement in the royalist journal *Mercurius Democritus* as appearing in an entertainment at the Red Bull which includes a display of rope, sword and country dancing.[32] The name was presumably a generic name like that of Jack Pudding, who had been found dancing on the ropes during the 1649 New Year's Day raid on the Red Bull. That Capon is alluded to as the prologue of *The Disease of the House* suggests that the playlet was performed, possibly on the stage of the same theatre. Certainly the text, one of the shortest of the pamphlet plays, could be prepared with little rehearsal for performance. *A Bartholomew Fairing* has for its prologue 'a pedlar in haste with an horn' suggesting that the horn, as with the playing of trumpets and drums by travelling players, was blown to summon an audience. The prologue to *A Tragicomedy Called Newmarket Fair or a Parliament Outcry of State Commodities* similarly creates an impression of performance. It is 'sung by the crier' and the stage direction for his entrance, bearing all the ensignia of monarchy, is visually evocative: 'with a crown and sceptre, a carkanet of jewels, two or three suits, with some robes of state'. In his departing shot the crier comments on the 'saint's market day' and recommends his audience to make a quick purchase and then watch the play:

> See but this play, and before you go away
> You'll say 'tis wondrous pretty.
> Welcome, welcome, with all my heart,
> For now I must go mind my part.

(p. 3)

'Mind my part', in the sense of 'learning one's lines', would seem to be a tantalizing allusion to the doubling of the prologue in an anticipated performance.

The relationship between the written and performed texts of the pamphlet plays is a curious one. Typographically, the plays represent texts for performance, containing as they do the list of dramatis personae, prologues and epilogues, stage directions and details of scene locations. While production of the pamphlet plays can only be conjectured from hints and allusions in the texts, the knowledge that illicit playing continued throughout the civil war years and the years of the Republic lends the conjecture more substance. Amongst plays from the old repertoires, it is reasonable to surmise that the political satires were some of the plays performed illicitly in private venues and at the public theatres. During the period, there was much emphasis on the publication of plays and it is often inferred that greater reading of dramatic texts became a substitute for performance.[33] By and large it must have been so, but, in the case of the popular pamphlet play, it seems unlikely that its audience comprised only the literate section of the male population. It may be conjectured that the playlets dramatizing the same rumours and smears as featured in the newsbooks were produced in tandem with them to ensure, through some kind of performance, a wider reception for such anti-parliamentary propaganda. The pamphlet play can be seen as an extension of the ballad in so far as it became part of a popular oral—as well as print—culture.

The two parts of *Crafty Cromwell*[34] reflect this hybrid of drama and journalism. Fantasy and rumour, characteristic of the royalist mercuries, combine with devices of earlier popular theatre, while the rawness of the plays, as a consequence of their hasty composition, is seen in some abrupt shifts in register and idiom. In Act 1 of the First Part, for example, two citizens, rehearsing familiar doctrines of passive obedience, express their loyalty to the King. In contrasting tone, Act 2 opens with the mock-tragic image of the ghost of Pym, the former leader of the House, in torment for his disloyalty to the King: 'I, whose projections grim and dangerous, brought a free people into slavery, incensing them against their gracious Prince and topsy turvy turned all Law and Right . . . I, that for the same am doomed for evermore to fry in flames.' In a bizarre mixture of elements, Act 3 introduces two Jesuit priests and the civil uprising against the King is portrayed as part of a Jesuit plot masterminded from Rome. The Chorus at the end of the act concludes: 'Lo from our cursed dissensions, and our wars, / How Rome gets strength, the whore of Babylon / Doth clap her hands, and laughs to see our jars.' Here, all the fantastic intrigues attributed to Rome, the 'whore of Babylon', in Elizabethan drama are revived, before the play returns to Cromwell, who discloses both his double-dealings with the King and his declaration to supplant him: 'Yet 'spite of fates, and men, I will be king.' The Second Part culminates with Cromwell's mock crowning, detailed in a substantial stage direction:

> Recorders. Enter Cromwell in state, a canopy borne over his head, by Harry Marten, Pride, Ireton, and Joyce. They place him in a throne, and then put a crown upon his head, then they bow the knee, saying (Omnes) 'Long live King Oliver.'

The visual image is accompanied by the plotting of Cromwell, Joyce, Ireton, Pride and Marten—all of whom were months later to sign the King's death warrant—to kill the King and dissolve Parliament. The play would seem to have been composed in order to fuel rumours circulating as early as 1648 that Royalists were to be massacred, that Cromwell was planning to be monarch and that quarrels among the army grandees were about to erupt.[35] In serving such propaganda, the text appeals to theatrical memory as it draws on a stock of images and familiar conventions detailed in the implicitly theatrical stage directions. These seem to be indicative of performance. While it might well have been difficult to represent the army grandees, on the other hand, the drama would have been effective if Cromwell, Ireton and Marten had been impersonated in caricature-like fashion. If read aloud as part of a royalist gathering, it is almost certain that some acting of parts must have accompanied the delivery of the racy dialogue.

As with the two parts of *Crafty Cromwell*, other plays appear not only to pick up a motif from a news pamphlet, so that the drama represents a satiric reworking of news communicated only days earlier, but also to anticipate the news bulletin itself. This can be seen in *Newmarket Fair*, printed in June 1649 with the facetious imprint 'At you may go look'. The scene is Westminster and the characters include Fairfax, the leader of the parliamentary forces, Cromwell's son-in-law Ireton, Mildmay, Pride and the wives of the generals. The comical piece attempts to present the immediate aftermath of the King's execution as a period of gross confusion and rivalry amongst the regicides. Fairfax, Cromwell, Ireton and Pride each bid for the royal regalia, culminating in a dispute between Fairfax and Cromwell. To Fairfax's suggestion that they share power, Cromwell contends: 'No, a crown admits no rival; I'll all or none. / He sits unsafe that doth divide his throne.' The scene becomes increasingly farcical as the two wives hurl insults at each other about their relative status, while Mildmay suggests that Cromwell and Fairfax should cast lots as to who should be king of England and that they should divide the spoils and offices between the Parliamentarians. As Cromwell and Fairfax conspire to extort money from the city, the arrival of a messenger precipitates the denouement. Letters announce that the navy has been defeated, Dublin has been taken by royalist forces, Levellers and Presbyterians have defected and 'which is worse, the people generally do our late actions curse'. The play's abrupt closure presents images which reflect some of the wildest fantasies of the royalist press. The regicides fall upon their swords and the crier extracts a political moral: 'All people here behold our miseries / Who lives by treason thus by treason dies.' In its less fantastic moments, the play anticipates, rather than represents, known events. On 4 July 1649, the royalist paper *The Man in the Moon* commented that 'an act was brought in and read for the sale of the goods of the late King; Newmarket Fair it seems is proclaim'd at Westminster' (M2r). Theatre becomes the effective vehicle for the carnivalesque metaphor of parliamentary proceedings as the transactions of a fair. When the farce was reprinted in 1661 it was apparently done so 'at the request of some young gentlemen to act in Christmas holidays'. This reference to acting might indeed suggest that there was a precedent in the form of an earlier private house performance.

The sequel, *The Second Part of the Tragicomedy Called Newmarket Fair or Mrs Parliament's New Figaries* (1649)[36]—perhaps a self-conscious comic allusion to the two-part Elizabethan dramas—is much longer and has an obviously more dramatic structure, being divided into acts and some scenes. From the reference to 'the Man in the Moon' on the title page, the author can be identified as John Crouch, who was also briefly associated with the royalist journal *Mercurius Melancholius*. The Prologue alludes to performance—whether literally or ironically, it is impossible to say—in its provocative assertion that the 'rebels' will rage to see themselves 'thus acted on the stage'. Less overtly farcical than its predecessor, the play opens with two loyalists, Constantius and Fidelius, alluding to the strange 'revival' of the regicides who had killed themselves in the earlier play. The characters comment on 'butchering Sacred Majesty' and Cromwell's projected campaign in Ireland. In the second act there is ludicrous black magic in the depiction of Hugh Peters, Cromwell's chaplain, who it transpires has resurrected the regicides. As a necromancer, Peters calls up the ghost of Issac Dorislaus, the Republic's ambassador to the Netherlands, who had been murdered by Royalists in April 1649. The ghost is conjured and 'appears from underneath the stage in fetters and flames of sulphur', threatening to take Peters with him. Again, the stage direction, with its suggestion of a trap beneath the stage, provides evidence of an actual or proposed performance. Throughout the play there is a concoction of sexual and political satire, news and farce typical of much royalist propaganda. Mrs Cromwell, for example, now wearing the Queen's jewels, is discovered 'behind the hangings' in bed with her paramour by the Jesuit Miles Corbet, who exclaims: 'Hell and damnation! what, are we all turned sodomites?' (3.5). Mrs Fairfax is represented as similarly libidinous, claiming that her husband is as impotent 'as a king is to England', while Fairfax is preoccupied with fears that he will be murdered by the Levellers. Ireton and Pride comment on the Irish campaign and the sequestration of royalist lands.

The play reveals the complex political alliances of the period, as it appears to support the Leveller constitutional document 'The Agreement of the People', in opposition to Parliament and the army grandees. In Act 5, Fairfax in his soliloquy castigates the Levellers and their demands: 'The devil stop your mouths, will nothing serve you but The Agreement of the People, The Agreement of the People. Are not the Parliament the people's representatives.' Thereafter, the theatrical dimension of the piece is apparent in the stage direction that Fairfax sleeps, while 'Enter three or four furies and antics dancing about him with their hands all bloody, and exit'. Fairfax is pinioned by the crowd and led away; the sheriffs appear, holding 'the Agreement of the People'. The proceedings are greeted with great satisfaction by the two Royalists, who remark on the fall of the general: 'Do not the Phaetons tumble now? Blood must be revenged; murder and patricide, although concealed long, at last betrays itself.' In an anarchic finale, Fairfax is discovered to be a ghost recalled by a necromancer. Lady Fairfax, who had spoken out forcibly against the King's execution, here kills Mrs Cromwell and is then carried off to prison by the people. The Epilogue spoken by the entire cast (stage direction *omnes*) strikes a familiar note of revenge, concluding with its appeal to the King in exile 'Come Royal Charles, and with a cloud of thunder / Disperse this bed of snakes and keep them under.' Thus, both the rhetoric and, particularly, the dynamics of the plot are very much geared to performance.

Intertextuality functions in the pamphlet play to the extent that the ideal reader or spectator was assumed to have been a regular theatregoer. Again and again, verbal resonances and dramatic motifs from Marlowe, Jonson and Shakespeare are used as if to appeal to a common dramatic culture.[37] Reassurance of cultural continuity is offered in the very familiarity of plot devices and stage action. In an ironic echo of Richard Brome's play concerning a beggar's commonwealth, *A Jovial Crew*, Samuel Sheppard, sometime printer and editor of the royalist newspaper *Mercurius Pragmaticus*, directed his playlet *The Jovial Crew* (1651)[38] at the radical religious sect of the Ranters. The structural parallels and contrasts between Brome's and Sheppard's plays are illuminating. In *A Jovial Crew*, the two daughters of the landlord Oldrents leave their father's home to experience for a summer the freedom of the beggar's life; in Sheppard's play, the two wives join the 'jovial' Ranters, anticipating a more hedonistic kind of social freedom. While drawing upon contemporary pamphlets which claimed to expose the Ranters and alleged abominations amongst members of the sect,[39] the play strongly evokes theatrical antecedents.

The title page of Sheppard's play states that the names of the characters are 'sorted to their several natures' and both are 'lively presented in action'. This concept of character is Jonsonian and indeed there is a recall of Pug in *The Devil Is an Ass* as, in the first scene, the devil accommodates himself amongst the Ranters:

> I have surveyed the universe, as France, Spain, and Italy, yet cannot parallel the ranters of this our English climate; I've blinded them with pleasures of this world, by putting on a mask of religion to make it no sin, that makes my proselytes run headlong down to the infernal lake, where Cerberus transports them to their supposed joy, where yet at last, into infernal flames at length they're cast. (p. 2)

The play here discloses its intertextual relationship with news pamphlets by drawing on their idiom. *Ranters of Both Sexes*, one of such pamphlets, had commented, 'It is no new work of Satan to sew heresies, and breed heretics, but they never come up so thick as in these latter times.'[40] It is, however, the theatricality of the play which is most apparent in the spectacular close to the first act when the Ranters dance a jig and sing in company with the devil, before he vanishes in thunder.

The play draws eclectically upon comic antecedents. At the opening of Act 2 the satire is directed at two citizen wives, Idlesby and Do-little, who are attracted to the supposed libertarian style of the Ranters, believing that they do nothing 'but acting good for one another, drinking love-healths, and amorous deportments'. The playlet ends in the vein of a rather savage citizen comedy with the cuckolded husbands taking vengeance upon their wives, but the play extends to more than sexual satire. The frontispiece has an apocalyptical caricature of the devil driving a chariot through a map of the British Isles (figure 1), conveying an image of the destruction of a nation caused by the anarchy of the sects[41] spawned by the Puritan revolution.

One of the final playlets to be published during the Republic was *The Ghost, or The Woman Wears the Breeches*,[42] a play which according to its title page had been written in 1640 but appeared only in 1653. It is longer than the average playlet and its elements of intrigue make it more complex than others of the period. The prologue, again, seems designed for performance, as agreement is reached with the audience, who are instructed to sit still, put down their wine and laugh, while the money

The Prologue.

Bedlam broke loofe? yes, *Hell* is open'd too :
Mad-men, & *Fiends,* & *Harpies* to your view
We do prefent: but who fhall cure the *Tumor?*
All the world now is in the *Ranting Humor.*

1   Frontifpiece, *The Jovial Crew or The Devil Turned Ranter.*

earned by the actors will enable them to drink the audience's health. As with *The Jovial Crew*, political satire is submerged in sexual comedy as Aurelia submits to her father's will and marries the elderly Philarchus. The destabilization of gender relations is present in the scene of Aurelia's wedding night, where there is a reversal of Shakespeare's *The Taming of the Shrew*. Aurelia insults and humiliates Philarchus, eventually forcing him to sign an agreement allowing her full sexual licence and free access to his fortune. The drama thus exemplifies David Underdown's thesis that inversion of government was seen to be accompanied by sexual inversion, in the sense that, for example, female petitioners acted independently and sects such as the Quakers offered greater opportunity for female self-expression.[43] The Friar, in his speech at the end of the first act, ostensibly commenting on the changing nature of personal affairs, makes such a connection in his teasing paradoxes: 'Tis a steady tottering state / Propt with love and shook with hate. / Like that I now am musing on to be / Relator of a joyful tragedy' (p. 7).

The image of the all-licensed female was likely to cause hostile reaction in the press, but here Philarchus is the object of derision and with justification Aurelia has the upper hand. To demonstrate her power, she tells her servant, who rejoices in the Jonsonian name of Engin, to take her husband's breeches—her 'shield'—tie them to a pole and carry them before her. If the play was performed, there may well have been a visual pun here, since the twin arms of England and Ireland, adopted by the Republic as part of its symbolism, were ridiculed by Royalists as resembling a pair of breeches.[44] Indeed, the prologue may be hinting at such an analogy when it states, 'about those breeches I have much to say'. While Aurelia's domestic revolution is only a temporary aberration, however, and gender inversions are thus contained, there is, in the carnivalesque image of breeches slung from a pole, the gleeful suggestion that the Commonwealth has produced subversion it cannot contain.

The pamphlet plays clearly derive from the popular literature of ballads, jest books and the anecdotes, scandals and satires which had circulated in the Elizabethan and Jacobean pamphlets. Moreover, as Lois Potter has observed of two early pamphlet plays, the *Mistress Parliament* dialogues, there is an exploitation of stage devices similar to those which were effective in the Martin Marprelate controversy of the late 1580s.[45] To this tradition of stage satire, defiant of and ultimately uncontrollable by authority, the pamphlet plays belong. Political subversions are mirrored by generic subversions. Even in a royalist play alluding to the regicide, *The Famous Tragedy of King Charles I*,[46] published immediately following the King's execution, there is a blurring and confusing of genres, as sexual satire and comic rhetoric co-exist with lofty sentiment and scenes of 'noble dying' in the persons of the Royalists Lord Capell and Sir Charles Lucas after the siege of Colchester. Cromwell speaks in mock-Marlovian rhetoric, dividing his energies between plotting the King's trial and execution and the seduction of Mrs Lambert, wife of one of his generals. The two threads are brought together in the final act, as his love-making ends abruptly with the arrival of Henry Ireton. Ireton, an instigator of the trial of Charles I and Cromwell's son-in-law, brings the news of the King's execution and a request to Cromwell to participate in the formation of the new Republic: 'We are now modellizing the Commonwealth, in the prosecution of which both soldiers and senators desire your aid.' Thus, following the collapse of the monarchy, a royalist play registers uncertainty about the future identity of the State, an uncertainty which is reflected in the play's varied generic associations.

Most of the pamphlet drama of the period is broadly royalist, although royalism appears as an allegiance adopted by a variety of groups, often by default. Alliances were often functional rather than ideological. A principal interest of the playlets lies in the very topsy-turviness they convey, as authors played off various factions and groupings: Leveller against army; Presbyterian against Independent; fabricated rivalry amongst Cromwell and the army grandees. In general, the pamphlet plays exploit intra-parliamentary differences and represent a guileful, nakedly ambitious Cromwell. The play form becomes the ideal medium for depicting the deceptions of Puritanism: self-righteousness is thus a mask for sexual transgression and hypocrisy. Subversion and chaos in the domestic sphere, and in particular sexual relations, mirror 'unnatural' inversions in the public sphere. Connections are made between personal and political authority in the invention of parliamentary sexual scandals and the libertarianism of the sects. David Underdown has drawn attention to the ways in which such metaphors of inversion could be differently applied. The 'world upside down' did have liberating and positive connotations for many.[47] On the other hand, in the periodical literature the view was often negative, as the King's execution was seen to unleash anarchic desires and ambitions.[48] To depict Cromwell and the major generals as libidinous undermined their political authority, while enabling Royalists to present an alternative form of masculinity illustrated in rhetorical closet drama.

CLOSET DRAMA

Under the Auspices column in their *Annals of English Drama*, Harbage and Schoenbaum classify most new writing of the Republic as closet drama, on the basis that there are no records of performance. But, as has been argued, pamphlet plays, which evince so many features of a performance text, may well have been acted in a variety of venues. It is clear that the categories by which it is generally helpful to analyse pre-civil-war drama need to be revised for the post-civil-war period. Closet drama composed in the tradition of Mary Sidney's *The Tragedy of Antony*, Samuel Daniel's *Philotas* and Fulke Greville's *Mustapha*—with its high moralizing sentiments, the presence of a Chorus and stark and relatively static plot construction—was read, either in solitude or declaimed in a controlled literary circle. It was favoured by the strongly Protestant Sidney circle because of its moral, sometimes didactic, tone and its unity of plot and genre. Here was no 'mongrel tragicomedy' deployed in the popular theatre so despised by Philip Sidney.[49] In contrast, in the aftermath of the civil wars, closet drama proper can be identified with the royalist party in opposition. Several plays were written during the Republic which do indeed conform to this tradition and some, like Mary Sidney's closet drama, were translations. Since such academic drama was never designed for the stages of either public or private theatres, it provided a readily available tradition for the continuation of political and rhetorical play writing. Indeed, in their observance of classical form, the plays contrast markedly with the hybrid form and ribaldry of the pamphlet play and the comic or farcical interlude. In Edmund Prestwich's translation of Seneca's *Phaedra* as *Hippolitus*, published in 1651, one of the dedications alludes to the devaluation of drama and the literary text, now supplanted by the wide circulation of pamphlets or 'mercuries': in 'this age of ignorance', readers 'think their eyes abused if fixed on aught but mercuries'. Prestwich's work might be seen as an attempt to regain the aesthetic high ground of drama rather than, as in the case of Christopher Wase's *Electra*, a political intervention. Apart from the obvious parallel of the wandering princes, Charles and Theseus, or the return of Theseus from 'night's gloomy coasts' as an optimistic political projection, there is no significant re-presentation of the story for the contemporary reader.

For the most part, the closet drama of the period suggests a deliberate, lofty political detachment, perhaps even withdrawal from events, by way of exemplifing stances of stoical fortitude associated with a certain kind of royalism.[50] William Lower, who had been a royalist captain and lieutenant-colonel during the civil wars, published two closet dramas, *Polyeuctes* (1655) and *Horatius* (1656), both translations from Corneille. Articulating elevated sentiments at moments of affliction, the plays refract idealized royalist attitudes. Their rhetoric makes them especially suited for reading aloud, as seems to have been Corneille's occasional practice. Following conventions of neo-classical drama they rigidly maintain the unities of place and time and demand very little in the way of staging.

In *Horatius: A Roman Tragedy*, the war between Alba and Rome is represented starkly in terms of family loyalties, articulated through the female characters, conflicting with loyalty to the State, expressed in terms of Roman warrior culture. Although he is married to Sabina from Alba, the Roman Horatius demands from his family absolute loyalty to Rome. After killing his sister, Camilla, because she had dared to attack Roman values for their inhumanity, he declares, 'Who is so bold to curse / His country, doth renounce his family' (4.6). But his crime is pardoned by the king, Tullus, because 'such servants are the wealth and strength of kings' (5.3). The play is set in a period, little dramatized, when Rome was a monarchical State. The setting enables the expression of absolutist sentiments. Tullus tells Old Horatius that he must dispense justice: 'It is by that a king makes himself / a demi-God' (5.2). It is this ideological perspective, rarely associated with Rome, albeit reflecting contemporary French absolutism, which gives the play a provocative edge. Such views offer a reaffirmation of royalism condoned within the cloak of translation.

Charles I was venerated by his adherents as a martyr who had died in defence of the Anglican Church, yet was denied a State funeral. In a

Wenceslaus Holler engraving, Charles's crown lies in the dust while a heavenly crown approaches him. It was such an identification, not only of Charles but of other executed Royalists as martyrs, that may have prompted Lower's translation of *Polyeuctes or the Martyr: A Tragedy*. Polyeuctes and Nearchus are described anachronistically as 'two cavaliers straightly tied together in amity', although they are of different religions. Polyeuctes is converted to Christianity and suffers persecution at the hands of the Emperor, Decius. Despite the pleas of his wife Paulina and her father, Felix, Roman senator and Governor of Armenia, Polyeuctes remains steadfast, telling Felix 'A Christian is at best, when he doth suffer; / The cruellest torments are but recompenses / Unto us' (5.2). Such is the power of Polyeuctes's resistance and his embracing of martyrdom that Paulina and Felix convert to Christainity, while Servius, on behalf of the Emperor, renounces the persecution of the Christians and utters a plea for tolerance. The sensibility of the drama is thus consonant with a certain royalist ethos and, as with the revenge play, it could be said that the 'martyr play' offered to the party in defeat a dignified accommodation and ennobled status. Consolation could be found in the dramatic reworking of ancient models of stoical fortitude.

The choice of any text for translation can be politically suggestive, even overtly referential. A particularly notable example is Christopher Wase's translation of *Electra* by Sophocles, which he presented to Elizabeth, younger daughter of Charles I. That the play was published in The Hague may have encouraged Wase to be quite explicit about the political intentions of his work. In his dedication he employs the familiar metaphor of the play as the mirror of 'men's actions' and then alludes to the topical resonances of the story: 'This dim crystal (sullied with antiquity and a long voyage) will return upon your Highness some lines and shadows of that piety to your deceased father which seats you above the age.' Dedicatory verses reiterate Wase's 'apt choice and seasonable translation of Electra in Sophocles'. By casting Elizabeth in the role of Electra, who remains faithful to the memory of her father Agamemnon following his murder by her mother, Clytemnestra, and Aegisthus and hopes for the vengeful return and restoration of her brother Orestes, Wase likens the House of Atreus to the House of Stuart and turns the fate of the Stuarts into a revenge tragedy. This revenge tragedy cannot, however, be read as a complete reflection of the times, since Sophocles' tragedy is impelled by crimes within the family. By Electra's reference in the text to her mother Clytemnestra, Wase has made a marginal note on the character of the Queen which begins, 'Here may not unproperly be urged the old caution, that similitudes run not upon all four' (p. 5). If the martyred Charles might be cast as the victim Agamemnon, the devoted Henrietta Maria could not be cast as the unfaithful, blood-stained Clytemnestra.

As a revenge tragedy for the royalist reader, *Electra* has the ideal conclusion. In place of Sophocles' chorus of Mycenean women, Wase has a 'quire' of maids of honour who rejoice in the revenge: 'Atreus's seed how hard oppressed, / Art thou at length arrived at rest / By this assay redressed.' Post-1649 loyalist pamphlets and newsbooks had likewise invoked the theme of revenge. The opening verses of the royalist journal *The Man in the Moon* in July 1649, for example, appeal to foreign powers as well as 'Irish, English, Scots' for vengeance to be exacted for the black deeds and hellish plots of the Parliamentarians. Revenge tragedy produces this wished-for closure. The Epilogue of *Electra*, addressed to Elizabeth, develops in two poems, 'The Return' and 'The Restoration', the parallels between her brother Charles and Orestes. There is a comment on the military might of the Commonwealth and the 'stiff yoke' it holds on the country's neck; yet 'Force can but in a Rape engage / 'Tis choice must make it marriage.' The return of Charles is projected as providentially ordained: 'And touched from Heaven with holy flame / His throne we plant, his foes we tame.' All in city and village, the poem promises, will welcome and give thanks for the return of the King. In its optimistic and highly specific projections, Wase's text thus goes well beyond the act of revenge represented off-stage in *Electra*.

DRAMATIC FORMS: INTERLUDES, DROLLS AND FARCES

The drama which proved most resilient to State opposition was that which had roots in popular pastime and non-commercial theatre: the interlude, jig or farce, or an entertainment which has been classified rather imprecisely as the droll, an abbreviation of 'drollery'. Droll, a post-Restoration term, as genre is somewhat misleading, since it has been used to incorporate such diverse dramatic forms as interludes, jigs, masques and plays in adapted and abridged form.

To add to the repertoire of jigs and interludes during the 1640s and 1650s, certain players began to abridge popular Elizabethan and Jacobean plays, the reduced versions being subsequently termed drolls. Two miscellanies of drolls entitled *The Wits or Sport Upon Sport* were published at the Restoration: the first compiled by Henry Marsh in 1662, with a second enlarged edition by the bookseller Francis Kirkman in 1672; and *II Wits or Sport Upon Sport*, published by Kirkman in 1673. The title pages of both editions of *The Wits* claim social inclusivity for the form: 'fitted for the pleasure and content of all persons, either in court, city, country, or camp'. Marsh recommends his collection not only to individuals but for the purposes of recitation or extempore performance, no doubt, recalling earlier informal theatre practice. Both prefaces maintain that the drolls were performed during the Commonwealth. A specific reference to actual performance at the time of the Rump Parliament (1648–53) is found in Marsh's final line, 'Pray remember the Rump drolls, and for their sakes, your old servant, H. Marsh.' The title page of

Kirkman's edition recalls performance 'on mountebank stage by strolling players, fools and fiddlers' while the Preface to *II Wits* refers to productions at Charing Cross and the Red Bull, and at fairs and inns.

A small number of interludes, which were later incorporated into the Restoration anthologies of drolls, was, however, published in c.1655 by the comedian and player Robert Cox, with the pieces advertised as having been performed on the stage of the Red Bull, the theatre with which Cox was associated. Cox had been mentioned in the details of a raid in June 1653 on a suburban theatre—probably the Red Bull—occasioned by the betrayal of two fellow actors.[51] According to the report, Cox had been employed by the rope dancers 'to present a modest and harmless gig called Swabber'. *John Swabber the Seaman*, a comic farce of cuckoldry, is included in Cox's collection, which provides the only sure evidence of the nature of the Commonwealth interlude and of which pieces were actually performed.

The generic hybridity of the volume is apparent in Cox's full title: *Actaeon and Diana: with a pastoral story of the nymph Oenone: followed by the several conceited humours Bumpkin the Huntsman, Hobbinal the Shepherd, Singing Simpkin and John Swabber the Seaman. Singing Simpkin* is also included in Restoration anthologies, but it is almost certainly Elizabethan, indicating the continuity of jig, interlude and droll.[52] In the title piece, *Actaeon and Diana*, as in *A Midsummer Night's Dream*, but in small compass, the mythic and popular co-exist to comic effect. The interlude begins with the entrance of Bumpkin, 'chief dog-keeper' to Actaeon, announcing that he is suffering from love sickness and that he has 'a horrible mind to be in love', but he is scorned by the girls dancing around the maypole. Since maypole dancing had been condemned in an ordinance of 1644 as a 'heathenish vanity' and the raising of maypoles was forbidden, such dramatic imagery would seem intentionally provocative as well as sexually suggestive. The young women sing enticingly, 'Then to the Maypole come away, / For it is now a holiday.' In contrast to their earlier disdain, the women now hang about Bumpkin and pull him down as he tries to extricate himself from these 'burrs'. The finale returns to the mythological, as Actaeon is pursued by his huntsmen and then borne away, while Diana dances with her nymphs. Within its brief confines, *Actaeon and Diana* plays with the forms of rustic comedy and pastoral, while maintaining the cultural appeal of popular pastime.

Kirkman's second collection of twenty-seven drolls reveals a diversity of dramatic form. Some, like *Bottom the Weaver*, extracted from the rustic scenes of *A Midsummer Night's Dream*, are much longer than others; not all are humorous, some are abridgements from masques and some are little more than a short dialogue. If, according to Kirkman's testimony, these pieces were performed during the 1650s we can see how the drama of the Commonwealth reveals itself as both backward- and forward-looking. As a prime example of such dramatic hybridity, the droll appropriates the jig, the play within a play and the moral interlude; but it can also be seen as the prototype of the burlesque drama associated with Thomas Duffet and the Shakespearian adaptations of Davenant and Dryden at the Restoration. Like the burlesque, the drolls were often derivative in their adaptation of scenes from popular plays by Shakespeare. *The Bouncing Knight*, for example, included in Kirkman's second collection, is an amalgam of various scenes in *1 Henry IV* in which Falstaff appears. Thus, we move from the tavern scene (3.3), in which Falstaff accuses Mistress Quickly of rifling his pockets, to Falstaff's comic soliloquy about his abuse of recruitment ('I have misused the King's press damnably'), followed by his preposterous claim that he has killed Hotspur. Such a redaction obviously depends on a folkloric appreciation of the character, divorced from any narrative framework. Other drolls in Kirkman's collection re-present scenes from plays by Jonson, Marston and Beaumont and Fletcher.

In a sense, Marsh and Kirkman created by their compilations a genre which was far from uniform in style or idiom. Marsh was not unaware of this, apologetically acknowledging in his preface that he has made of a fluid a solid body. By gathering extant Commonwealth and early Restoration drama and presenting it under the identity of a collection, the compilers imply homogeneity where there is only miscellany. Nevertheless, the prefaces of Marsh and Kirkman provide some evidence that abridgements and redactions of Elizabethan and Jacobean plays, as well as jigs and reworkings of masques, continued to be performed during the years of the civil wars and the Republic.

DRAMA AND METAPHOR

Writing was a safe outlet for the Royalist in defeat, a notion suggested by one of the contributors to the commendatory verses prefacing *Electra* in lines which are quoted as an epigraph to this Introduction. It was also one of the few defiant gestures left to the defeated party. While the pamphlet plays, like the royalist journals, can be said to represent the novel dressing up of elite culture in a popular idiom, the more conventionally genre-based plays continue to respect antecedent dramatic conventions. However, themes and motifs of rebellion and usurpation, of lost and wandering monarchs, took on a highly charged significance following the regicide and after the defeat of Prince Charles at Worcester. The use of fictional or historical locations to provide a gloss on contemporary politics represents the continuation of the familiar and pleasurable use of metaphor as a means of evading censorship and deciphering meaning.

The majority of the full-length plays written after 1649 are broadly royalist; but the ideas they express are by no means unequivocal. As Susan Wiseman has incisively demonstrated, binary opposites of Royalist and Parliamentarian represent an over-simplification of variegated and complex ideological positions in the period.[53] In particular, loyalty to the royalist cause was sometimes combined with ambivalent feelings about the defeated monarch. Indeed, several of the following plays register a sense of political disillusionment and distrust of declared beliefs. From the other side of the ideological divide, a seemingly republican play like *Cicero* (included in this volume), while reinforcing the values of the Commonwealth, discloses a sense of unease at potential dangers to the new dispensation.

A play which quite explicitly responds to crises of government is *The Rebellion of Naples or the Tragedy of Massenello*,[54] whose author chooses, unsurprisingly, to hide his identity. The title page simply refers to the author as a gentleman who was an eyewitness to events 'where this was really acted upon that bloody stage, the streets of Naples.' Typical of so many earlier Jacobean plays is the disclaimer in the address to the reader that the dramatist is offering any allusion to contemporary events: 'I assure you the times are busy with me and not I with the times.' The play's topicality is none the less surface-deep. The Viceroy's imposition of excise taxes was bound to evoke memories of the deeply unpopular levies imposed by Charles I during his personal rule.[55] There may, also, have been a more immediate association with the taxes levied on London to finance the civil wars, the unpopularity of which led to the burning of the Excise House in Smithfield in 1647. Published in the year of the King's execution, the play exposes the fundamental causes of rebellion, while also relaying apprehension about its consequences. Persuaded by his secretary Genuino, General Tomaso Massenello, a one-time fisherman, agrees to lead the people's rebellion and presents himself as a popular leader with a sense of patriotic responsibility. Massenello tells Genuino that he will take action only for 'the good of the Republic'. But such honourable intentions are short-lived, as first Massenello is persuaded to act out of self-interest and then he becomes literally mad with power.

The Epilogue, which is spoken by Massenello, seems to be having it both ways in warning both the ruler of the consequences of the abuse of power and the people of the detrimental effects of rebellion:

> Let kings beware how they provoke
> Their subjects with too hard a yoke,
> For when all's done, it will not do,
> You see they break the yoke in two:
> Let subjects no rebellion move
> On such pretences least it prove
> As sad a thing (which God forbid)
> And fatal as to us it did.

(p. 76)

As the Epilogue intimates, *The Rebellion of Naples* treads a cautious middle ground between political extremes. The Viceroy is certainly not a complimentary image of Charles I, assuming that an analogy is to be drawn: the ruler's weak, vacillating personality and susceptibility to poor counsel are seen as responsible for the city's conflicts. Yet the cause of liberty, with all its noble pretensions, degenerates readily, if somewhat unconvincingly, into tyranny. The populace are fickle and undiscerning, lacking the judgement to resist the sovereign abuse of power.

As in a number of Renaissance plays, Sicily was the fictionalized location of John Tatham's *The Distracted State*. Tatham's career illustrates the difficulty of defining playwrights by their political allegiance. He had earlier been associated with the Red Bull, but he wrote a number of plays during the Commonwealth and he was to compose the Lord Mayor's shows in 1657 and 1658, and at the Restoration.[56] *The Distracted State*, a tragicomedy, was one of the few plays to be licensed and was duly entered in the Stationers' Register on 23 November 1650. The entry states that the play had been written as early as 1641; but the reference to an earlier date of composition may well have been a smokescreen to ease the licensing procedure, since the drama certainly discloses a preoccupation with political events in the period post-1642 which is unlikely to owe its inspiration to mere premonition.[57] The epigram 'Seditiones sunt Reipublicae ruina' is an indication of how the term *respublica*—the Commonwealth—had in a sense become a contest of meaning, as Tatham focuses on the destruction of the body politic through the 'sedition' of usurpation.

While adapting familiar Renaissance themes of usurpation, rebellion and deposition, *The Distracted State* demonstrates a marked ideological flexibility unthinkable in earlier plays. As in *The Rebellion of Naples*, Tatham attempts an overview of the causes and condition of a usurped government. Agathocles, who is vehemently opposed to the new regime, and Epecides comment on the responses of the people and, in the words of Epecides, their manipulation: 'It is pretended / The people's pressures and continual clamours / Enforced the war' (Act 1, p. 3). But the same speaker offers a balanced view, conceding that 'The state was much distempered and Evander [the deposed king] / Was not without his faults'. Agathocles, however, remains staunchly loyalist, claiming that those who have supported the *coup* justify themselves in terms of 'providence and justice' and exaggerate the faults of the monarch:

> People disposed for change
> Survey the vices of their prince through optics
> That rather multiply than lessen them;
> And what is in themselves but criminal
> Is in their prince held horrid, as the symptom
> To the disease of tyranny.
>
> (Act 1, p. 4)

In the play's rapid reversals such professed loyalty is to assume an ironic note. There are no fewer than four further rebellions, and, rather as in *The Tempest*, usurpation generates more of the same. At one point, Agathocles and Epecides express their disillusionment with monarchy and speak in favour of republicanism:

Agathocles. How sweet and freely Rome enjoyed herself,
　　'Til she submitted to the power and pride
　　Of one man's rule. Tell me what good did ever
　　Kings bring into our country, that we might not
　　Have purchased without 'em? Ills they have
　　Almost incredible; our coffers emptied,
　　To fill their treasury, and maintain their riot.

(Act 4, p. 24)

Epecides agrees and proposes that the country should be 'governed by three or ten, as did the Romans'; in response, Agathocles advocates yet further democracy, proposing that elected governors will each have only one year in power and will be accountable to their successors. But in the final act, when Agathocles realizes that power may be within his grasp, he repudiates such an ideology and reveals by his seizure of the crown his own lust for absolute power. There is a further revolt from within the army before the return and restoration of Evander. Sicily, exclaims Evander, has been 'beaten and banded to promote the ends of turbulent spirited men'. Following the restoration of the legitimate king, the drama ends with a general pardon and an improbable moment of reconciliation between Evander and the dying officers who had staged the last rebellion. Ostensibly, *The Distracted State* is a play about the familiar Elizabethan theme of the evils of usurpation. Power becomes a tyrant's charter. But, composed in such a radically different context from that of its antecedents, the play is more explicit in its critique of monarchy. Evander is recognized as a flawed king, as are all his successors, and absolute power is seen to corrupt. Other forms of government are at least contemplated and eloquently articulated, if not ultimately endorsed. Moreover, the play's resolution is as much concerned with the reconciliation of warring factions as it is with monarchical restoration.

Attesting to the comparative freedom with which royalist dramatic texts could be circulated, two tragicomedies, *The Just General* and *The Loyal Lovers*, by Major Cosmo Manuche were licensed and published in handsome quartos.[58] *The Just General* was entered in the Stationers' Register in November 1651 and, by using his army title and in dedicating his work to the Earl of Northampton, Manuche made no attempt to conceal his allegiances. Northampton wrote plays and through the auspices of his patronage Manuche's works may well have been performed at Castle Ashby, Northampton's home. But Manuche, like John Tatham, Richard Flecknoe and William Davenant, appears to have adjusted to the Commonwealth under Cromwell, petitioning the Protector in 1656 for recompense for 'making discoveries of the disturbers of our present happy government'.[59] Such accommodations seem to be reflected in the elusiveness of the plays' ideological preoccupations and their conciliatory resolutions.

Although *The Just General* begins with the announcement of 'a cessation of arms on both sides', the dramatic focus is not the war but on the love of Amasius, the king, for Aurelia, a match considered unequal by his general, Bellicosus. It has been suggested that a possible parallel could have been drawn between Amasius's desires and Charles's insistence on marrying the Catholic Henrietta Maria.[60] But the drama cannot be said to operate at an analogical level. The loyalist Bellicosus, portrayed as the model courtier-adviser, is an anti-type of Charles's ill-advising counsellors. When Aurelia becomes the victim of a plot and disappears, Amasius, convinced that Bellicosus has murdered her, leaves the court in disguise. The tragicomic motif of the wandering, disguised ruler might be said to contain additional resonances in 1651 when, after the Battle of Worcester, Charles Stuart was forced to flee England incognito, and rumours abounded of his whereabouts. The General is offered the crown, but, in a romantic and loyalist representation of events, he at first declines it, while the King's supporters swear they will never acknowledge any other king until the death of Amasius is confirmed. Possibly this scene brings to mind allegations of Cromwell's aspirations to power and, more particularly, royalist propaganda which maintained that he aimed for nothing but the throne (although Cromwell was not in fact offered the crown, which he declined, until 1657). Interestingly, particularly in the light of Manuche's supplication to Cromwell, in his play the General does accept the crown, in the conviction that only by doing so can he save the country from anarchy.

The Just General negotiates both literal and allegorical meanings concerning the relationship between monarch and subject. At the local level, it has been suggested that the play dramatizes the dangers inherent in a ruler's untimely desertion of his kingdom, exemplified in Charles I's departure from London in 1642.[61] Less specifically, the play is a performance of loyalism and of fortitude, as Bellicosus remains faithful to the King in extremity, even to the extent of sentencing his own son to death for his unwitting participation in the plot to kill Aurelia, and immediately restores the crown to Amasius on his return. Yet the play resists any explicit political engagement. Like Manuche's other play of the period, The Loyal Lovers, the drama notably relegates the war to its margins in order to focus on the tragicomic material, reflecting a genre which, with its ultimate denial of disaster, regained popularity during the Commonwealth.[62] In the tragicomic form of both The Just General and The Loyal Lovers there is a fluidity in political stance. In the former, a general assumes the authority of a king, while in the latter factional intermarriage between the daughter of a committee man and a loyalist-type figure symbolically provides a resolution to political conflict.

From Shakespeare and Jonson to Massinger and Thomas May, ancient Rome had long served dramatic purposes as a political paradigm of republican, imperial or transitional government. In the non-dramatic writings of the period, it was common to invoke the spirit and mixed constitution of the Roman Republic and to hope that Britain was 'building a new Rome in the West'. Analogies between Cromwell and Julius Caesar as military leaders and, pejoratively, through their imperial ambitions, as destroyers of republican values, were made.[63] Allusion to classical historians and poets who had celebrated the Roman Republic or criticized the Empire—notably Livy, Tacitus and Lucan—was central to the culture of the English Republic, although, as David Norbrook has commented, English admirers of the Roman Republic were never particularly sanguine about the political future.[64] This seems to be the case with the author of one of the most significant plays of the period, included in this edition, *The Tragedy of that Famous Orator Marcus Tullius Cicero*, which was published in 1651. Although the author draws on earlier Renaissance translations of Cicero's moral and philosophical works—*De officiis* and *Tusculan Disputations*—it is with Cicero as advocate of the Roman Republic that the play is primarily concerned. With many backward glances at the politics of the Republic, the play engages with the period between the assassination of Julius Caesar in 45 BC and the subsequent civil wars and establishment of the triumvirate. The collapse of the Republic is foreshadowed as the imperial ambitions of both Antony, who engineers the death of the patriotic Cicero, and Caesar Octavius are unmasked. Heightened drama stems from the conflict between Cicero, the honourable patriot and public orator, and the loose-living, vengeful Antony, who is intent on sacrificing the public good to personal advantage. The author of this academic play was steeped in his classical sources and the play was evidently intended as a sustained political meditation on forms of government and the dangers to the fledgling English Republic of unchecked individual ambition leading to dictatorship.

Within familiar genres, new plays written during the Republic self-evidently engage with pressing political and ideological preoccupations. In a sense drama with its metaphoric inventiveness became a repository for—in the main royalist—hopes, fears and plain wish-fulfilment. Not all the plays were licensed, but the fact that a number were suggests some acceptance of the act of play writing in the cultural life of the Commonwealth. Several—Manuche's tragicomedies for example—may have been performed under private auspices as well as licensed for the press. Despite the apparent restriction on theatre production, dramatists continued to conceptualize their plays in terms of performance. An elaborate dumb show presaging the fall of the monarch is described in an initial stage direction of *The Rebellion of Naples*. The final scene of *The Just General* represents in high theatrical fashion the peripeteia of tragicomedy as the General's son who had unsuccessfully contrived to marry Aurelia, and his jealous lover Artesia, are led in for execution, only to be saved by the sudden reappearance of the King. In a scene which cries out for theatrical realization, 'the executioner prepares to strike', but the King orders him to stay and then 'discovers himself'. In the final focus on the return of the lost king the genre of romance is evoked. New plays of the Commonwealth self-consciously make a direct appeal to a theatrically literate reader and/or amateur performer. The pleasures of the text are thus bound up not only with allusions to and deciphering of contemporary politics but with the participation in familiar stage and dramatic practice.

THEATRICAL ACCOMMODATIONS

In his tribute to Oliver Cromwell, *The Idea of his Highness Oliver, late Lord Protector with certain brief reflections on his life*, published in 1659 after Cromwell's death, the priest, poet and playwright Richard Flecknoe had mused that 'Men of Estates and Fortunes always comply with the present times and seek not (with hazard to make them worse) to better their conditions' (p. 45). It was in this spirit that William Davenant, who was indebted to Flecknoe's ideas of a reformed stage, officially revived and produced drama governed by new theatrical aesthetics.

Flecknoe first made a bid to realign and reconstitute the drama by seeking the patronage of Lady Elizabeth Claypole, Cromwell's daughter. In dedicating *Love's Dominion* (1654) to Claypole, Flecknoe made a strong plea for the revival of drama, which is desired by 'the nobler and better sort'. The play was advertised as 'a dramatic piece full of excellent morality' and written as a pattern for the reformed stage. Suggesting a redefining of drama, Flecknoe claims that 'actions', 'opera' or 'works' would all be more apt designations than 'plays'. A restored, reformed stage, he argues, should be welcomed by the dispensation of the Cromwellian Protectorate and could, he suggests, be subject to moral censorship:

> I deny not but aspersions (these latter times) have been cast upon it by the ink of some who have written obscenely and scurrilously . . . but instead of wiping them off, to break the glass, was too rigid and severe. For my part I have endeavoured here the clearing of it, and restoring it to its former splendour, and first institution (of teaching virtue, reproving vice, and amendment of manners) so as if the rest but imitate my example, those who shall be enemies of it hereafter, must declare themselves enemies of virtue, as formerly they did of vice: whence we may justly hope to see it restored again, with the qualification of an humble coadjutor of the Pulpit, to teach morality, in order to the others divinity, and the moulding and tempering men's minds for the better receiving the impression of godliness. (A4v)

A similar line had been offered by Davenant in *A Proposition for the Advancement of Morality by a New Way of Entertainment of the People* (1653), presented to the Council of State, in which he argues the moral and socially educative advantages for the lower classes of a reformed stage, which he too suggests could be subjected to censorship.[65] Davenant advocates that the subject matter of the reformed drama would be heroic and the actions depicted would be inherently virtuous. His propositions were followed up three years later with a further apology for public entertainment in a letter to John Thurloe, Cromwell's Secretary of State and occasional licenser of the press.[66] Here economic, pragmatic and ideo-logical reasons are further offered to support a theatrical revival. The extent to which London had been impoverished by the absence of the court, and its desertion by Royalists, enabled Davenant to argue that the gentry must be encouraged to reside in the City by the allure of 'pleas-ant assemblies', so that wealth can circulate. In contrast to the argument of his earlier document, Davenant emphasizes that the clientele he now proposes to attract are the gentry. It is doubtful whether economic reasons alone could have persuaded the council to grant permission for what Davenant terms 'moral representations'. The clue to the eventual theatri-cal revival lies in the final paragraph of the letter, in which Davenant pro-poses his subject: 'If moral representations may be allowed . . . the first arguments may consist of the Spaniards' barbarous conquests in the West Indies and of their several cruelties there exercised upon the subjects of this nation: of which some use may be made.' The perceived political utility of the project, specifically in negative representations of Spain, an imperial rival, must have been a highly significant factor in the govern-ment's decision to sanction public performance.

Appropriately, the theatrical revival, in the private space of Rutland House, began with a debate about the nature of drama. There are two parts and two rhetorical exchanges to *The First Day's Entertainment*, whose very title draws attention to the novelty of the performance. The first debate is between Diogenes, the cynic philosopher who was alleged to have spent his life in a tub, and Aristophanes, the satiric playwright, and the second is set between a Frenchman and an Englishman. In the first dialogue, Diogenes voices and possibly anticipates objections to recitative and scenic drama. Music is a deceitful art, leading to the 'evil of extremes' of feeling and transporting an audience 'beyond the regions of reason'. Scenes are deceptive of place and motion and, argues Dio-genes, may only inculcate the evil of deception in general. Aristophanes refutes such literalism with a reiteration of the therapeutic, moral and aesthetic refinement of drama. Music 'unites and recollects a broken and scattered mind; giving it sudden strength to resist the evils it hath long and strongly bred'. Pictorial representation, as in the uses of scenes, is 'the safest and shortest way to understanding'. The playwright dismisses Diogenes' claim that the tendency to use the remote past in dramatic rep-resentations makes their subject matter less credible by arguing that the past works with greater subtlety on the intelligence. Predictably, the victory lies with Aristophanes, who defeats his antagonist by arguing that, since Diogenes is himself 'the worst representation of morality', he is justly afraid to be portrayed in the theatre. At the close of the dialogue, in a graphic rejection of anti-representational argument, Diogenes is forced to retreat to his tub.

In the second dialogue, with its cultural references to Parisian style and manners, the emphasis shifts. Here the argument would seem to be clearly directed at a former aristocratic audience, since it runs counter to the

nationalist ideology promoted by the Republic. The Parisian refers to the
long association of the English gentry with French modes of conduct:

> but though you have frequently the pride to disdain the behaviour of other
> nations, yet you have sometimes the discretion to send your sons abroad
> to learn it. To Paris they come: the School of Europe, where is taught the
> approaches and demeanours towards power: where they may learn honour,
> which is the generous honesty, and confidence which is the civil boldness
> of courts.

In the context of a bid to revive public drama, the allusion to courts modelled on the French style is curious. The Queen Dowager was of course
French, and Davenant had spent part of his exile at her *émigré* court in
Paris, an experience shared no doubt by some of his audience. But it is
possible that the royalist perspective was not as apparent in performance
as it is in the printed text: according to a government informer who
attended the performance, the declamation concluded with a song in
praise of Cromwell which is notably absent from the published text.[67]

The Epilogue of *The First Day's Entertainment* initially appears to be
an apologia for the absence of familiar dramatic constructions and conventions, which may disappoint an audience with expectations of a revival
of theatre as it was:

> Perhaps some were so cozened as to come
> To see us weave in the dramatic loom:
> To trace the winding scenes, like subtle spies,
> Bred in the Muses camp . . .
> To watch the plot's swift change and counterturn:
> When Time moves swifter than by Nature taught
> And by a Chorus miracles are wrought;
> Making an infant instantly a man:
> These were your plays, but get them if you can.

The lines recall the Prologue of the 1616 Folio text of *Every Man in His
Humour*, so that Davenant's comments on the 'lost' drama are mediated
through Jonson's critique of the looseness of romance and, in particular,
Shakespearian plotting. Despite the challenge to the audience in the final
line, it is possible to read the Epilogue as suggesting that the audience
has experienced less a culturally compromised art form than innovatory
drama produced for a new age.

Davenant, ever the entrepreneur, succeeded where Flecknoe failed, in
gaining the Republic's sanction for the performance of his entertainments—three other pieces followed *The First Day's Entertainment*—but
it was Flecknoe's continentally influenced theories of a scenic drama communicated in recitative music which influenced Davenant's work of the
period. Flecknoe's *Ariadne Deserted by Theseus and Found and Courted
by Bacchus*, published but not performed in 1654, set out in theory and
action ideas for new stage practice. In his preface Flecknoe asserts that,
in course of travelling in Italy, he 'found that music I intended to intro-

duce, exceedingly in vogue': that is, recitative music, which he claims has immense emotive power through its association with poetry. In a second short preface, Flecknoe traces the development of his interest in the form: 'Tis many years since I proposed unto a sovereign Prince the congruity, that as their persons, so their music, should be elevated above the vulgar, and made not only to delight the ear, but also their understanding, not patched up with songs of different subjects, but all of one piece, with design and plot.' 'All of one piece' carries a fairly clear refutation not only of the Renaissance drama with its inclusion of songs, ballads and jigs but of the different musical composites of masque and anti-masque.

Again, there is no record of any performance of Flecknoe's final operatic entertainment published in 1659, *The Marriage of Oceanus and Britannia*. Flecknoe's work, however, demands more elaborate stage effects than do Davenant's texts, and it is possible that restrictions on the scope of production rather than any official prohibition hindered its staging. The opera is described as 'an allegorical fantasy, really declaring England's riches, glory and puissance by sea' and as such is a celebration of the naval power of the first Protectorate. In its allegorical representation of imperial expansionism under Cromwell, Flecknoe is drawing on earlier imagery of the Republic. Marchamont Nedham had translated John Selden's *Mare Clausum* (1635) as *Of the Dominion or Ownership of the Sea* (1652), in which the frontispiece has Britannia, signifying the English Republic, with the crown at her feet and with Nepture urging her to expand her empire (figure 2). In Flecknoe's work Britannia first appears in the second 'part'—Flecknoe avoids the masque term of 'entry'—reflecting on her present happiness in contrast to the recent miseries of the civil wars; nevertheless, she orders Oceanus to desist from his pursuit of her until she has become 'the most renowned and opulent / Of all the isles with circling waves / You ever yet surrounded have'. The third part depicts Oceanus announcing his partisanship for the English naval forces opposed to the Spanish and promoting England as a colonizing power. In projecting such imperial expansionism, Flecknoe is drawing on imagery of the Republic which had earlier been mobilized by Davenant in *The Cruelty of the Spaniards in Peru*.

The same celebration of 'Englishness', and in particular the nation's military and naval power, is present in all of Davenant's entertainments dating from the Protectorate: *The Siege of Rhodes, The Cruelty of the Spaniards in Peru* and *The History of Sir Francis Drake*. In theatrical form these dramas are the most innovatory works of the Republic; but, in adapting such nationalist themes as the apocryphal colonization of Peru and Drake's plundering voyages to South America, Davenant produced a drama which harked back to Elizabethan foreign policy. This was, of course, a safe enough subject, and it was also one which had a unifying appeal. The Cromwellian Protectorate spoke the language of Elizabethan expansionism. It had been a familiar theme of the news journals that, if the Stuarts had been Tudors, England would not have suffered the same religious,

2 Frontispiece, Marchamont Nedham's translation of Selden, *Of the Dominion or Ownership of the Sea.*

political and economic ills and would still have been recognized as a European power. When in 1628 the nephew of Francis Drake published *Sir Francis Drake Revived*—the source for *The History of Sir Francis Drake*—he called on his title page for 'this effeminate age' to follow 'his noble steps for gold and silver'.[68] In reviving such Elizabethan material and making a connection with Cromwellian foreign incursions, Davenant is contributing to the re-formation of an earlier English national identity in a guise which is compatible with the ideology of the Republic.

At the same time as depicting a military ethic, *The Siege of Rhodes*, the first of the narrative dramas, reveals a remarkable recovery of dramatic form, with the five entries closely resembling acts and the love plot between Alphonso and Ianthe complicating the historical action. Here, the debate between love and honour with which Alphonso wrestles refers back to the ideological conflicts in Davenant's pre-civil-war drama and adumbrates the concerns of later plays by John Dryden in particular. As is also the case with *The Cruelty of the Spaniards in Peru*, *The Siege of Rhodes* makes an appeal to both sides of the civil wars divide.

It is revealing to study the later reception of Davenant's dramatic output during the Republic. Dryden, in his preface to *The Conquest of Granada*, 'Of Heroic Plays: an Essay' (1674), commented that, in order not to offend 'those good people, who could more easily dispossess their lawful sovereign than endure a wanton jest', Davenant had been 'forced to introduce the example of moral virtue, writ in verse and performed in recitative music'.[69] Whether Davenant's innovations in form and content were entirely due to the pressures of censorship, as Dryden implies, is doubtful. Like Flecknoe, Davenant seems to have seen the Commonwealth as an appropriate time to experiment with the semi-operatic practice which was proving so influential in French and Italian courts. His aspirations for a musical and scenic stage antedated the civil wars: in 1639 he had been granted a patent for an aborted project for a playhouse 'wherein plays, musical entertainments, scenes, or other like presentments may be presented'.[70] Neither was the appeal of the entertainment limited to the Republic; all were republished at the Restoration, when *The Siege of Rhodes*, with its Second Part, although acted not sung, continued to be popular.

The composite forms of *The Siege of Rhodes*, *The Cruelty of the Spaniards in Peru* and *The History of Sir Francis Drake* defy easy classification. No doubt their indistinct or novel generic identity allowed them to circumvent the prohibitions on the public performance of plays. In the correspondence about *The Siege of Rhodes* accompanying a copy of the work which Davenant sent to Bulstrode Whitlocke, a former Master of the Revels at the Inns of Court, and subsequently Cromwell's ambassador to Sweden, Davenant referred to his work as 'opera'.[71] But this is a loose and no doubt strategic use of the term, recalling Flecknoe's similar attempt to redefine drama, rather than an evocation of the specific Italianate form. It would have been indiscreet to refer to these entertainments as masques, recalling associations with Stuart court culture; yet the Stationers' Register does describe *The Siege of Rhodes* as masque, and manifestly the works do appropriate some of that genre's formal elements for distinct ideological purposes.

The contributions during the Commonwealth of Davenant, and indirectly of Flecknoe, to such changes in theatre practice were far-reaching and cannot be overestimated. Without doubt, the political had helped to define the aesthetics of drama, as the settlements of the 1650s stimulated its formal reinvention and a small-scale theatrical revival. It has been said that the execution of Charles I marked the end of the Renaissance. Despite the self-conscious allusion and appeal to Renaissance dramatic conventions and motifs, the drama of the English Commonwealth did indeed mark a decisive break with elements of the past. Scenic theatre had replaced the bare Renaissance stage and its fluent dramatic production. The appearance of Catherine Coleman as Ianthe in *The Siege of Rhodes* prepared audiences for the given of Restoration theatre: female impersonation of the woman's part. Blank verse was no longer the dominant verse medium. Conquest plays were to enjoy a vogue, and love and honour, however parodied, were to endure as themes in the plays of Dryden. In theatrical terms the period which was once regarded as a dramatic backwater provided the impetus for so much that was to follow. From the irreverent treatment of the Shakespearian text to the sensational political drama and satire of the Exclusion crisis to the opera of Purcell to the classical ethos of Nathaniel Lee, prototypes were developed in the years of the English Republic.

NOTES

1 Prefatory verses to Christopher Wase's translation of *Electra* (1651).
2 Leslie Hotson, *The Commonwealth and Restoration Stage* (New York, 1928; reprinted 1962).
3 See Potter, pp. 261–304; Dale B. J. Randall, *Winter Fruit: English Drama 1642–1660* (Lexington, 1995); Wiseman, pp. 1–7.
4 See David Norbrook, *Writing the English Republic: Poetry, Rhetoric and English Poetics 1627–1660* (Cambridge, 1999), pp. 98ff.
5 *Acts and Ordinances of the Interregnum, 1642–1660*, edited by C. H. Firth and R. S. Rait, 3 vols, London, 1911, I, pp. 26–7.
6 See Gosson, *The School of Abuse* (1579), Stubbes, *The Anatomy of Abuses* (1583), *The Second Part of the Anatomy of Abuses* (1583), Rankins, *A Mirror of Monsters* (1587), Prynne, *Histrio-mastix, The Player's Scourge* (1633).
7 See Christopher Durston, 'Puritan Rule and the Failure of Cultural Revolution, 1645–1660' in *The Culture of English Puritanism, 1560–1700*, edited by Christopher Durston and Jacqueline Eales (London, 1996).
8 *Perfect Occurrences*, 1–8 October 1647, p. 281.
9 *Diary of John Evelyn*, edited by E. S. De Beer, 6 vols (Oxford, 1955), I, p. 539.
10 See E. K. Chambers, *The Elizabethan Stage*, 4 vols (Oxford, 1923), 4, p. 324.
11 *Mercurius Anti-pragmaticus*, 28 October–4 November 1647, p. 2.
12 *Mercurius Democritus*, 1–8 June 1653, p. 463.

13 James Wright, *Historia Histrionica: An Historical Account of the English Stage showing the ancient use, improvement and perfection of dramatic representations in this nation* (London, 1699), p. 7.

14 See Judith Milhous and Robert D. Hume, 'New Light on English Acting Companies in 1646, 1648, and 1660', *Review of English Studies*, 42:168 (1991), 487–509.

15 *The Perfect Weekly Account*, 6–13 October 1647, p. 2^v.

16 *A Perfect Diurnal of Some Passages in Parliament*, 18–25 October 1647, p. 1774.

17 Firth and Rait, *Acts and Ordinances*, 1, p. 1027.

18 *The Kingdom's Weekly Intelligencer*, 9–16 January 1649, pp. 1210–11.

19 *Perfect Occurrences*, 29 December 1648–5 January 1649. See Blair Worden, *The Rump Parliament 1648–1653* (Cambridge, 1974), pp. 15, 23–6.

20 See Margot Heinemann, *Puritanism and Theatre: Thomas Middleton and Opposition Drama under the Early Stuarts* (Cambridge, 1980).

21 See *Middlesex County Records*, edited by J. C. Jeaffreson (1887; reprinted 1972), 3 vols, 3, p. 279.

22 Wright, *Historia Histrionica*, p. 9. Rich fought for Parliament in the first civil war and then, in late 1647, turned to the royalist cause. He was executed in March 1649. Later theatrical performances may have taken place under the auspices of Isabella, dowager Countess of Holland.

23 See below, pp. 11, 21–2.

24 See *Renaissance Drama by Women: Texts and Documents*, edited by S. P. Cerasano and Marion Wynne-Davies (London, 1996), pp. 127–30.

25 See W. P. Williams, 'The Castle Ashby Manuscripts', *The Library*, 6th series, 2:4 (1960), 391–412.

26 See *The Letters of Dorothy Osborne to William Temple*, edited by G. C. Moore Smith (Oxford, 1947), pp. 172–3.

27 See F. S. Siebert, *Freedom of the Press in England 1476–1776* (Urbana, 1965), pp. 179–233.

28 Siebert, pp. 172–5; Joseph Frank, *The Beginnings of the English Newspaper 1620–1660* (Cambridge, Mass., Harvard University Press, 1961), pp. 230ff.

29 It is not clear what is meant by 'beneficial second day' since the irregular practice from the 1630s was to award profits from the third day of the production to the author. I owe this point to Andrew Gurr.

30 See *Middlesex County Records*, 3, pp. 197–8.

31 *A Bartholomew Fairing* (1649), Wing 981, BL (E.572/7).

32 See *Mercurius Democritus*, 2–9 March 1653.

33 See Louis B. Wright, 'The Reading of Plays during the Puritan Revolution', *Huntingdon Library Bulletin*, 6 (1934), 73–108.

34 *Crafty Cromwell or Oliver Ordering our New State: A Tragicomedy* (1648), Wing C6772: BL (E.426/17); *The Second Part of Crafty Cromwell or Oliver in his Glory as King: A Tragicomedy* (1648), BL (C. 71. b 36/2).

35 See Frank, p. 162.

36 *The Second Part of the Tragicomedy called Newmarket Fair or Mrs Parliament's New Figaries* (1649), BL (E.565/6).

37 See Lois Potter, 'Marlowe in the Civil War and Commonwealth: Some Allusions and Parodies' in *'A Poet and Filthy Playmaker': New Essays on Christopher Marlowe*, edited by K. Friedenreich, R. Gill and Constance B. Kuriyama (New York, 1988), pp. 73–82.

38 *The Jovial Crew or The Devil Turned Ranter* (1651), Wing S3166, BL (E.621/7).

39 See *Ranters of Both Sexes, Male and Female: being thirteen or more, taken and imprisoned at the gate-house at Westminster, and in the new prison at Clerkenwell* (June 1651) and *Strange News from Newgate and the Old Bailey: or the proofs, examinations, declarations, indictments, conviction and confessions of J. Collins and T. Reeves, two of the ranters taken in More Lane* (January 1651).

40 *Ranters of Both Sexes*, p. 4. See also *Mercurius Democritus*, 2–9 March 1653, p. 272.

41 The verbal imagery of devilish destruction is contained in the pamphlet by John Taylor, *Ranters of Both Sexes*: 'Thus the devil shows by his raging, that his reigning draws towards an end . . . but his whole and many general drift ever have been, and ever will be, to disturb and destroy the Church of God, to sow his mischievous fares of damnable errors and mingle his hellish seed of sects and schisms with the pure and all-saving word of God' (p. 4).

42 *The Ghost, or The Woman Wears the Breeches* (1653), Wing 641; BL (E.710/8).

43 David Underdown, *A Freeborn People: Politics and the Nation in Seventeenth-century England* (Oxford, 1996), pp. 92–107.

44 See Sean Kelsey, *Inventing a Republic: The Political Culture of the English Commonwealth 1649–1653* (Manchester, 1997), p. 102.

45 See 'The *Mrs Parliament* Political Dialogues', edited by Lois Potter, *AEB (Analytical and Enumerative Bibliography)*, N.S. 1 (1987), 101–70, p. 111.

46 *The Famous Tragedy of King Charles I* (1649), Wing C384, BL (C.34.b.10).

47 See Christopher Hill, *The World Turned Upside-down: Radical Ideas during the English Revolution* (Harmondsworth, 1975), pp. 14–38; 361–86.

48 See Underdown, *A Freeborn People*, pp. 90–111.

49 See Philip Sidney, *A Defence of Poetry* in *Miscellaneous Prose of Sir Philip Sidney*, edited by K. Duncan Jones and J. A. van Dorsten (Oxford, 1973), p. 114.

50 See Raymond A. Anselment, *Loyalist Resolve: Patient Fortitude in the English Civil War* (Newark, NJ, 1988), pp. 13–20.

51 See *Mercurius Democritus*, 22–29 June 1653, p. 467.

52 *Singing Simpkin* almost certainly goes back to the sixteenth century. On 21 October 1595, there was an entry in the Stationers' Register for 'a ballad called Kemp's New Jig betwixt a soldier and a miser and Sym the clown'. See C. R. Baskervill, *The Elizabethan Jig* (Chicago, 1929), p. 238.

53 Wiseman, p. 9.

54 *The Rebellion of Naples, or The Tragedy of Massenello* (1649), Wing B, T199; BL (E.1358/2).

55 For possible reflections in the play on Charles's rule in the 1630s, see Geoffrey Aggeler, 'The Rebellion in Cavalier Drama' *Western Humanities Review*, 5:32 (1978), 53–75.

56 For a case study of John Tatham, see Wiseman, pp. 165–89.

57 See J. M. Wallace, 'The Case for Internal Evidence (10): The Date of John Tatham's *The Distracted State*', *Bulletin of the New York Public Library*, 64 (1960), 29–40.

58 See Wayne H. Phelps, 'Cosmo Manuche, Royalist Playwright of the Commonwealth', *English Language Notes*, 16:3 (1979), 207–11.

59 *CSPD*, 1655–56, p. 348. See also Phelps, p. 209.

60 See Aggeler, 'The Rebellion in Cavalier Drama', p. 63.

61 See Aggeler, 'The Rebellion in Cavalier Drama', p. 64.

62 See Lois Potter, ' "True Tragicomedies" of the Civil War and Commonwealth' in *Renaissance Tragicomedy*, edited by Nancy Maguire (London, 1987), pp. 196–217.

63 See David Armitage, 'The Cromwellian Protectorate and the Language of Empire', *The Historical Journal*, 35:3 (1992), 531–55, p. 532.

64 Norbrook, *Writing the English Republic*, p. 34.

65 See James R. Jacob and Timothy Raylor, 'Opera and Obedience: Thomas Hobbes and "A Proposition for Advancement of Morality" by Sir William Davenant' in *The Seventeenth Century*, 6:2 (1991), 205–50. 'A Proposition' was published anonymously in 1653, but dated 1654.

66 See C. H. Firth, 'Sir William Davenant and the Revival of Drama during the Protectorate', *English Historical Review* (April 1903), 103–20.

67 *CSPD*, 1655–56, p. 396.

68 'Sir Francis Drake Revived' in *Documents Concerning English Voyages to the Spanish Main 1569–1580*, edited by I. A. Wright (1932; reprinted Nendeln/ Liechtenstein, 1967), pp. 245–326.
69 'Of Heroic Plays; An Essay', in *Essays of John Dryden*, edited by W. P. Ker, 2 vols (Oxford, 1900), 1, p. 149.
70 *CSPD*, 1638–39, p. 604. See also Mary Edmond, *Rare Sir William Davenant* (Manchester, 1987), p. 75.
71 *The Diary of Bulstode Whitelocke 1605–1675*, edited by Ruth Spalding (Oxford, 1990), p. 449.

A NOTE ON EDITORIAL PROCEDURE

The works by William Davenant and James Shirley included in this volume are unusual in their formal design. Part masque, part drama and part chamber opera, *Cupid and Death*, *The Siege of Rhodes*, *The Cruelty of the Spaniards in Peru* and *The History of Sir Francis Drake* have no specific generic identity. In the 1650s they were variously described as 'opera', 'masque' and 'moral representation'. Terms such as 'act' and 'scene', which would have evoked theatrical models, are avoided and replaced by the masque term 'entry'. Yet, in structure, the entries in *Rhodes* and *Drake*, in particular, more closely resemble an act of a play rather than the more loose form of the masque entry.

Such indistinct generic type presents particular problems for the editor faced with different conventions for the editing of masques and for plays. In order to preserve the dramatic quality of the pieces, I have departed from the usual convention in editing masques of continuous line numbering. I have treated each entry as an act—although the term was strenuously avoided in the attempts to revive the drama—and numbered accordingly. I have attempted to preserve a distinction between conventional stage directions on one hand and the descriptions of the scenic stage and dramatic commentary, which are peculiar to Davenant's texts, on the other. The former are numbered from the previous line, as they would be in a play, while the latter are treated substantively.

INTRODUCTION

The Tragedy of that Famous Roman Orator Marcus Tullius Cicero was published anonymously in 1651.[1] Even by the norms of disclosure during the Republic, there is nothing in the publication details of the play to aid the reconstruction of its auspices, intended readership or ideological perspectives. The play was unlicensed, and it contains no paratextual material in the form of dedications or addresses to the reader. The text bears the signs of a drama which had been economically printed, compressed as it is into double columns with the play set to end on an exact gathering.

There is no textual or external evidence that *Cicero* was ever performed. Nevertheless, several of the scenes make dramatic sense only if staged and there is a liveliness of movement not present in closet drama, as the focus switches from public to domestic locations. Lois Potter has suggested that *Cicero* was composed as a schools play, on the grounds that it contains several parts for boys.[2] This notion is supported by several scenes containing quasi-philosophical debates, reminiscent of textbook learning, which have no real bearing on the sequence of political events. But, as will be argued, the drama seems to have been written with a specific intuition of the contemporary relevance of the Ciceronian material, and this purpose would require a more initiated audience reception than that of a schools play.

The play focuses on the last year in the life of Marcus Tullius Cicero, the greatest orator of the Roman Republic. In particular, the circumstances leading to Cicero's death are represented as closely bound up with the transmutation of Roman sovereignty from the Republic to the rule of the triumvirs, Mark Antony, Caesar Octavius and Marcus Lepidus: the starting point of Shakespeare's *Antony and Cleopatra*. Cicero's faith in the old Republic and his fear of its passing, echoed in the Chorus of senators, resound throughout the play. The author offers an historical long view. The decline of Rome is represented as having begun with the first civil war between Pompey and Julius Caesar and the subsequent dictatorship of Caesar. Caesar's assassination functions variously and ambiguously in the drama: it is an act of liberation from tyranny, yet one which brings retribution upon Rome. In the prologue, which recalls the opening of Jonson's *Catiline* with Sulla's ghost, the ghost of Julius Caesar, appearing eight months after his assassination, promises not personal retribution, as in the vein of the Elizabethan avenger, but civil bloodshed: 'The days of Sulla shall return, and blood / Swim down thy streets in as profuse a flood, / As ere his black proscriptions made.' Moreover, the ghost predicts, in the loss of Rome's 'sacred tongue', the death of Cicero. Act by act, the play works through the following year: Act 2 dates to March and April 43BC, Act 3 to July and August, Act 4 to October and November and Act 5 December 43 BC.

In his prologue Caesar styles Cicero 'the great patrician of the speaking art'; it is in the arts of persuasion, as a lawyer and as an orator, rather than by birth, that Cicero is styled patrician. Both in Jonson's *Catiline* and in *Cicero*, he is despised by opponents for his non-aristocratic origins. Cicero had indeed risen from a comparatively humble family in Arpinum, outside Rome, and he was never part of a charmed aristocratic circle. In *Catiline*, Cicero is dismissed by Sempronia, a noblewoman in the thick of Catiline's conspiracy, as an 'inmate', a new man, who is unelectable because of his non-patrician origins (2.5.115–16). In *Cicero*, Antony is similarly dismissive of the ex-consul, while implicitly acknowledging Cicero's oratorical skills: 'I will make that inmate know what 'tis to write my life' (5.5.63–4). It is Cicero's 'writing' of Antony's life which initiates another pattern of revenge in the play.

SOURCES AND INTERTEXTUALITY

Sources for *Cicero* include Plutarch's ' The Life of Marcus Antonius' and 'The Life of Cicero', books 46 and 47 of the *Roman History* of Dio Cassius and books 3 and 4 on the Civil Wars of Appian's *Roman History*. The author of the play must also have been familiar with the annotated *Works* of Cicero, edited by Dionysius Lambinus,[3] which went through numerous editions in the late sixteenth and early seventeenth centuries. First published in London in two volumes in 1585, the second volume is prefaced by a life of Cicero which associates the orator's death with that of the Republic. In his preface Lambinus praises Cicero for his virtues and love of his country, his acute insight into Antony's ambitions being undermined by his imperfect judgement of Octavius's purposes. Lambinus depicts Cicero, as does the play, as a defender of republican liberties and this political assessment is also present in Joseph Webbe's *The Familiar Epistles of M. T. Cicero*, published in English in 1620. In his address to the reader, Webbe eulogizes Cicero as 'glorified with these testimonies: of preserver of the city; defender of all men; and father of his country. And came to be of that authority, that he was one of those which commanded kings and potentates' (sig. A7v). Lambinus's life and Webbe's brief commentary may have shaped the representation of Cicero as orator and hero of the Republic, although from the numerous echoes of Cicero's writings the author of the play clearly drew far more directly on Cicero's own works.

The *Philippics*, Cicero's orations attacking Antony for his appropriation of power after the death of Caesar, which were delivered to the Senate or, as in the case of the *Second Philippic*, circulated amongst Cicero's friends, are directly referred to in the play. The first Chorus alludes to them when it celebrates Cicero's active intervention as advocate for Rome, pleading the city's griefs. In his first soliloquy at the opening of Act 1 scene 2, Cicero rehearses the *Second Philippic* as he professes his love for the Republic and condemns Antony as 'traitor to the freedom of his country'. Here, as elsewhere, Cicero is using the term 'Republic' to denote the old system of government by the Senate which had been eroded by the powers of individuals during the previous decade. Addressing the Senate later in the play, in a speech closely modelled on the *Fourteenth Philippic*, Cicero honours those who had died opposing Antony at the battle of Mutina. The close citation of the orations reveals the author's classical humanist education, and by mediating the text through Cicero's persuasive tracts, the drama endorses Cicero's view of his opposition to Antony as the cause of constitutional government against tyranny. Taking into account the machinations of Octavius Caesar, the reality was more complex, but for the author of *Cicero* his hero is the apostle of liberty and honour set against the despotic threat of Antony.

The verbal resonances from the Roman plays of Shakespeare and Jonson's *Catiline* indicate the author's—not unexpected—familiarity with them; although there is a notable shift of emphasis in *Cicero* towards the advocacy of republican government. The aftermath of Caesar's assassination—the period covered by *Cicero*—is, interestingly, the hiatus in Shakespeare's treatment of Antony and Roman politics in *Julius Caesar* and *Antony and Cleopatra*. The author of *Cicero* selects and discards material from the Shakespearean tragedies. Caesar's ghost in the opening scene of *Cicero* recalls all the omens preceding his assassination which are vividly described by the conspirators in *Julius Caesar*. Caesar's reference to the appearance of the screech owl in the marketplace at midday—not in Plutarch—borrows directly from Casca's account to Cicero in *Julius Caesar* of the prodigies he claims to have witnessed. Yet in the latter play, Brutus, the arch conspirator, rejects the idea of including Cicero in the plot against Caesar on the grounds that Cicero 'will never follow any thing / That other men begin' (2.1.149–50). This dismissal of Cicero is in marked contrast with the love and admiration Cicero expresses for Brutus in his own play. Shakespeare's representation of a magniloquent and magnanimous Antony in *Antony and Cleopatra* finds little expression in *Cicero*, where Antony is intent only on furthering his political ambitions and exacting his revenge on Cicero. Following both Plutarch and Dio Cassius,[4] Antony and his wife Fulvia are represented as taking sadistic pleasure in the apt form of their revenge, as Antony gives orders that Cicero's head and hands be placed on the rostra 'where he vomited / His Philippics against me'. The one sure intertextual moment is in the image of Antony after his defeat at Mutina. Here, in his soliloquy in Act 3, he gives voice to the stoical fortitude for which he is grudgingly commended by Octavius in Shakespeare's play (1.4.56–72).

The author of *Cicero* exposes Cicero's lack of political acumen in his dealings with Octavius, a point glossed over by Plutarch. In a scene which evokes the overreacher of Jonson's *Sejanus* and Chapman's *Bussy D'Ambois*, Octavius first appears in soliloquy exposing the ambitions which Cicero so greatly underestimates: 'Now Caesar summon thy whole self: thou art \ But yet a stripling, and must arm thyself \ With providence unknown in these few years' (3.2.1–3). While Cicero fails to recognize such designs, believing that he can use Octavius to draw support away from Antony with a view to regaining republican liberties, the senator Piso and the tribune Salvius are quick to detect that 'the boy will prove at length another Julius'. A further example of Cicero's political misjudgement is his naive assumption that Octavius will recall Marcus Brutus. This is a miscalculation which prompts his brother's more astute interpretation of Octavius's character and political ambitions (3.3). It is such dramatic tensions and ironies that suggest the play's antecedents in popular, as much as academic or closet, classical tragedy.

CICERO, CLASSICAL REPUBLICANISM AND CONTEMPORARY CONTEXT

Cicero is remarkable in that it is the first and only play in a long line of classical tragedies set in republican and imperial Rome to be written and possibly performed under a republican dispensation. It may be conjectured that the writing of the play was begun only months after the establishment of the English Republic. The Act of March 1649 had declared that the office of king or the reposing of power in any single person was unnecessary, 'burdensome and dangerous to the liberty, safety and public interest of the people, and that for the most part, use hath been made of the regal power and prerogative to oppress and impoverish and enslave the subject'.[5] Such are truly Ciceronian sentiments. The immediacy of *Cicero* to the formation of the Republic allows a freer and more expansive treatment of classical republicanism which is apparent when comparison is made with a generic predecessor, *The Tragedy of Cleopatra, Queen of Egypt*, the work of the republican Thomas May. May's *Tragedy of Cleopatra* was acted in 1626, first published in 1639 and reprinted in 1656. In its early scenes, *Cleopatra* adumbrates those fears, fully articulated in *Cicero*, that the evolving power struggles of the triumvirate are destroying the Republic. Like Shakespeare's *Antony and Cleopatra*, the play opens with a dialogue between Romans discussing Antony's infatuation for Cleopatra, but unlike Shakespeare the focus soon shifts from the personal to the political. Canidius dismisses as irrelevant Plancus's comments on Cleopatra as being the ruin of Antony:

> have we
> Time to dispute his matrimonial faults,
> That have already seen the breach of all
> Rome's sacred laws . . .
> It was the crime of us, and fate itself

> That Antony and Caesar could usurp
> a power so great.
>
> (1.1)

In contrast with Shakespeare's *Antony and Cleopatra*, the transition from Republic to empire is not subordinate to the volatile relationship of the protagonists. What Shakespeare sidelines in the transmutation of republican politics becomes an increasing preoccupation from the time of May's composition of *Cleopatra* to the endorsement of republicanism in *Cicero* in 1651.

In its appeal to Ciceronian civic and moral values, *Cicero* is an intervention in the cause, prevalent in the 1650s and earlier, of classical republicanism and can be viewed in the context of other texts appealing to the tradition of republican government in classical Rome. This ideological position was loosely associated with such literary and parliamentary figures as James Harrington, Thomas Chaloner, George Wither, Algernon Sidney and Thomas May.[6] For such men, the political and moral values of the old Roman Republic were revered and to be recovered. In *The Modern Statesman* of 1653, the republican poet George Wither, for example, discusses the character of a nation in terms of Ciceronian *honestum*:

> but where we see virtue as the throne in a nation, there we may foretell a blessing . . . and where vice predominant, that its attendant ruin is not far off; and for this the before-mentioned commonwealth of Rome affords us an example in both kinds which as it grew up by virtue to an unparalleled height, so by vice was its strength broken.[7]

Wither entitles a subsequent chapter 'Of the piety of the Romans'. *Pietas*, in the classical sense of civic and personal integrity combined with respect for the gods, 'bridles the unruly, strikes awe where reason cannot persuade. If piety is taken away so then is all fidelity, justice, purity.' Alluding to Cicero's *De Natura Deorum*, Wither claims that society cannot exist without it (p. 67). The theme of piety was expounded also by James Harrington in his self-styled 'political romance', *Oceana*, published in 1656. In the preliminaries in which he outlines the principles of government, Harrington equates piety with 'the goods of the mind', virtue and wisdom, which must contest the rule of self-interest:

> Wherefore if we have anything of piety or of prudence, let us raise ourselves out of the mire of private interest unto the contemplation of virtue, and put an hand unto the removal of this evil from under the sun: this evil against which no government that is not secured can be good; this evil from which the government that is secure must be perfect . . . from those principles of power which balanced upon earthly trash, exclude the heavenly treasures of virtue, and that influence of it upon government which is authority.[8]

Here, it would seem that Harrington is putting his own Christian gloss on Cicero's axiom that we cannot be just unless we be imbued with *pietas*.

Harrington's concern with piety, by which he means a sense of duty and loyalty to one's country and family, is reflected in *Cicero*. Caesar's ghost predicts that, in the ensuing civil conflict and moral inversions following the collapse of the Republic, piety will 'be treason to the State'. In agreeing to the proscription of Cicero, a man whom he had addressed as 'honoured father' and father of his country, Octavius reveals not only his callous pragmatism but his rejection of the traditional republican moral values. Young Quintus Cicero, Cicero's nephew, in contrast, dies through his act of piety, in his refusal to betray his father and uncle in the face of torture. Piety, not stoicism—that other doctrine which had shaped Renaissance thought—is the cardinal virtue represented in the play.

It is tempting to read political allegory into the play as certain commentators have done. Lois Potter sees the play as supportive of the Commonwealth.[9] In the figure of Octavius purporting to avenge Julius Caesar, an analogy with the young Charles II is made, specifically in the lines of the third chorus:

> O what a golden age we enjoyed
> Under the reverend Saturns of the State.
> But now an upstart, scarce unboyed,
> Unto an age of iron gives new date.

(3.13.45–8)

Thus the play warns that, should a monarchy be returned in the guise of Octavius/Charles Stuart, it would mark not the restoration of the golden age, as in earlier Stuart iconography, but the onset of a base and oppressive one.

Dale Randall has suggested that the author of the play was a 'highly literate sort of English Ciceronian, apparently supportive of mixed government in which the Parliament had a major voice'. But Randall too proceeds to carry the Commonwealth analogy further, in suggesting representations of Charles I, his son, the future Charles II, and Cromwell in the characters of Julius Caesar, Octavius and Antony.[10] Responding to the play in less personalized terms, Susan Wiseman regards it as distinctive in its sympathetic treatment of the republican cause and consistent in its attempt to associate monarchy with bloodthirsty despotism and republicanism with public and civic virtue.[11] It has been suggested that the language of classical humanism could be appropriated equally by believers in kingship or by advocates of mixed government,[12] and interestingly such ambivalences are borne out by a further interpretation of the play as royalist. Nigel Smith, noting its publication so immediate upon the regicide, has labelled *Cicero* as early royalist propaganda and a 'fully fledged antirepublican play'.[13]

These various and contradictory responses, all by historically minded critics, attest to the play's fascinating multivalency of meaning, as well as its avoidance of direct allegorical association. That the play resoundingly endorses the values of the Republic before Julius Caesar's assumption of supreme power would seem to be beyond question. Moreover, by the time the play was completed, probably in late 1650, Cromwell's career as Lieutenant General of the army had begun to suggest parallels with that of the Roman dictator. Cromwell had already broken the resistance of the Irish and was well on the way to the subjugation of Scotland. Charles II was crowned at Scone on 1 January 1651, to which news Cromwell allegedly responded, 'They are now crowning the black boy, but I may get crown and head yet.'[14] Apocryphal or not, the story attests, as do a number of news and dramatic pamphlets,[15] to the fact that Cromwell was perceived by critics—Royalist, leveller and, less vocally, republican—as aspiring to that office which he had helped to destroy.

The play would seem to anticipate and echo those fears about the precariousness of the republican experiment which were expressed by classical republicans in the 1650s.[16] James Harrington had castigated the 'execrable reign of the Roman emperors' which he saw as arising from the military strength of Julius Caesar. Algernon Sidney had taken the contemporary parallels further, glorifying the English Republic as combining the best elements from the republics of Sparta, Rome and Venice.[17] Sidney had likened Cromwell to Caesar and the more republican Henry Ireton (Cromwell's son-in-law, army officer and regicide) to Pompey, Caesar's political and military rival during the last years of the Republic.[18] According to conversations which had taken place in France and were recorded by his French contact, Sidney had commented that, if Ireton had not died (his death having occurred in 1650), the Republic would have been established and 'he would have prevented Cromwell from aspiring to domination'. That Cromwell, for his part, was not averse at least to the iconography of Caesar is suggested by his retention of Mantegna's 'Triumphs of Caesar' from the collection of the late King's goods before their sale in 1649 (figure 3).[19]

The author of *Cicero* may have chosen circumspectly to remain anonymous. In its figuring and prefiguring of events from 1649 to 1653—the regicide to Cromwell's rise to power, leading to his forcible dissolution of the Long Parliament in April 1653—the play is remarkably prescient. The role of the army is recognized as the crucial factor in the rise of both Antony and Octavius. The army asks for the consulship on behalf of Octavius (3.5) and, when this is denied, the Senate learns that 'the army's fired for the late repulse'. Arguably, the play can be read as a veiled warning of the threat posed to the young Commonwealth by the army grandees and by Cromwell himself as army chief.

The final link in the chain connecting the play with the classical republicanism of the 1650s is Harrington's *Oceana*, a text that seems to share some of the same ambiguities as *Cicero*. Harrington's fantasy commonwealth Oceana is, of course, a thinly veiled image of England, based on what Harrington saw as the models of Rome and Venice. In Oceana's transmutation from monarchy to a republic, Harrington comments approvingly that the balance of state authority changed in a way quite

3   Andrea Mantegna, Canvas IX of *Triumphs of Caesar: Caesar on his Chariot*.

contrary to the experience of Rome. In the case of Rome, when the power base changed from popular to oligarchical or monarchical, 'as by example of Rome in the time of the triumvirs', it became 'altogether incapable of a commonwealth'.[20] The Oceanic commonwealth, by contrast, is fashioned by the lawgiver, the Lord Archon, who significantly resigns supreme power once the constitution has been established.

Harrington dedicated *Oceana* to Cromwell, who is represented in the work as Olphaus Megaletor, Lord Archon, the sole legislator. Yet, despite such apparent sympathies, the work still encountered publication difficulties. According to Harrington's late seventeenth-century biographer the republican John Toland, opposition to *Oceana* came from 'those who pretended to be for a commonwealth'; the work was seized and conveyed to Whitehall. Harrington appealed to Cromwell's daughter, Elizabeth Claypole, and gave his assurance that 'it was only a kind of political romance so far from any treason against her father'. Yet Cromwell, on reading the text, took a contrary, if tolerant, view, commenting, according to Toland, that Harrington sought 'to trepan him out of his power, but that what he got by the sword he would not quit for a little paper shot'.[21] Toland offers his own gloss on Harrington's text with his summary comparison of Cromwell and Caesar: 'Julius Caesar, Oliver Cromwell, and such others as at any time enslaved their fellow citizens, will be for ever remembered with detestation, and cited as the most execrable examples of the vilest treachery and ingratitude.'

If indeed the military dictatorship of Julius Caesar functioned in the language of classical republicanism as a warning of Cromwell's aggrandizement, then it is perhaps not surprising that the author of *Cicero* chose to leave no traces of his identity. The play, as has been argued, is above all a representation of civic and republican humanism threatened by military pragmatism. Yet, like *Oceana* with its representations of the lawgiver as both type and anti-type of Cromwell, there is an ambiguity to *Cicero*. Caesar's assassination serves only to prove his popularity as his avengers assume power and establish a dictatorship even more aggressive than his. The reversals in the state, despite the cruelties visited upon their opponents by the main protagonists, may not ultimately be so tyrannous as Cicero fears. The third chorus pleads that 'the sceptre should know some measure / That being servile we may yet seem free', a wish that is fulfilled in Octavius, whose system of government, while effectively autocratic, retained much of the façade of the old, free Republic. Annabel Patterson's classic thesis that texts composed under conditions of censorship display a certain functional ambiguity[22] would seem to be applicable to the unlicensed, anonymous *Cicero*.

Erasmus, attacking earlier extreme Ciceronianism, had argued that, since Cicero was a man of his own time, so the modern Ciceronian must likewise be a man of his time. Stressing the irrecoverability of Cicero's Rome, Erasmus eloquently pronounced on the chasm of cultural difference between himself and Cicero: 'I stand on another stage, I see another theatre, yes another world.'[23] The author of the first English play to focus on Cicero may, on the contrary, have imagined that he stood on a similar political stage to that occupied by Cicero and, like his tragic hero, may have been intent on employing the persuasive arts to raise spectres of tyranny.

A NOTE ON THE TEXT

There is only one edition of *The Tragedy of that Famous Roman Orator Marcus Tullius Cicero*. This edition is based on the copy of the play in the British Library (Q), checked against a copy held in the Bodleian Library, Oxford. The quarto is divided into acts, but not scenes. This edition follows the general editorial principle of establishing scene breaks where there is a clearing of the stage. Although the play is far from a closet drama, the text contains comparatively few stage directions. Expan-

sion and additions to stage directions, recorded in square brackets, have
been made where necessary to clarify stage action.

In scenes which consist of dialogue between Marcus Tullius Cicero and
his brother Quintus, the quarto uses the nomenclature 'Marcus'. To avoid
confusion in these instances, I have silently emended 'Marcus' to 'Cicero'.

NOTES

1 In one British Library copy, Thomason has altered the date to February 1650. Wing
   attributes the play to Fulke Greville. This ascription has been rejected or ignored
   by commentators on the play.
2 Potter, p. 295.
3 Dionysius Lambinus, *Ciceronis opera omnia quae constant* (Paris, 1565–66).
4 See Plutarch's *Life of Cicero* in *Fall of the Roman Empire*, trans. Rex Warner
   (Harmondsworth, 1958), p. 360 and *Dio's Roman History*, trans. Ernest Cary
   (London, 1917), Book 47, pp. 131–3.
5 *Acts and Ordinances of the Interregnum, 1642–1660*, edited by C. H. Firth and
   R. S. Rait, 3 vols, 1911, 2, pp. 18–19.
6 Blair Worden, 'Classical Republicanism and the Puritan Revolution', in *History and
   Imagination: Essays in Honour of H. R. Trevor Roper*, edited by Hugh Lloyd-Jones,
   Valerie Pearl and Blair Worden (London, 1981), p. 184.
7 George Wither, *The Modern Statesman* (1653), pp. 65–6.
8 James Harrington, *The Commonwealth of Oceana*, edited by J. G. A. Pocock
   (Cambridge, 1992), p. 19.
9 Potter, p. 296.
10 Dale B. J. Randall, 'The Head and the Hands on the Rostra: *Marcus Tullius Cicero*
   as a Sign of its Time', *Connotations*, 1:1 (1991), 34–54, p. 50. See also John
   Morrill's reply, 'Charles I, Cromwell and Cicero (A Response to Dale B. J. Randall)',
   Connotations 1:1 (1991), 96–102.
11 Wiseman, pp. 74–9.
12 Markku Peltonen, *Classical Humanism and Republicanism in English Political
   Thought 1570–1640* (Cambridge, 1995), pp. 1–17.
13 Nigel Smith, *Literature and Revolution in England, 1640–1660* (New Haven and
   London, 1994), p. 84.
14 Quoted in *The Writings and Speeches of Oliver Cromwell*, edited by W. C. Abbott,
   4 vols (Oxford, 1939; reprinted 1988), 2, p. 385.
15 See General Introduction, pp. 11–14.
16 See also Sarah Barber, *Regicide and Republicanism: Politics and Ethics in the
   English Revolution 1646–1659* (Edinburgh, 1998), pp. 202–20.
17 See Jonathan Scott, *Algernon Sidney and the English Republic, 1623–1677*
   (Cambridge, 1988), p. 15.
18 Scott, *Algernon Sidney*, p. 105.
19 *The Late King's Goods: Collections, Possessions and Patronage of Charles 1 in the
   Light of the Commonwealth Sale Inventories*, edited by Arthur MacGregor (London
   and Oxford, 1989), p. 227.
20 Harrington, *Oceana*, p. 61.
21 See *The 'Oceana' of James Harrington and his Other Works . . .*, 'with an exact
   account of his life prefixed by John Toland' (London, 1700), pp. xix–xx.
22 *Censorship and Interpretation* (Madison, 1984).
23 Erasmus, *Ciceronianus*, in *Collected Works*, vol. 6, edited by A. H. T. Levi (Toronto,
   1986), p. 383.

The Tragedy of that Famous Roman Orator Marcus Tullius Cicero

London

Printed by Richard Cotes, for John Sweeting
at the Angel in Popes-head Alley.

1651

THE PERSONS OF THE PLAY

The Ghost of JULIUS CAESAR
MARCUS TULLIUS CICERO
QUINTUS CICERO, *his brother.*
MARCUS ANTONIUS, *formerly Consul, now at enmity with the Senate.*
OCTAVIUS CAESAR ⎫
LEPIDUS ⎭ *Generals for the Senate.*   5
PUBLIUS SERVILIUS ⎫
PISO ⎬ *Senators.*
CALENUS ⎭
SALVIUS ⎫   10
CARNUTIUS ⎬ *Tribunes of the people.*
PUBLIUS APULEIUS ⎭
MINUTIUS, *Praetor.*
POPILIUS LAENAS, *a colonel.*
CORNELIUS, *a centurion.*   15
QUINTUS JUNIOR, *Quintus Cicero's son.*
PHILOLOGUS, *a scholar, Quintus Cicero's man.*
CLODIUS ⎫ *commanders in Lepidus's army, friends to Marcus*
LAELIUS ⎭ *Antonius.*

---

19. LAELIUS] LEANAS Q.

1. *JULIUS CAESAR*] Gaius Julius Caesar (100–44 BC), the greatest Roman general and the most significant figure in Roman politics of the period antedating the play. After his conquest of Gaul (modern France) between 58 and 50 BC, Caesar had fought and won a civil war against Pompey the Great, a war which eventually left him in complete control of the Roman empire. Though a dictator, Caesar was not a repressive ruler. Nevertheless, in March 44 BC a group of aristocrats led by Brutus and Cassius, resenting his monopoly of political power, assassinated him, thereby inaugurating a new round of civil upheaval.

2. *MARCUS TULLIUS CICERO*] Cicero (106–43 BC), the hero of the play, and Rome's greatest orator. His finest hour had been his suppression of the 'Conspiracy of Catiline' in 63 BC, since when his career had been in eclipse. In late 44 BC, however, after Caesar's assassination and the arrival in Rome of Caesar's young heir Octavius, Cicero thought he saw a chance to restore the 'republic', government by senate and people such as had existed before Caesar's dictatorship. The play follows the progress of his attempts until his murder in December 43 BC.

3. *QUINTUS CICERO*] Marcus Cicero's younger brother (102–43 BC), a significant public figure in his own right, also murdered in December 43 BC.

4. Consul] The consulship was the highest political office of the Roman State. There were two consuls at any one time, holding office for one year only. The second most powerful office was the praetorship.

5. *OCTAVIUS CAESAR*] known by modern scholars as Octavian. He later became the first Emperor, Augustus.

11. Tribunes of the people] officials whose special duties lay in defending the rights of the common people.

19. *LAELIUS*] Laelius appears as 'Leanas' in 'The Persons of the Play', but is referred to as 'Laelius' throughout the text.

LAUREAS, *a poet.* ⎱
TYRO, *a great pretender to history.* ⎰ *Marcus Cicero's men.*   20
[Members of] The Senate
Chorus
POMPONIA, *wife to Quintus Cicero.*
FULVIA, *Marcus Antonius's wife.*   25
Centurions
Lictors
Soldiers
Messengers
[Phillis   ⎱
Clarinda ⎰ *servants to Pomponia.*   30
Galla]   ⎰

The Scene: ROME

---

21. pretender to history] an aspiring historian.

22. *Senate*] a body consisting of current and former State officials. Its function was in theory to advise elected officials and nothing more, but it had become, in time, effectively the ruling body of the State. At this juncture (44 BC), it had about a thousand members.

23. *Chorus*] it is probable that members of the Senate formed the Chorus. This doubling of Chorus and Senate would mean that the Chorus would have to enter and exit at the end of Acts 1–4.

27. *Lictors*] attendants of public officials.

I, purae Cicero pater loquelae,
I, jurista Quiritium supreme,
Post passas Latii furentis iras
I pernix, fuge, et Alitis Sabaei
Surgentis tepido ex rogo renatis   5
Vestitus calamis, petas Asylum
Magni pectoris, aurei, sereni,
In quo Mercurius, Themista, uterque
Divini soboles Jovis triumphat,
Hermes eloquii fluentis autor,   10
Aequi diva parens Themista Juris.

1–11.] Go, Cicero, father of pure discourse, go, greatest lawyer of the Romans, after the widespread anger of raging Latium [area around Rome], go swiftly, flee and clothed in the reborn plumage of the Phoenix which rises from the smouldering pyre, seek the refuge of a great breast, golden and unclouded, in which Mercury and Themis reside [i.e. Mercury as Eloquence, Themis as Justice]—both offspring of divine Jove—rest triumphant, Hermes [i.e. Mercury] the fount of flowing eloquence, Themis the divine parent of just law.

[Act 1 Scene 1]

        [Enter] JULIUS CAESAR's *Ghost.*

Caesar. What, not one prodigy to rouse thee, Rome,
   And give loud warning that great Caesar's come?
   What, not one peal of thunder to proclaim
   And echo from thy seven proud hills the fame
   Of my arrival? Is my weight so light   5
   It cannot force one dismal groan to affright
   And wake thy genius? Is the ground thus rent,
   And Julius like an exhalation sent
   From the black womb of hell, yet cannot strike
   An earthquake in thy breast? I like, I like   10
   Such dire forerunners. What? Before my fall,
   In Rome's great Forum, upon every stall
   A bird of night was perched in midst of day,
   And when black night her mantle did display
   (As if the Stygian people had forsook   15
   Their pitchy harbours, and possession took
   Of the upper world) the air was filled with streams
   Of rolling fires, and the presaging dreams
   Of citizens were broke by dismal frights
   Caused by the confused noise of walking sprights: 20
   And is my rise so full of silence?   *Thunder*
              So,
   Now stubborn Rome, I'll thunder forth thy woe.
   Caesar must be revenged, and to thy cost.
   Alas, thou canst not bribe my wrongèd ghost
   With the vain fiction of thy Julian star.   25

  1.1.0.1.] Caesar's ghost appears eight months after his assassination on 15 March 44 BC. At the time of his death, Caesar had established himself as dictator in Rome. See Jonson, *Catiline*, which opens with the appearance of Sulla's ghost.
  1. *prodigy*] an omen; something abnormal or monstrous.
  4. *seven proud hills*] Rome famously covered seven hills.
  7. *genius*] spirit of Rome.
  13. *bird of night*] the screech owl, a bird of ill omen. See *Julius Caesar*, 1.3.26.
  15. *Stygian people*] the dead, people from the underworld.
  20. *sprights*] spirits.
  25. *vain ... star*] In July 44 BC, four months after Julius Caesar's assassination, a comet appeared. It was interpreted by the Romans to be Caesar's soul ascending to heaven to join the gods and was named the Julian star. Caesar here asserts that the interpretation was wrong: his soul is in the underworld, like any ordinary human dead, and treating him as a god will not conciliate his angry ghost.

Were I but stellified indeed, I'd mar
Thy pride with such an influence should convey
Submission through thy blood, and cast a ray
Should light a sun to rule the Roman world
Without a colleague: yet this fate is hurled   30
Through thy own blindness on thy cursèd head,
And with such plagues to usher it as thy dead,
Thy butchered Julius from his soul abhorred.
My glory was, that Fortune did afford
That royal power to do the good I would,   35
And nature heart to will the good I could.
But I was too, too mild; a heavier hand
Shall make thee stoop to sovereign command
And kiss the yoke, though sullied first and dyed
In thine own gore. A scourge shall check thy pride;   40
The days of Sulla shall return, and blood
Swim down thy streets in as profuse a flood
As e'er his black proscriptions made: the sword
Shall be as free as then. The slave his lord,
The wife her husband shall betray; the son,   45
Thinking the vital thread of his father spun
To a too tedious length, and that his feet
Travel too slowly to the grave, shall greet
His age with death. The senators shall drink
Of the same cup of slaughter too, and think   50
The burden easy, for a sudden death
Is sweet to them that scorn a slavish breath.
Each proscript's head shall bear a weighty rate,

---

28. blood] blond Q.   35. the good] thee good Q.

26. *stellified*] transformed into stars.
27. *influence*] emanation from the stars (*OED*).
28–31. *cast a ray . . . cursèd head*] a complex word play. Were Caesar really a star, he says, he would use his light to kindle a sun to dominate the world. But 'sun' is a pun; Caesar would also make his adopted heir ('son'), Octavius, monarch of Rome. As it is, the Romans are bringing this fate upon themselves without his intervention.
30. *without a colleague*] i.e. unlike a traditional consul, Octavius will rule as an absolute monarch. Traditionally, Rome was ruled by two consuls.
34–6. *My glory . . . could*] By his victory over Pompey and his supporters in the civil war, Caesar secured absolute control ('royal power') over the Roman empire. But he was a mild ruler. What Caesar here claims is that his achievement or 'glory' was that, while his successful military career gave him the power to do good, he was already naturally disposed to do so.
39. *kiss the yoke*] The yoke was an arch of three spears, symbolizing the wooden cross-piece harnessed to oxen, under which defeated enemies were made to march (see 1.2.224).
41. *days of Sulla*] Victor in the civil war of the 80s BC, Sulla captured Rome and avenged himself brutally against his enemies.
43. *proscriptions*] Proscription was a process whereby people, in this case enemies of Sulla, were outlawed and their lives and property made forfeit. Caesar is predicting the proscription of political opponents, 43–42 BC, carried out by the triumvirate, of which Cicero was the most prominent victim.
53.] i.e. there will be a considerable reward for those who turn in alleged enemies of the State.

And piety be treason to the State.
Thus, Rome, shalt thou be plagued, and among   55
Thy other evils lose thy sacred tongue,
The great patrician of the speaking art.
Then shall thy griefs lie fettered in thy heart,
And speak no other language but of tears;
Words shall be strangled by thy stupid fears.   *Exit.*   60

[Act 1 Scene 2]

Enter CICERO.

Cicero. Now ought we to give thanks unto the gods
That now at length the fathers of the public
With free unforced judgements dare lay open
The sick distempers which disease and trouble
The body politic. Methinks in this   5
I see some gleam of liberty break forth
And promise to the State a milder sunshine
Than, since our late unbridled Phaetons
Usurped the Roman heaven, we have been blessed with.
As for myself, though now grown old and feeble   10
In my loved country's service, I have yet
As good a heart as ever to defend her.
What, though my voice did seem a while suppressed,
My heart did nourish an untainted love
Of the Republic, which in zealous flames   15

54.] 'Piety' is a translation of the Latin *pietas*, the duty owed to one's country, parents, family or gods. Under normal circumstances, the right thing for relatives of the proscripts to do was to lend them all the help they could. But, Caesar says, it will be a sign of the topsy-turvy nature of the times that the laws passed by the triumvirate will make such 'piety' an act of treason.

57. *patrician*] aristocrat. The reference is to Cicero, an aristocrat, or master, of the oratorical arts.

1.2.2. *fathers . . . public*] members of the Senate, often referred to as 'fathers' (*patres*). The 'public' is the *respublica*, the Roman word for the State.

4. *distempers*] disturbance; disorder.

8. *unbridled Phaetons*] Phaethon had asked the sun, his father, to let him guide the solar chariot for a day. But the immortal horses bolted with him and he was killed by a thunderbolt from Zeus to prevent the world from being set on fire. Here, Cicero refers specifically to the powerful individuals—Pompey, Crassus and Caesar—who had in recent years taken power away from the Senate and into their own hands. The upshot had been civil war between Pompey and Caesar.

13.] After Caesar's assassination, Antony almost immediately took his place as sole ruler of Rome. Cicero was dismayed by events: he had hoped that the killing of Caesar would bring about a restoration of the old system of government by Senate and people. Nevertheless Cicero did not feel there was anything he could do, and he consequently stayed out of public view. It was only when Octavius arrived on the scene, splitting the erstwhile supporters of Caesar between Antony and himself, that Cicero saw a way to resist Antony by manipulating the rival factions.

15. *Republic*] Cicero uses the term to denote the old system of collective government by the Senate which had been eroded by the power of individuals during the previous decade.

Has now discharged itself in the face of Antony,
That traitor to the freedom of his country.
I did defend, while but a youth, the State;
I will not, now I am grown old, forsake it.
I have condemned the swords of Catiline;   20
I will not now fear his.
Some twenty years ago, I well remember,
I said death could not to a consular
Be immature; how much more truly now
May I pronounce unto an agèd man?   25
Now may I wish for death, yet from my heart
Two things I do desire, and pray for: one,
That I may leave the Roman people free:
The immortal gods cannot bestow upon me
A greater blessedness. The other's this: 30
That all may meet with a proportioned fate,
As their deserts have been unto the State.

Enter LAUREAS [, *a poet*].

Laureas. Your brother Quintus, sir.
Cicero.   Entreat him hither.

Enter QUINTUS *and* PHILOLOGUS.

Brother, you're welcome: How does thy Pomponia
And my young cousin?
Quintus.   Both my wife and son   35
Are (heaven be thanked) as well as my best wishes
Can fancy they would have them; and my wife
Presents her love, my son his duty, to you.
Cicero. They cannot by a better messenger,
For you are monarch of Pomponia's love,   40
And sovereign of his duty; these are titles
Good in economy, but once thrust out
Make heavy hearts in State when they return.

---

16. *now ... Antony*] probably a reference to the writing of the *Philippics*.

18. *I did defend...*] The remainder of this speech is a close translation of the end of the *Second Philippic*.

20. *Catiline*] an impoverished patrician whose attempted rebellion was suppressed during Cicero's consulship in 63 BC. This was Cicero's proudest moment.

23. *consular*] an ex-consul.

24. *immature*] premature, untimely.

31–2.] i.e. that fate may reward everyone as their actions towards Rome (good or bad) deserve.

32.1. *LAUREAS*] Tullius Laurea, a devoted ex-slave of Cicero, was also a poet. See 5.8.166–9.

35. *cousin*] a close relative, here Cicero's nephew, the son of his brother Quintus Cicero.

41–3. *these ... return*] i.e. it is good and appropriate to be able to use words like 'monarch' and 'sovereign' in the home and family (oeconomy, from the Greek *oikonomia*, origin of our word 'economy', literally means 'domestic management'), but they

You have not heard of Antony's proceedings
Since he departed to Brundusium?   45
Quintus. Not one word.
Cicero.   I collect the consul's drift;
But why do I the State that injury
To style him Consul that so governs it,
That leads his life so, and was so created?
His aim I know is at those four legions   50
Transported from the Macedonian province
At his appointment thither by his brother.
'Twere dangerous he should win them; but I have
A surer confidence in the martial legion,
For it has ever been extolled as much   55
For its integrity to the State as prowess.
The fourth is under conduct of the Quaestor,
Egnatuleius, a brave citizen
And valiant man, so that I cannot doubt
But he'll be partly frustrate.   60
Then Caesar's posting to Campania
Puts me in hope: 'tis to procure the colonies
There resident to side with him against
Antonius; for you know the noble youth
Will not be checked by him. But brother Quintus,   65
I have some private matters which require
A more retired conference; take a seat.
              [*Quintus and Cicero withdraw and sit down.*]
Laureas [*to Philologus*]. How does my fellow academic? Canst
       Digest my lord's discourse of *summum bonum*?
Philologus. 'Tis somewhat tough, methinks; but Laureas,   70

---

are unwelcome in the State. The comment is an early indication of the play's republican leanings.

45. *Brundusium*] modern-day Brindisi; a harbour on the Adriatic coast of Italy, of importance as the starting point for the crossing to Greece and other eastern countries. Antony was thus able to take control of four legions arriving from Macedonia and with them could more easily control events in Rome.

46. *collect*] infer.

the consul's] Antony's. Antony was consul in 44 BC.

49. *was so created*] Antony was effectively elected consul because Caesar so decided, not by constitutional process.

54. *the martial legion*] the name of a particular legion (army unit), derived from the name 'Mars', god of war.

57. *The fourth*] the fourth legion.

conduct] command.

Quaestor] minor Roman official.

60. *partly frustrate*] met with some resistance.

61. *Caesar's . . . Campania*] Octavius, grand-nephew and adopted son of Julius Caesar, is in Campania, south of Latium, near Naples.

62. *colonies*] settled by ex-soldiers as reward for services to the State, an important potential source of support.

69. summum bonum] the ultimate good; Cicero had written *De Finibus* ('On Ends') which discussed the theories as to the nature of the ultimate good of the three leading

Which hadst thou rather be? An Epicure?
A Stoic? or Peripatetic? Tell me.
Laureas. Why, faith, before I was infranchised, boy,
The Stoic would have furnished me completely;
I should have laughed a cudgel in the face,   75
And swore a bed of straw had been as soft
As wool, or down of ermines. I should then
Have stood as stout as Atlas with a burden
Weighty as his upon my brawny shoulders.
But since I did with thee shake off the name   80
And nature of a slave, and serve my lord
More for affection than constraint, I could
Sometimes methinks shake hands with Epicurus.
                              [*Cicero and Quintus approach.*]
Cicero. It must be so. But, brother, since your haste
Hinders your longer stay, let me entreat you,   85
Philologus a while may bear me company.
Quintus. With all my heart.
Cicero.   My love unto Pomponia.
Quintus. I will; farewell.
Cicero.   Farewell, good brother Quintus.
                                        Exit QUINTUS.

Philologus and Laureas, come let's hear
How you have relished your philosophy.   90
Philologus. My lord, your Laureas relishes extremely,
For he is almost turned an Epicure.
Cicero. An Epicure!
Laureas.   Not I, my lord. I told him

---

philosophical schools—the Epicureans, Stoics and Peripatetics. What follows is a light-hearted discussion of ancient philosophical principles.

71. *Epicure*] member of the philosophical school of Epicurus, which regarded pleasure as the ultimate good, and thus gained a reputation for luxurious living.

72. *Stoic*] member of a philosophical school founded by Zeno. Stoic philosophers had a reputation for endurance and resilience.

Peripatetic] member of school of philosophy founded by Aristotle.

73. *infranchised*] set free.

boy] Philologus is younger than Laureas (see 1.2.123 and note). In Plutarch's life of Cicero, he is described as a young man educated by Cicero in literature and philosophy.

77. *down of ermines*] fur of the ermine or stoat.

78. *Atlas*] hero who held up the heavens, a Stoic symbol of the wise and self-sufficient man.

90. *relished*] taken pleasure in.

93–116. *Not I . . . . unhead me*] Laureas and Philologus are dealing in caricatures of Stoic and Epicurean philosophy. Laureas has stated that while he still had the difficult life of a slave the Stoic philosophy—associated with toughness and resilience—would have suited him, but now that he has been freed and enjoys an easier life, he is more suited to Epicureanism, with its reputation for luxury and comfort. But here Laureas proceeds to assert that he really has nothing in common with Epicureans at all: Epicurus advocated retirement from the outside world, which Laureas here rejects.

93–110. *I told . . . goodness*] Laureas means that a truly virtuous man should not

Virtue, which in a proud conceit neglected
The due preservatives of the weaker nature   95
And was estranged from that first-born dictate
Of making nature's union, if it were possible,
Immortal, by a competent cherishing
Of either part, and in an ecstasy
Like an intelligence, all soul and reason,   100
Was wholly taken up with mental beauties,
Was like a table furnished with rare viands,
But not a dish prepared with condimental
Provocatives to make the relish kind.
For virtue is, we know, a fruitless, rude,   105
Impolished treasure, without use and action,
Which give it taste and life. Now to the use:
Health, wealth and liberty are requisite,
Though not essential unto virtue's self,
That root of goodness. Thus you may see, my lord,   110
Laureas is neither Epicure nor Stoic.
'Twas only the comparison which made
Your shallow-brained scholastic think I was
One of the kitchen; but were I a hog
Of Epicure's fraternity, yet his brain   115
Should not be the Atlanta to unhead me.
Cicero. Why, here's no sign of Epicure in this:
'Tis current and authentic.
Philologus.   True, but sir,
He harped upon another string even now.
Yet, since he is so cunning, pray, my lord,   120
Let me be stoical a while, and try
Whether he be found as he pretends.
Laureas. Pish, there's a face to act a Stoic with!
Make me believe the goddess Venus thought
She was embraced by Mars, when 'twas young Adon   125

---

lose himself in abstract theorizing and neglect the needs of the body, but should engage
in the real world.

    104. *to make . . . kind*] i.e. to make the flavour pleasant.

    113. *scholastic*] an abusive name for a scholar; someone with only superficial edu-
cation and understanding.

    114–15. *One of . . . fraternity*] Epicurus's championing of pleasure as the *summum
bonum* led to much unjustified abuse of the Epicurean school, such as the charge that they
were gluttons, no better than pigs, who had thought only of their bodily satisfaction.

    116. *Atlanta*] a mythical heroine who took part in the hunting and killing of the
Calydonian boar.

    118. *current and authentic*] correct and accurate.

    123. *there's . . . with*] Laureas is mocking Philologus because he does not have the
severe countenance to match the stern philosophy (see 1.2.73 and note).

    124–6. *Make me . . . dallied*] Mars, a god, and Adonis, a young mortal, were both
lovers of Venus. Philologus is as far from looking like a Stoic as Adonis was from resembling Mars.

With whom she dallied. Give me one shall look
With as severe a countenance as Cato
When he unshackled his heroic soul.
Cicero. No more of him, I pray, unless you would
Make fountains of my eyes. But Laureas, 130
You have the fittest visage for a Stoic:
It shall be your part.
Laureas.   Then, my noble lord,
Suppose I had ingrossed the Stoic wisdom
Within my bosom, and were now brought forth
To some unheard of torture: thus I'd stand, 135
                [*Moves to centre stage*]
And thus I'd dare the utmost of their furies.
Vain mortals, do you think my fearless soul
Is capable of pains? Why, tear this flesh
From off my bones, you touch not me: for know
This is not Laureas, but his robe. Extract 140
The very quintessence of the strongest poisons,
I'll quaff it as I would divinest nectar,
And think it but a draught of immortality.
Cast me alive into a den of lions,
I will embrace my destiny and deem 145
The loudest accent of their spacious throats
But as a trumpet to proclaim my triumphs.
I would not bellow in Perillus's engine,
But, like the swan in Tiber's silver streams,
Sing my own dirge with an unwrinkled note. 150
Nay, more than this, the disunited heavens
Tumbling upon my head should not affright me.
Yea, the confused rattling of their ruins
Should be as ravishing harmony to my ears
As now they make in their celestial spheres. 155
Now, sir, suppose the anger of some tyrant
Had thrust me from the bosom of my country,

127–8. *Cato . . . soul*] Marcus Porcius Cato, a Stoic philosopher and opponent of Julius Caesar in the recent civil wars, committed suicide in 46 BC rather than fall into Caesar's hands. Cicero considered him a martyr to the cause of freedom.
   133. *ingrossed*] absorbed.
   137–88.] Laureas enacts an amusing and melodramatic version of a Stoic facing painful death. The Stoics believed that external circumstances could not affect a wise man's peace of mind.
   148. *Perillus's engine*] Perillus constructed a bronze bull for Phalaris, tyrant of Agrigentum. Criminals were placed inside it and roasted alive, their screams giving the impression that the bull was roaring. The first victim of the machine was Perillus himself.
   149. *like the swan*] The swan was supposed to sing most sweetly just before it died.
   150. *unwrinkled*] Smooth, clear.
   155. *celestial spheres*] The heavenly bodies in their orderly circular movements ('spheres') were each supposed to make a noise which together created a perfect harmony, the 'music of the spheres'.

From the embraces of a faithful spouse,
And the sweet pledges of our mutual loves,
And I were wandering in some wilderness,   160
Within whose gloomy shades was never heard
The Daulian minstrel, but the boding tones
Of owls and night-ravens, and in every bush
Lay couched a lion, tiger, or a wolf:
Would I sit musing in a dumpish passion   165
And cry, O times! O manners! No my lord,
A wise man does not tie his house or home
To the tuition of one private Lar,
Nor does he bound what men their country call
To the straight limits of one State or kingdom.   170
Though Thule were the place of my nativity,
Yet should the Gades be my country too.
I have a little world within my self,
And shall one narrow landskip claim me hers?
Now for those petty dangers I defy them: 175
A wise man carries in his sacred front
The character of majesty, which brutes,
Though ne'er so wild and savage, must adore.
As for my wife and children, they were given me
Not for eternity, and as good be severed   180
By exile as by death: had I still lived,
Dividing my indulgent soul among them,
I might perhaps have seen my loving wife
Ravished before my face, I might have seen
My children's brains knocked out against the stones   185
And dashed in my own wounded eyes; but now
I shall not view those clouds. *Thus had I been*
Unhappy, had I not unhappy been.
And now my honoured lord, with wonder hear

---

159. *the sweet . . . loves*] i.e. our children.
162. *Daulian minstrel*] nightingale. In myth, originally a woman, Philomela, from
the town of Daulis in Greece. Raped and mutilated by Tereus, she was later transformed
into a nightingale to avoid his further wrath after the murder of his son at the hands
of his wife, Procne, Philomela's sister.
  boding] presaging; portending.
165. *dumpish*] melancholy.
166. *O times! O manners!*] *O tempora! O mores!* An exclamation by Cicero from
the start of one of his best-known speeches, the *First Catilinarian* of 63 BC.
168. *tuition*] care.
  Lar] household god.
171. *Thule*] proverbially the northernmost part of the inhabited world.
172. *Gades*] modern Cadiz, in the far south of Spain.
174. *landskip*] landscape.
176. *sacred front*] i.e. face.
187–8. *Thus . . . been*] i.e. had I not experienced the (apparent) misfortune of being
exiled, I would have been truly unhappy seeing violence to my family. Italic type is conventionally used in the printing of this period for sententious expressions.

How in a yet unparalleled affliction   190
Your Stoic Laureas would demean himself.
Suppose my lord—oh, how my heartstrings ache
To utter it! Yea, it makes me clean forget
The Stoic whom I personate: I say,
Suppose—oh, hold me, good Philologus,   195
The very thought will strike me dead—suppose
My bosom friend, my faithful Pylades,
My second self, even my Philologus,
Were whipped clean through the streets of Rome and cudgelled
Till his bones cracked again, do ye think I'd weep?   200
Lift up my eyes and cry, O cursèd heavens,
Which suffer innocence thus to be afflicted?
No, my lord, I'd do an act of wonder
Which after ages should admire: I'd down,
And in the cellar all my sorrows drown.   205
Cicero. Is it come to this? You are a wanton, Laureas.
Laureas. 'Tis stoical, my lord.
Cicero.   Well, let it be so.
But since you think you could so sweetly sing
In the engine of Perillus, let me hear you
Out of it. For I'm persuaded you might frame   210
Your voice a great deal better to a song
In a far colder place.
Laureas.   'Tis true, my lord;
But I spoke like a Stoic.
Cicero.   Be not modest.
Begin: but let your song be sage and grave,
Such as a vestal need not blush to hear.   215
Rip up the vices of the State, that while
You sing, my wounded heart may bleed for sorrow.
[*Laureas sings.*]
How happy was the Roman State
When her chiefest magistrate
Was raisèd to the fasces from the plough;   220

---

203. No] Now Q.   217.1. *Laureas sings*] Song Q.

---

191. *demean*] conduct.
197. *Pylades*] in myth, the loyal companion of Orestes.
204-5. *I'd down ... drown*] a joke, since a true Stoic wise man would have no
sorrows to drown.
205. *cellar*] i.e. wine cellar.
206. *wanton*] rogue.
214. *sage*] wise, solemn.
215. *a vestal*] The vestal virgins were six aristocratic women who acted as priest-
esses of Vesta, goddess of the hearth, for at least thirty years, during which time they
were obliged to maintain strict sexual purity.
217.1. Laureas sings] Laureas's song celebrates the values of the Republic that
Cicero wants to restore.
220. *fasces*] bundles of rods around an axe carried by the attendants of Roman
officials (lictors), symbolic of their power, as elected officials, to punish wrongdoers.

When such as Cincinnatus swayed
The helm of the commonwealth, and made
Her proudest adversaries humbly bow
To the self-same yoke wherewith they used to check
The stubbornness of the toiling heifer's neck?   225

How sacred was the Roman name,
How shining was our virgin fame,
When in their homes our bravest men
Had nothing glorious but themselves;
When he who now in quarries delves   230
For golden ore as low as Pluto's den
Was deemed a parricide, and had the doom
Of one who rent his mother's sacred womb?

How happy were we then, how blessed,
When the Republic was possessed   235
Of those ancient palinures?
When Curius and Fabricius led
Her armies, which for dainties fed
On boiled turnips? Then the easy cures
Of her more temperate body soon were wrought,   240
Her health with little loss of blood was bought.

But since the Asian luxury
Has crept into our veins, and we
No less for fame in dishes strive
Than if we had the conquest won   245
Of the stout Hamilcar's son,

---

221. *Cincinnatus*] Lucius Quinctius, an exemplar of humility; he came from his farm to be dictator in 458 BC. On defeating the Aequi he resigned and returned to his farm.

222. *the commonwealth*] the State, a common translation of the Latin *respublica*.

223–4. *humbly . . . yoke*] Defeated enemies of Rome were made to undergo the humiliating ceremony of 'passing under the yoke' (see 1.1.39 and note).

230–3. *when he . . . womb*] a reference to the mythical Golden Age, a time of moral purity before the invention of supposedly immoral activities like mining. The latter was judged as equal to a crime of violence and punished as such.

231. *Pluto*] god of the underworld.

232. *parricide*] vicious criminal, traitor.
had the doom] i.e. suffered the fate.

236. *palinures*] guides, pilots.

237. *Curius and Fabricius*] Manius Curius Dentatus and Gaius Fabricius Luscinus, two Roman generals of the third century BC who were later regarded as the paradigms of the frugality and incorruptibility on which the success of Rome had been built.

242. *Asian luxury*] Romans traced their (perceived) moral decline to, amongst other things, the annexation of the Greek Kingdom of Asia (modern western Turkey) to the Roman empire in 133 BC. It was an extremely rich country which brought unprecedented wealth and luxury to Rome.

246. *stout . . . son*] Hannibal, leader of the Carthaginians.

Or brought the treacherous Syphax home alive
To grace our triumphs: now a thousand pains
Lie brooding in the State's corrupted veins.

The commonwealth is full of tumours,   250
And each day repugnant humours
Threaten the downfall of this frame;
Her constitution is too weak
To harbour such guests, and not break,
Unless some pitying deity quench the flame.   255
Be thou our Aesculapius, mighty Jove,
And send some healing influence from above.
Philologus and Laureas together.
Be thou our Aesculapius, mighty Jove,
And send some healing influence from above.
Cicero. So here's a song has fire in it, poetry;   260
Oh, 'tis the language of the gods when virtue
Is made her theme; they prostitute the muses,
And turn Parnassus to a stews, that clothe
Their unwashed fancies in these sacred weeds.

Enter QUINTUS.

Cicero. Brother, so soon? Your countenance methinks   265
Tells me your bosom travails with some news,
And fain would be delivered.
Quintus.   Sir, Octavius
Is with an army at the gates.
Cicero.   Octavius?
Why, that's not Hannibal.
Quintus.   But the citizens
Suspect a more than panic treachery;   270
For those that saw the consul and Octavius
So lately reconciled in the Capitol,

247–8. *Syphax . . . triumphs*] Syphax was an African chief, ally of the Carthaginians, defeated by Scipio Africanus in the late third century BC. A triumph was a procession through Rome, in celebration of a major military victory, in which defeated captives and victorious soldiers were paraded. Also the betrothed of Sophonisba, the heroine of Marston's play *Sophonisba: The Wonder of Women*.

256. *Aesculapius*] god of medicine and healing.

263. *Parnassus*] a Greek mountain, sacred to the Muses, goddesses of poetry. *stews*] brothel.

264. *unwashed fancies*] licentious imaginings.

266. *travails with*] is troubled with.

267–8. *Octavius . . . gates*] an event which occurred on 9 November 44 BC.

269. *Hannibal*] Hannibal's threatening appearance before the gates of Rome (see 1.4.32) represented in Roman folklore one of the moments of the greatest peril in the city's history. Cicero is suggesting that the threat which Octavius poses to Rome is hardly of the same order.

270. *a more . . . treachery*] a co-ordinated plan.

271. *the consul*] Antony.

272. *Capitol*] one of the seven hills of Rome, site of the temple of Jupiter Optimus Maximus (Jove), the most important in the city.

Will not believe these forces are contracted
To oppose Antonius; but that covertly
Both have complotted one to aid the other   275
In the promotion of their aims; that Antony
May gain the sovereignty, and Octavius
Revenge on those which slew his uncle Julius.

Enter TYRO.

Tyro. Carnutius, sir, the tribune of the people,
    Desires some conference with your lordship.
Cicero.   Quintus,   280
    He is a professed foe to Antonius,
    And friend to Caesar. Bring the tribune in.

Enter CARNUTIUS.

Carnutius. Octavius is returned.
Cicero.   Aye, so I hear.
Carnutius. And brought along with him ten thousand soldiers.
    I have explored his aims, and they are whole   285
    For opposition of the consul Antony,
    Whom he has much endamaged.
Cicero.   How, Carnutius?
Carnutius. By spies, which he has closely had about him
    Still crossing and opposing his proceedings,
    And with such good success, as now the legions   290
    Are even upon desertion of his party,
    Especially the fourth and martial.
Cicero.   Tribune,
    Inform the people how the youth's affected,
    And I'll procure he shall be straight brought in;
    For I'm persuaded, since he is returned   295
    Antonius' enemy, the provident Senate
    Will not be so injurious to the State
    And their own safeties, as deny him entrance.
    Yea, I presume they will with glad consents
    Meet the first motion of his entertainment.   300
Carnutius. They will, no doubt. Come, let's dispatch, my lord.
                                        Exeunt.

---

275. *complotted*] conspired.

278. *his uncle Julius*] Octavius was adopted as Julius Caesar's son in his will, but was in fact his grand-nephew.

282. *Caesar*] Octavius.

287. *endamaged*] caused damage to.

293. *how . . . affected*] i.e. the way Octavius is inclined. At this time he was still only nineteen years old.

296. *provident*] far-sighted, prudent.

299–300. *they will . . . entertainment*] The Senate will agree with the first senator to suggest that Caesar should be welcomed.

301. *dispatch*] act quickly.

[Act I Scene 3]

Enter PISO [, *a* Senator] *and* SALVIUS [, *a* Tribune].

Salvius. Methinks the admittance of Octavius
    Will much endamage Antony.
Piso.   I fear it,
    And doubt not but he will be shortly here:
    But what dost think of this young upstart, Salvius?
    It cannot enter Piso's head, that zeal   5
    To the Republic does incite him to it.
Salvius. Faith, Piso, my opinion is this: I doubt
    The boy will prove at length another Julius.
Piso. And so think I.
Salvius.   Was it ever known a youth
    Of his hot spirit was so much devoted   10
    Unto his country's cause without some plot
    To strengthen his ambitious aims? Well, Piso,
    I am persuaded Caesar's heart and countenance
    Are not correlatives.
Piso.   And I fear our orator,
    Although he think himself a profound statist,   15
    Is but, as it were, a visor, which Octavius
    Covers the face of his close projects with:
    Well, mark the end, these now are but surmises,
    But they may prove oraculous. Let this pass.
    I think if Antony come he will not stay: 20
    You know he has determined to be master
    Of the Cisalpine province.
Salvius.   True, he has.
Piso. Now when he's gone to Gaul, if Cicero
    Advise the Senate anything against him,
    It must be our parts to oppose their counsels.   25
Salvius. It must. I'll second you, you know I may
    Do much by virtue of the tribuneship.
Piso. 'Tis true, you may do much indeed.

Enter Messenger.

Messenger.   The consul

    1.3.7. *I doubt*] I suspect.

    14. *Are . . . correlatives*] i.e. what Octavius *appears* to want and what he really wants bear no relation to each other.

    15. *statist*] statesman, politician.

    16. *visor*] mask.

    19. *oraculous*] as accurate as oracles, (truthful) prophecies of the future.

    22. *Cisalpine province*] Northern Italy; at this time a separate province of the Roman empire. It had been given to Antony as his responsibility for five years, but he had first to remove Decimus Brutus, one of the assassins of Caesar, who had taken control of it.

    25. *counsels*] resolutions.

    27–8. *you know . . . tribuneship*] Tribunes had the right to veto actions of other magistrates or decisions of the Senate.

Antonius is arrived, and, Lucius Piso,
Desires your presence; to you, Salvius,   30
He sends his love, and prays you to repair
Unto the Senate which is newly convocated.
Salvius. Piso, return my love, I'll thither straight.   *Exeunt.*

[Act 1 Scene 4]

   Enter QUINTUS, [*and his wife*] POMPONIA.

Pomponia. How does my brother Marcus Cicero?
Quintus. Well, my Pomponia, but would be far better
 Could he once see the commonwealth in health.
Pomponia. Why, husband; what, have States diseases too?
Quintus. They have, my sweet, and as old fathers die   5
 To make room for posterity, so chance
 Quits ancient States, that from their ruins may
 New ones arise. States have their several ages
 Which carry some analogy with ours.
 Their small beginnings are their infancies;   10
 Their bold exploits to propagate their glories
 Are like the flashes of ambitious youth;
 When they are mounted to the highest pitch
 Decreed them in the starry consistory,
 They are arrived to a state much like   15
 That which in us doth bear the name of manhood.
 They stand not long on this high tower of glory,
 But stealingly, as we, do fall away;
 Their sprightly vigour like a full-blown rose
 Droops and decays, they suddenly contract   20
 Distempers, grow diseased, and finally
 Sink down into the grave of their own ruins.
 The Babylonian and the Persian monarchies
 Died of a surfeit; then the Macedonian
 Of a seditious quarrel in the humours   25
 Striving to be predominant;
 Greece of a meagrim; Carthage first was caught
 With an unruly fever, which at last
 Degenerated to an ague, and

1.4.6. *chance*] fortune.
5–38] Cf Marchamont Nedham, *The Case of the Commonwealth of England Stated*
(1650), chapter 1, 'That governments have their revolutions and fatal periods'.
 14. *starry consistory*] the court of heaven, i.e. the sky.
 18. *stealingly*] gradually, stealthily.
 23–30. *Babylonian ... death*] great world powers of the past.
 24. *of a surfeit*] of excessive indulgence i.e. of having too much power.
 25. *seditious quarrel*] civil conflict. Macedonia was very prone to conflict within the
ruling family.
 27. *meagrim*] sick or nervous headache.
 29. *ague*] a violent or malarial fever.

Was quickly seconded by death. But Rome   30
(Only she never felt an ague yet,
Unless when Hannibal was at her gates)
Is whole infected with a various mixture
Of all together; she's even grown a spittle,
An hospital of diseases, which will sink   35
Her glories to the first and ancient nothing:
But may that day be leaden heeled, nor fall
Within the compass of this age.
Pomponia.   Fie, husband,
This passion is not Roman. We may raise
Our spirits with hopes of better times;   40
Caesar affords us comfort.
Quintus.   True, Pomponia,
But Rome has had a long sucession
Of State usurpers; when this Hydra's head
Is cut away, another may bud forth.
Pray heaven we have no cause with that old Beldam   45
Of Syracusa, in our fruitless wishes
To dig our ancient tyrants up again.

                    Enter CICERO.

Welcome from the Senate, brother, pray what news?
How were things carried?
Cicero.   Nothing done at all.
The consul Antony came without all doubt   50
To censure Caesar's doings, but his mind
It seems was changed; for having said a little
Touching the provinces and Marcus Lepidus,
But not a word of Caesar, he departed.
Quintus. And what will follow, think you?
Cicero.   Sure he will not   55
Stay long in Rome, for, as I hear, 'has sent
His army to Ariminum, no doubt
With an intent to follow. Then besides
I think he dares not stay for fear of Caesar;
For he returned, though proudly, yet but weakly,   60
With only one Praetorian cohort with him.

---

32. *when Hannibal . . . gates*] See 1.2.269.
34. *spittle*] distinguished from a hospital, as being of a lower class (*OED*).
37. *leaden heeled*] slow in coming.
43. *Hydra's head*] Antony. The hydra was a monster destroyed by Hercules. It had multiple heads, and whenever one was severed two more would grow in its place.
45–6. *Beldam . . . Syracusa*] a witch who brought old tyrants back to life.
53. *Marcus Lepidus*] a senior Roman politician and general, currently governing the provinces of Gallia Narbonensis and Near Spain. He would become the third member of the triumvirate, but at this stage was claiming to be loyal to the Senate.
56. *'has*] he has.
57. *Ariminum*] modern Rimini; an important road centre, the key to Cisalpine Gaul.
61. *Praetorian cohort*] a small group of soldiers which acted as a general's bodyguard.

But 'tis grown something late, I must intreat you
To let my cousin Quintus guide me homeward.
Quintus. He will be proud to do you such a service.   *Exeunt.*

[Act 1 Scene 5]

Enter ANTONY.

Antony. What evil genius crosses me? the fourth
          And Martial legions sided with Octavius?
          For so I have received intelligence;
          Well I'll to Alba, whither, as I hear,
          The Martial legion have betook themselves.   5

Enter FULVIA [, ANTONY'*s wife*].

          I will not thus be thwarted by a boy,
          A mongrel; sooner shall a bee or gnat
          Stop the proud eagle in his airy course,
          And heaven be scaled by a band of pygmies.
          Let Cicero call him Rome's Junonian boy,   10
          And truly golden offspring of his mother,
          Let the whole Senate hug him, as they do;
          Yet will I choke and ruin all their hopes,
          I'll send him naked home to his first nothing,
          And make him answer to Thurinus. What!   15
          Is not the family of the Antonii
          Derived from Anton, son to Hercules?
          And shall these sons of earth confront me thus?
          The stellified Alcides shall not lose
          The cheerful lustre of his rays, to see   20
          His blood run muddy in his issue's veins.

Enter ANTONY] *Enter* ANTONIUS Q.

63. *my cousin Quintus*] i.e. Quintus junior, Cicero's nephew.

1.5.0.1. *Enter* ANTONY] The events described date this scene to 28 November 44BC.
1. *genius*] spirit.
4. *Alba*] Alba Fucens, a strategic town in central Italy. The 'Martial' legion had deserted Antony for Octavius and occupied this town.
7. *mongrel*] i.e. not of pure aristocratic blood, as Antony was.
9–10. *Let Cicero . . . mother*] One of Antony's main lines of attack on Octavius was to accuse him of low birth, claiming that his mother was a nobody. Cicero had contradicted these attacks and here Antony parodies what Cicero had said: Octavius's mother was like Juno, mother of the gods, and Octavius's birth correspondingly noble.
15. *Thurinus*] a name used by Octavius earlier in life, which Antony takes to refer to his relatively humble origins in a town called Thurii.
18. *sons of earth*] i.e. sons of mortals, as opposed to Antony who traced his ancestry to the god Hercules. There is a further allusion to the mythical race of Giants, sons of Earth, who revolted against Jove, king of the gods, their rightful ruler, just as (Antony suggests) the humble Octavius is rebelling against the aristocratic Antony.
19. *The stellified Alcides*] Alcides is another name for Hercules. He was deified after his death. His transformation into a god was associated with a constellation called 'Hercules'.

Fulvia. I like this spirit, Mark. Methinks I see
    The world already prostrate at thy feet.
    Cherish this fire: oh, wert thou all composed
    Of these heroic flames, Fulvia would be   25
    To such a Jove another Semele.
Antony. Spoke like thy glorious self: yet, Fulvia,
    Passion or indiscretion may condemn him,
    But when I weigh his actions in the balance
    Of serious and more accurate construction,   30
    I find he has no base or common soul,
    And does as well inherit Caesar's heart,
    And courage, as his name. Besides he has
    The counsels of experienced heads to steer
    His actions by, so that he's now above   35
    The pitch of my disdain: with strong-nerved eyes,
    Like a young eagle, he confronts our sun.
Fulvia. What, cooled so soon? Octavius an eagle?
    A scarab, rather. He an eagle, Antony?
    He's but a Ganymede in an eagle's claw: 40
    The Octavian family never yet was nest
    To such a kingly bird. But who I pray
    Are those experienced heads you talk of? what?
    Is that tongue-valiant Cicero worth the fear
    Of Fulvia's Antony?   45
    No doubt but he who has of late divorced
    His wife Terentia, and in her place
    Made a young girl his consort, may as soon
    Supplant Antonius, and set up that boy:
    Oh, 'twas great policy to exercise   50
    Himself upon the weaker sex at first.
    Your turn is next: the hawk thus tries his talons
    Upon some meaner prey before he ventures
    To grapple with the eagle or the heron.
Antony. I think Minerva's self dwells in thee, Fulvia: 55
    Such words as these might fire the coldest bosom,
    And by strong alchemy transmute a heart
    Of leaden temper to a golden purity.

---

26. *Semele*] beloved of Jove, consumed by flames when she insisted that the god visit her in his real form.

32–3. *And does . . . name*] Though by blood Julius Caesar's grand-nephew, Octavius was adopted by him in his will and following convention took his name, changing from Gaius Octavius to Gaius Julius Caesar Octavianus.

35–6. *he's now . . . disdain*] i.e. he no longer deserves my contempt.

39. *scarab*] beetle.

40. *Ganymede*] a Trojan prince, carried off by Jove (in the form of an eagle) to be his cupbearer and lover.

47. *Terentia*] Cicero's first wife. In 47 or 46 BC, after thirty years of marriage, Cicero divorced her and married a very young woman named Publilia.

50. *great policy*] devious course of action.

55. *Minerva*] goddess of wisdom and of war.

Were young Octavius indeed an eagle,
And nested in the bosom of great Jove,   60
I'd pluck him thence. As for that Cicero,
My fear, if I had any, should not be
Pitched on so base an object. I will make
That inmate know what 'tis to write my life;
H'ad been as good have published to the world   65
The mystic name of Rome. But let that Cerberus
Proceed to belch his poisonous vomit forth
At view of light; yet shall his unwashed mouth
One day repent that biting impudence.
Fulvia. And there may come a time when Fulvia   70
Shall be revenged on his wormwood jeers.
Oh, how my entrails boil! my heart's on fire:
Had I his damned tongue within my clutches,
This bodkin should in bloody characters
Write my revenge.
Antony.   Come Fulvia, be content;   75
Let him triumph, and in his proud conceit
Frame to himself a conquest great as Jove's
Over those sons of earth, and parallel
His verbal thunder with the voice of heaven.
Yet may I one day be that stronger Typhon   80
Shall cut the sinews of his insolence,
And place thee Juno in this Rome's Olympus.
Come kiss me, sweeting. Though the drowsy Sol
Have not yet left the bosom of his Thetis,
Yet here's no nightly shade, for from thine eyes   85
Breaks a more glorious day. I could, my beauty,
For ever dwell in thy divine embraces,
But I must leave thee, yea and that before
Aurora's first blush gilds the East; thou know'st
My army is sent before unto Ariminum,   90
And I must follow. I will have the province

---

64. *inmate*] stranger or, more disparagingly, 'intruder'. Antony is alluding to Cicero's non-aristocratic origins. See Jonson, *Catiline*, 2.2. 'He is but a new fellow, / An inmate here in Rome.'

65. *H'ad*] he would have.

66. *mystic name*] i.e. the name of Rome's protective deity which was kept strictly secret. If enemies came to know the name it was thought they could summon up the deity and persuade it to remove its protection from the city.

66. *Cerberus*] monstrous three-headed watchdog of Hades, the classical hell.

71. *wormwood jeers*] bitter, scolding taunts. A reference to the *Philippics*.

74. *bodkin*] hairpin.

77. *Frame to himself*] i.e. devise in his own mind.

79. *verbal thunder*] Jove's weapons in his fight against the Giants ('sons of Earth') were thunder and lightning.

80. *Typhon*] a monstrous enemy of Jove.

83–4. *Sol . . . Thetis*] i.e. the sun has not risen; Thetis was a goddess of the sea.

89. *Aurora's . . . blush*] the first signs of the dawn.

Of Decimus Brutus; aye, I will, that's certain,
By fair or foul means. Julius my colleague
Returned from Gaul so happily established,
Great Pompey's self was vanquished by his eagles.   95
I know an army will be soon sent after,
And war proclaimed against me as an enemy
To the State, if once I offer violence
To Decimus, but I'm resolved, and should
The whole world rise against me, what I've said   100
I'll prosecute to ruin or fruition.
Only, my Fulvia, do but thou molest
My foes at home by opposite authority.
There's Lucius Piso, Lucius Philippus,
Fufius Calenus, Salvius, Lucius Caesar,   105
Servius Sulpicius too, and many others
My special friends: thou mayest solicit them,
They'll not be backward in my glorious cause.
Come, I'll go kiss the pledges of our bed,
And then for Mutine; there my hopes are fed.   *Exeunt.*   110

[*Enter* Chorus *of* Senators.]

Chorus. Is there such sweetness in dominion?
Or is it only fond opinion?
Is there such pleasure in the height
Of greatness? Or is it mere conceit?
Sure if the glories of a throne   115
Were in their proper colours shown,
It would appear the highest place
Is pleasant only in the face;
A king is but a royal slave,

---

92. *Decimus Brutus*] one of the assassins of Julius Caesar. He had been provincial governor of Cisalpine Gaul, and refused to accept the validity of the law which handed the province over to Antony. Antony's attempt to force Brutus to give way led him to the siege and battles of Mutina.

93. *Julius my colleague*] Julius Caesar, Antony's colleague in the consulship before his death. He had conquered the whole of Gaul in campaigns between 58 and 50 BC.

95. *eagles*] ensigns i.e. Caesar's forces.

102–3.] Cf comments about Fulvia's warlike activities in *Antony and Cleopatra*, 2.2.46–7 and 65–8.

104–6. *Lucius . . . Sulpicius*] political figures who would be willing to support Antony, and argue his case, in Rome. Salvius would later repent of his support for Antony (see 3.7) and be the first to die in the proscriptions (see 5.3).

109. *pledges of our bed*] our children.

110. *Mutine*] a pun: the town of Mutina in Cisalpine Gaul (modern Modena) where Decimus Brutus was based; but also 'mutiny', rebellion against established authority, such as the Senate.

110.1. *Chorus*] The Chorus, in denigrating monarchy and extolling republican liberty, expresses sentiments which chime with parliamentary abolition of kingship.

112. *fond*] foolish.

118. *in the face*] to outward appearance.

And rule a vassallage more brave.   120
A sceptre's but a glorious name,
A crown the burden of the same
Proud front which it adorns; but peace
And steadfast joy with full increase
Salute the cottage of the swain.   125
There quiet harbours, where disdain
Doth fix a scornful brow, but where
The eye of envy's feasted, there
A thousand discontents do dwell.
Oh, 'tis a second, second hell.   130
Why then, O why, distressèd Rome,
Do thy vipers rend thy womb,
To be possessors of a light
So prejudicial to the sight?
Unhappy Rome, did Julius die   135
For affected tyranny?
And must Antonius inherit
The aims of his ambitious spirit?
Yet in this, thrice happy State,
That thou hast an advocate   140
Dares plead thy griefs, and to his face
Tell thy proud enemy he is base,
Base in his life, and base to thee,
An hater of thy liberty.
Oh, hug so rare a statist's worth,   145
Let thy matrons carol forth
His praise, and crown his agèd hairs:
Not with laurel wreaths, but prayers.
Long mayst thou live, brave man, and have
When dead a soft and peaceful grave!   150

---

120. *vassallage more brave*] i.e. only a higher form of servitude.
126–30.] A contrast is being drawn between the life of the peasant ('swain') and the life of the ruler. The latter seems more desirable, but although the peasant's existence is regarded with contempt, it none the less has the advantage of being peaceful, whilst the ruler's life, for all the envy it excites, is in fact a living hell.
133–4. *light . . . sight*] Political power seems to be desirable but in fact causes great suffering to anyone who possesses it. As such, it is like a light (such as sunlight) which, though superficially attractive, can cause blindness.
140. *advocate*] i.e. Cicero.

ACT 2

[Act 2 Scene 1]

[*Enter* CICERO.]

Cicero. So now methinks I see our common foe
　　Already crushed with ruin; he shall know
　　Ambition is a precipice, and the sky
　　At which he aims his shafts to be too high.
　　Were it the cause though, 'twere ground enough　　　5
　　To build a settled confidence upon.
　　An honest cause in mouth of ruin sings,
　　'Tis the good genius of a State, and brings
　　Down Jove himself to side with her: but more
　　'Tis Brutus whom Antonius copes with, Brutus　　　10
　　The omen of whose very name and blood
　　Fatal to State usurpers were sufficient
　　To fortify our drooping souls, and raise them
　　From thought of servitude. But then besides,
　　Three armies have we sent to succour him:　　　15
　　Two under Aulus Hirtius, and Pansa,
　　Our late elected consuls. Young Octavius
　　Have we made general of the third: a youth
　　Ordained by heaven to do his country good.
　　And yet before this war was brought about,　　　20
　　What oppositions did I meet withall.
　　Piso withstands it, Salvius seconds him,
　　The consular Calenus makes a third.
　　The matter is adjourned, till at the last
　　Ambassadors must be sent to Antony　　　25
　　To treat of peace; a thing, in my conceit,

2.1.1. *our common foe*] i.e. Antony.

5–6.] If Cicero's only grounds for optimism were the fact that Antony was aiming too high, and bound eventually to fall, then that would be enough. But in fact there are, as Cicero goes on to say, further grounds for confidence: namely that Antony is facing the redoubtable Decimus Brutus.

10–14. *'Tis Brutus . . . servitude*] Decimus Brutus was allegedly descended from the semi-mythical Lucius Junius Brutus who killed Tarquin the Proud, the tyrannical last King of Rome, and established government by elected officials. It was following the example of this ancestor that Decimus Brutus, Marcus Brutus (one of the leaders of the conspiracy) and others assassinated Julius Caesar, another perceived tyrant. Brutus's very name will thus restore confidence to the opponents of Antony. It offers the promise that this new tyrant, Antony, will be dealt with in the same way as Brutus's ancestor had dealt with Tarquin.

15. *him*] i.e. Decimus Brutus.

17. *our . . . consuls*] consuls for 43 BC.

26. *conceit*] opinion; estimation.

Of little credit to the senators.
For what could be more base, more full of levity,
Than to send messengers of peace to him
Whom, but a little before, they had condemned   30
As enemy to his country and Republic,
By several decrees, as Caesar's honours,
The great rewards of the legions that forsook him,
The assignment of the Consuls to the wars?
As also their most ample commendations   35
Of Brutus and his army, which the province
Of Gaul did plainly intimate. Moreover,
There was great danger in it; for could the city
Be safe, when it should Antony immure,
Or rather Antonys within her bosom,   40
Which like a nest of serpents would torment her,
And never cease to stab with baneful stings
Till they had wrought a passage to the heart?
Lastly, it was not possible there should
Be peace confirmed with him, for not the Senate   45
Nor citizens could affect him, nor he them.
Both had condemned him, he injured both.
Well, legates are dispatched; yet nothing done;
Antony is still as insolent as ever.
Then must a second embassy be enterèd;   50
And I am one elected for that service.
O heavens! with what distempered, wounded eyes
Should I have looked that monster in the face!
Who in a public concion had decreed
My goods unto Petissius of Urbin,   55
One who but newly from the utter shipwreck

---

56. shipwreck] shipwreak *Q*.

32–4. *as . . . wars*] i.e. such as the honours which the Senate had awarded to
Octavius (in return for his opposition to Antony), the rewards it paid to the legions
which deserted Antony, and its instructions to the consuls (the highest office in the
State) to take command of the armies against Antony. Cicero is arguing that all these
measures showed that the Senate (rightly) regarded Antony as a threat to Rome who
had to be crushed; it was inconsistent now to dignify Antony by sending ambassadors
to discuss peace terms with him.
35–7. *their . . . intimate*] Senate had implied its approval of Brutus by giving him the
province of Gaul.
37–43. *Moreover . . . heart*] It would actually be positively dangerous to come to
terms with Antony, and reconcile him with the State, since he and his followers would
continue to undermine Rome from within.
46. *affect him*] be on good terms with him.
48. *legates*] messengers.
54. *concion*] A concion (Latin *contio*) is a public meeting called by an official such
as (in this case) a consul.
55. *Petissius of Urbin*] a bankrupt supporter of Antony. Many of the details of this
passage derive from Cicero's *Twelfth Philippic*. This dates the episode to the beginning
of March 43 BC.

Of a no mean but rich inheritance
Has crept to those Antonian rocks for shelter?
My tender eyeballs never could have borne
The hated sight of Saxa, Capho, Bestia,   60
Hostilius and Vesenius. Oh, I should
Have seen the very visage and aspect
Of civil war itself. But this legation
Was found at length a mere device and trick
To hinder with delays the Senate's care   65
In preparation for the war. Yet, see
A new demure obtruded; Marcus Lepidus,
Our general beyond the Alps, exhorts
The Senate by ambassadors to the peace.
Hereat the former advocates take heart,   70
And plead the authority of Lepidus,
As if that plea could quench the zealous flames
Which were then kindled in the Senate's breasts.
But all in vain. Our armies are launched forth
Against that archpirate of the State, Antonius.   75
And now we daily with our prayers solicit
The ears of heaven to free the commonwealth
Of such a dangerous and infectious plague,
Which like a gangrene would run on and spread
To the destruction of the body politic.   80
But to strike down such monsters Jove has thunder,
And we have arms to press this viper under.   *Exit.*

[Act 2 Scene 2]

Enter POMPONIA.

Pomponia. Phillis come hither.

[*Enter* PHILLIS.]

Phillis.   Madam.
Pomponia.   Are the rooms
Perfumed as I commanded?
Phillis.   Yes.
Pomponia.   And all things
Done as I gave directions?
Phillis.   All things, Madam.
Pomponia. Well.

                                      Exit PHILLIS.

            But I need not be so punctual.
My brother Marcus, as he is no stranger,   5

60–1. *Saxa . . . Vesenius*] acolytes of Antony, whom Cicero would be obliged to meet
in Antony's camp if he were to go on the proposed embassy.
67. *demure*] delay.

2.2.4. *punctual*] punctilious.

So not so curious as our other Romans.
As for myself, I'm none of those which waste
Whole mornings in the fruitless contemplation
Of their supposèd beauties in a glass.
I have not learned to paint and daub my face   10
With borrowed colours; mine's a native grace,
And, if it please my Quintus, 'tis enough.
Nor am I in the list of those which spend
Their husbands' faculties on loose attires,
On rings, and bracelets, or a glittering toy   15
To dangle in my ear. My ornaments
And jewels are the virtues of my Quintus.

Enter PHILOLOGUS.

Philologus. Madam, my lord your brother's newly entered.

Exit POMPONIA.
Manet PHILOLOGUS.

Enter LAUREAS and TYRO.

Laureas. Here's a triplicity of libertines!
How does my little Philologus?   20
Philologus. O sir, the better
To see your stoicship in health: but, sirrah,
What is yon Tyro doing?
Laureas.   Ha! let's see.
Why, poring on a fragment of Herodotus,
The grandsire (as he calls him) of historians,   25
A kind of vermin he's enamoured with:
And he himself has got an itching humour
To be of that fraternity.
Philologus.   I'faith!
Nay then, we'll furnish him. Most learned Tyro,
Have you not heard the news?
Tyro.   Ha. News? What news?   30
Philologus. Why, 'tis reported, and that credibly,
How Atlas, being weary of his burden,
As sure he well may be, and if you ever
Beheld his picture with that mighty globe
Upon his back, he looks but sourly on it: 35
Well, Atlas, being weary as I told you,
To ease his shoulders, lifted up his arm,
Some say it was his right arm, some his left;

---

6. *curious*] particular, difficult to satisfy.
14. *faculties*] resources.
attires] gowns.
20. *little*] earlier described as 'boy' (see 1.2.73 and note).
24. *Herodotus*] the Greek historian described by Cicero as 'the father of history'.
29. *furnish him*] provide him with the ability and material to be an historian.
32. *Atlas*] See 1.2.78.

But that's not so material, you observe!
Lifting his arm above his head to keep   40
The sphere a while from his back, he chanced to thrust
His thumb into a star, and burnt it off.
Laureas. Tyro, he's misinformed; 'twas thus, old boy:
About the time when the all-seeing sun
Mounted the raging lion's back, this Atlas,   45
This living column of the archèd heavens,
Distilling from his hot and sweating brows
As much salt waters as might turn a sea
Fresh as our Tiber to a brinish sourness;
And truly, were that scorching season constant,   50
Well might the nation of philosophers
Cease their intestine broils about the saltness
Of the vast ocean, and determine safely
The sweat of Atlas were the genuine cause;
Well, Atlas sweltering, as I said, and sending   55
Whole clouds of vapours from his boiling entrails,
Erects his brawny arm, and so sustains
That azure fabric, while he stoops to reach
A draught or two of Nilus in his palm;
But as he stoops, he thus behind him throws   60
His leg, and by ill fortune popped his foot
Into the hot Trinacrian hill; and so
(O sad disaster!) burnt his little toe.
Tyro. I thought your mount at length would be delivered
Of a ridiculous mouse. But what's this all?   65
Philologus. Aye, there's enough at once, too much will glut you.
Tyro. Glut me! by Castor, I'm as lank and thin
As if chameleon-like I had been fed
Of nought but air. This have I only chewed on
Since (to usurp Laureas' inspired notion)   70
The sun lashed up his fiery team from the
Blushing ocean.
Laureas. How the rogue hobbles! 'Slight he makes the muses
Halt, and their god Apollo go on crutches.

44–5. *when ... lion's back*] i.e. when the sun enters the constellation of Leo.
58. *azure fabric*] sky.
59. *Nilus*] the River Nile.
62. *Trinacrian hill*] the volcano Etna, on the island of Sicily (Trinacria).
64–5. *I thought ... mouse*] an anachronism: Horace (a generation later) warning poets against employing a style too grand for their theme, wrote, 'the mountains will labour and bring to birth a ridiculous mouse' (*Ars poetica*, 139).
66. *glut you*] i.e. fill you to excess.
67. *by Castor*] a common expletive. Castor was one of Leda's twin sons, the other being Pollux.
68. *chameleon-like*] Chameleons were thought to subsist on air alone (see *Hamlet*, 3.2.91).
71–2.] the day dawned. Tyro is imitating Laureas's pompous style.
73. *hobbles*] limps i.e. produces poor rhetoric.
'Slight] by God's light.

Philologus. No matter, Laureas, you must attribute it   75
    To the faintness of his stomach, which I'll quicken
    With some supply. Stay here, while I go in,
    And if I meet with an extravagant capon,
    Or some such pilgrim, I'll direct him hither.
Laureas. Well said; but sirrah, you know what I love,   80
    A cup of rich Falern, you rogue, or some
    Extracted nectar of the Formian grape.
Philologus. I'll furnish you immediately.   *Exit.*
Laureas.   I wonder
    What foolish humour Pindarus was in,
    When he begun his poems with the praise   85
    Of that weak element, water: 'slight, blind Homer
    Was an old soaker at it, and the father
    Of our brave Roman Laureats, Ennius,
    Before he dipped his sacred quill in blood,
    Would steep his brains in this Castalian liquor;   90
    Drenched in this juice he could more proudly look
    Bellona in the face than e'er Achilles
    Dipped by his mother in the Stygian lake.

          Enter PHILOLOGUS [*carrying a fowl*].

Laureas. So soon, Philologus?
Tyro.   What's here?
Philologus.   Why, Tyro,
    The remnant of a martyred quartered goose.   95
Tyro. I thought in truth this would be one of your
    Extravagant pilgrims; for it is reported,
    That geese have travailed on their feet to Rome
    Even from the marishes of the Morini.
    What bird is this? 'Tis a young goose, I warrant.   100
Laureas. How, a young goose?
Philologus.   He's one that said so, rather.
Tyro. No, rogue, I'll leave that title to philosophers,
    With whom the geese are so enamoured.

---

78. *extravagant*] wandering.
capon] castrated edible cock (*OED*).
81–2. *Falern . . . Formian grape*] famous types of Roman wine.
84–90. *Pindarus . . . liquor*] Pindarus was a Greek lyric poet of the sixth and fifth
century BC, whose *First Olympian* began 'Water is the best thing of all'. Horace claimed
in his *Epistles* (1.19) that Homer was fond of wine and that Ennius, a Roman epic
poet, would never compose poetry without first getting drunk.
90. *Castalian liquor*] Castalia was a spring on Mount Parnassus associated with the
Muses. Laureas thus means, 'inspirational wine'.
92. *Bellona*] goddess of war. Ennius is imagined actually taking part in the wars he
described. See *Macbeth*, 1.2.55.
92–3. *Achilles . . . lake*] warrior and hero of Homer's *Iliad*. He was plunged by his
mother into the river Styx when an infant and rendered invulnerable except in the heel
by which she held him.
99. *marishes . . . Morini*] marshes in the coastal region of modern Belgium.
101. *He's one . . . rather*] i.e. a goose, an idiot. Geese were proverbially stupid.
103. *with whom . . . enamoured*] possibly a play on 'goose' as prostitute.

For I have read in story of one Lacydes,
Of your bald tribe, affected by a goose   105
With such an ardent zeal that day and night
Abroad, at home, at board, and in his bed,
She would be with him: and I am persuaded
There are but few of that profession
Can leap a span from goose.
Laureas.   The rogue's satirical.   110
Tyro. Nay, there are poets too of this affinity.
Know you not Anser, he who sings the praise
Of Antony in verse?
Laureas.   And witty too.
Philologus. But 'tis a partridge, Tyro.
Tyro.   Ha! a partridge.
Laureas. Come, leave this prattle, he will tell you now   115
How Mulciber the Ferrian prince was hawking,
And a poor partridge, such a one as this,
Mewted in its mouth, only for sincere dread
Of the pursuing hawk: but you, young rascal,
Here's that has life in it.
      Drinks to Philologus.   Philologus, come.   120
Philologus. Historical Tyro.   *Drinks to Tyro. Tyro takes
                                  it [i.e. a goblet of wine].*

Tyro.   What's this?
Laureas.   'Tis wine, pure wine.
Tyro. But Romulus,
The father of this city, knew not wine;
Milk was his drink.
Laureas.   That was in Rome's infancy.
Come, drink, you coxcomb.
Tyro.   Ha, methinks it smiles   125

---

120. Philologus, come] *Phil.* Come Q.

---

104. *Lacydes*] a Peripatetic philosopher who had harboured unusually strong affection for his pet goose.
      105. *bald tribe*] philosophers.
      110. *leap . . . goose*] possibly an allusion to 'goose', a board game introduced to
England in 1597 and popular in the seventeenth century. A player who landed on a
square marked with a goose moved forward ('leaped'?) double the number of his throw.
If playing games was associated with children, Tyro is claiming that few philosophers
are even capable of children's games.
      112. *Anser*] a pun: Anser was a Roman poet and supporter of Antony whose name
is the Latin word for goose.
      113. *partridge*] possibly a pun on partridge as a broadside of cannon shots. Philo-
logus may be suggesting that Anser is more 'partridge' than 'goose' in firing broadsides
at Antony's enemies.
      116. *Mulciber . . . prince*] Vulcan, god of metal smelting: 'Ferrian prince' means
'prince of iron'.
      118. *Mewted . . . mouth*] tore at its moulting feathers.
      125–6. *it . . . maiden*] The wine is as inviting as a seductive woman. Tyro speaks as
if intoxicated.

Like an ungirdled maiden.
Laureas.   Are you there?
Philologus. I see these scribbling fablers are sly creatures.
Laureas. There's my lord's biting mastix Sallust, lately
   Was found at the sport.
Philologus.   Ay, and I think belaboured
   To the purpose for his pains.
Tyro.   'Tis something pleasant.   130
   'Twere good this vacuum were again replenished.
Laureas. Come, come, let's fall aboard.   *They eat.*
Tyro. I see you rascals, you are no Pythagoreans.
Philologus. Why, Tyro? We are as still as they.
Tyro.   'Tis true.
   But they, t'enure themselves to abstinence,   135
   Would cause a table to be richly furnished
   With costly viands, and then sit them down
   To feast their eyes upon the several dishes,
   But not to taste a bit, for when their mouths
   Had watered long o'er the enticing dainties,   140
   A waiter was commanded to remove,
   And so with empty stomachs all departed.
Laureas. A fine device to make a living ghost on.
   But Tyro, here boy.   *Drinks.*
          Wine, why, 'tis the soul
   Of history; methinks in this small glass   145
   I see a volume of brave heroes' acts
   In letters capital: here I read the trophies
   Of Bacchus fetched from the remotest India;
   Here I peruse the battle of such fame
   Between the Centaurs and the Lapathites,   150

128. Sallust] Salust *Q*.

126. *Are you there?*] i.e. are you with us?
127. *scribbling fablers*] historians.
128. *my lord's . . . Sallust*] Sallust was an historian who, at the time of the play, was believed to be the author of a surviving speech attacking Cicero. A 'mastix' is a 'scourge', 'critic'.
128–30. *There's . . . pains*] On the basis of his previous statement, Philologus jokingly implies that Tyro is sexually cunning. Sallust was said to have been caught by Annius Milo in adultery with his wife, 'soundly beaten with a whip and only let go when he had paid over a sum of money' (Aulus Gellius, *Attic Nights*, 17.18).
131. *vacuum*] empty goblet.
133. *Pythagoreans*] Pythagorean philosophers believed that the soul was released from the body by cultivation of abstinence and purity.
134. *still*] unperturbed in mind, the object of the Pythagorean school of philosophy.
145–51. *methinks . . . things*] Laureas is seeking to establish that wine is 'the soul of history'. He describes famous events from mythical history associated with the consumption of wine. Bacchus, the god of wine, conquered India; the Lapiths and Centaurs became involved in a murderous fight at the marriage of Pirithous as a consequence of heavy drinking; and the Greeks were able to enter and sack the city of Troy because the Trojans had been celebrating (with drink) what they mistakenly took to be the withdrawal of the Greek army.

The sack of Troy, and many other things
As well recorded in this fluid monument
As in the strongest adamantine tables.
Tyro. I may in time make use of this sweet doctrine.

Enter CICERO, QUINTUS, QUINTUS JUN.

Laureas. My lord, by Phoebus.
Cicero.   So, so, I perceive   155
You have been at it, 'tis well done. But Tyro,
What news from Mutine? You were ever wont
To be inquisitive.
Tyro.   None but this my lord:
'Tis for a truth given out, that Decimus
From the beseigèd town conveyed a letter   160
To the army of the consuls by a kestrel.
Cicero. How weak, alas, to what small purpose tend
The plots of State usurpers in the end!
How are Antonius' projects crossed! He thought
With scouts and trenches to cut off intelligence   165
Between the consuls and the town, and spread
Nets o'er the surface of the neighbouring river,
Lest the swift waves should carry Brutus' counsels.
But all in vain, if through the yielding air
A wingèd post his embassy may bear.   170

Enter POMPONIA.

Pomponia. Alas, my lord, the town is full of uproars:
Some cry out Antony, some, we are undone;
Some, Marcus Brutus must be called home.
Cicero. Tyro, go see whence springs this sad confusion.
                                        Exit TYRO.
Pomponia. Some answer it is now too late, and others   175
Affirm it were best to fly to him for succour.
There's not a throat but hoarse with cries; an eye
But drowned in floods of tears. The cause I know not.
But yet I fear.
Cicero. If Antony have won the day (which heaven   180
And heaven's all-seeing monarch Jove forbid),
We are undone, there is no hope of succour
Except in Brutus, which must be attained

---

153. *adamantine tables*] tablets made of strong rock.
155. *Phoebus*] the god Apollo, often identified with the sun.
158. *inquisitive*] eager for knowledge.
159. *Decimus*] Decimus Brutus, currently besieged in the town of Mutina.
173. *Marcus Brutus*] one of the two leaders, with Gaius Cassius, of the plot to assassinate Julius Caesar. Both had fled Rome for Greece and the eastern empire soon after Caesar's death.
183. *Brutus*] i.e. Marcus Brutus, not Decimus Brutus.

Not by his coming, but our flight to him,
Unless the common voice mistakes, and danger   185
Be not so nigh our doors as it infers.
But yet my soul is quiet, which was ever
Wont to anticipate the common ills
In her oraculous auguries.

Enter TYRO.

Tyro.   My lord,
There is a rumour spread throughout the city   190
That Antony has overthrown the consuls,
And is now coming with his troops to Rome.
Quintus. Great Jove defend us.
Cicero.   Heaven avert this evil.
Tyro. And the Antonians within the city
Are flocked together into Pompey's court.   195
Cicero. No doubt to broach some mischief against the State.
Tyro. My lord, 'tis broached already; for there is raised
Another bruit without all doubt by those
Pernicious citizens, only to divert
The concourse of the people from your lordship,   200
That on the Ides of April you've determined
To usurp the fasces.
Cicero.   Sure thou art deceived:
'Tis meant some ambitious thief, or sword player,
Or some new minted Catiline.
Tyro.   No, my lord;
You are the man.
Cicero.   O heavens, that I who ruined   205
The counsels of base Catiline, should now
Turn Catiline myself! Is any man
So lost, so wicked to raise this of me?
So rash, so furious to believe it? Heavens!

Enter PUBLIUS APULEIUS [, *a* Tribune].

Alas good tribune, how is Cicero wronged!   210
Apuleius. I know you are, and therefore in a concion

---

195. *Pompey's court*] the *Porticus Pompei*, a park built by Pompey the
Great (Caesar's opponent in the civil wars) in 55 BC, adjacent to his great
theatre.
198. *bruit*] rumour.
200. *concourse . . . people*] popular opinion.
201. *Ides of April*] 13 April (the Ides are the 13th, except in March, May, July and
October when they are the 15th).
202. *fasces*] symbol of power (see 1.2.220); therefore, usurp power.
203. *sword player*] gladiator.
204. *Catiline*] revolutionary of the 60s BC. See 1.2.20 and note.
211. *concion*] see 2.1.54.

Before the people have I urged your innocence,
And partly choked the rumour. I proposed
All your endeavours for the public State
Before their censures, and the whole assembly   215
Pronounced they never yet could find you guilty
So much as of a thought against the welfare
Of the Republic: [*Shouts are heard*] but what noise is this?
Quintus. Hark, the late cries are turned to shouts methinks.
Quintus jun. I hear a cry of victory in the streets.   220
Cicero. Tyro, go see again, my heart presages
          Some sudden good.
                                        Exit TYRO.
Pomponia.   Hark, hark, the noise increases.
Quintus. Aye, and approaches nearer too methinks.
Apuleius. 'Tis at the doors.   [*A shout*]

                    Enter TYRO *and a* messenger.

Tyro.   Here's one, my lord, can tell you.
Messenger. The consuls (worthy sir) have won the day.   225
These will inform you better.   [*Hands him*] *letters. Cicero reads.*
Cicero.   Brother Quintus,
          A word or two in private. [*They withdraw.*] Antony
          Is put to flight, but Hirtius slain, and Pansa
          Dangerously wounded; for some private reasons
          Best known unto myself, I will conceal   230
          The consul's death, which I may do completely,
          For here's a letter sent from Hirtius
          Unto the Senate of a former victory:
          This will remove suspect.   *Shout* [*off-stage*]
Tyro.   The Roman people
          Wait at the door to bring you to the Capitol.   235
Cicero. Thanks to the gods! This day we'll dedicate
          To Jove and Mars, the savers of our State.
                    Exeunt [CICERO, QUINTUS, QUINTUS JUN.,
                              PUBLIUS APULEIUS, TYRO *and* messenger].
Laureas. [*To Pomponia*] Nay, madam, stay, I feel an ecstasy
          Steal through my breast, and fire my pliant soul.
          You shall not go without a hymn of victory.   240
Pomponia. Phillis, Clarinda, Galla, quickly come,

                    [*Enter* POMPONIA's servants.]

          Laureas begin, and these shall sing the Chorus.

---

224. [*A shout.*] *Enter* TYRO *and a* messenger.] *Enter* TYRO *and a* messenger. *A Shout.*
Q.

---

213. *proposed*] set forth.
228. *Hirtius . . . Pansa*] the two consuls for 43 BC, both opponents of Antony.
Hirtius was killed in the fighting at Mutina, Pansa mortally wounded.
235. *Capitol*] site of the temple of Jove, where thanks were offered after a particularly significant military victory.

The Song

Have you not heard the city's cry,
How the people vent their joys
In the welcome, welcome noise   245
Of victory?
The Capitol returns their shout again,
As if itself would learn their joyful strain.

Chorus
Let Echo sing with long-spun notes,
And Philmels carol from their lubric throats;   250
Let hills rebound,
And valleys sound
Io *triumphe!*

The streets are filled with cheerful glee,
And the common mirth is shown   255
In the pleasant, pleasant tone
Of liberty;
For now our consuls have delivered Rome,
And the disturber of her peace o'ercome.

Chorus
Let Echo sing with long-spun notes,   260
And Philmels carol from their lubric throats;
Let hills rebound,
And valleys sound
Io *triumphe!*

Great Jove, we bless thy patronage;   265
By whose high auspice Rome is saved
The Roman State, and kept unslaved
From inbred rage.
And Mars, we praise thee, by whose aid have stood
The Roman walls so long, though built in blood.   270

Chorus
Let Echo sing with long-spun notes,
And Philmels carol from their lubric throats;

260–4]. Let Echo sing with, &c. *Q.*

242.1. *The Song*] The song celebrates Antony's defeat.
247. *returns*] echoes.
250. *Philmels*] nightingales (see 1.2.162 and note).
lubric] smooth, fluent.
253. Io triumphe] a ritual cry of the triumph ceremony.
266. *By whose high auspice*] by whose divine guidance.
270. *Roman . . . blood*] Romulus, the founder of Rome, killed his twin brother, Remus, in the course of its foundation.

Let hills rebound,
And valleys sound
Io triumphe!   *Exeunt.*   275

[Act 2 Scene 3]

> *Enter* [CICERO *and members of*] Senate
> [, PUBLIUS SERVILIUS, PISO, CALENUS].

                                                    A shout

Cicero. Honoured and conscript fathers, if those days
     Appear to us with far more welcome rays
     Wherein we are preserved, than those wherein
     To breathe this common air we first begin,
     Because our safeties have a sure fruition   5
     Of gladness, but our births a frail condition,
     And that we do our safeties entertain
     With pleasure, but nativities with pain:
     How ought we then to embrace this happy light
     Which has redeemed us from that sad affright   10
     Raised by domestic furies? Yet we will not
     Return unto our civil robes, till tidings
     Be brought of Brutus' safety, for this war
     Was undertaken for his aid and succour
     Against those enemies of the State, and is not   15
     Complete but with his freedom first recovered.
Servilius. Although I am not, Cicero, of your mind
     Concerning the retaining of this robe
     Of war, yet I determine public prayer
     Be made to all the gods for twenty days   20
     In the three generals' names.
Cicero.   Which twenty days
     Publius Servilius, I enhance to fifty,
     Since they are granted not to one but three.
Piso. But, Marcus Tullius, my opinion is
     This day to put our civil garments on,   25
     And to resume the sage again tomorrow.

2.3.1. *conscript fathers*] translation of *patres conscripti*, another word for senators. This debate took place in the Senate on 21 April 43 BC. The material here is largely derived from Cicero's *Fourteenth Philippic*.

1–8. *those . . . pain*] The day which brings salvation is more pleasurable than the day of our birth, since salvation is a more secure condition than birth, and birth a painful experience.

9–11. *How . . . furies*] possibly an oblique allusion to the close of the English civil war.

12. *civil robes*] non-military wear. It was traditional for all Romans to wear the *sagum* ('sage'), a military cloak, when the State was at war. Cicero wants to remain in the sage until Decimus Brutus's safety is secured.

21. *three . . . names*] Hirtius, Pansa and Octavius (see 1.2.228).

22. *inhance*] expand.

Calenus. And 'tis my judgement too.
Cicero.   Yes, 'twould be grateful
    To the immortal deities to depart
    To put the sage on from their hallowed altars
    To which we came arrayed in civil robes?   30
    'Twere most enormous, and against religion.
Calenus. Then, Cicero, your terms are too, too harsh.
    You brand them with the name of enemies;
    'Tis too severe a style. We will allow them
    To be called wicked and audacious citizens,   35
    But not their country's foes; and for this cause
    The consuls Hirtius, Pansa, with Octavius
    Are not to be entitulèd generals.
Cicero. If the Antonians are not enemies,
    Then 'twas a great impiety to slay them;   40
    And if it were impiety to slay them,
    How can we hope our solemn supplication,
    Decreed for their destruction, should be pleasing
    To the immortal deities? But, Calenus,
    Know I am not contented with a word   45
    Of such a slight conceit. If any man
    Will furnish me with one of deeper stain,
    I'll burn it into their names; for, even by those
    Which spilt their sacred blood for us at Mutine,
    I know they do deserve it. As for the consuls   50
    And young Octavius, whom we made our chiefs,
    Their brave deserts have made them generals,
    For now that prince of outlaws is o'erthrown;
    The very sun was happy, which before
    He hid his beams, beheld the breathless trunks   55
    Of those dead parricides, and Antony
    For very fear with few associates fly.
    Therefore I thus decree that in the names
    Of the three generals, fifty days together
    Be supplications made, which I will frame   60
    In the most ample words I can contrive.
    Then for the legions, we renew the promise

---

27. *grateful*] pleasing, agreeable: here used ironically by Cicero whose meaning is, in fact, that it would be irreverent to arrive in civil robes only to have to leave and reappear wearing the sage once more. He prefers that they remain in the sage throughout.

33–8. *enemies . . . generals*] Cicero wants to have Antony and his supporters pronounced *hostes*, 'enemies', i.e. people who have by their actions forfeited the rights of Roman citizens. A successful commander could only be awarded the title *imperator*, 'general', if he had defeated *hostes* rather than Roman citizens.

38. *entitulèd*] entitled, called.

42. *supplication*] prayer of thanksgiving to the gods.

45–6. *I . . . conceit*] i.e. I am not happy just to call them enemies.

53. *prince of outlaws*] i.e. Antony.

Of their rewards, which we decreed before,
Should be performed when the war was finished:
But as for those which perished in the battle,   65
We will the pensions were decreed for them
Be (as 'tis just and requisite they should be)
Paid to their parents, brothers, wives and children.
Some of the Martial legion to our grief
But their own glory fell with victory.   70
O happy death which, being nature's due,
Was for their country's welfare suffered. You
Borrow your glorious names from Mars, that he
Who for the nations' good did Rome decree,
Might seem to have ordained you for Rome's.   75
Fame shall erect you Mausolean tombs:
Death caught in flight is backed with infamy,
'Tis glorious to die with victory;
For in the fight Mars, to oblige the rest,
Is wont for pledges to select the best.   80
Therefore those impious foes whom you have slain,
In hell now suffer their deserved pain;
But you who poured forth your latest spirit
In sacred victory, shall now inherit
Those blessèd fields where pious souls are sainted.   85
What though your lives were short! They were untainted.
And the blest memory of your deaths shall climb
Beyond the confines of all-wasting time.
Therefore, most valiant while you lived, but now
Most holy soldiers, it goes well with you,   90
Your shining virtues shall not clouded lie
In the black dungeon of obscurity:
Not your surviving kindred, but all Rome,
Senate and people, shall erect your tomb.
There shall be built a stately monument   95
With words engraven, whose meaning shall present
Your deeds unto eternity; that they
Which see that frame, and read your acts, may say
These were the men that loved their country's good,
And bought her freedom with their dearest blood;   100

   69–70. *Martial legion*] The Martial legion, originally under Antony's command, had gone over to Octavius (see 1.2.292). A number of soldiers from this legion fell at Mutina, bringing glory to themselves by their heroic deaths (Cicero suggests), but grief to those left behind.
   73. *Mars*] father of Romulus (see 2.2.270 n.) and thus ultimately responsible for the foundation of Rome.
   73–5. *that . . . Rome's*] i.e. just as Mars has directed Rome's military victories he has also given the Martial legion a special role in those triumphs.
   76. *Mausolean tombs*] The magnificent tomb of Mausolus, King of Caria, was one of the Seven Wonders of the World.
   79–80.] Mars sacrifices the best soldiers in place of the majority.
   83. *latest spirit*] last breath.

And now for guerdon of their loyalty
Have seized a crown of immortality.

Exeunt omnes.
A shout.

[*Enter*] CHORUS [*of* Senators].

Chorus. How wildly fortune sports with mortals! Now
        She shows a face as black as night,
        Anon becalms her stormy brow,   105
        And outvies Apollo's light.

        We float upon the surface of this main,
        Now sinking into Scylla's jaws,
        Anon we check our fears again
        With hope and comfort's milder laws.   110

        The world's great empress, the blind queen of chance,
        A fairer pattern never drew
        Of her own unconstant glance,
        Than our native Rome can show.

        Alas! How did we whilome fear the waste   115
        Done in the poor Brundusium?
        When Caesar with maturer haste
        Strikes all those bleeding sorrows dumb.

        Then what a sad confused distraction late
        With horror did surprise our ears?   120
        How each heart did antedate
        A tempest in their troubled fears?

        When on a sudden (mighty Jove be praised)
        The welcome news of victory
        Serened those storms, and shouts are raised   125
        Which echoed from the harmonious sky.

        O may this fleeting, fickle goddess here
        Securely, softly sit her down,
        And sleep as long as Phoebe's dear
        On towering Latmus's sacred crown.   130

---

    101. *guerdon*] reward.
    106. *Apollo's light*] the sun.
    108. *Scylla's jaws*] Scylla was a sea monster who inhabited a cave in the Straits of
Messina, seizing and devouring approaching mariners.
    115. *whilome*] at one time.
    115–16. *the waste ... Brundusium*] In Brundisium in late 44 BC, attempting to
bring the legion from Macedonia under his control (with a view to dominating events
at Rome), Antony had executed large numbers of mutinous soldiers.
    117. *Caesar with maturer haste*] Octavius was also raising troops. More successful,
he reached Rome before Antony could.
    129. *Phoebe's dear*] Endymion, a handsome youth with whom Diana (Phoebe),

O that the wakeful Genius of this place
Would but present her with a potion
From Lethe fetched, might make her face
Forget its frown, and feet their motion.

Now Rome is Mars his darling Aphrodite;   135
O that some deity would set
To take them in this happy plight
A lasting adamantine net!

Listen, great Jove, with what devotion sings
The voice of newborn liberties;   140
O that some god would clip the wings
Of unconstant victory!   [*Exeunt.*]

---

the moon-goddess, fell in love. The goddess put him to sleep for eternity on Mount
Latmus.
    131. *wakeful Genius*] guardian spirit.
    133. *Lethe*] a river in the underworld, the water of which had the property of
causing forgetfulness.
    135. *Rome . . . Aphrodite*] Mars, god of war, loves Rome as much as he does his
mistress Aphrodite, i.e. war will never leave the city alone. The Chorus expresses the
wish that this damaging 'attachment' between Rome and the war god should come to
an end, i.e. that war should cease.
    136. *O that . . . net*] Homer recounted how Hephaestus caught his wife, Aphrodite,
commiting adultery with Ares (Mars in Latin) and trapped them *in flagrante delicto* by
means of an invisible but unbreakable net.

ACT 3

[Act 3 Scene 1]

Enter ANTONY *in a mourning gown; the hair of his head and*
beard very long and uncombed, [with] Soldiers.

Antony. Come fellow soldiers, cheer your drooping spirits,
    Behold the camp of Lepidus. This weed
    Black as my fortunes, these uncombèd locks,
    This rusty long-grown beard, this meagre visage,
    Emblems of my distress, might make the bowels   5
    Of ravenous wolves and tigers yearn with pity,
    But they are Romans, and have Roman hearts.
    Come, come, the day may shine, when with delight
    We shall recount the sorrows of this journey;
    When by our fires, in bosom of our wives,   10
    Our children too, and faithful friends about us,
    We shall discourse unto their greedy ears
    Our travails through the Alps, and glory in them;
    How every weary step presented us
    With some new precipice; how we eased our limbs   15
    Not on the soft repose of downy beds,
    But on a frigid and congealed heap
    Of snowy fleeces, with some rugged crag
    To be our pillow. You shall then deride
    The Roman pomp, and when you see an ear   20
    Hung with a jewel, tell them 'twas not so
    With you, when whilome on the Alpine cliffs
    Your hairs were linked with chains of dangling icicles.
    What a brave glory will it be at a feast,
    Amongst the abundance of the Roman luxury,   25
    To tell them how your welcome drink was once

3.1.0.1. Enter ANTONY] After his defeat at Mutina (Modena), Antony retreated with
his army through the Alps, in very difficult conditions. He camped at Forum Iulii
(modern Fréjus in southern France) close to the armies of Marcus Lepidus and Lucius
Munatius Plancus, which were nominally on the side of Cicero and the Senate. Antony
was confident, however, that he could persuade the generals and their armies to join
them. Here, he approaches Lepidus's camp, to this purpose.
    mourning gown] a black robe.
    2. *Behold . . . Lepidus*] Presumably Antony gestures upstage to the bounds of
Lepidus's camp. The scene suggests double staging with upstage (back) and downstage
(front) denoting the camps of Lepidus and Antony respectively and a neutral area
between the trenches.
    weed] mourning garments.
    20. *Roman pomp*] the rich and elaborate ceremonies of the Roman State, such as
the victorious procession known as the triumph.

Not the sweet nectar of the Lesbian grape,
Or Formian wines presented in a cup
Of gold engraved with antiques, or in crystal
Prized more for its fragility than worth,   30
But that which once Darius so esteemed,
The muddy water of a tainted puddle
Scooped with a hollow palm into your mouths;
And that your viands were not Lucrine oysters,
The dainties of Cercei, or wild fowl   35
Procured as far as from the River Phasis,
But beasts whose stinking flesh would make the stomach
Of your luxurious citizen disgorge,
Roots, wild fruit, and the very barks of trees.
Thus, faithful partners of my travails, shall we   40
Solace ourselves, when these unwelcome clouds
Are blown away. I'm now to throw the dice,
Pray heaven the chance be good; retire you something.

                                   Exeunt [Antony's] *soldiers.*

Enter [CLODIUS *and* LAELIUS *with*] Soldiers *as in Lepidus's camp.*

                    [ANTONY *approaches Lepidus's camp.*]
First Soldier. What discontented wight is this approaches
    Our trenches in this mournful garb and habit?   45
Second Soldier. By Mars, he looks like a *memento mori.*
Third Soldier. Sure I have seen thy face.
Antony.   You have, no doubt.
    And if my eyes deceive me not, I see
    Clodius and Laelius there among you, two
    That would have known me once.
Clodius.   It may be so.   50
Laelius. But if we cannot call you now to mind,

---

44. First Soldier] 1 Soldier *Q.*   46. Second Soldier] 2 Soldier *Q.*   47. Third
Soldier] 3 Soldier *Q.*

27–8. *Lesbian . . . Formian*] two varieties of high-quality wine.

31. *Darius*] King of Persia, defeated by Alexander the Great, King of Macedonia.
He was subsequently assassinated by another Persian, Bessus. As he lay dying, a Macedonian gave him water. Darius exclaimed that he had now reached the depths of his
misfortune since he could not repay his benefactor.

32–9.] See Octavius's comments on Antony's defeat at Modena in *Antony
and Cleopatra*, 1.4.56–72. Both Shakespeare and the author of *Cicero* follow
Plutarch.

34–5. *Lucrine . . . Cercei*] The Lucrine lake (near Naples) and Cercei, a seaside town
fifty miles south-east of Rome, were both famous for their oysters.

36. *Phasis*] a river running into the Black Sea, regarded in classical times as the fron-
tier between Europe and Asia. Antony means 'procured from the very farthest reaches
of Europe'.

40. *travails*] troubles, sufferings.

44. *wight*] person.

46. memento mori] a skull, or similar object, acting as a reminder of human
mortality; the words mean literally, 'remember that you have to die'. A Renaissance
rather than a classical motif.

I hope you will impute it to your habit
And our forgetfulness, but not to pride,
Or scorn of misery.
Antony.   No I do not, Laelius.   55
For I may well seem strange to thee, who am
Grown almost out of knowledge with myself;
Yet have I not forgot my name, which while
I was more happy was Antonius.
Clodius. Alas, I know you, sir, to my grief.
Antony. But now I will not arrogate that name,   60
For being fallen from what I was, I must not
Make myself what I am. Alas, I thought not
Then, when Antonius was Antonius,
Fortune would e'er malign me so as make me
An eyesore to myself. Brave Romans, here   65
You see a wretch thrown from the height of greatness
To feed on carrion, and, in fellowship
Of beasts, drink water out of tainted quagmires.
Some remnants of my army are surviving
Which have with many a weary step passed o'er   70
The rugged Alps, and here attend the sentence
Of life or ruin from your mouths.
Omnes.   Alas!
       [*Exit* CLODIUS, LAELIUS *and several of the* Soldiers.]

              Enter LEPIDUS.

Lepidus. How's this? Antonius in a mourning habit
Close at my trenches, and with fawning words
At parley with my soldiers?
[*To soldiers off-stage*]   Sound the trumpets,   75
And drown this Siren's language, or we are lost.   *Exit.*
                                        Trumpets sound.
Antony. I had but two poor engines by whose help
I thought the fortress of these soldiers' hearts
Might be subdued, my habit and my speech;
And one's already frustrate, 'tis no matter.   80
Though with this more than Corybantian noise
My words are swallowed, yet my miseries
Shall speak as loud as thunder in the ears

---

52. *habit*] dress.
60. *I will . . . name*] i.e. I will not call myself that name.
67. *carrion*] rotting flesh; garbage.
71. *here*] i.e. in southern France (following his retreat through the Alps). See 3.1.0.1.n.
72.1. Exit CLODIUS . . . *Soldiers*] For staging purposes, some soldiers must exit, to
return moments later with comrades (see 3.1.88.1).
76. *Siren's language*] language of the Sirens who were enchantresses with voices so
beautiful that sailors passing their island and hearing their singing would land and die
of hunger.
77. *engines*] means.
81. *Corybantian noise*] The Corybantes were mythical attendants of the goddess
Cybele who accompanied their rituals with wild music.

Of these relenting Romans, for I see
Tokens of pity in their looks. Well, here   85
Like a decayèd statue will I stand
And speak a mute oration, that may chance
Advance my hopes to the height of wished fruition.

Enter Soldiers *as in Lepidus's camp.*

First Soldier. See where he stands.
Second Soldier.   Is that Antonius?
First Soldier. The same, or rather not the same Antonius.   90
Third Soldier. 'Fore Jove, 'tis pity, he's a proper man.
Fourth Soldier. Methinks he looks vile thin about the gills.
Second Soldier. He stands by heaven like a mercurial index.
Fourth Soldier. Even such a meagre face for all the world
    Has Saturn's statue in the capitol.   95

Enter CLODIUS *and* LAELIUS *in women's attire.*

Fourth Soldier. But stay, what's here, a brace of cockatrices?
    Whither so fast, my pretty mincing damsels?
    We must not part thus, come, come.
Clodius.   Say you so?
        With a box on the ear strikes him down.
Soldiers. Ha, ha, ha!
Fourth Soldier. What female devil tro was it? By Jove,   100
    My ear is as hot as limping Vulcan's anvil.
Soldiers. Ha, ha!   *Exeunt.*
            [CLODIUS, LAELIUS, ANTONY *remain.*]
Clodius. Now, noble Antony, I see we are
    As much unknown to you in this disguise
    As you to us, when first you did appear   105
    So far unlike our late renowned consul;
    But, sir, to put you out of doubt, I'm Clodius.
Laelius. And I am Laelius.
Clodius.   Both come to recomfort
    Your wretched fortunes.
Antony.   Friends, I can but thank you.
Laelius. 'Tis more than we deserve yet.
Antony.   'Tis as much   110

89. First Soldier] 1 Soldier *Q.* Second Soldier] 2 Soldier *Q.*   91. Third Soldier] 3
Soldier *Q.*   92. Fourth Soldier] 4 Soldier *Q.*

89. First Soldier] same soldier as at 3.1.44, while other soldiers represent new characters who have not yet seen Antony.
91. *he's a proper man*] he was a handsome man.
93. *like a mercurial index*] i.e. thin, like the mercury in a thermometer.
95. *Saturn's statue*] The god was represented as a very old man.
95.1. Enter ... women's attire] Clodius and Laelius have assumed a disguise in order
to defect from Lepidus's camp.
96. *cockatrices*] prostitutes.
100. *tro*] possibly slang for 'trollop', a slut.
101. *limping ... anvil*] the anvil of Vulcan, the lame god of metalworking.

As my forlorn estate can now afford.
Laelius. Your state's forlorn no longer than you please:
     Take heart, the camp is ready to receive you.
Clodius. Aye, and to kill the general Lepidus
     If you'll but say the word.
Antony.   Again I thank you,   115
     And will not die a debtor; nay, I must
     Die both a debtor, and ungrateful too.
     The courtesy is so great, my best endeavours
     Will be too feeble ever to requite it.
     Yet shall the general Lepidus live for me,   120
     I will not raise my fortunes by his fall.
Clodius. Then, sir, tomorrow morning shall our camp
     Expect you with your soldiers, and the trench
     Be levelled against your coming.
Antony.   Clodius
     And Laelius, the restorers of my life,   125
     I were a foe to my own happiness,
     And which is more, respectless of your kindness,
     If I should fail.
Clodius.   Then Antony, till then,
     Farewell.
Antony.   Farewell, farewell good Laelius.
                                   Exeunt CLODIUS *and* LAELIUS.
     Why now methinks I'm Antony again;   130
     I gratulate my Alpine travails now.
     Who in a state so hopeless as was mine
     Would not for such an issue feed on dogs,
     Or cats, or worse than both an age together?
     Well, I'll unto my fellow travailers,   135
     This news will make them frolic. Thus the day
     Ushered with darkness sends the sweeter ray.   *Exit.*

[Act 3 Scene 2]

                    Enter [OCTAVIUS] CAESAR.

Caesar. Now Caesar, summon thy whole self, thou art
     But yet a stripling, and must arm thyself
     With providence unknown in these few years.
     The senators, those Nestors of the State,

---

111. *forlorn estate*] pitiful condition.
123–4. *trench . . . coming*] Clodius will betray the camp by filling in the trenches to allow Antony to enter.
131. *gratulate*] rejoice in.
134. *an age together*] for all time.

3.2.3. *providence*] foresight.
4. *Nestors of the State*] i.e. aged politicians. Nestor is a character of advanced age in the *Iliad*.

Disturb the fair praeludium of my glories.   5
They have created Decimus their general
Against Antonius, robbed me of my triumph,
And jealous of my fortunes, closely practise
To win the soldiers from me; but I am not
So weak a politician, on such terms   10
To part with these fair hopes. If this contempt
Be cast upon me, Antony yet living,
What would they do if he were once extinguished?
Well, I'll no longer be deluded thus.
I'll do what Pansa on his deathbed wishèd me,   15
Even this, acquaint myself with Antony,
And Lepidus, to whom no doubt he is joined.
Then will I send centurions to the Senate,
To ask for me, in name of the whole army,
The consulship. If it be denied, I am determined   20
To march myself to Rome, and gain by force
What fair means cannot win. They who intend
Betimes to compass their wished journey's end
Must take the day before them; so must I
Set forth at morning of my age, and ply   25
My youthful sinews in this task of glory,
Crowning my spring with harvest, that the story
Of Caesar's forward years may be as bright
As others' lives, and send as fair a light.   *Exit.*

[Act 3 Scene 3]

Enter CICERO, *and his brother* QUINTUS.

Cicero. Brother, I am much perplexed about this Caesar:
He has so fixed his hopes upon the consulship
There's no removing him.
Quintus.   I always feared
What the immoderate honours which the Senate
Conferred upon him would at length produce.   5
For if Antonius from deceased Caesar

---

5. *praeludium*] prelude; beginnings.
6–7. *They have created ... triumph*] With Hirtius dead and the other consul Pansa
dying, the Senate made Decimus Brutus commander-in-chief of the forces against
Antony. Although both Octavius and Brutus had commanded at Mutina, only Brutus
was awarded a triumph.
23. *Betimes*] early in life.
compass] accompish, reach.
28. *forward*] early.

3.3.4. *immoderate honours*] excessively generous award of honours. At the beginning of January 43 BC, Cicero had persuaded the Senate (in his *Fifth Philippic*) to give
Octavius a series of special and unconstitutional powers, in an attempt to legitimize his
command of the army. Constitutionally speaking, Octavius was far too young to qualify
for any of them.

Took his occasion to usurp the State;
What hope, may we suppose, will he put on,
The author of whose confidence is not
A murdered tyrant, but the Senate's self?   10
And truly, brother, you are to be blamed
For the same flux of honours with the rest.
Cicero. Why Quintus, he deserved them and more
While he stood constant to his country's cause;
As for myself, the dignity which I   15
Decreed him was but just and necessary;
For you well know the name of general,
Though it was somewhat too much for his age,
Is not convenient only, but essential
To the well governing of so great an army.   20
Now since Octavius has abused both that
And other favours, 'tis his own ambition
And not my fault, unless I must be censured
As guilty of another's misdemeanours.
Quintus. You must, if you might have prevented it,   25
Which moderation would have done. But now
That Caesar who (as you were wont to say)
Flowed from the fountain of your counsels, sullies
All your intendments; for alas what good,
What profit gain we by the overthrow   30
Of Antony, since for reward Octavius
Requires succession in his tyranny?
Since he who vindicated one, begins
Himself another ill, as black as that,
And like to take a deeper root and footing?   35
Cicero. Nay, prithee Quintus, do not aggravate.
The youth, I hope, is not so lost to goodness,
So desperately given, but I may win him
To have some pity on the State, to tender
The safeties of well-minded citizens,   40
Especially of my beloved Brutus.

---

12. *flux*] flow; flood.
15. *dignity*] honour.
17. *the name of general*] One of the honours given Octavius was *imperium pro prae-tore*, effectively the right to command an army.
19. *convenient*] useful.
28. *Flowed . . . counsels*] a claim actually made by Cicero in a letter to Marcus Brutus, meaning that Octavius derived the inspiration for his actions from the advice given him by Cicero. This exchange between Cicero and his brother owes much to the arguments made by Cicero and Marcus Brutus in extant letters exchanged between them. The author of *Cicero* has made Quintus a mouthpiece for sentiments which were in fact expressed by Brutus.
28-9. *sullies . . . intendments*] spoils your intentions.
33. *vindicated one*] took vengeance for one crime.
36. *aggravate*] make the situation worse than it is.
41. *Brutus*] Marcus Brutus.

Quintus. What if he will not? Shall we not be safe
    But under his protection? Heaven defend us,
    What would the noble Brutus say of this,
    Should he but hear it: do you think he'd brook   45
    His safety should be so demissely begged
    Of him that's heir to Julius, whom he slew?
    Why, now you put the reins of tyranny
    Into his hand, and indiscreetly kindle
    The fire already glowing in his breast,   50
    He'll raise his thoughts to fancy certainties,
    And hasten to maturity what yet
    Is scarce conceived in the womb of his ambition,
    When he perceives the authors of our liberty
    Commended to his care, and that by you   55
    Who have been hitherto the chiefest prop
    And pillar of it; why consider, Marcus,
    The very name of Caesar seems to incite him
    Against those which slew his uncle.
Cicero.   Cease, good Quintus,
    You wrack me too severely.

Enter TYRO.

Tyro.   My good lord,   60
    The centiner Cornelius, from the general
    Octavius Caesar, waits to speak with you.
Cicero. He must be mildly handled.
Quintus.   As you please.
Cicero. Well, bring him in.
                          Exit TYRO.

Enter again TYRO *with* CORNELIUS.

Cornelius.   The general Octavius
    Salutes your lordship not by me alone,   65
    But by these letters.   *Delivers and Cicero reads.*
           Sir, I must intreat you
    In the name of the whole army to repair
    To the Senate.
Cicero.   Yes, Cornelius I will,
    And glad I am to hear the noble Caesar

---

  45. *brook*] allow.
  46. *demissely begged*] humiliatingly gained.
  51. *raise . . . certainties*] entertain the possibility of real power.
  54. *authors of our liberty*] assassins of Caesar.
  58. *The very . . . Caesar*] As heir and adopted son of Julius Caesar, Octavius was determined to take vengeance on his killers, Marcus Brutus and Gaius Cassius in particular.
  60. *wrack*] torture.
  61. *centiner*] centurion, army officer.
  68. *repair*] go; make your way.

Is in good health.
Cornelius.   Farewell, my lord.
Cicero.   Farewell.   70

Exit CORNELIUS.

Brother, here's that I feared so much: there are
Four hundred soliders in the army's name
Come to intreat for him the consulship.
'Tis Caesar's own device, I fear, although
He makes it not his, but the army's suit.   75
What's your advice?
Quintus.   Why are you doubtful, brother?
Ne'er give your voice, lest what you have achieved
Against Antonius now degenerate
From the fair glory of a valiant mind
To an opinion of slavish fear.   80
Nay worse, 'twill occasion to the world
To brand you with hypocrisy, and say
Your deeds have tended not to root out tyranny,
But rather to obtain a milder master.
You know the times; a magistrate is made,   85
Do what he can, the common mark of slander.
The best State-pilots oft are overwhelmed
With the foul sea of an opprobrious mouth,
Their virtues branded with the name of vice,
Their diligence of deceit; but to consent   90
To this ambitious suit for Caesar, were
To expose yourself to a deserved censure
And such a one would taint your worthiest actions.

Exeunt.
Except TYRO.

[*Tyro*] *takes out a table-book, and writes,* [*reading aloud:*]
Calendis Sextilibus Anno ab urbe condita Septingentensimo vicen-
simo. Cornelius with other centurions and soldiers, to the number of   95
400, came in the behalf of the whole army to Rome, to ask of the
Senate the office of consul for their general Octavius Caesar.
Tyro. Now, as it is the custom of historians,
Let me a little descant on this business.
There is a whispering rumour that Octavius   100
Slew Hirtius in the tumult of the battle,

---

94. *Calendis . . . vicensimo*] Cal. Sex. An. ab. urb. cond. D.CC.XX *Q.*

77–80.] Quintus is suggesting that Cicero should say nothing, lest the reputation for courage which he has won as a consequence of his successes against Antony be replaced by a reputation for cowardice and servility.

93.3. table-book] pocket notebook.

94. Calendis . . . vicensimo] a Roman date, 'On the first of August in the 720th year after the foundation of Rome'. Rome was traditionally founded in 753 BC, so 43 BC should actually be the 711th year (DCCXI). This event in fact occurred a little before the beginning of August. Tyro is writing his history.

99. *descant*] give an opinion.

And poisoned Pansa at Bononia,
By his physician Glyco; now, methinks,
This sudden suit for the consulship confirms,
At least makes more suspicious, that report.   105
Nay more, I hear he is reconciled to Antony
Upon a sudden; this is something too.
I know not what will follow; but 'tis doubtful.
So, now I care not if I go and read
Two or three pages of that liquid volume   110
Commended to me by my cousin Laureas.

[Act 3 Scene 4]

Enter [members of] Senate [, PUBLIUS SERVILIUS, PISO, CALENUS],
    CORNELIUS [, *a Centurion] and [other]* Centurions.

Cornelius. My lords, the senators, we here are come
    To ask for Caesar our victorious general,
    In the behalf and name of the whole army,
    The office of the consul, and expect
    Your present answers to our just request.   5
    We hope his age will be no greater bar
    To him, than it has been before to others.
    Corvinus was but yet a youth, and Scipio
    No more, when they were both created consuls,
    And yet the State repented them of neither.   10
    We might produce the examples of great Pompey
    And Dolabella, but we hope 'tis needless.
Centurion. Cornelius speaks the language of us all.
Cornelius. And the whole army, Fathers, speaks in us.
Cicero. What is your counsel, conscripts?
First Senator.   Marcus Tullius,   15
    Our liberty's at stake in my opinion,
    And would be ruined should we grant the suit.
Second Senator. 'Tis palpable.
Third Senator.   We must not give such reins

---

15. First Senator] 1 Senator Q.   18. Second Senator] 2 Senator Q. Third Senator]
3 Senator Q.

---

102. *Bononia*] modern Bologna.
106. *liquid volume*] wine.

3.4.6–12. *We hope . . . Dolabella*] Octavius was still only nineteen. The Roman constitution was unwritten but, as a rule, one could not be elected consul before the age of
forty-two. Cornelius here cites great figures of Roman history who under extreme circumstances became consul before the correct age: 'Corvinus' is Marcus Valerius Corvinus, a semi-mythical hero of the fourth century BC; 'Scipio' is Scipio Africanus the
Younger, who captured and destroyed the city of Carthage in 146 BC; 'Pompey' is
Pompey the Great, Julius Caesar's main opponent in the recent civil war, and 'Dolabella'
is Publius Cornelius Dolabella, Cicero's son-in-law, who assumed Caesar's consulship
after Caesar's assassination. All held their first consulship before the age of forty-two.
14. *conscripts*] senators.

To this ambitious youth.
Fourth Senator.   I know not one
    In all our order will consent unto it.   20
Fifth Senator. The tribunes are against it.
Cicero.   Salvius too?
Fifth Senator. Ay, he especially.
Sixth Senator.   And I.
All.   And all.
Cicero. Inform him, good Minutius.
Minutius. The senators do all intreat the army
    To be a while contented with the honours   25
    Already heaped on your general,
    The worthy Caesar, and the State's preserver.
    When they shall judge it timely and convenient
    He shall, I know't Cornelius, have both this
    And other dignities with a full hand.   30
    While others rule, yet those that do obey
    Are no less part of the commonwealth than they.
Cornelius. Minutius, you may keep your sentences,
    For they nor your fair language shall persuade us
    To leave the prosecution of our suit.   35
    It seems the conscript fathers are against it;
    But this shall do it, if the Senate
    Will not.   *Shows them the pommel of his sword.*
Minutius. Hence, traitorous varlet, dost thou threaten us?
                            Exeunt CORNELIUS *and* Centurions.
First Senator. How's this?
Second Senator.   So boisterous? Then I fear a storm.   40
Cicero. A strange affront.
Minutius.   What heavy tyranny
    Must we expect from Caesar's consulship,
    Whose agents dare thus check this sacred order?   *Exeunt.*

[Act 3 Scene 5]

                    Enter POMPONIA, [*and*] PHILOLOGUS.

Pomponia. What, is the Senate yet broke up, Philologus?
Philologus. Yes, newly, Madam.
Pomponia.   Where is my husband Quintus?
Philologus. Gone but to accompany my lord, your brother,

---

19. Fourth Senator] 4 Senator *Q.*   21. Fifth Senator] 5 Senator *Q.*   22. Sixth
Senator] 6 Senator *Q.*   40. First Senator] 1 Senator *Q.* Second Senator] 2 Senator
Q.

---

    23. *Minutius*] a praetor. In the absence of the two consuls (both of whom were now
dead) the praetors were the most powerful officials in the State and were in charge of
proceedings in the Senate.
    33. *sentences*] statements, but with a suggestion of the Latin term *sententia*, meaning
the opinion or decree of the Senate.
    41. *strange affront*] exceptionally great insult.

Home to his house. He will be with you straight,
For so he bade me tell you.   *Exit* PHILOLOGUS.
Pomponia.   'Tis enough,   5
    Why what a piece of idle vanity
    Is woman to be so inquisitive?
    My ear now itches, till I hear the affairs
    Debated in the Senate. I have read
    A very pretty fiction, now I think on it;   10
    How the first mover, being, cause, or nature,
    Or fate or fortune, call him what you will,
    When he first framed the fondling sex of women
    In his Promethean shop, did form the heart,
    The mind, the soul, or whatsoe'er you call   15
    That inner pilot of this floating clay,
    Of strange and various matters, whence they did
    Derive their strange qualities and conditions.
    A slut was formed of as foul a sow;
    A subtle housewife of a crafty fox;   20
    A gluttonous and lazy crone of earth;
    A woman turning like a weathercock
    With the fond wind of cross and foolish humours,
    Smiling and frowning oft times in an hour,
    As false as winter sunshine or a shower   25
    In summer, was composed of the ocean.
    And so of all the rest, but she whose ears
    Tingle as mine with this inquisitive itch,
    Had, as the fable fancies, for her sire
    A dog. But yet methinks I cannot find   30
    Myself in all this brood; for though I have
    A fond desire to hear, yet say I little,
    I bark not, mine's a harmless folly which
    Is never like to change me to a bitch
    As it did the Trojan Hecuba.   *Exit.*   35

[Act 3 Scene 6]

Enter PISO *and* FULVIA.

Piso. Come, Fulvia, cease these sorrows, for thy husband
    Has now shook off the chains that kept him down.

---

18. their strange qualities] their as strange qualities Q.

3.5.9–10. *I have ... fiction*] Pomponia had read a misogynistic poem by the early
Greek poet Semonides of Amorgos which traced the various characters of women to
the different animals from which they had been created.
    13. *fondling*] endearing, affectionate.
    14. *Promethean shop*] In Greek mythology, Prometheus made the human race,
including Pandora, the first woman, out of clay; 'shop' here means workshop.
    16. *floating*] vulnerable.
    32. *fond*] foolish.
    35. *Trojan Hecuba*] wife of Priam and Queen of Troy. She was turned into a dog after
the fall of Troy, a story told in Euripides's *Hecuba*, a popular play in the Renaissance.

The frozen Alps have brought him to a fortune
Which may weigh down the thought of past afflictions:
He's fellow general with Lepidus,   5
Nay, he alone rules all, and Lepidus
Has but the naked name and title only;
And now they have repassed the Alps altogether,
With seventeen legions, as I am informed,
Besides ten thousand horsemen. Nay, Octavius   10
And he are now for ever reconciled;
Here's that will add authority to my words.
                                              Delivers a letter. She reads.
Fulvia. Octavius is our own; confirmed, confirmed,
      By a more natural tie than friendship.
Piso.   How?
Fulvia. He must now call me mother; for the daughter   15
      Of Fulvia is decreed his spouse.
Piso.   Indeed!
Fulvia. Ay, and Octavius too has passed the Rubicon,
      And is now marching hither with eight legions.
      So Cicero, I think, has lost his shelter.
      Now shall my husband Antony and I   20
      Be for his stabbing jeers at length revenged.
      Piso, I thank you, all my cares are vanished.   *Exit.*
Piso. This woman's now secure, but I have eyes
      Which stay not at the superficies,
      But pierce to the centre and the heart of things.   25
      I am afraid this friendship is not real,
      And but to compass his own ends. He creeps
      Into acquaintance with Antonius,
      That by his aid I doubt himself may win
      A good success to his ambitious aims;   30
      As first to seat himself in the consulship,
      Next to root out the Macedonian chiefs
      Brutus and Cassius; but will this be all?
      Will he sit still and on this height determine
      To fix the pillar of his hopes? No, no,   35
      Ambition cannot brook plurality.
      Only one Neptune in the sea doth dwell,
      One Jove in heaven, and but one Dis in hell:

3.6.15. *He must . . . mother*] To cement the new alliance, Octavius married Antony's stepdaughter (Fulvia's natural daughter) Clodia.

17. *Rubicon*] the boundary of Italy and Cisalpine Gaul. To cross this border was a clear act of war against the government in Rome.

24. *superficies*] surface.

29. *doubt*] fear.

32. *Macedonian chiefs*] Caesar's assassins, Marcus Brutus and Cassius, are now in Macedonia (now in northern Greece).

34–5. *Will . . . hopes*] i.e. will this be the limit of his ambition?

37–8. *Neptune . . . Jove . . . Dis*] divine rulers of the sea, sky and underworld, respectively (Dis is another name for Pluto). Piso predicts that the alliance cannnot last. An audience would have been aware that it did not: civil war again erupted between

> Heaven, hell, and raging sea have each but one,
> And he or Antony must rule alone.   *Exit.*   40

[Act 3 Scene 7]

Enter SALVIUS [*and*] CICERO.

Salvius. Alas good Cicero, 'twas not hate to you
    Nor love unto Antonius that I did it,
    But pure devotion to my country's cause.
Cicero. But my immoderate hate of Antony
    (I now confess it) blinded my discretion,   5
    And carried me too inconsiderately
    Unto this dangerous planting of Octavius.
Salvius. 'Twas that I feared, and therefore did withstand you.
    You favoured Caesar, and maintained his youth
    In opposition of Antonius,   10
    Lest Antony should get the upper hand;
    I favoured Antony, and opposed your counsels,
    Lest Caesar should ascend too high a pitch.
    Your aim was to beat down a reigning tyranny,
    Mine to keep down springing ambition;   15
    Yours to oppress Antonius culminant,
    Mine to suppress rising Octavius; both
    Good in the intent, though in effect pernicious.
Cicero. Sure some superior power has ordered this,
    And made us instruments of our own subversion;   20
    But this afflicts me most, that these calamities
    Should happen at a season so unfortunate,
    When Brutus and Cassius are so far remote,
    Nor furnished neither to oppose such violence.

Enter APULEIUS.

    You look, good Tribune, as if horror dwelt   25
    Upon your brows; what tidings, Apuleius?
Apuleius. My lord Octavius is directly coming
    To the city with an army of eight legions;
    Antonius too and Lepidus are come
    With mighty forces into Italy   30
    Only with this intent, to second Caesar.
    The streets are filled with tumult and confusion.
    Some run about not knowing what to do,
    Others remove their families and goods
    Into out-villages, or stronger places   35
    Within this city.
Salvius.   Heaven defend us, Cicero,

Octavius and Antony in the late 30s BC. Octavius was triumphant and became the first emperor of Rome, Augustus.

3.7.16. *culminant*] at the height of his power.

Alas we are undone.
Apuleius.   The Senate, sir,
Is now in consultation of some course
Whereon to pitch. Your presence is expected.
Cicero. No doubt it is; but I'll absent myself.   40
The conscript fathers may themselves determine
What's best in this, necessitating straight
For their own safeties: I should say the State's,
But there the choice is crossed; as for myself,
Nothing can come amiss. I've lived too long   45
To see this day: the fathers forced to yield
(As now they must) to the ruin of their liberty.
Oh, 'tis a corrosive to my soul to think on it.
'Twere good you two would go and take your place.
Both. We will, and that with speed; farewell.
Cicero.   Farewell.   *Exeunt.*   50

[Act 3 Scene 8]

                    Enter [four Senators].

First Senator. We must be speedy, fathers. What's your counsel?
Second Senator. 'Twere best in my opinion to dispatch
A message to him to present him with
The consulship.
Third Senator.   Ay, that's the safest way.
Fourth Senator. But the army's fired for the late repulse.   5
How shall we stay their furies?
Second Senator.   We'll decree
To the whole eight legions twice so much in gift
As we have promised to the two.
First Senator.   How say you?
Are you content?
Omnes.   Content! We must of force.
First Senator. See what the tribunes say to it.
Second Senator.   They consent,   10

0.1 *four* Senators] Senate Q.   10. *First Senator*] *1 Senator* Q. *Second Senator*]
Senator Q.

41. *conscript fathers*] senators.
44. *crossed*] difficult.
48. *a corrosive*] destructive.

3.8.5. *fired for*] angry at.
late repulse] the initial rejection of Caesar's request for the consulship.
6–8. *We'll decree . . . two*] Two legions, the fourth and the Martial (see 1.2.53–60;
1.5.1–2), had deserted Antony and had been promised financial reward by the Senate
for doing so. Now the Senate hoped to conciliate *all* of Octavius's troops, not only the
fourth and Martial, with rewards.
9. *Content*] translates the Latin word, *placet*, 'I approve'.

Forced by the same necessity as we.
First Senator. Come then, let's speedily dispatch the legates.

Exeunt.

[Act 3 Scene 9]

Enter CICERO.

Cicero. How will this royal city now become
    A nest of vultures! and her senators
    Be made a wretched prey to ravenous talons!
    Will Caesar think himself secure while men
    So much addicted to the State survive?   5
    No; tyranny's suspicious, he'll unhead them,
    Lest happily they should beget young Brutes.

Enter SALVIUS.

    Salvius, what news?
Salvius.   What news! Why, Caesar's consul.
    Legates are sent unto him with the offer.
Cicero. Heavens! What a tide of woes must Rome expect,   10
    When she must lift the axe to her own head?
    That Brutus were at home now! We would lose
    Our dearest blood, before our liberty.
    Thrice happy you, which in the Mutine field
    Gave up your lives! You breathe not with the rest,   15
    To taint your former glories with black treason
    To your own country's freedom; in soft peace
    Rest your immortal souls. But wretched we,
    That for one tyrant, now are plagued with three.

Enter QUINTUS.

Quintus. Brother, the Africk legions are arrived.   20
Cicero. Arrived, Quintus?
Quintus.   Marcus, 'tis most certain.
Cicero. Nay, then we will not on such feeble terms
    Part with our country's freedom. Salvius, come.   *Exeunt.*

---

   12. *legates*] ambassadors (to Octavius).

   3.9.7. *Brutes*] a pun: (violent) 'animals', children of the 'prey' attacked by the vultures; and 'Brutuses', 'tyrant-killers'.

   14–15. *you . . . lives*] those who died during the resistance to Antony at Mutina in 43 BC.

   19. *now . . . three*] Antony, Octavius and Lepidus, who called themselves a 'triumvirate', 'government of three men'.

   20. *Africk legions*] two legions, still loyal to the Senate, from the Roman province of Africa (modern Tunisia). Their arrival raised hopes of a last-minute reprieve, but they quickly deserted to Octavius.

[Act 3 Scene 10]

Enter [four] Senators.

First Senator. What have we done, my lords? Given up our liberty,
　　Without the shedding of one drop of blood?
　　'Twill grow a custom for ambitious men
　　To usurp the offices of State, if thus
　　The consulship be made a prey to force;　　　　　　　　5
　　Nay, rather let's oppose and bear the assault,
　　Till Decimus or Plancus come and succour us.
　　Let's fight till our life's latest breath be spent,
　　Rather than leave a gap for tyranny,
　　Never before attempted with success.　　　　　　　　10
　　There was, there was that virtue once in Rome,
　　When her brave worthies would not stand aghast
　　At such a threatened storm as this, but strike
　　The bolt from hand of the usurping Jove
　　Durst venture once to raise it. Conscripts, what!　　　15
　　Have we let dull and rust the glorious edge
　　Of that heroic boldness? Or is it only
　　Imprisoned in the sheath? Let's draw it out:
　　Nor fail our country, but would uphold her cause,
　　While we have hearts, and hands, like true-born Romans.　　20

Enter CICERO.

Cicero. Fathers, you were too forward in the dispatch
　　Of your legation to Octavius.
　　You will repent it.
First Senator.　　　　　　Marcus Tullius, why?
Cicero. The Africk legions are arrived.
Second Senator.　　　　　　　　　Arrived?
　　Then let the messengers be called back.　　　　*Exit.*　　25
Cicero. Fathers, I need not urge how bright and glorious
　　Is zeal unto the common cause. I know
　　You prize it as the jewel of your lives,
　　And you do well: for 'tis a music which
　　Will, like the note of the Caystrian bird,　　　　　　30
　　Stick by you till your latest gasp; and then
　　Be your good genius mounting to the skies
　　Your wingèd souls, where being stellified
　　You shall with shining optics see how weak
　　A nothing is this molehill earth whereon　　　　　　35
　　Poor mortals toil so; there you shall behold

3.10.7. *Decimus or Plancus*] Decimus Brutus and Lucius Munatius Plancus, both
currently commanding troops loyal to the senate in Gaul.

30. *Caystrian bird*] swan, common on the banks of the River Cayster in modern
Turkey (see 1.2.149 and note).

32. *genius*] attendant spirit who conducts the soul from this world into the next.

How feeble, how ridiculous a madness
Is fond ambition. But I lose myself
In this divine and pleasing contemplation.
Come, let's dispose ourselves for opposition.   40
Senators. With all our hearts. Heaven prosper the attempt.   *Exeunt.*

[Act 3 Scene 11]

    Enter [OCTAVIUS] CAESAR, [CORNELIUS,] Captains, Soldiers.

Caesar. How's this? The Senate so unconstant? Well.
    Cornelius, take some certain horsemen with you,
    Post to the city, and assure the people,
    I come not with intent to raise a tumult,
    But on fair terms of peace; make haste before,   5
    And I will follow with all speed I can.   *Exeunt.*

[Act 3 Scene 12]

    Enter POMPONIA *and* QUINTUS JUN.

Pomponia. So studious, Quintus, in such times as these?
Quintus. Yes, Madam, therefore because the times are such
    Though Caesar be a youth as well as I,
    Yet he is one of deeper undertakings
    Than can be founded by such heads as mine;   5
    Pray heaven they puzzle not the piercing judgements
    Of our grave senators.
Pomponia.   And 'tis my prayer,
    But what is it you are reading?
Quintus.   'Tis a book
    My uncle Marcus wished me to peruse.
Pomponia. You cannot better spend your morning's leisure   10
    Than after his prescriptions. Time's a treasure.
    A day is like a costly ring of gold,
    And morning is the diamond of that ring.
    But tell me something which your book contains
    Worthy our hearing.
Quintus.   Madam, the whole volume   15
    Is like a gallery hung about with pictures
    Of filial piety. Here on trembling shoulders,

0.1. QUINTUS JUN.] Young Quintus *Q.*

    3.11.2. *certain*] dependable.
    3. *Post*] make haste.
    5. *before*] i.e. 'ahead of me'.

    3.12.4. *undertakings*] enterprises, objectives.
    5. *founded*] attempted, initiated.
    8. *book*] anachronistic in the modern sense; the main vehicle of Latin literature was
the papyrus roll.
    17. *filial piety*] respect shown by children to parents.

More framed than those of Hercules, which upheld
The heavenly orbs, one bears aged father
Through midst of flames, and so conserves that being   20
Which was the spring of his. Another bears
Her on his pious back who in her womb
Bore him. Here one sustains her mother's life
With the same food wherewith her own first breath
Was by that mother cherished; these were deities   25
In nature's heaven, and have now an Elysium
Not to inhabit only, but to rule.
Yet that which makes me most admire is this,
That the mute son of Croesus should unloose
The fetters tied by nature to his tongue,   30
And cry, kill not the king.
Pomponia.   To save our parents
Is the first law and dictate nature writes
In our hearts' fleshy tables; therefore did she
Articulate the undistinguished murmurings
Of his chained tongue, lest by her fault that law   35
Should want its force and vigour in the youth.
Quintus. Methinks I envy the example.
Pomponia.   What?
Would you your father should be so endangered
That you might save him?
Quintus.   No, not for a world.
But who knows what this age doth travail with?   40
Pomponia. True. But the precedent coheres not; you,
The heavens be thanked for it, were not born dumb.
Quintus. 'Tis a great benefit; but yet methinks
I could incarcerate, as he freed his voice,
To save a father. I could win by bridling   45
As great a name, as he by giving reins
To stupid nature; such an act would come

---

23. Bore] Bare Q.

___

18. *framed*] sturdy.

18–19. *those . . . orbs*] In the course of one of his twelve labours, Hercules persuaded Atlas to fetch the golden apples for him from the Garden of the Hesperides. In
return, he took over Atlas's task of supporting the heavens for a time.

19. *one bears . . . his*] Aeneas carrying his father, Anchises, from burning Troy.

21–5. *Another . . . cherished*] Quintus here refers to various mythical examples of
filial piety.

26. *Elysium*] in Greek mythology, the state or place of the blessed after death.

29. *the mute son of Croesus*] In the first book of his *Histories*, Herodotus recounts
how Croesus, King of Lydia, was defeated by Cyrus, King of Persia. During the fighting, when a Persian soldier was on the point of attacking Croesus, his mute son discovered the power of speech and cried out, 'Man, do not kill Croesus'.

33. *fleshy tables*] the writing-tablets metaphorically constructed by our hearts.

40. *travail with*] bring to birth.

44. *incarcerate*] imprison my voice; go mute.

45. *bridling*] suppressing.

Within the verge of praise, whereas his does not
Without the internals.
Pomponia.   Go, you make me sad.

                                        Exit QUINTUS.

What genius has informed my Quintus' fancy,   50
That he still meditates on such examples?
Pray heaven my husband never prove an object
For him whereon to exercise this piety.   *Exit.*

[Act 3 Scene 13]

                    Enter CICERO.

Cicero. Still do I strive against the stream and, like
    A silly lark, mount the enraged wind,
    Which, if I do not poise my actions well,
    Will carry me away. We thought the gods
    By their auspicious providence had sent   5
    The Affrick legions to our succour; but
    They are revolted from us, and their captains
    Taken to favour. Only one Cornutius,
    Scorning to beg life from this second Caesar,
    Has like a second Cato slain himself.   10
    And I would follow him, but that the good
    And safety of my country is my remora.
    I will for the present seek Octavius' favour.
    It cannot be a stain to Cicero,
    Since all have done it already but myself.   15

                Enter [three] Senators.

First Senator. Have you made peace with Caesar?
Cicero.   I have sued it
    By mediation of his friends, and now
    Wait to accost him; sure he is at hand.
Second Senator. He is indeed; hark how the people shout.   *Shout.*

            *Enter [*OCTAVIUS*] CAESAR *and others.**

Third Senator. Health to the worthy and victorious consul.   20

---

16. First Senator] Senator Q.   19. Second Senator] Senator Q.   20. Third Senator]
Senator Q.

48. *verge*] boundary.
49. *internals*] physical impediment.
53. *piety*] duty.

3.13.2. *silly*] helpless.
3. *poise*] keep in balance.
8. *Taken to favour*] gone over to Octavius.
Cornutius] a praetor in command of one of the legions.
12. *remora*] impediment; what restrains him. The remora is a sucking fish which
was believed to have the power of holding back the progress of a ship.

Caesar. Fathers, I thank you.
Cicero.   Hail to noble Caesar.
Caesar. My honoured father!
Cicero.   'Tis too high a title
    For Marcus Tullius Cicero.
Caesar.   Now you wrong me,
    The parent of my country must be mine.
    But yet I must be bold to tell you, sir,   25
    You have been something sparing of your courtesies;
    You are the last of all my noble friends
    That come to welcome my return from Gaul.   *Exeunt.*
                                             A shout

           [*Enter*] Chorus [*of* Senators].

Chorus. Oh, what a wounding shout was this!
    'Tis even as baneful as the mandrake's note,   30
    The shrieks of damned souls, the hiss
    Of scorpions, adders, or the siren's throat.
    Let it be strangled, 'tis a sound
    Will wake pale death from his Cimmerian cell,
    'Twill rend a passage through the ground,   35
    And bring the furies from their court of hell.
    The barbarous Thracians, though they sing
    Their dead unto their graves, would howl to see
    So black, so venomous a sting
    Enter the body of their State, as we.   40
    For these are but Sardonian smiles
    Which dance upon our brows; this fading mirth
    Will prove an embryon, and beguile us
    When we shall find it stillborn at the birth.

---

24. *parent . . . country*] Cicero had been declared *parens patriae*, 'parent of his country', for his achievement in crushing the conspiracy of Catiline during his consulship in 63 BC.

30. *baneful*] poisonous.

mandrake's note] an allusion used several times by John Webster. See *The Duchess of Malfi*, 2.5.1. The mandrake, a poisonous plant, had a forked root which could resemble a caricature of the human form. If uprooted, it reputedly shrieked and had the power to madden.

34. *Cimmerian cell*] dark and gloomy cell, i.e. the underworld. The Cimmerians were a mythical people who lived in a land of mist and cloud at the edge of the earth. In Homer's *Odyssey* this was also the location of the entrance to the underworld.

36. *furies*] avenging powers of the underworld.

37. *Thracians*] Many unusual customs were attributed to the inhabitants of Thrace (roughly modern Bulgaria), including celebration and feasting at funerals.

41. *Sardonian smiles*] sardonic; bitter. A fatally poisonous herb grew in Sardinia (Sardonia) which, if eaten, caused the facial nerves to contract into a smile.

Oh, what a golden age we enjoyèd   45
Under the reverend Saturns of the State.
But now an upstart, scarce unboyed,
Unto an age of iron gives new date.
What power this ruin on us flings?
Julius is turned his genius, we fear,   50
And lent him Tityus's vulture's wings
To enhance the swiftness of his proud career.
If such a little time as scant
Full twenty summers have a consul bore
Of such a growth, so culminant;   55
What may we think alas of twenty more?
Others, when in this sacred way
Of honour they had travailed but so far,
Would sit them down, and sagely say,
Death was mature unto a consular.   60
But this young minion of blind chance
Like a sky-climbing eagle still will tower
Until he shall himself advance
Unto a sovereign independent power.
Heavens! if it be your sacred pleasure   65
To put a period to our liberty,
Oh, let the sceptre know some measure,
That being servile we may yet seem free.

45–6. *golden . . . State*] Saturn was overthrown by his son, Jove, and came to Italy,
where he presided over a Golden Age of peace and innocence. The Golden Age was
followed by the current Iron Age of violence and vice. By 'Saturns of the State' is thus
meant, 'great politicians of our virtuous past'.

47. *unboyed*] past adolescence.

50. *Julius . . . genius*] The spirit of Julius Caesar has entered Octavius.

51. *Tityus*] a giant punished for assaulting the goddess Leto by having his liver
attacked by vultures for eternity.

60. *Death . . . consular*] a statement made in Cicero's fourth speech against Catiline
in 63 BC, and repeated in his *Second Philippic* (see 1.2.18n.).

68. *That . . . free*] a wish which was fulfilled. Having defeated Antony, Octavius
established a system of government which, while effectively autocratic, retained much
of the appearance of the old, free Republic.

ACT 4

[Act 4 Scene 1]

[*Enter*] CICERO.

Cicero. Now we are past recovery, lost for ever.
　　Our new-made consul, made indeed, but not
　　Elected, for election is an act
　　Of will not voice, of an internal sufferage,
　　Not outward sound; this consul, whom our fears,　　　5
　　Not our consents or votes, have dignified,
　　Hangs o'er us like a full and pregnant cloud
　　Ready to pour a tempest on our heads.
　　Our forced hands delivered him the axe
　　To punish State-malingers but, alas,　　　　　　　10
　　He whets it for the necks of our preservers.
　　I, only I, am blamed: ungrateful city!
　　They are not Caesar's honours which afflict us,
　　But his new-entered friendship with Antonius,
　　Which was the only rock my best endeavours　　　15
　　Were ever pressed to avoid, lest the Republic
　　Should suffer wreck upon it. I thought the way
　　To keep him distant with Antonius,
　　Was to advance him to a requisite power
　　Of opposition: 'las we but conjecture　　　　　　20
　　And guess at the events of things. Our knowledge
　　Cannot arrive to an infallible certainty
　　Of the success of matters; 'tis a privilege
　　Peculiar only to the gods, and is
　　Derived to us weak mortals not by nature,　　　　25
　　But extraordinary participation.
　　Since therefore 'tis the unknown event alone,
　　Not the perverseness of my soul, which crosses
　　The seeming good appearing in my counsels,
　　Why am I made the mark of accusation?　　　　　30
　　But 'tis the custom of the times, I will not

4.1.3–6. *for . . . dignified*] Octavius has not gained his position as consul through the official election process. See 3.3.95–108.
　4. *internal sufferage*] private assent.
　9. *axe*] fasces (see 1.2.220 and note).
　21. *events*] outcome.
　21–6. *our . . . participation*] As humans, we do not naturally have the capacity to see the future: it is vouchsafed only to some of us under unusual circumstances.
　27–30.] i.e. why am I criticized for the unfortunate outcome of events, when it is my quite human inability to foresee the future, and no wickedness on my part, which has made my advice inadequate?

Deject myself for this; the innocence
Which I am armed with is enough to raise me
From such servility, but yet I'm grieved
For the sure ruin of my country's freedom,   35
For my dear Brutus, and the noble Cassius.
The other consul, Quintus Pedius,
Has published a decree wherein they're sentenced
With interdiction of fire and water.
Of fire and water! Can they then constrain   40
The fountains of our eyes to cease their course?
Brutus shall have these waters, till we have wept
Their currents dry; and then our hearts shall send
Whole clouds of vapouring sighs to feed new showers.
But as for fire, they want it not; their breasts   45
Cherish the flame of an unmoved zeal
Unto their country's liberty, which cannot
Be quenched but with their blood; this Caesar knows,
And therefore that he may with doubled power
Oppress the heroic bravery of their spirits,   50
Has reconciled Antonius and Lepidus,
Those two pernicious monsters, with the Senate,
And now he is returned again toward Mutine,
No doubt to join with those two plagues, and there
Contrive the ruin of the commonwealth.   55
For State usurpers think of nought but blood;
When they consult, 'tis to devour the good.

                    Enter QUINTUS.

Quintus. Brother, how dost?
Cicero.   Think'st, my beloved Quintus,
   I can be healthful when the State's diseased
   Whereof I am a member?
Quintus.   'Las, 'tis true,   60
   Too true; the commonwealth's diseased indeed,
   Sick at the heart, faints, can no longer stand,
   Lies bedrid, and like fierce Procrustes' guests
   Must be distended or abbreviated
   To the pleasure of her lord, the worst of thieves;   65
   For Caesar, Antony and Lepidus

---

32. *Deject myself*] be cast down.
37. *Quintus Pedius*] Octavius's uncle and fellow consul, who outlawed the assassins of Julius Caesar.
39. *interdiction...water*] The standard Roman fomula for outlawing somebody prohibiting them from receiving fire or water, the basic necessities of life.
53. *Mutine*] with a pun on 'mutiny'.
60. *member*] 'member' meaning limb and participant. There is a persistent association between the body politic and Cicero's body.
63. *Procrustes*] a bandit who would lie his victims on a bed. If they were too short for it, he would stretch them; if too long, cut them down to size.

Are met together not far off from Mutine,
And in an island round environed
With a small river, without any company,
Are as I hear consulting.
Cicero.   What a hell   70
Will this poor city be, when such a three,
Like Minos, Aeacus and Rhadamanth,
Sit on the life and death of her best statesmen?
Quintus. 'Tis to be feared indeed they will play Sullas.
But who can help it? If the gods will throw   75
Destruction on us, we must not complain,
For they're above us, and it were but vain,
For who can alter the decrees of fate?
Alas we are but mortal, and the state
Of this life's pilgrimage is full of woe.   80
Better die once, delivered with one blow,
And in one's country's cause, than living die
Wounded with sight of bloody tyranny.
Cicero. Now Quintus speaks like his own virtuous self.
This language melts me into fire and air;   85
I am sublimed, and ready to take flight
In ecstasy from this unwieldy lump.
Come, let's retire into my garden; there
Proceed in this divine discourse, 'twill make
My soul disdain with earthly mould comply,   90
And raise her thoughts to immortality.   *Exeunt.*

[Act 4 Scene 2]

Enter [OCTAVIUS] CAESAR *solus.*

Caesar. How full of fate and horror is this morning?
She comes not tripping on the mountains' tops,
But moves with drooping pace, and leaden heels.
Her eyelids are not rosy, nor her brow
Gilded with that sweet beauty it was wont;   5
What, has she changed colours with her Memnon?

---

67. *are met together*] In October or November 43 BC, Antony, Octavius and Lepidus met on a small island in the River Lavino near Bononia (Bologna) to cement their alliance and arrange for the removal of their enemies (and raising of funds) by proscriptions.

72. *Minos . . . Rhadamanth*] the three judges in the underworld who meted out punishment to the dead. The triumvirs are arrogantly imitating these divine figures in handing out punishment to the victims of their proscriptions.

74. *Sullas*] On the dictator, see 1.1.41 and note.

86. *sublimed*] sublimated, refined. Term used for material converted to vapour from solid form.

89–91. *'twill . . . immortality*] the philosophical discussion will raise Cicero's soul to such a state of rapture that it will take leave of his body.

4.2.6. *Memnon*] son of Aurora (the dawn) and a black African.

Or is she sick, and so has bound her head
In this black veil of clouds? Alas, alas,
'Tis lest her eyes behold our blacker deeds.
Myself, Antonius, and Lepidus   10
Have, like the three Saturnian brothers once,
Amongst us shared the Roman world, as if
It were our own inheritance, and now
We must complot a tragedy. The proscripts
Must be culled out; shall Cicero then die?   15
Alas, how piety struggles in my breast.
This mouth, this tongue which now must speak his death,
Was wont to call him father; shall I then
Become a parricide? Suppose I do;
He that aspires to govern without check,   20
Must set his foot upon his father's neck.
It is a maxim long since practised
By Jove himself upon his father Saturn.
But words oblige not to a natural duty.
I did but call him father; and if now   25
I yield consent unto his death, I do it
As he is Marcus Cicero, a stranger
To Caesar's blood. But Cato thought him worthy
The honoured title of his country's parent.
And shall Octavius ruin so great worth?   30
Be still, my melting passions; he must die.
And therefore 'cause he is his country's parent,
He, that is Caesar's friend, must be a foe
Unto his country's freedom, which he prizes
Above his life, and for this cause must lose it.   35
Shall he then die? Ambition says he must.
But piety forbids; but piety
Must not be sided with ambition.
It must be so. Antonius shall have Cicero,
Antonius then shall give me Lucius Caesar,   40

---

11. *Saturnian brothers*] The three sons of Saturn, Jupiter, Neptune and Pluto, divided the world between them.

14. *proscripts*] those who were 'proscribed' or outlawed. On proscription, see 1.1.43n.

14–43.] see *Julius Caesar*, 4.1.1–9, where Antony, Octavius and Lepidus meet to decide upon the proscripts.

18. *was wont . . . father*] a detail derived from Plutarch's biography of Cicero.

19. *parricide*] the perpetrator of a serious crime (originally, one who murders his father), see 1.2.232n and 2.3.56.

23. *Jove . . . Saturn*] Jove overthrew his own father, Saturn, to become king of the gods.

24–5. *But . . . father*] 'Father' was just a term of honour Octavius used to Cicero; it did not oblige him to treat him like his real father.

28. *Cato*] a Roman politician of celebrated integrity (see 1.2.127). He had supported the award to Cicero of the title 'parent of his country', in 63 BC.

40–1. *Antonius . . . Paulus*] Octavius refers to the coming proscriptions. They were notoriously callous, and this is exemplified by the fact that Octavius allowed the name

And Lepidus shall yield his brother Paulus.
Ambition thus must thought of pity smother,
Even towards a father, uncle, or a brother.   *Exit.*

[Act 4 Scene 3]

Enter LAUREAS.

Laureas. Heavens! What a dismal time is this! The dogs,
　　As if they were transformed into wolves,
　　Gather together, and do nought but howl;
　　And wolves, as if they were changed into dogs,
　　Have left the woods and traverse through the streets.   5
　　A bull was heard send forth a human voice,
　　An infant newly born to speak; a shower
　　Of stones descended from the troubled skies,
　　And in the air was heard the cries of men,
　　Clashing of armour, and a noise of horses.   10
　　Shrill trumpets sound; the statues of the gods
　　Sweat drops of blood, and some were touched from heaven.
　　Many of the temples too are thunderstruck.

Enter TYRO.

　　Tyro, were ever known such tragedies?
Tyro. Never was imminent calamity   15
　　Threatened to Rome, but 'twas thus ushered, Laureas.
　　I might allege the wretched fall of Crassus,
　　When such a purple flood of Roman gore
　　Discoloured Lucan's field.
　　But the not yet cured dire Pharsalian blow   20
　　Shall speak for all. Rome scarce e'er knew a prodigy
　　Which was not previous to that bloody day,
　　The sun and moon eclipsed, Etnean flames

---

of his erstwhile ally (and 'father'), Cicero, to go on the list, Antony that of his uncle,
Lucius Caesar, and Lepidus that of his own brother, Lucius Aemilius Paullus. The latter
two managed to survive by escaping abroad.

　　4.3.1–13.] Such omens are common harbingers of disaster. See *Hamlet*, 1.1.114–25;
Macbeth, 2.4.1–19; *Julius Caesar*, 1.3.3–32.
　　12. *touched from heaven*] struck by lightning.
　　16. *ushered*] preceded.
　　17. *allege*] cite.
　　wretched . . . Crassus] Marcus Licinius Crassus was one of the most powerful figures
(along with Pompey and Julius Caesar) of the previous generation. He was killed, and
his army destroyed, by the Parthians at Carrhae in 53 BC. As he set off on this campaign, there were believed to have been many ominous warnings from the gods of what
was to come.
　　19.] a corrupt line. The meaningless 'Lucan's' may conceal the family name of
Crassus: Licinius.
　　20–1. *the not . . . all*] At the battle of Pharsalus, 48 BC, Caesar defeated Pompey;
but the ills are still not cured as the civil war continues.
　　23. *Etnean flames*] fire from the volcano, Etna; another omen.

Obliquely darted on the Italian shore,
The vestal fire extinct, the native gods   25
Weeping; state-changing comets, monstrous births,
The groans of ghosts from out their troubled urns,
With many more.
Laureas.   But the Hetruscian soothsayers
Will descant better on these things than we.
Tyro. 'Slight, thou sayest true, and now I think on't, Laureas,   30
We'll try if we can search what they determine,
Sure they have done by this their immolations.   *Exeunt.*

[Act 4 Scene 4]

   Enter [CICERO, *members of the*] Senate *and* [*five*] Soothsayers.

Cicero. You, the most reverend of Hetruscian Vates,
To whom is known the births and deaths of States;
You who by art unlock the pole, to whom
Is made apparent fate's intended doom
By entrails' deep inspection, or by thunder,   5
A hairy star or some such boding wonder,
Inform us what the angry destinies
Threaten in these portentous prodigies,
But be not enigmatical, nor shroud
Your speeches in a dark mysterious cloud,   10
As did the sibyls and the Delphic nun.
Let your inspired numbers evenly run
With obvious and unfolded sense, that so
We may conceive the essence of our woe.
The Ancientest of
the Soothsayers. Then fathers, hear your dismal fate.   15
Your freedom shall be lost, your State
Converted to a monarchy,

---

25. *vestal fire*] the fire in the temple of Vesta, which it was the duty of the Vestal Virgins (see 1.2.215 and note) to keep alight. Extinction of the fire spelled catastrophe for Rome.

27. *state-changing comets*] a pun: comets which change their shape; and comets which signify political change in the State.

28. *Hetruscian soothsayers*] The art of soothsaying ('haruspicy') originated amongst the Etruscans, a people of central Italy.

30. *'Slight*] i.e. 'By God's light'.

32. *immolations*] sacrifices of animals.

4.4.1. *Vates*] prophets.

3. *unlock the pole*] reveal the secrets of the sky.

6. *hairy star*] the literal meaning of the Greek word 'comet'.

11. *sibyls ... Delphic nun*] The sibyls and the Pythia, priestess of Apollo at Delphi, were famous prophets. They couched their prophecies in obscure language.

12. *numbers*] verses. The soothsayers' response will be in verse.

And all be slaves but only I.   *Stops his breath,*
                                                 and falls down dead.
Senator. What means the agèd prophet?
Cicero.   Fallen down?
    Is it some powerful ecstasy or death?   20
Second Soothsayer. Our brother from his clay is flown,
    And sealed your destiny with his own.
    Thrice happy he, that now is blest
    With a true Elysian rest,
    And shall not see the tide of woe   25
    Which on survivors' heads will flow.
The Third. Like our brother's vital thread
    Who now lies before us dead,
    Your twine of liberty is broke,
    And Romans must expect the yoke.   30
The Fourth. What the destinies have made
    A firm decree, and he hath said,
    No human power can disannul,
    'Tis signèd in your speaking bull.
The Fifth. When Romulus first founded Rome,   35
    He fixed his crown by Remus' doom,
    And built his monarchy in blood;
    Now shall return that antique power,
    Not re-established with a shower
    Of that salt humour, but a flood.   40
Cicero. Well, what the fates have destined, human power
    Is not of strength to cancel; if I die,
    (As sure my blood must help to make the stream)
    I will die willingly; 'tis a noble death
    Not to survive one's country's liberty.   45
    If gods might taste of death, then would they die.

        The soothsayers over the dead corpse sing this song.

First Brother. Art thou dead?

46.1. *Q adds after this line* 1 Brother, 2 Brother, 3 Brother, 4 Brother.   47. First
Brother] 1 Q.

────────────────────────────

18.1. stops . . . dead] As in the author's source (in Appian, *Civil Wars* 4.4), the oldest
soothsayer holds his breath until he dies in order to avoid the coming enslavement of Rome.
    21. *brother*] i.e. fellow soothsayer.
    29. *twine of liberty*] cord of freedom.
    33. *disannul*] cancel, abolish.
    34. *speaking bull*] the edict which you spoke.
    36. *Remus' doom*] Romulus, the founder of Rome, was able to found the city only
after killing his own twin brother, Remus. The city was thus founded by an act of
bloodshed.
    38. *antique power*] monarchy.
    40. *salt humour*] blood.
    47. *First Brother*] The designation 'brother' for each of the four soothsayers empha-
sizes the mystic communion of the scene.

Second Brother. Art thou fled?
Third Brother. Art thou gone,
Fourth Brother. All alone?   50
First Brother. To the shades below,
Second Brother. To the desert cells,
Third Brother. Where glowing darkness dwells,
Fourth Brother. And cloudy woe;
First Brother. Where ne'er was known   55
Second Brother. A cheerful tone,
Third Brother. Where wretched souls
Fourth Brother. Like Stygian owls
Together. Have no joy of one another?

First Brother. Thou art dead;   60
Second Brother. Thou art fled;
Third Brother. Thou art gone
Fourth Brother. All alone
First Brother. To the groves below,
Second Brother. Where sacred choirs   65
Third Brother. Inspired with holy fires
Fourth Brother. In triumph go,
First Brother. Where songs of mirth
Second Brother. Are carolled forth,
Third Brother. Where blessèd souls   70
Fourth Brother. In nectar bowls
Together. Drink and solace one another.   *Exeunt with the carcass.*

[Act 4 Scene 5]

                    Enter CICERO *reading.*

Cicero. O vitam vere vitalem! sed beatam etiam mortem quae
        ad beatissimam vitam aditum aperiat!
        Most true, for did we die like savage beasts
        Returning to a former airy being,
        No one part of us free from dissolution,   5
        Death were a plague, and did not harbour in it
        The sweetness which they talk of; for I think
        To be, is better, though in restless troubles,
        Than not to be at all; 'twere senseless, impious

---

48. Second Brother] 2 *Q.*   49. Third Brother] 3 *Q.*   50. Fourth Brother] 4 *Q.*
3. for did we die] for we die *Q.*

---

52. *desert*] desolate.
58. *Stygian owls*] Owls were associated with night and, hence, the underworld. The
Styx was a river of the underworld.

4.5.1–2.] 'O life that is truly full of life! But blessed also the death that opens the
way to most blessed life.' The following soliloquy draws on the thinking of Cicero's
Tusculan Disputations.
8–9. *To be . . . at all*] recalls Hamlet's meditation on suicide, *Hamlet*, 3.1.56–90.

To say the power that's president of nature   10
Infused into us such a love of union
In this compounded frame without some blessing
In the continuance; but a mere cessation,
A sinking into nothing, though it pains not,
Yet 'tis no blessing, nor can properly   15
Be said to take our cares and sorrows from us,
Or us from them, but rather and more truly
Us from ourselves. I cannot think the gods
Were so unkind, so sparing of their blessings,
Or feebly stored, as to bestow a nothing   20
On the two pious sons of Argia,
On Agamedes and Trophonius;
For pray, what goodness can be couched in that
Which cancels being, that is one with goodness?
But do we live then? Can I think the soul   25
Survives, when in an urn's forgetful chest
The mournful treasure of our ashes rest?
See how my panting, struggling soul contends
To harbour the belief: alas, methinks
'Tis no small argument to ground our hopes on,   30
To see how sweetly good men entertain
The weakest motion for a future life;
To see them, how even shaking hands with death,
They are more sprightly and replete with vigour,
Yea oftentimes oraculous, as if   35
Something lay caged within that was not mortal,
But were new rapt with joy of better state
And even then seizing on divinity,
When wicked men are full of discontents,
Tortured with furies, which their consciences   40
Present them in the ugliest shapes: is't fancy?
Or is't a fear their sullied names will stink
In the nostrils of posterity? 'Tis neither.
For if the first; why then are not the good
Subject to the same commotions, whose diseases   45
And bodily distempers are the same?
But if the second; then might they be free,
To whose enormous actions darkness only

---

20. *feebly stored*] impoverished.

21. *the two pious sons of Argia*] Cleobis and Biton, sons of a priestess of Hera (Juno) at Argos in Greece. The oxen drawing their mother's chariot became exhausted, and the brothers themselves took their place and pulled it to the temple. Their mother prayed to the goddess to grant them the greatest gift that could be bestowed on humans in return for this display of filial duty, and the two died that very night.

22. *Agamedes and Trophonius*] two architects in a story similar to the previous one and told, likewise, in Cicero's *Tusculan Disputations*. They built the temple of Apollo at Delphi. Once finished, they asked the god to give them the highest gift a man could receive, and died soon after.

32. *weakest motion*] weakest belief.

And secret angels have been conscious.
Therefore by this it seems that Tityus' vulture,   50
Ixion's wheel, and the Tantalian fruits
Are not mere bugbears, but some mystic emblems
Of the succeeding pains of guilty souls.
Thus have I argued, yea and partly satisfied
My own weak reason. Yet our great philosophers,   55
In the discussing of this weighty matter,
Fare much like naked men in stony fields:
They can with ease beat down another's reasons,
But cannot save their own, alas, from falling;
They can offend a wise antagonist,   60
Weaken his grounds, but not defend themselves.
Whither, alas, shall our endeavours tend
When we are blind in knowledge of our end?

                        Enter LAUREAS.

Laureas. My lord, there's one without would speak with you
    From the triumvirs.
Cicero.   The triumvirs, Laureas?   65
Laureas. Yes, so he says.
Cicero.   Oh, from Antonius,
    Caesar and Lepidus. Send for Quintus to me,
    For Salvius, Otho, Publius Apuleius,
    And other of my friends, you know.
Laureas.   I fly.
Cicero. But charge none enter till they hear from me.   70

                                            Exit LAUREAS.

    From the triumvirs? Have they then usurped
    A new-coined office? What will now become
    Of those that have the old ones? What? why, have
    Their reverend heads struck off like Tarquin's poppy!

                        Enter QUINTUS.

    Brother, how is it you are here so soon,   75

50–1. *Tityus'* ... *fruits*] three miscreants supposedly enduring unending punishment
in the underworld. Tityus endured having his liver gnawed by a vulture for eternity and
Ixion was tied to a constantly turning wheel. Tantalus was perpetually thirsty and
hungry. He stood in water up to his chin, with a branch of a fruit-tree just above his
head. But whenever he stopped to drink or reached for the tree the water flowed away
and a gust of wind blew the branch out of reach.

52. *bugbears*] imaginary terrors.

55. *weak reason*] i.e. 'my poor intellect', in implied contrast with the great philosophers who follow.

72. *a new-coined office*] a newly invented political office.

74. *Tarquin's poppy*] The son of Tarquin the Proud, last King of Rome, gained
control of the nearby city of Gabii and sent a messenger asking his father for advice
on what to do next. Tarquin said nothing but walked into his garden and struck
off the heads of the tallest poppies. His son understood his advice and had all the
most powerful men in Gabii put to death. The story is told in Livy's *History of
Rome*.

Since 'tis but now I sent to intreat your company?
Quintus. A brother should not stay till he be sent for,
 When he suspects his presence will be useful;
 I had some doubtful notice of this messenger
 Which now within waits for admittance.
Cicero.   Quintus,   80
 How I am blest in such a careful brother!
 Thus, when the Argive King was vexed with doubts,
 And called a council of the Grecian peers,
 Only his brother Menelaus came
 Of his own free accord.
Quintus.   It should be so.   85
 Why had we else one father, why one mother,
 If not to live like brothers?
Cicero.   True, good Quintus,
 I could even weep to see this piety
 Flow so divinely from thee; now if ever
 Our States require our mutual aids and counsels. 90
 But what dost think this messenger may bring?
Quintus. No good I warrant you, perhaps our deaths.
 Can we expect from those three Roman furies
 A milder sentence?
Cicero.   Why, I will embrace it. *[Prays]*
 Father and ruler of the lofty sky,   95
 What way thou pleasest lead, and grant that I
 May follow with no sad or grieved blood,
 Nor like an ill man bear what fits a good.

  Enter SALVIUS, APULEIUS *and other friends of* CICERO.

Cicero. Friends, you are welcome. You shall hear anon
 Why you were sent for. Now call in the messenger. 100

    Enter Messenger.

Messenger. I cannot, sir, say health unto your lordship,
 Until yourself confirm it, which you may,
 As will appear by this.   *Delivers a letter.*
     Nay, good my lord,
 Give these the hearing of it, for the affair
 May crave their judgements.
Cicero.   Then you know it.
Messenger.   Partly.   105
Cicero. Read you it, Quintus.
Quintus.   No, my mouth shall never
 Speak my own brother's sentence.
Cicero.   This is fond.

---

 79. *doubtful notice*] fearful intimation.
 82. *Argive King*] Agamemnon, commander of the Greek army during the siege of Troy. The episode is related in Homer's *Iliad.*
 94. *embrace it*] welcome it.
 107. *fond*] foolish, foolishly affectionate.

Quintus. Pray heaven it prove so.
Marcus.   Will you read it, Salvius?
Salvius. You must excuse me, Cicero.
Cicero.   Say you so?
    Then, Apuleius, you must be the man.   110
Apuleius. Sir, by no means, if your own brother dare not;
    Pray pardon me.
Cicero.   Indeed! then read it, you.
First Friend. Not I, my lord.
Second Friend.   Nor I.
Third Friend.   Nor I.
Fourth Friend.   Nor I.
Cicero. Then, Marcus Tullius, sit thee down and read,
    No doubt, thine own proscription.
Omnes.   Heavens defend!   115
               (CICERO *reads.*)
    Marcus Antonius Imperator, Augur, Triumvir, to Marcus Tullius
    Cicero, Consular, Greeting.
    We the triumviri Marcus Antonius, Marcus Lepidus, and Octavius
    Caesar (Ventidius being chosen consul in his room)
Cicero. Ventidius, consul in Octavius's room,   120
    And he triumvir? this afflicts my soul.   (*Reads.*)
    are for the space of five whole years appointed with full and
    absolute authority for the re-establishment of the commonwealth;
    and you, Cicero, are now in my hands; yet have I so mitigated my
    just conceived indignation toward you, that if you will but burn 125
    your orations which you call your Philippics, compiled out of
    malice and rancour against me, you shall live; otherwise—
        Yours, if perverseness make you not your own foe.
Cicero. You shall be soon informed which way I am resolved to take.
Messenger. I'll wait your lordship's pleasure.   *Exit.* 130
Cicero. Friends, here you see the slender twine whereon
    My aged life depends.
Salvius.   Too true, my lord.
Cicero. Your counsel, brother.
Quintus.   Mine is resolute.
Cicero. The better, let me hear it.
Quintus.   This it is:
    Defy him.
Salvius.   Hold, I hope you will not, Quintus,   135
    Be your own brother's headsman, that but now

---

113. First Friend] 1 Friend. Q. Second Friend] 2. Q. Third Friend] 3. Q. Fourth
Friend] 4. Q.

---

  116. Imperator] honorary title of successful general.
  Augur] a type of Roman priest.
  120–1. *Ventidius . . . triumvir*] On becoming triumvir, Octavius resigned his consulship. Publius Ventidius, a supporter of Antony, became consul in his place for the last
few weeks of 43 BC.
  136. *headsman*] executioner.

Could not be won so much as read the letter,
Lest you should speak his sentence.
Apuleius.   Good my lord,
    Preserve yourself for better times; the State
    Will lose its soul, when 'tis deprived of you.   140
Salvius. 'Twill be a breathless trunk, a lifeless carcass,
    When you are gone; which were the only blood
    And sinews of her liberty.
First Friend.   Alas!
    We shall be preyed upon by ravenous vultures,
    And those insulting eagles of ambition.   145
Second Friend. Think but of this, when Catilines arise,
    Where shall we find new Ciceros to oppose them?
Third Friend. Where shall oppressed and wronged citizens
    Find upright patrons, that will stick to justice,
    Not fearing to incur a great one's frown?   150
    They may as soon climb up to heaven, and bring
    Astrea down again; unhappy Rome!
Quintus. I do confess, good friends, the commonwealth
    Will miss a Cicero; and that my brother,
    If we respect the wishes of the people   155
    And wants of the Republic, has not yet
    Lived half of half his time; but if we cast
    A backward eye upon his glorious actions,
    Has lived a goodly age, and cannot now
    Die immaturely. Look upon the State   160
    Of present things, the downfall of our liberty
    (And heaven knows what calamities will follow).
    I think you cannot be so much his foe,
    As not to say, he has now lived too long.
Apuleius. Ah! but the public good's to be preferred   165
    Before respects of private consequence.
Quintus. But Publius, the State is now so wounded
    That there's no hope of cure, and therefore may
    Our old physicians safely give it o'er.
    Were he an Aesculapius that could put   170
    New life into a State, as once that son
    Of Paean did to Virbius, I should then
    Blaspheme great Jove himself, should he but aim
    His triforked flames against him; but for one
    Now sinking of himself into his grave,   175
    And such a one as Cicero, in these times,

---

    149. *patrons*] The term 'patron' translates the Latin *patronus*, an advocate or
defence lawyer.
    152. *Astrea*] goddess of Justice who fled the earth at the end of the Golden Age.
    159–60. *cannot . . . immaturely*] See 1.2.22–4.
    170. *Aesculapius*] god of medicine.
    171–2. *that son . . . Virbius*] The hero Hippolytus was brought back to life by Aes-
culapius, son of Apollo (Paean), and thereafter was called Virbius.

When such men's ages are but vain, what sepulchre
Can be more fit, more glorious than the fame
Wherein his country's freedom lies enclosed?
If he now die, he shall be buried   180
With the renownèd Pompey, son and father;
With Catulus, Petreius and Afranius;
Yea with Antonius that brave man, unworthy
His noble stock should bear so foul a branch.
But if he live, with whom I pray wilt be   185
But Caphos, Saxas and Ventidii?
Therefore good brother, (I confess my eyes
Do swim with tears, yet shall my words proceed
From a courageous mind) be still thyself;
To the huge volume of Antonius' faults   190
Add one crime more, even Cicero's death; 'twill stick
Upon his name with a more lasting blot
Than the most heinous of his other villainies.
For, should his future deeds pronounce him parallel
To the great Alexander or Alcmena's son,   195
From whom he fetches his vain pedigree;
Should after ages wonder at his acts,
And say, why this, and this, and this he did!
Built such a city, conquered such a country,
Thus and thus many times triumphed, with kings   200
And queens to follow his victorious chariot;
Yet, for a period to each glorious sentence,
Some honest standerby will sighing say,
But he killed Cicero. Cicero shall still,
Much like Prometheus' vulture, rend and tear   205
The very heart and liver of his name.
Let Antony proscribe thee, let him, Marcus,
Why, he can do it but once, and that's some comfort;

---

181. *Pompey . . . father*] Pompey the Great (Gnaeus Pompeius Magnus), killed in Egypt in 48 BC after his defeat by Julius Caesar at Pharsalus. His elder son, also Gnaeus Pompeius Magnus, died later in the same civil war.

182. *Catulus . . . Afranius*] Quintus Lutatius Catulus was a senior conservative politician of the previous generation. Marcus Petreius and Lucius Afranius were commanders on Pompey's side in the civil war against Caesar. Both died during its course.

183. *Antonius . . . man*] Marcus Antonius, successful general, fine orator and grandfather of Mark Antony. He died in 87 BC. Cicero had as much respect for this man as he had disdain for his grandson.

186. *Caphos . . . Ventidii*] see 2.1.60 and note.

195. *Alcmena's son*] Hercules, from whom Antony claimed to be descended (see 1.5. 18n).

200-1. *triumphed . . . to follow*] In the ceremony of the triumph, prisoners were led in tow. The triumphant general rode in a special chariot.

202. *period*] conclusion.

205. *Prometheus' vulture*] Prometheus was punished for defying the gods by being tied to a rock and, like Tityus, having his liver gnawed by a vulture for eternity.

207. *proscribe*] outlaw (see 1.1.43); mark out for death (see 4.2.15).

But thou shalt proscribe him unto eternity.
It is not thy proscription he remits,   210
But closely sues a pardon for his own.
Believe me Marcus, 'tis the meanest part
Which can be given, or taken from thee; that,
That's the true Cicero which Antonius knows
Cannot be proscribed but by Cicero.   215
If Antony deceive, and break his faith,
(As faith is seldom found in such as he)
Then thou must die. Suppose he do perform it:
Then must you live a vassal to his tyranny;
Now which is to be chosen, death or servitude,   220
I leave it to yourself, and your own judgement.
Yet my beloved brother, by our loves,
By thy now well spent three and sixty years,
By thy renowned consulship, the sacred
And (if thou wilt) the everlasting memory   225
Of thy admired eloquence, by these
And all that's dear unto thee, I adjure thee,
Die not confessing that thou wouldst not die.
Cicero. Friends, I am bound unto your cares, and thank you
That not affection only, which were fond,   230
But the Republic's good, has been the motive
Of your persuasions. Well; I promise you
I will do nothing unbeseeming Cicero.
Frame your hopes' complement by this. I shall
Dispatch the messenger myself.
Salvius.   Good Cicero,   235
Remember us and Rome.
Apuleius.   We were not born
('Tis your own saying) for ourselves alone.
Our country claims a part.
Cicero.   Farewell, farewell,
Farewell, my friends; but Quintus, let me have
Your company.
Quintus.   You shall.
Apuleius.   Nay then I fear.   240
                           Exeunt [except CICERO *and* QUINTUS].
Cicero. Come brother Quintus, thou hast bravely argued;

---

210. *remits*] cancels.
223. *three and sixty years*] Cicero was born in 106 BC.
227. *adjure*] entreat.
228. *die . . . die*] i.e. die stoically.
234. *Frame . . . this*] i.e. Rest assured in this.
237. *'Tis your own saying*] not really, in fact. In *De Officiis*, I.22., Cicero quotes a remark of Plato, 'we were not born only for ourselves, but our country claims a share of our existence'.
240. *Nay . . . fear*] i.e. I fear what Cicero's intentions are, given that he wants to speak with Quintus alone.

Why weep'st thou?
Quintus.   Do you then approve my language?
      I will unsay it.
Cicero.   Nay, thou shalt not, canst not.
      Come, come, let's in, thyself shall only hear
      How I will send defiance to Antonius.   *Exeunt.*   245

[Act 4 Scene 6]

                    Enter LAUREAS *and* TYRO.

Laureas. What think'st thou, Tyro, that my lord admits
      None but his brother Quintus to the delivery
      Of his reply?
Tyro.   I cannot guess the reason.
Laureas. Methinks he should not bar their longing ears
      The hearing, if he does intend acceptance   5
      Of the triumvirs' proffer. But I fear
      He does not prize his life at such a rate.
Tyro. Tush, life is precious.
Laureas.   But honour more;
      And what is life?
Tyro.   'Tis nature's gift.
Laureas.   A poor
      And worthless jewel fastened by a hair   10
      To the ear of vanity.
Tyro.   It is the fair
      And sprightly shine of this compendious world.
Laureas. And from what Phoebus is that lustre hurled?
Tyro. The soul.
Laureas.   A short-lived day, a twilight sun,
      Whose fading beauties cease when scarce begun.   15
      But honour is a day that knows no night,
      And ever triumphs in immortal light.
      I think Antonius might have done more wisely,
      And might have sooner compassed his desires,
      If he had only sent him life, without   20
      The intimation of those harsh conditions;
      For so he could not, in my slender judgement,
      On such applausive terms have contradicted
      The proffered benefit of his life, and then
      I am persuaded fully that my lord   25
      Would ne'er have let posterity have known
      His hate to Antony, from whom he should
      Have deigned the acceptance of a slavish breath.
Tyro. Come, prithee leave, I shall despair anon.   *Exeunt.*

4.6.13. *from what Phoebus*] from what sun: Phoebus Apollo was, amongst other
things, the sun god.
    21. *intimation*] announcement.
    23. *applausive*] worthy of approval.

[Act 4 Scene 7]

Enter CICERO *solus.*

Cicero. Now I have sealed my fate, I must expect
          The second message for my head. I must?
          What, may not man unlock this cabinet,
          And free the heavenly jewel of his soul?
          A wise man stays not nature's period but,   5
          If things occur which trouble his tranquillity,
          Emits himself, departing out of life
          As from a stage or theatre, nor passes
          Whether he take or make his dissolution,
          Whether he do it in sickness or in health.   10
          'Tis base to live, but brave to die by stealth,
          This is the daring Stoics' glorious language.
          I was myself, too, of the opinion once;
          But now I find it impious and unmanly.
          For as some pictures drawn with slender lines,   15
          Deceiving almost our intentive eyes,
          Affect us much, and with their subtleties
          Woo us to gaze upon them, but are found
          By skilful and judicious eyes to err
          In symmetry of parts, and due proportion;   20
          Even so the Stoics' arguments are carved
          With seeming curiousness, almost forcing judgement,
          And carry with them an applausive show
          Of undeniable verity, yet well scanned
          They are more like the dreams of idle brains   25
          Than the grave dictates of philosophers:
          The wise Pythagoras was opinioned better,
          For most divinely he forbids us leave
          The corps due guard without our captain's licence.
          And to speak true, we are but usufructuaries,   30
          The god that governs in us is proprietary.
          A prisoner breaking from his gaol or hold,
          If he be guilty, aggravates his guilt;
          If innocent, stains even that innocence
          Which might perhaps have brought him clearly off.   35
          'Tis so with us; our magistrate, I mean

4.7.5. *nature's period*] the end which comes to life in the natural course of things.
11. *die by stealth*] i.e. by suicide.
12. *the daring Stoics*] Stoic philosophy advocated suicide under certain circumstances, as a rational alternative to natural disadvantages such as disease.
22. *curiousness*] carefulness.
27–9. *Pythagoras . . . licence*] According to Plato's *Phaedo*, the Pythagoreans were
opposed to suicide on the grounds that man belongs to God and has no right to do
away with himself without divine permission.
29. *corps due guard*] soldiers stationed as sentinels, with a pun on corps/corpse.
30. *usufructuaries*] persons who have temporary use of fruits or profits of an estate.
31. *god . . . proprietary*] The ownership of the body is divine.

The power that's sovereign of this natural frame,
Has sent us (Plato says from heavenly mansions)
Into this fleshy prison; here we live,
And must not free ourselves, but patiently   40
Expect our summons from that sacred power
By his lieutenant, death. For otherwise
We become guilty of a greater sin
Than parricide itself, no bond of nature
Being so near as of one to himself.   45
The Grecians knew this, when they judged the body
Of Ajax who had slain himself, unworthy
The common rites of burial. Careful nature
Has fenced our hearts about with certain bones,
Fashioned like swords; and shall we break the guard?   50
No, rather let us wait the will of th'heavens,
And, when we hence are warned by their ordinance,
Let us depart with glad and joyful hearts,
And think ourselves delivered from a gaol,
Eased of gyves and fetters, that we may   55
Remove unto our own eternal dwelling;
For, without doubt, that power that gave us being,
Did not beget and foster us for this,
That having suffered on this stage of life
Thousand afflictions, infinite calamities,   60
Quotidian toils, and all in virtue's cause,
We should for guerdon fall into the gulf
Of an eternal death, and non-subsistence.
Yea, rather let us cherish this belief
That there's another haven provided for us,   65
A blessèd refuge for our longing souls.
Armed with a settled confidence of this,
Like Socrates I will outface my death,
And with the same fixed spirit resign my breath.

Enter QUINTUS.

How now?
Quintus.   O brother, there's no remedy   70

37–9. *The power . . . prison*] familiar idea derived from Plato, that the body is the
prison of the soul.
44. *parricide itself*] see 4.2.19 and note.
47. *Ajax*] Greek hero of Trojan war who went mad and committed suicide when
the weapons of the dead Achilles were given to Odysseus. In Sophocles' *Ajax*, an influential play, Ajax was refused burial by the commanders of the Greek army.
49–50. *certain . . . swords*] the ribs.
52. *when . . . ordinance*] i.e. when the gods order us to depart from life.
55. *gyves*] shackles.
61. *Quotidian*] daily.
62. *guerdon*] reward.
68. *Socrates*] the great Greek philosopher. He was executed for his beliefs in 399
BC and, according to Plato's description in *Phaedo*, faced death with great composure.
outface] confront fearlessly.

        But die we must, or save ourselves by flight.
Cicero. Why? if the destinies have so determined,
        Welcome the easer of our woes, sweet death.
        But what's the matter, Quintus?
Quintus.   The triumvirs
        Are posting with a threatening speed to Rome;   75
        They come like thunder, and are bringing with them
        A bloody tempest.
Cicero.   Who can help it, brother?
        Yet we'll incline the times' malignity.
        The heavens must not be tempted; we are to keep
        This fortress of our lives safe from invasion;   80
        Why did they else entrust us with it? Now
        That cannot be without the use of means;
        We must not look to escape the jaws of Scylla,
        When by our own improvident carelessness
        We are engulfed already. He that thinks,   85
        Surrounded with his enemies, to 'scape
        (As Homer fables in the Trojan war)
        Enveloped with a cloud, may be deceived.
        No Quintus, we will fly, or, if that word
        Be, as the Stoics prattle, not beseeming   90
        A prudent man, we will give way to the times.
        We will depart.
Quintus.   But whither?
Cicero.   Whither, Quintus,
        But into Macedon to my dearest Brutus?
        Prithee see all things suddenly prepared;
        We'll first unto my house at Tusculum;   95
        Thence to Astyra, so to Macedon.

                                          Exit QUINTUS.

        I have a heart dares meet a thousand deaths,
        But yet my soul is grieved to see these days.
        Are all my labours come to this? My watchings?
        My cares and services for the public good?   100
        The dangers which I daily have incurred
        By opposition of new-springing tyranny?
        Are all, all my endeavours come to this,

---

    78. *Yet . . . malignity*] i.e. we must be expedient.

    79–80. *The heavens . . . invasion*] Cicero suggests that to contemplate suicide is to
risk losing the gods' favour.

    87. *As Homer . . . war*] In Book 3 of the *Iliad*, Homer described how Paris escaped
from Menelaus after the goddess Aphrodite (Venus) shrouded him in a cloud and spirited him away.

    90. *as . . . prattle*] In the *De Finibus* (see 1.2.69 and note), Cicero criticizes the Stoics
for using unfamiliar and new-fangled language. The Stoic ideal was the wise man or
prudens, the origin of 'prudent'.

    94. *suddenly*] without delay, immediately.

    95. *Tusculum*] a town ten miles outside Rome where Cicero owned a country house.

    96. *Astyra*] Astura, a town on the coast, 35 miles south-east of Rome, site of another
of Cicero's properties.

That they now seem to have precipitated
This ruin on us, rather than withstood it?   105
Unhappy Rome! The deities decreed
This downfall of thy liberty; for never
Could all our labours have been so pernicious,
Unless there had a greater power disposed them
To this sad end; which was the sole Charybdis,   110
Whence we directed thy now shipwrecked bark.
This sinks me in a sea of grief. Thy senators
Shall die like victims, ruffians be the priests;
And thou the altar. In their wretched entrails
A dismal horrid augury shall be written,   115
Even thy eternal bondage to oppression.

Enter QUINTUS, POMPONIA, QUINTUS JUNIOR, *muta persona.*

Cicero. Are all things ready?
Quintus.   Yes, or will be straight,
    But the triumvirs are not with such haste
    Posting to the city, as I was informed,
    Yet there are certain centiners they say   120
    Coming as harbingers.
Cicero.   Believe me Quintus,
    We have the greater reason to be packing;
    These are the lightning previous to that thunder,
    Whereof you spake before. And lightning strikes not
    The humble cottage, but the towering edifice.   125
    I see the loved objects which imprint
    Those characters of sadness in thy visage.
    Grieve not, Pomponia, thou art happy, sister,
    Thou mayst remain in thine own native Rome.
    No Antony thirsts for thy blood, thou mayst   130
    In peace adore the deities of thy country,
    Yea and the Lares of thy private house;
    When such as we must leave our ancient homes,

106–11.] Cicero is exculpating himself from any blame in Rome's destruction, which
he concludes can have been determined only by the gods.

110. *Charybdis*] a sea-monster which occupied the opposite side of a channel (the
Straits of Messina, between Italy and Sicily) from Scylla. This part of Cicero's speech
is constructed around the image of Rome as a sinking ship caught in the jaws of this
monster.

113. *victims*] i.e. sacrificial victims.

114. *And . . . altar*] i.e. Rome will be the site of the 'sacrificial' slaughter of its
senators.

wretched entrails] An important form of haruspicy (see 4.3.28 and note) involved
inspecting the entrails of sacrificed animals for omens (auguries) as to future events.

116.1. QUINTUS JUNIOR, *muta persona*] i.e. the actor playing Quintus junior does
not speak.

120. *centiners*] centurions, junior army officers.

121. *harbingers*] forerunners; foretellers.

132. *Lares*] Roman gods of the home.

Yea and our country, to a heavier woe.
Pomponia. And that 'tis grieves me brother; what content,   135
 What pleasure can I take in anything,
 When my beloved Quintus is departed?
 My life will not be vital. O my Quintus,
 Soul of my soul.
Quintus.   Pomponia, do not weep,
 Tears are an ill presage to such a journey.   140

    Enter LAUREAS, TYRO, PHILOLOGUS.

Cicero. What, are the litters ready?
Laureas.   Yes, my lord.
Quintus. My life, Pomponia, now farewell.
Pomponia.   Nay husband,
 I'll see you setting forth, I will enjoy
 As long as possible I may thy sight,
 Heaven knows if ever I shall see you more.   145
Cicero. Nay sister, now your grief is too extreme.
Pomponia. It cannot, brother.
Cicero.   Yes, for though you part,
 Thy loving spouse shall leave behind his heart.
        Exeunt omnes.

    [*Enter* Chorus.]

Chorus. Where is that ancient beauty, Rome,
 Was wont to shine   150
 About thy head? Where are become
 Those rays divine?
 Survey thy fortunes, stupid city,
 Look, look and know
 Thyself turned monument of pity,   155
 A map of woe.
 But thou are deaf; well vaunting, stand
 And tell't about,
 It was thy once renownèd hand
 Thrust Tarquin out;   160
 Proclaim it, citizens, that you
 Did Melius quell,
 That Cassius and Manlius too,

---

138. *My life ... vital*] My life will not be a real life.
153. *stupid*] stupified, insensible.
157. *well-vaunting*] extol.
160. *Tarquin*] last King of Rome, deposed, according to tradition, by Lucius Junius Brutus in 509 BC (see 2.1 10–14n).
162. *Melius*] Spurius Maelius, a semi-mythical figure who attempted to become tyrant of Rome but was killed (in 439 BC).
163. *Cassius*] Spurius Cassius Vecellinus, executed in 486 BC because he was believed to be aiming at kingship.
Manlius] Marcus Manlius Capitolinus, executed as punishment for his tyrannical ambitions, in 385 BC.

Your victims fell.
Boast this, and more, do, but withall   165
With horror say,
You did it only to install
Worse plagues than they,
That you one viper of the State
Have changed for three;   170
And for a worse triumvirate
A monarchy.
Alas, alas, where shall we shroud
Our wretched heads?
For this threatening pendulous cloud   175
Wide ruin spreads.
Our ship upon a rock is cast,
Our sail yards mourn,
The north wind has beat down our mast,
Our sheets are torn;   180
Our cables too (alas!) are lost,
Oars have we none,
And that which grieves and cuts us most,
Our pilot's gone.
What helps, weak vessel, on this shelf   185
Thy birth divine?
In vain, in vain, thou vaunt'st thyself,
A Pontic Pine;
In vain thou invocat'st thy two
Tyndarian gods,   190
They are to anticipate such woe
Too weak by odds.
Then since poor wretches, ah! we must
Ourselves compose
To bear each rigid storm, each gust,   195
Each wave that flows;
Oh, let us pray, this dangerous flood
Does not become
A dead sea, or a sea of blood,
And its own tomb.   *Exeunt.*   200

180. sheets] sheet] *Q.*

---

181. *cables*] ropes, attached to ship's anchor.
184. *Our pilot's gone*] i.e. Cicero.
188. *A Pontic Pine*] timber from the Black Sea, such as might be used to construct a ship. This chorus owes a lot to the fourteenth poem of Horace's first book of *Odes*, on the ship of State.
190. *Tyndarian gods*] Castor and Pollux, sons of Tyndarus, protectors of sailors.

ACT 5

[Act 5 Scene 1]

Enter SALVIUS *and others.*

Salvius. Friends, you are welcome. Why so sad, I pray?
    Those looks befit not feasts; invest your brows
    In the glad livery of smiles. Be merry;
    Mirth is the only essence of a feast.
    But ah, how ill does this dissembled jollity 5
    Suit with my inside, or the times. I have
    Invited you this night unto a supper,
    The last, for ought I know, that I shall taste
    In your desired companies. 'Tis true:
    The tribuneship was ever till this day 10
    Esteemed holy, and of sacred power;
    But from those men which coin new offices,
    What must the old expect but foul misprision?
    Should Jove himself come down from his Olympus,
    Not shadowing his deity with a veil, 15
    But in his most godlike majesty, I think
    For one Lycaon, he might now find three,
    And such that would with more unheard of savageness
    Feast his divinity; not with some poor infant,
    But even their mother's flesh, I mean their country's, 20
    And 'stead of nectar give him blood to drink.
    You know how, fraught with zeal unto the cause
    Of the Republic, I have now cashiered
    And quit that sink of villainous rebellion,
    Antonius' party, and have stuck to Cicero, 25
    The truest patriot Rome was ever blessed with;
    And can I hope to meet with milder storms
    Than those whose only distant apparition
    Has made him timely seek another harbour?
    Which from my soul I wish he may obtain. 30

5.1.0.1.] The scene is located at the tribune's house.

2. *invest*] clothe, cover.

12. *which coin new offices*] referring to Antony, Octavius and Lepidus's creation of the unprecedented office of 'triumvir for the re-establishment of the commonwealth' (see 4.5.64–73).

13. *misprision*] corruption, abuse of public office.

17. *Lycaon*] king of Arcadia who fed the flesh of a child to Jove, to test whether he really was a god, and was turned into a wolf as a consequence.

21. *nectar*] the drink of the gods.

23. *cashiered*] cast off.

28. *apparition*] appearance.

Nay, rather if that good man feared a shower,
I must expect a tempest; for our nature
Hates more implacably a declined friend
Than a continued foe. Since, therefore, Antony
And his two fellow plagues are now approaching,   35
Since there are centiners arrived already,
Their fatal Mercuries, perhaps, to extinguish
Those careful eyes whose restless vigilance
Has been employed in service of the State,
(As sure they come to some such bloody end)   40
Let me enjoin you with the same solemnity
As parting friends take leave of one another.
Yet mingle something of the Thracian mirth
Among your sighs; let's laugh away our sorrow,
We may perhaps with Pluto sup tomorrow.   *Exeunt.*   45

[Act 5 Scene 2]

Enter Centurion, Soldiers.

Centurion. Come soldiers, Salvius Otho, as I hear,
Is frolic with his neighbours at a feast.
We'll spoil their second course. You know the price
Whereat the heads are rated by the triumvirs.
Come, follow me.   *Exeunt.*   5

[Act 5 Scene 3]

A table is discovered. SALVIUS *and his friends. To them the* Centurion.

Centurion. Nay stir not, sirs, be still, and keep your places,
Lest your own folly make yourselves co-partners
In this man's fall, which must be sudden—Tribune.
                              Pulls Salvius over the table
                              by the hairs of the head.
                              A curtain drawn.

Enter Centurion *with Salvius's head.*

Centurion. Now for Minutius.   *Exeunt.*

32–4. *for . . . foe*] Salvius had formerly been a supporter of Antony (see Act 1, esp.
1.5.105 and 3.7).
37. *Mercuries*] i.e. messengers. Mercury, the messenger of the gods, also summoned
and guided the dead to the underworld.
43. *Thracian mirth*] see 3.13. 37n.
45. *We . . . tomorrow*] i.e. in the underworld.
38. *careful*] watchful.

5.2.0.1.] Salvius was the very first victim of the proscriptions.
2. *frolic*] merry, enjoying himself.
4. *the heads are rated*] They (literally) have a price on their heads.

5.3.4. *Minutius*] See 3.4.23 and note.

[Act 5 Scene 4]

           Enter MINUTIUS *disguised* [, *with* Lictors].

Minutius. Nay leave me, sergeants. I am still Minutius,
   Although disguised, and if you longer stay
   Those very ensigns of my praetorship
   Will soon betray me, and perhaps the axe
   Which you there carry may strike off my head.   *Exit.*   5
Lictors. Alas, alas, but lest our too much piety
   Prove our own lord's destruction, let's be gone.   *Exeunt.*

[Act 5 Scene 5]

           Enter Centurion, Soldiers

Centurion. He cannot be escaped far, that's certain.
   What should the Lictors else do here? Go search.
                          Exeunt milites.
   Yet Marcus Tullius, with whose execution
   We were most strictly charged, is escaped,
   With Quintus Cicero. But the colonel,   5
   Popilius Laenas, and Herennius
   I hope will overtake them.

         Enter Soldiers *with Minutius's head.*

Soldier.   Here's the head
   Of that tall poppy.
Centurion.   Why, 'tis bravely done.
   Come, there are more such cedars to be lopped.   *Exeunt.*

[Act 5 Scene 6]

              Enter QUINTUS.

Quintus. They say the golden and the silver age
   Was then, when frugal mankind was content
   With those displayed riches which the earth
   Invests herself with, and her concealed entrails

    5.4.1. *Nay ... sergeants*] Minutius is addressing the attendants ('lictors') who are
carrying the *fasces,* emblems of his political office.
    3. *praetorship*] second most important magistracy in Rome.
    4. *axe*] of the fasces.
    6. *piety*] dutifulness.

    5.5.2.1. *milites*] soldiers.
    5. *colonel*] translating the Roman rank *tribunus,* a senior officer. Herennius was a
centurion. The details of the deaths of Quintus Cicero and his son and Cicero himself
are derived from the end of Plutarch's biography of Cicero.
    8. *tall poppy*] allusion to the myth of Tarquin (see 4.5.74 and note).

    5.6.1–9. *the golden ... moves*] On the Golden Age, see 1.2.230 and note, 3.13.45
and note. Sometimes the myth included a Silver Age which came after and was less

Were not rent up in quarries deep as hell,   5
For those pernicious world-disturbing metals;
For sure this is the age of gold and silver,
When those two precious perils are the poles
And hinges of the world, whereon it moves;
I might perhaps with my belovèd brother   10
Have been secure and safe, whereas being forced
For lack of money to return, each step
I take is ready to surrender me
Into the hands of death.

Enter QUINTUS JUNIOR.

Quintus jun.   O father, father,
Your treacherous servants have betrayed you, come   15
For heaven's sake, come, death, death is at your heels.

Exeunt.

[Act 5 Scene 7]

Enter Centurion, Soldiers.

Centurion. Bring his son hither, though you find not him.
Exeunt Soldiers.
Quintus returned! I wonder where's his brother.

Enter Soldiers with QUINTUS JUNIOR.

Soldier. Himself we cannot find, but here's young Quintus.
Centurion. Come youngster, where's your father, quickly tell me.
Quintus jun. O that I knew, my ever honoured sire,   5
The place of thy abode, alas; or whether
Thou are yet living, or hast now breathed forth
Thy sacred spirit! For a thousand pains,
My breast all gored with darts, hands cut with chains,
Famine or sword, or all, should never move   10
Me make a rupture in my filial love.
Centurion. Cease this dissembling language, and reveal him,
Or by the heavens thou diest.
Quintus jun. No, villainous centurion, threaten life.
If I knew where my reverend father were,   15
That would extort it soonest. 'Tis my wish

---

ideal than the Golden, but still far better than what followed. Here Quintus suggests that the current decadent age, in which money (made of these metals) is so crucial, is the real 'age of gold and silver'.
   8. *perils*] i.e. the cause of peril.
   11–12. *forced . . . return*] Cicero and his brother and nephew have left Rome to evade capture, but Quintus senior and junior have had to return to Rome to obtain money to fund their escape. There they are betrayed and killed.
   5.7.1. *him*] i.e. Quintus senior.
   14–17.] Death is no threat to Quintus who would sooner die than betray his father.

     I may soon quit this life.
Centurion.   With stripes, with wounds,
     With torments worse than death; impetuous pains
     Shall rend thy secrets from thy stubborn breast.
Quintus jun. Pish! These are nothing, threat more and heavier,   20
     Expose me to the ravenous lion's paw;
     Fling me into some common jakes, or dungeon,
     Wind off my flesh with pincers, do, and cram
     Young vultures with the bits before my eyes;
     Yet had I hid my father, as you deem,   25
     I would never betray so dear, so sacred,
     So glorious a treasure.
Centurion.   Take him thence,
     And torture this fond elf till he confess.
                    Exeunt Soldiers *with* QUINTUS JUNIOR.

           [*Enter*] QUINTUS *above.*

Quintus. Oh, what a virtuous son have I! Was ever
     Such piety in so few years? He dares   30
     The extremest of their tortures, with a spirit
     Constant as virtue's self. See how they wrack him!
     My melting bowels yearn within me; oh!
     Each stripe they give him cuts my very soul.
     See, see, they are even weary of tormenting,   35
     And yet the youth still firm. O piety!

     Enter soldiers *with* QUINTUS JUNIOR, *as from torture.*

Centurion. What? Where's his father? Has he yet confessed?
Quintus jun. Confessed, Centurion! No I will not, cannot,
     I am not Juno's Iris, that my eyes
     Should reach from hence to Macedon.
Centurion.   To Macedon?   40
     Why, his own servants say he is returned.
Quintus jun. Such slaves as they would betray their master,
     If he were in their clutches; may not they
     Cheat thee as well?
Centurion.   'Tis folly to conceal
     What force shall soon unbosom; speak,   45
     Where is he?
Quintus jun. What's that to thee? I dare the worst, Centurion,
     Thy malice can inflict.
Centurion.   Nay then, I see
     I must myself chastise you; come, ye weasel.

---

  18. *impetuous*] violent.
  22. *jakes*] privy.
  25. *deem*] believe, imagine.
  39. *Iris*] Iris, often equated with the rainbow, was the messenger of Juno, queen of
the gods. The sense is apparently that she can see a long distance from her elevated
position in the sky.

Enter QUINTUS.

Quintus. Nay hold, Centurion, here I am before you,   50
        Quintus the father whom you seek for.
Quintus jun.   Ah,
        What mean you, father, that you thrust yourself
        Into the jaws of certain fate? I could
        Have spit defiance in the face of cruelty,
        Though she had harboured in her friendlike looks   55
        A thousand deaths.
Quintus.   Indeed I do believe it,
        And let me kiss thee for thy piety;
        But old unfruitful stocks must be cut down,
        When their decaying and now sapless heads
        Keep off the quickening sunbeams from the young   60
        And hopeful tenderlings which they overtop.
        Suppose, my son, I had still lived, and thou
        Been made a prey to their relentless rage,
        I should have died too: for my bloodless loins
        Are dry and barren; but in thee my son,   65
        I shall survive myself.
Centurion.   Ha, ha, ha!
Quintus. I hope you do not mock at my calamity.
Centurion. Survive in him? Ay, so you shall, and both
        Be ferried over the Stygian lake together.
Quintus. What! Must my son then die? What has he done,   70
        Alas?
Centurion. 'Tis crime enough to have a life.
Quintus. Then kill me first, for sure I shall anticipate
        Your bloody hands, if I but see him slain.
Quintus jun. Nay, on my knees with suppliant breath, I beg
        I may die first, it is a boon I shall   75
        Prize even above my life.
Centurion. We'll soon decide your controversy, you shall die
        together.
        (*Both* [*are*] *slain.*) Take hence the bodies and unhead them
        quickly.   *Exeunt.*

[Act 5 Scene 8]

Enter POPILIUS LAENAS [, *a* Colonel] *with* CICERO'S *head and hands.*

Popilius. A princely gift, by Jove; Popilius Laenas,
        Thou hast now played the royal butcher. On,
        And let Antonius bless his longing eyes
        With sight of such a welcome present. Ha!

76. your controversy] you controversy Q.

69. *the Stygian lake*] The River Styx had to be crossed before entering the underworld.
    75. *boon*] favour.

Is this that Cicero's head that thundered so   5
In our tribunals? Ha! is this that mouth
Was wont to spit such lightning? Or are those,
Those hands which whilome thumped our rostra so?
Ay, even the selfsame head, and mouth, and hands.
Then Antony triumph, thy foe is dead,   10
The trophies of his fall, these hands, this head.   *Exit.*

[Act 5 Scene 9]

Enter POMPONIA, LAUREAS, TYRO.

Laureas. Dire, horrid, bitter fates! Did Rome e'er see
  A cruelty of such a high degree?
  Whose griefs shall I first publish? Thine,
  Unhappy widow? Or the State's? Or mine?
  Thine that hast lost so excellent a brother?   5
  The State's, that cannot now produce another,
  So reverend a patriot? Or mine own,
  That have now lost so good a lord? I groan
  Under the burden of my loss, nor can
  Summon the smallest character of man   10
  Into my wounded breast.
Pomponia.   Come, Laureas, come,
  Expound the series of his death; my heart
  Is turned adamant, I cannot weep,
  Stupidity has seized me, and methinks
  I feel a kind of pleasure in the story   15
  Of woes complete and perfect. I am even
  Transformed to a statue. Small griefs mourn,
  But great ones, such as mine, much like the head
  Of the deformed Gorgon, turn to stone,
  And make us our own sepulchres.
Laureas.   Good Tyro,   20
  Tell thou the tragic story, for my voice
  Is strangled by a throng of struggling sighs,
  Crowding from out my wounded breast.
Tyro.   Then thus.
  Departing hence we went to Tusculum,
  Where hearing of these outlawries and proscriptions,   25
  They suddenly determined for Astyra.
  So we conveyed them both into two litters,
  Weak as they were, alas; but on the way

5.8.6. *tribunals*] law courts.
8. *rostra*] the platform in the Roman Forum from which speeches were delivered.

5.9.12. *series*] sequence.
19. *deformed Gorgon*] Medusa, a monster whose head, severed by Perseus, was so horrible to look at ('deformed') that it turned all viewers to stone.
20. *sepulchres*] i.e. (stone) tombs.

Your husband calling to his sad remembrance
That at his fatal setting forth he took   30
But little money with him, and his brother
My lord had scarce sufficient for himself;
He thought it best in such an urgent straight,
His brother should hold on, while he himself
Returned home to furnish him with necessaries,   35
And so to haste and overtake him; this
They both agreed upon, and so embracing,
Tears trickling down their cheeks, they took their leaves
Of one another.
Laureas.   Thus departing souls
Do bid adieu unto their fading mansions,   40
For never nature strove so much, as when
This honoured pair sighed forth their last farewells.
'Twas a sad omen that they ne'er should meet.
Tyro. My lord being come at length unto Astyra,
Found a ship ready and embarked immediately,   45
And with a fair and prosperous gale of wind
Sailed along the coast unto Mount Circe,
And there he landed; but on other thoughts
He went aboard again, for 'twas his mind
To be conveyed by sea unto his farm   50
Which is by Capua. But before we landed,
Rowing securely by the pleasant shore,
Our linens swelling with the Etesian gales,
Which in the summer season fan that tract,
A shoal of crows came waving through the air,   55
As we conjectured from a little temple
Standing upon the shore, and dedicated
To god Apollo; these most strangely crying
Lighted upon our sailyards, with their bills
Pulling the cords, which made our heavy hearts   60
Presage some sinister and dismal luck
Then imminent; yet being come aland,
We brought him to his house, where he reposed
Himself a while, to see if he could sleep.
Laureas. Unhappy sleep! For straight this drowsy brother   65
Was seconded by his pale sister, death.
Tyro. But lo, the former shoal with louder cries
Came hither also, beating 'gainst the windows,

---

43. they] thy Q1.

---

40. *fading mansions*] i.e. dying bodies.
41. *strove*] i.e. fought against their decision to part.
47. *Mount Circe*] Circaeum: a promontory near Circeii (see 3.1.34–5 and note).
51. *Capua*] a town 15 miles north of Naples.
53. *linens*] sails.
Etesian gales] cool north winds, common in the Mediterranean in high summer.
65. *this drowsy brother*] i.e. sleep, in mythology the brother of Death.

'Till some of them got in, and never ceased
'Till with their bills they had plucked off at length   70
The clothes wherewith his face was covered.
We, seeing this, were angry with ourselves
As too, too negligent of our master's safety,
Saying, we were more vile than savage creatures,
Should we still tarry in that fatal place,   75
And see perhaps our lord before our eyes
Cruelly butchered; wherefore with all speed,
Partly by force, and partly by entreaty,
We carry him again unto his litter,
And so in haste departed towards the sea;   80
But being come into a shady wood
Which the sun never pierces with his beams
To glad the widowed earth—
Laureas.   A place decreed
By fate, I think, for such a villany;
For should the sun have seen so foul an act,   85
He would have turned retrograde, and hid
His visage from such cruelty—
Tyro.   Well here,
In this same gloomy canopy of horror,
Popilius Laenas overtook the litter.
Pomponia. Who? He whose cause my brother Marcus once   90
Pleaded before the judges, when he was
Accusèd for his father's death?
Tyro.   The same.
We stood prepared to spend our dearest blood,
Before we would have seen our master slain;
But ah! my lord commands us not to stir,   95
And to speak truth, it was in vain, for Laenas
Had armèd soldiers with him, and was followed
By other centiners. Then, O then my lord
Thrust out his agèd head from forth the litter,
And taking, as his manner was, his beard   100
In his left hand, and looking manfully
His headsman in the face, he stoutly said,
Come soldier, come, strike off this head of mine.
Laureas. We stood like statues with our trembling hands
Before our wretched eyes, for 'twould have struck   105
A tiger with remorse to have beheld him.
Tyro. Then Laenas with a thrice repeated stroke
Hacked off his head; there was scarce blood enough
Fell from those agèd veins to stain the sword,

---

86. *turned retrograde*] turned back, reversed its course in the sky.

90–2. *He whose . . . death*] a detail derived, like most of the rest of the scene, from the end of Plutarch's biography of Cicero.

108–9. *there . . . sword*] expressing the belief that the blood of the elderly was thin or had dried up. See 5.7.64–5 and Lady Macbeth's lines in *Macbeth*, 5.1.37–9.

And prove it conscious of so foul a murder.   110
Laureas. Thus was divided from his breathless trunk
   That sacrary of learning, where the graces,
   Graces that never had a Cytherea
   To be their mistress, moved in their right spheres;
   Where Hermes was enthroned, that winged patron   115
   Of heaven-born elocution, but without
   His filching art, for that State-piracy
   The bribing science was as far from him
   As Themis' self; where Pallas too was lodged,
   Not she that strove with Venus for an apple   120
   On the Idean hill, but such a one
   That deemed externals but as chaff and dust,
   In lieu of inward beauties, which inform
   The intelligences of our souls, and make them
   Comply with heaven and immortality;   125
   Lastly, where all the deities invested
   In their divinest purities, did dwell
   As 'twere in a compendious capitol.
Tyro. But Cicero's reverend head was not enough;
   The hands that wrote those glorious Philippics   130
   Must be cut off too.
Laureas.   Those illustrious hands
   Which once held up this tottering commonwealth,
   And set her on her feet, when she was falling
   From her proud orb into a gulf of fire.
Tyro. That head, those hands, are both divorced and severed 135
   From his now mouldered carcass, and no doubt

131. hands] hand Q.

---

110. *conscious of*] guilty of.
112. *sacrary*] shrine, temple.
113. *Graces*] goddesses of charm, elegance and beauty, constantly attendant on Venus (Cytherea).
114. *moved ... spheres*] i.e. the Graces which inhabited Cicero had more serious and appropriate concerns than love.
115. *Hermes*] the Roman Mercury, winged messenger of the gods, patron god both of the art of oratory and persuasion, and of theft (the 'filching art'). This speech of Laureas repeats much of the material from the opening Latin epigram.
117–18. *that State-piracy ... science*] The bribing of voters was an extremely common practice in Roman politics.
119. *Themis*] goddess of Justice or Righteousness.
Pallas] the goddess Minerva (Greek Athena) who, according to myth, took part in the 'Judgement of Paris' on Mount Ida (near Troy) to decide who was the most beautiful between herself, Venus (Aphrodite) and Juno (Hera). More commonly, though, she was associated with the cultivation of wisdom and the liberal arts (compare 1.5.55 and note).
126–8. *Lastly ... capitol*] Cicero is the amalgam of all the most perfect aspects of the gods.
128. *capitol*] the religious focal point of Rome (see 1.2.272 and note). Cicero has become the embodiment of Rome.
132. *once ... commonwealth*] referring to the events of 63 BC (see 2.2. 204n).
136. *moldred*] rotted, decayed.

Are by this time Antonius' game and sport;
For Laenas posted with them to the city.
Pomponia. Why, here's a story at whose sad relation
　　Democritus might change his laughing humour　　　　140
　　And side with Heraclitus. As for me,
　　I cannot weep; but Laureas, prithee tell me,
　　How came Popilius to find you out?
　　Methinks he could not, without information,
　　So shrewdly light upon the self same way　　　　　　145
　　Which you had took before him; was it fate?
Laureas. 'Twas fate, that's certain madam, 'twas, but ah,
　　There was an engine which the destinies
　　Did make their agent.
Pomponia. 　　　　　　　Whom?
Tyro. 　　　　　　　　　　　　Philologus.
Pomponia. Philologus?
Laureas. 　　　　　　　Aye, he betrayed your brother,　　　150
　　The oracle from which he learned the mysteries
　　Of pure philosophy. He, he it was
　　Who, being left behind us at the house,
　　Revealed the way we took unto the colonel.
Pomponia. And where's the villain?
Laureas. 　　　　　　　　　　Brought by Laenas hither,　　155
　　To be rewarded of Antonius
　　As a service of egregious merit.
Pomponia. Aye, so he shall, I'll see his wages paid.　*Exit* POMPONIA.
Laureas. Come, Tyro, since our day is set forever,
　　We'll live like owls, those citizens of night.　　　　160
　　Like owls indeed, but like Athenian owls;
　　Thou shalt sublime thy pen, and write the life
　　Of our deceased Lord, that spotless life,
　　Which virtue's self might make her meditation.
　　Tyro, thou shalt, and I, poor Laureas, I　　　　　　165
　　Will sit and sigh forth mourning elegies

140–1. *Democritus ... Heraclitus*] two Greek philosophers, the first with a reputation for bright humour, the second for melancholy. Thus Seneca, *De tranquillitate animi*, 15.2: 'Let us imitate Democritus rather than Heraclitus. For the latter wept whenever he used to go out, whilst the former laughed.'

157. *egregious*] an ambiguous word meaning both 'very good' (from the point of view of Antony) and 'very bad' (from the viewpoint of Pomponia and Laureas).

160. *live like owls*] i.e. live in darkness, now that the light which Cicero brought to their lives has been extinguished.

161. *Athenian owls*] Owls were the symbol of the goddess Athena (Minerva) and, hence, of her city, Athens. Athens was renowned for its achievements in literature.

162. *sublime thy pen*] raise your literary aspirations high enough to undertake a biography of the great man, Cicero.

write the life] Marcus Tullius Tiro, Cicero's loyal ex-slave, went on to write a biography of his former master after his death.

165–7. *and I ... death*] Part of a poem by Laureas (Tullius Laurea) in honour of Cicero, written after his death, is preserved by Pliny the Elder (*Natural History* 31.8), who remarks that 'even Cicero's servants drew inspiration from that mighty genius'.

Upon his death; he, while he lived, good man,
Delighted in my muse, and now my quill
Shall consecrate his name to the Muses' hill.   *Exeunt.*

[Act 5 Scene 10]

>   *Enter* ANTONY, FULVIA. POPILIUS LAENAS *crowned,*
>   CICERO'S *head in one hand, and his hands in the other.*

Antony. Laenas, 'twas nobly done, and thou hast well
          Deserved that crown which circles in thy temples.
          The head of Marcus Tullius Cicero!   *Takes it of Popilius.*
          Why, 'tis a kingly present, Ha, ha, ha!   *Derides and misuses it.*
                    [*Rolls Cicero's head as if it were a bowl.*]
Fulvia. To me.
Antony.   Rub and a good cast. Ha, ha, ha!   5
                    [*Rolls the head to Fulvia.*]
Fulvia. Bravely bowled, i'faith.
          Come up here.
                    Takes it up, and sitting down places it upon her knees.
          [*Addressing Cicero's head*] Now I'll be revenged
          For your tart, nipping jeers—yes, reverend sir,
          Fulvia's indebted to the State—too long.
          The no whit covetous wife of Antony,   10
          Whom you describe without all contumely,
          Owes the third pension to the Roman people.
          Indeed! but does she? Yes, nor will I wrong

0.1. *Enter* ANTONY] *Enter* ANTONIUS Q.   10. The no whit] *Philologus.* The no
whit] Q.

---

169. *consecrate . . . hill*] i.e. make Cicero a sacred theme of poetry. The Muses' hill
is Mount Helicon, which often stands for poetry as a whole.

5.10.2. *Deserved . . . temples*] The historian Appian tells us that Antony was so
delighted by Popilius Laenas's murder of Cicero that he gave Laenas a crown, or
garland, and a large sum of money as a reward.

5. *Rub*] a reference to the practice of rubbing or polishing the surface of a bowl
before it is thrown, to smooth its motion.

cast] throw.

9–12. *Fulvia's . . . people*] A 'pension' is a payment. Fulvia is ironically quoting
something said by Cicero in his *Second Philippic* (113). Cicero repeatedly accused
Fulvia in this speech of corruption. He combined this slur with the fact that, before
marrying Antony, she had been married to two other opponents of the Senate, Publius
Clodius and Gaius Scribonius Curio, both of whom died violent deaths. Cicero mali-
ciously suggested that it was being married to Fulvia which had brought about their
deaths and said that she had 'owed the third instalment [i.e. the death of her third
husband, Antony] to the Roman people over long'. Fulvia here suggests that what she
really 'owes to the state' is not Antony but Cicero's tongue.

10–16. Q's attribution of these lines to Philologus would seem to be mistaken: he
is not listed in the entry and the sentiment is particularly suited to Fulvia (see
5.10.14.1n).

11. *contumely*] reproach, disgrace. Fulvia is, of course, being ironic.

The people of their due, the debt's thy tongue.
                              Cuts out his tongue.
Here take it. I warrant him for barking now.   15
'Twill make a better football than a bowl.   *Kicks it away.*
Antony. Have at it.   *Quoits the hands to the head.*
          Take them, good Popilius,
And place them on the rostra, where he vomited
His Philippics against me. Let his head
Be set betwixt his hands, 'twill be a brave   20
And goodly spectacle.
Popilius.   I will, my lord.   *Exit.*
Antony. Do Fulvia stab it; give it as many wounds
As Julius Caesar had, whose horrid murder
That worm extolled as an heroic deed.
Well I must leave you for a while to meet   25
My colleagues, Lepidus and Octavius Caesar.   *Exit.*
Fulvia. That such a paltry thing as this should make
So great a bustling in a commonwealth?
I heard my husband once compare his lungs
To Vulcan's bellows, and his head to Etna,   30
His words to flame, and this his tongue to fire.
But now I think 'tis quenched, it burns not now;
Nay, 'tis as cold as stone, no thunder in it,
No lightning flies from it. Sure this is not that
Herculean tongue that lately was so weighty,   35
That it could crush such giants of the State
As it hath done to nothing? Yes, the same.
Then, Fulvia, march along, and banish fear.
Thou hast the tongue upon thy silver spear.   *Exit.*

[Act 5 Scene 11]

Enter POMPONIA.

Pomponia. Anger will me strength. Bloody Antonius,
          Thou shalt not thus evade. As once the stout
          And stern Amazon foiled the Grecian rout,

14.1. Cuts out his tongue] Fulvia exacts the revenge she had earlier desired. See
1.5.73–5.
    17. Quoits] throws like a quoit.
    23. *as many wounds*] According to Plutarch's life of Caesar, Caesar is said to have
received twenty-three wounds at the hands of his assassins.
    24. *extolled ... deed*] repeatedly, in the *Philippics*.
    30. *Vulcan's bellows*] Vulcan, god of metalworking, was believed to have his
forge beneath Mount Etna, which explained the smoke and flames which came out
of it.

    5.11.2. *evade*] escape.
    3. *stern Amazon*] Penthesilea, a female warrior who fought for the Trojans during
the siege of their city.
    the Grecian rout] the Greek army.

Or as the enraged Maenas armed with thyrse,
With pace directed by inspired force,   5
Affrights the woods, and quite distract makes gush
The blood which she perceives not, will I rush
Upon these Roman cannibals. If I die,
I shall enjoy my Quintus' company.
Alas, alas! what foolish rage is this?   10
We must appeal to heaven when we are wronged,
And not be our own carvers. Such State giants
Must have a Jove to curb them. Yet, Philologus,
That traitorous villain, that ungrateful wretch,
Whom not my husband's manumission,   15
Nor the divinest precepts of my brother,
Could keep within the bounds of faith and piety,
He, he shall rue it if I live, base caitiff!

                                                          Flourish.

         Enter ANTONY, LEPIDUS, OCTAVIUS, PISO *and others.*

[*To Antony*] Cruel triumvir, though thou hast unlived
My honoured husband, my belovèd son,   20
Though thou has slain my brother, and with him
Rent up the very groundwork of our Capitol,
And shown more cruelty to those sacred relics
Of his dissolved corpse, than victory
Did perpetrate on the Aemathian Perseus   25
Or the triumphed Jugurth, and King Syphax,
Or Hannibal himself, not one of whom
Was sent defective to the lower shades
With members violated; yet I come not,
Like the poor widowed Hecuba, to rail   30
And tell thee to what depth thou hast transgressed
The laws of goodness, and religious nature,
Making thyself the hate of men and gods,
Nor do I come to beg thy infamous sword
To rip that womb whose fruit thou hast destroyed,   35
Though I would hug my destiny. No, Antony,

4–7. *the enraged … perceives not*] A Maenad was a female worshipper of the god
Dionysus (Bacchus), who carried a special staff or thyrsus and ran wild, in a trance,
around the countryside, ripping animals limb from limb.
12. *carvers*] executioners.
12–13. *State … Jove*] See 1.5. 18n.
15. *manumission*] setting free of a slave.
18. *caitiff*] despicable, cowardly person.
25–7. *Perseus … himself*] major foreign enemies of Rome, all eventually defeated
by the Romans.
28–9. *was … violated*] None of the defeated enemies of Rome had their bodies
mutilated.
30. *Hecuba*] Queen of Troy, who in Euripides' *Hecuba* (see 3.4.35 and note)
delivered a long speech condemning Polymestor, King of Thrace, for the murder of her
son.

But only to put up a fair petition,
Whose grant will somewhat wipe away the rust
Which sullies thy bad name, and make posterity
Say thou didst something worthy of a Roman,   40
And thy renownèd stock; and this it is,
By all that's dear unto thee, I beseech thee,
Shelter not treason, but deliver me
The villain that betrayed my brother Marcus.
Antony. Philologus?
Pomponia.   Aye, he sir.
Antony.   Bring him forth.   45
Though such a treason was expedient,
Yet such a traitor must not live.
Octavius.   My lord,
You are most just in it.
Lepidus.   So says Lepidus.
Piso. 'Tis god-like equity.

Enter [Soldier] *with* PHILOLOGUS.

Antony. Pomponia, take him, he's at your disposing.   50
Pomponia. You heard that, varlet, now you're mine again;
I'll make you prey to a more hellish vulture
Than that of Tityus, thou thyself shalt slice
Thy own foul flesh by morsels off, and make
Thy own gaunt entrails thy own sepulchre;   [*Philologus falls*   55
                                          to his knees.]
Nay, 'tis in vain.
Philologus.   For heaven's sake, good my lord.
                              She drags him out.

Enter POPILIUS LAENAS.

Popilius. My lord, the tribune Publius Apuleius
Is with his wife escaped away by flight.
Antony. No matter, my long wished for aim is won.
And Cicero slain, the whole prescription's done.   60

Finis

---

47. Octavius] Caesar *Q.*   59–60.] *in italics, Q.*

38. *rust*] stain.
   41. *thy renownèd stock*] For Antony's illustrious ancestry, see 1.5. 18n and 4.5.185 and note.
   53. *Tityus*] See 3.13.51 and note and 4.5.50 and note.
   54–5. *and make . . . sepulcher*] Plutarch records the story that Pomponia made the treacherous Philologus cut off his own flesh little by little and eat it.
   60. *prescription's done*] the order given by Antony, with a punning allusion to the form that it took: proscription.

INTRODUCTION

The Republic is generally perceived as having been implacably hostile to theatrical entertainment. Such a perception is modified, however, by what we know of the performance of James Shirley's *Cupid and Death*, which is recorded on the title page of the first edition as taking place in the presence of the Portuguese ambassador in March 1653. Prefacing the first quarto, the printer's address to the reader reveals that Shirley had originally composed the masque for private entertainment, possibly at his school in Whitefriars, before the later, more public production. According to the address, the performance for the ambassador was not solicited by Shirley and nothing has survived amongst State papers to suggest that it marked a formal occasion. Nevertheless, Portugal was one of the first of the European powers to recognize the Commonwealth and in 1653 its ambassador, the Count of Peneguiaõ, was admitted to several private conferences with Cromwell before he met the Council of State.[1] Since both states sought to benefit from a treaty which was to be ratified in July 1654, the entertainment of the ambassador may have formed part of a diplomatic exercise.

Whatever the impetus behind the production, the selection for the occasion of an entertainment by Shirley was a cautious one. Although Shirley had been a prominent court dramatist and writer of masques during the Caroline period, he had largely withdrawn from post war cultural politics.[2] Unlike his younger contemporary Davenant, he had not become involved in attempts to revive the drama, choosing instead to publish old plays with new dedications while turning to the profession of schoolmaster and producing a Latin grammar. Several of his plays were published for the first time during the 1650s, and it is interesting to note that, as in *Cupid and Death*, he is not uncritical of royalist culture. In the dedication to *The Politician* (1655), for example, he refers to former 'abuses of the common theatres' and implies that opposition to drama is not endemic in the Commonwealth: there remain many lovers of 'exiled poesy' when it is presented 'without the stains of impudence and profanation'. A similar circumspection is evident in the critique of the cavalier gentry which appears in the first entry of the published text of *Cupid and Death*.

The narrative outline of *Cupid and Death* is loosely based on two popular fables from Aesop, 'Of Cupid and Death' and 'Of Cupid, Death and Reputation'. The first describes how the 'two great furies' rested at an inn and how their respective arrows were confused, subsequently wreaking havoc on the battlefield and at court. Love and Death retain some of each other's arrows, giving rise to the moral that 'age burns with love, while youth cold agues shake'. The second Aesopian fable has Love and Death in a contest with Reputation, in which the latter is represented as supreme. To these moralistic tales the dramatist has added broad comic elements together with mythological refinements consonant with the court masque. Shirley's narrative redaction begins with the preparations at the inn for the arrival of the 'immortal guests' Cupid and Death. This setting allows for the introduction of the comic figures of the Host, sporting anti-quated trunk hose and cross-gartered stockings, and his Chamberlain. Before the pair depart, the Chamberlain decides to exchange their arrows. As a result, whenever Cupid shoots, lovers die, and when Death fires his arrows, enemies become comrades and old people are rejuvenated. This confusion of arrows is yet another representation of the familiar Renais-sance conjunction of love and death, but in Shirley's version it is given a comic source. The Chamberlain's ruse is an act of revenge against Love for sending him 'a hard hearted baggage' as his wife. Yet the trick rebounds on him when Death, shooting Cupid's arrows, causes him to fall in love with two apes, and there follows the grotesque spectacle of the Chamberlain courting the fairground animals.

Shirley's immediate source was the translation of Aesop's fables by his friend John Ogilby, to which, with Davenant, he had written a dedica-tion.[3] The verse paraphrases of the tales in four books are particularly interesting for their contemporary political nuance. Ogilby fully exploits the characteristic application of the bestiary to accommodate pertinent political and social meanings. In book two, for example, in the twenty-ninth fable, 'Of Birds and Beasts', Ogilby recounts the hostilities between the birds and the beasts, and in particular the treachery of the bat. The story is used to point up the moral that, while just men are valiant and honest, treacherous men will make any compromise in order that 'they from sequestration be secure' (Cc3v). This is a fairly unambiguous allu-sion to those sometime Royalists who sought accommodation with the Commonwealth to preserve their estates from confiscation. 'The Parlia-ment of Birds', the fortieth tale in the second book, is again explicit in its political allegorizing, beginning, as it does, with the deposition of Saturn by Jove and the birth of a second age: 'Then civil war turned kingdoms into States' (Gg3). The whole fable becomes a metaphor for the over-throw of the monarchy and the establishment of the Commonwealth. By ejecting 'their king and lords of prey', the birds 'reduce' the kingdom 'to a popular State' but in their parliament they are divided about whether to make war on men. They are defeated by fowlers and the emergent State is overthrown. The fable ends with the caution, 'When civil war hath brought greater nations low, / Destruction comes, oft with a foreign foe.'

The use of such politically symbolic material might give rise to certain assumptions as to Shirley's purpose. It is significant, however, that in his choice of fable Shirley actually steers away from ideological moralizing, choosing instead to include comment that would have been amenable to the Commonwealth. The lively exchanges between the Chamberlain and the Host about the qualities of the various guests provide the occasion for humorous derision of a decadent nobility. The Chamberlain describes the drunken behaviour of the gentry while judging that their 'dancing days are done'; the Host retorts that such habits are now out of fashion. Contemporary comment is sustained in the discussion of Love's companions, Folly and Madness, whom the Chamberlain dismisses as worthless, fit only 'to be o'th' privy council'. Since the Commonwealth Council of State had replaced the monarchical institution of the Privy Council, the object of the satire is clear. In the opening scene the masque is thus expressly dissociated from royalist interests. The second edition of 1659, based on the production of the masque in Leicester Fields, omits all these lines, which suggests that the passages were incorporated in deference to the public occasion of the masque's earlier performance; their inclusion a political rather than a dramatic expedient.

The 1653 edition of *Cupid and Death* describes the work as a masque, although this designation is lacking in the second edition of 1659. Certainly, it demonstrates many features of the masque, as a spectacular entertainment incorporating song and dance within a poetic and dramatic framework. A characteristic of the Stuart masque was the anti-masque, a comic or grotesque scene containing a dance which preceded the splendid pageant of the masque proper. Intermixed with the story of the grim reaper and the waywardness of Cupid are the dance of satyrs and apes and the scenes of aged lovers courting, which correspond to the anti-masque. Again, certain scenes in *Cupid and Death* evoke Shirley's earlier masques *The Triumph of Beauty* and *The Triumph of Peace*. There is, for example, in *The Triumph of Beauty* a moment when Mercury descends and dancing shepherds are dispersed. In *Cupid and Death*, Mercury also descends and conducts Nature to the Elysian fields to witness the eternal happiness of the slain lovers, who participate in a grand dance. The climax of the entertainment is reached with Mercury's appearance followed by the formal dance of the principal masquers, who were probably pupils of the choreographer, Luke Channen, and not courtiers as in earlier masques. Scenic changes and the projected use of machinery for the conveyance of the gods again suggest a production which bore some resemblance to the elaborate engineering of Caroline court entertainments. There are three changes of scene: the inn and its location; the garden of love; and, finally, the Elysian fields. Unlike Davenant's later dramatic experiments, *Cupid and Death* allows for some spectacular staging, particularly in the descent of Mercury upon a cloud to dismiss the dancing satyrs and apes and in the appearance of the winged Cupid in the lovers' garden.

Although such dramatic and theatrical qualities are reminiscent of the anti-masque and masque of the Jacobean and Caroline court, there are subtle distinctions of both style and structure which distinguish Shirley's appropriation of the genre for the Commonwealth. There is a stronger dramatic sense in *Cupid and Death* than in the earlier masques. The rustic humour of the Host and Chamberlain has antecedents in Elizabethan comedy. For the narrative thread of suicidal Despair and his comic revitalisation, Shirley turns to the familiar motifs of the morality play. The non-dramatic elements of *Cupid and Death* are more integral to the text than in previous masques so that songs are interspersed with the narrative and not, as, for example, in *The Triumph of Peace*, sung only after the foolings of the anti-masque. Further, masque and anti-masque are part of the same dramatic event. What we have in essence is a masque which is popular in appeal and freed from its more esoteric mythological associations.

The 1653 production was a collaborative affair of author, the choreographer, Luke Channen, musicians and unknown scenic designers. The printer's address singles out the gentlemen dancers as 'masters of their quality' and it has been suggested that the set dances were designed first and the libretto written around them.[4] The music, to which Christopher Gibbons, the eldest son of Orlando Gibbons, contributed, has not survived, although the autograph libretto by Matthew Locke, 'The Instrumental and Vocal Music in the Moral Representations at the Military Ground in Leicester Fields', which was composed for the revival in 1659, is extant. Locke's autograph score almost certainly contains additional instrumental music to that played in earlier performances and it is clear that the last two entries, apart from a few lines spoken by the Chamberlain, were sung almost entirely in recitative. The typography of the dramatic texts—mostly roman, not italic, type—suggests that these entries consisted of spoken dialogue in earlier performances.

The masque was revived several times in the twentieth century for amateur performance, including a production at the Glastonbury Summer Festival in 1919.[5] With Nahum Tate's *Dido and Aeneas* (1689), *Cupid and Death* was performed at the London Opera Festival in 1929–30. In 1983 the Consort of Musicke, directed by Anthony Rooley, revived the masque for the Flanders Festival in Bruges, describing it as 'the first English comic opera'.[6] The production was staged the following year at the Royal Festival Hall.

A NOTE ON THE TEXT

Cupid and Death offers no particular editorial problems. The edition of 1653 (Q1) was authorized by Shirley and forms the copy text of this edition. It has been collated with the quarto of 1659 (Q2) and with the edition by B. A. Harris (Harris). Matthew Locke's autograph score and the edition of this prepared by Edward Dent in *Musica Britannica II* (1951) have been consulted. The score for the song which concludes the second entry is reproduced in Appendix I. I have departed from the usual convention in editing masques, that of continuous line numbering. The masque divides into five entries and each entry advances the narrative in a formal way, reminiscent of the act of a play. Each section (apart from entry one) consists of a number of dances, narrative development, a song which reflects on the action and a chorus which makes a final comment. To preserve this formal design and to enhance the dramatic quality of the masque, I have adopted separate line numbering for each entry.

NOTES

1 See *The Writings and Speeches of Oliver Cromwell*, edited by Wilbur Cortez Abbott, 4 vols (Oxford, reprinted 1988), 3, p. 35.
2 See Sandra A. Burner, *James Shirley: A Study of Literary Coteries and Patronage in Seventeenth-century England* (New York and London, 1988), pp. 177–97.
3 See John Ogilby, *Fables of Aesop Paraphrased in Verse* (1651).
4 See production notes by Anthony Rooley to a recording on compact disc of *Cupid and Death* (also incorporating John Blow's *Venus and Adonis*) by the Consort of Musicke, directed by Anthony Rooley, 1990 (Deutsche Harmonia Mundi, D-7800, Freiburg), pp. 18–19.
5 See *Cupid and Death*, edited by Bernard Harris, in *A Book of Masques*, edited by T. J. B. Spencer and S. W. Wells (Cambridge, 1967), pp. 378–9.
6 See *Opera*, 34:11 (1983), 1225–7, p. 1225.

Cupid and Death
A Masque

As it was presented before his Excellency the Ambassador of Portugal
upon the 26 of March, 1653.

Written by J.S.

London.

Printed according to the author's own copy, by T.W. for J. Crook and J. Baker,
at the sign of the ship in St. Paul's Churchyard, 1653.

DRAMATIS PERSONAE

[HOST
CHAMBERLAIN
CUPID
FOLLY
MADNESS   5
DEATH
DESPAIR
NATURE
MERCURY
Lovers   10
Two old men
Two old women
Six gentlemen
Satyr
Two apes]   15

---

1. *HOST*] Innkeeper.

2. *CHAMBERLAIN*] attendant at an inn, in charge of the bedchambers.

3. *CUPID*] Son of Venus, the boy-god of love. In the Renaissance Cupid was represented as blind. One tradition saw in blind Cupid a symbol of unenlightened animal
passion, whereas Neoplatonic thinking recognized a more exalted conception of blind
Cupid. See Wind, pp. 52–4.

9. *MERCURY*] identified with the Greek Hermes, messenger of the greater gods. A
popular subject in Renaissance art was Mercury teaching Cupid to read. See Wind,
p. 80.

14. *Satyr*] woodland semi-demonic figure, usually of human form, but with the ears,
legs and tail of a goat.

THE PRINTER TO THE READER

This masque was born without ambition of more than to make good a private entertainment, though it found, without any address or design of the author, an honourable acceptation from his Excellency the Ambassador of Portugal, to whom it was presented by Mr Luke Channen, etc.

It had not so soon been published, for the author meant all civilities to all persons, but that he heard an imperfect copy was put to the press with an addition before it of some things that should be obtruded by another hand, which the author's judgement could not consent to.

The scenes wanted no elegance or curiosity for the delight of the spectator. The musical compositions had in them a great soul of harmony. For the gentlemen that performed the dances, thus much the author did affirm upon sight of their practice, that they showed themselves masters of their quality.

5

10

The Printer to the Reader . . . quality.] *Q1; not in* Q2.

---

2. *private entertainment*] The masque was probably first performed by boys from the school in Whitefriars where Shirley was teaching.

3. *honourable acceptation*] favourable reception.

4. *the Ambassador of Portugal*] the Count of Peneguiaõ, who was negotiating a trade treaty with the Republic.

4–5. *Luke Channen*] or Channell. He was later dancing master for the Duke's Company, and with Matthew Locke and Joseph Priest composed music and choreographed dancing for Davenant's adaptation of *Macbeth*. Pepys records visiting his dancing school on 25 September 1660 (Pepys, 1, p. 253).

6. *It had . . . published*] i.e. it would not have been published so soon (after its performance).

6–7. *civilities . . . persons*] respect, presumably to those who had collaborated in the 1653 production.

8–9. *addition . . . consent to*] i.e. an unauthorized passage tacked on to the beginning of the work.

10. *scenes*] slides painted in perspective at the back and sides of the stage as a decorative adjunct and to reflect variation of mood and some change of location in the masque. There are three scene changes in *Cupid and Death*.

wanted] lacked.

curiosity] ingenuity.

11. *musical compositions*] It is probable that Christopher Gibbons (1615–76) was the major, possibly the sole, contributor for the first production in 1653. His setting of the song at the close of the second entry, 'Victorious men of earth', was printed in that year. Matthew Locke (c.1621–77) and Christopher Gibbons composed the music for the Leicester Fields showing in 1659.

CUPID AND DEATH

The Scene: *A forest, on the side of a hill a fair house representing an inn or tavern, out of which cometh an* HOST, *being a jolly, sprightly old man, his cap turned up with crimson, his doublet fustian, with jerkin and hanging sleeves, trunk hose of russet, stockings yellow, cross-gartered; after him, a* CHAMBERLAIN.

Host. Are all things in their preparation,
    For my immortal guests?
Chamberlain.   Nothing is wanting
    That doth concern my province, sir; I am
    Your officer above stairs. The great chamber
    With the two wooden monuments to sleep in   5
    (That weigh six load of timber, sir) are ready.
    That for the Prince d'Amour, whom we call Cupid,
    I have trimmed artificially with roses
    And his own mother's myrtle. But I have
    Committed sacrilege to please the other;   10
    Death does delight in yew, and I have robbed
    A churchyard for him. Are you sure they'll come
    Tonight? I would fain see this dwarf called Cupid;
    For the other, I look on him in my fancy,
    Like a starved goblin.
Host.   Death, I must confess,   15

0.1] A Masque *Q1; not in Q2.*   0.2. FIRST ENTRY] *Q2.*   9. his own mother's] *Q1;* own mother's *Q2.*

   1.0.3. *fustian*] coarse cloth made of cotton and flax.
   0.4. *jerkin*] close fitting jacket or short coat.
   trunk hose] full bag-like breeches covering the hips and upper thighs (*OED*). By 1653 they would have been considered old-fashioned.
   0.4–5. *stockings . . . cross-gartered*] This may be a recollection of Malvolio's appearance as a suitor to Olivia in *Twelfth Night* (2.5.190–5). As early as 1602 cross-gartered yellow stockings would have been seen as old-fashioned and comical.
   3. *province*] office, function.
   4. *Your . . . stairs*] i.e. chamberlain, responsible for the preparation of bedchambers.
   5. *wooden monuments*] ornate, four-poster beds.
   7. *Prince d'Amour*] recalling Davenant's Caroline masque, *The Triumphs of the Prince d'Amour* (1636).
   8. *artificially*] with a deliberate design.
   9. *mother's myrtle*] myrtle, sacred to Venus and an emblem of love.
   11–12. *Death . . . him*] the yew, associated with sadness, often grown in churchyards.
   14. *fancy*] imagination.
   15–18. *Death . . . feeding*] i.e. death may not cut his prey with such relish as we carved up the deer on our last hunt but, like the cormorant, he has an insatiable appetite.

Cuts not so many inches in the say
As our last venison; 'tis a thin-chapped hound,
And yet the cormorant is ever feeding.
Chamberlain. He is kin to the devouring gentleman
   Of the long robe—
Host.   That has bespoke a chamber   20
   In the college among the bears, and means to be
   In commons with them.
Chamberlain.   But, good sir, resolve me,
   Are they good-spirited guests? Will they tipple
   To elevation? Do they scatter metal
   Upon the waiters? Will they roar, and fancy   25
   The drawers, and the fiddles, till their pockets
   Are empty as our neighbour's drone? And after
   Drop by degrees their wardrobe? And in the morning
   When they have daylight to behold their nakedness,
   Will they with confidence amaze the streets,   30
   And in their shirts to save their pickled credits,
   Pretend a race, and trip it like fell footmen?
   These rantings were the badges of our gentry,
   But all their dancing days are done, I fear.
Host. These were the garbs and motions late in fashion   35
   With humorous mortals; but these guests are of

19–22. He . . . them] *Q1; not in Q2.*

16. *say*] assay, in hunting, cutting up of the slain deer.
17. *thin-chapped*] reduced in size, emaciated.
18. *cormorant*] a bird reputed to have a voracious appetite.
19–20. *He . . . robe*] an allusion to the alleged rapacity of lawyers.
20. *long robe*] the dress of the legal or clerical profession.
20–2. *That . . . them*] Harris quotes *Taylors Wit and Mirth*, 'I landed him at the Bears College on the Bankside, alias Paris Garden.' Paris Garden in Southwark was a centre of bowling and gambling. Customers for the theatre and bear gardens landed at Paris Garden stairs, where they stopped for refreshment. But perhaps the meaning here is less literal: one who has bespoke (engaged) a room in the commons (company) of louts (bears) and intends to board with them.
22. *resolve me*] dispel my doubts; free me from anxiety.
23–4. *tipple to elevation*] drink to raise the spirits.
24–5. *scatter . . . waiters*] i.e. do they tip the waiters well?
metal] coins.
25. *roar*] emit outbursts of boisterous laughter.
25–6. *fancy . . . fiddles*] favour the barmen and the fiddlers.
27. *drone*] i.e. an idler, a non-worker.
27–8. *And after . . . wardrobe*] gradually lose all their apparel.
30. *amaze the streets*] cause great astonishment in the streets.
31–2.] i.e. to save their reputations after such loutish behaviour, they pretend to compete in a race and thus nimbly escape.
32. *fell footmen*] cunning competitors in a foot-race.
33–4.] i.e. such roistering behaviour used to characterize the gentry, but their days of revelry are now over, I'm afraid.
33. *rantings*] dissolute, unruly behaviour.
35. *garbs*] prevailing modes of fashion.
36. *humorous*] subject to different humours, i.e. moods and states of mind.

No human race.
Chamberlain. 'Pray, what attendance have they?
Host.   Love has two
Gentlemen that wait on him in his chamber,
Of special trust; he cannot act without them.   40
Chamberlain. Their names, sir, I beseech you?
Host.   Folly and Madness.
Chamberlain. A pair of precious instruments, and fit
To be o'th' privy council.
Host.   We may see
What most of our nobility are come to.
Chamberlain. Sure they are well descended, sir.
Host.   The fool   45
Could ride a hundred mile in his own pedigree,
And give as many coats—
Chamberlain.   Fools' coats, there are
Enough to wear them.
Host.   —as he had acres in
Eleven fat lordships,
And played at duck and drake with gold, like pebbles.   50
Chamberlain. Was this man born a fool?
Host.   No, but his keeping
Company with philosophers undid him,
Who found him out a mistress they called Fame,
And made him spend half his estate in libraries,
Which he bestowed on colleges, took the toy   55
Of building quadrangles, kept open house,
And fell at last most desperately in love
With a poor dairy maid, for which he was begged—
Chamberlain. A fool?
Host.   —and leads the van in Cupid's regiment.

42–4. and fit . . . come to] *Q1; not in Q2.*   55. bestowed on colleges] *Q2, Harris;*
bestowed colleges *Q1.*

37. *No human race*] a pun on the race run by the gentry. Cupid and Death are
immortal.
42. *precious instruments*] worthless tools.
42–3. *fit . . . council*] That the line is omitted in *Q2* suggests an intentional pejora-
tive reference to the King's Privy Council, which was replaced by the Council of State
in the Commonwealth.
46.] could trace far back the ancestral line.
47–8. *And give . . . them*] a pun on the heraldic coats of the gentry, which the chamberlain likens to the traditional garb of the fool, the motley coat: i.e. many of the gentry,
being fools, are subject to the fashion.
49. *fat lordships*] vast estates.
50. *duck and drake*] the pastime of throwing a flat stone over the surface of the water
so as to cause it to rebound or skip as many times as possible before sinking (*OED*).
51. *this man*] i.e. Cupid's companion.
55–6. *took . . . Of*] amused himself by.
56. *quadrangles*] a reference either to the quadrangles of the colleges which Folly
endowed or to the extravagant design of his residence.
58. *for . . . begged*] because of which he was reduced to penury.
59. *van*] foremost position.

Chamberlain. What was the madman, sir?   60
Host. A thing was born to a very fair *per annum*,
    And spent it all in looking-glasses.
Chamberlain.   How?
    That's a project I never heard on, looking-glasses!
    How many did he break, sir, in a day?
Host. They broke him rather, in the right understanding;   65
    For nature having given him a good face,
    The man grew wild with his own admirations,
    And spent his full means upon flatterers
    That represented him next to an angel.
    Thus blown up, he took confidence to court   70
    A lady of noble blood and swelling fortune;
    Within three days fell sick of the small pox,
    And on the fourth ran mad, with the conceit
    His face, when he recovered, would be like
    A country cake from which some children had   75
    New picked the plums.
Chamberlain.   A brace of pretty beagles.
Host. They are here.
Chamberlain. I see not Death.
Host.   He's the last thing we look for.

                              [*Exit* CHAMBERLAIN.]

    Enter CUPID, FOLLY, MADNESS; *the* HOST *joins with*
                 them in a dance.

                  Song

      Though little be the God of love,
      Yet his arrows mighty are,   80
      And his victories above
      What the valiant reach by war;
      Nor are his limits with the sky;
      O'er the milky way he'll fly,
      And sometimes wound a deity.   85
      Apollo once the Python slew,
      But a keener arrow flew
      From Daphne's eye, and made a wound

---

61. *fair* per annum] good annuity.
70. *blown up*] with an inflated opinion of himself.
73. *conceit*] a fanciful notion.
76. *plums*] dried raisins or currants.
A brace . . . beagles] The suggestion would seem to be that Folly and Madness scent
out or hunt down Love.
78.3. *Song*] Locke's score shows that the song was sung by a soprano and bass, with
lines 84–5 and 94–5 sung in chorus.
84. *milky way*] figuratively, the way leading to heaven lit by the stars.
86. *Python*] serpent, guardian of the oracle at Delphi, slain by Apollo.
88. *Daphne's eye*] Daphne was a nymph who spurned Apollo's love; pursued by
him, she was turned into a laurel tree.

For which the God no balsam found.
One smile of Venus, too, did more   90
On Mars than armies could before:
If a warm fit thus pull him down,
How will she ague-shake him with a frown!
Thus love can fiery spirits tame,
And, when he please, cold rocks inflame.   95
        [*Exeunt* CUPID, FOLLY, MADNESS *and the* HOST.]

[SECOND ENTRY]

Enter DEATH; *he danceth the second entry; after which, he speaks.*

Death. Holla! within!

                Enter CHAMBERLAIN.

Chamberlain.   You are welcome gentlemen; ha!
    Quarter, oh quarter! I am a friend, sir,
    A moveable belonging to this tenement
    Where you are expected. Cupid is come already,
    And supped, and almost drunk. We have reserved   5
    According to order, for your palate, sir,
    The cockatrice's eggs, the cold-toad pie,
    Ten dozen of spiders, and the adders' tongues
    Your servant Famine, sir, bespoke.
Death.   Live, live.   *Exit.*
Chamberlain. I thank you, sir! [*To himself*] A curse upon his
        physnomy!   10
    How was I surprised! 'Twas high time to comfort me,
    I felt my life was melting downward.
[*Despair. (Within)*]   Death, O death!
Chamberlain. Who's that? I do not like the voice. What art?

            Enter DESPAIR *with a halter.*

---

89. *balsam*] balm.
90–100.] i.e. Venus, the goddess of love, has more power over Mars, god of war, than any army. In many Renaissance idylls the victorious Venus is depicted, having subdued Mars, playing with his armour. See Wind, p. 89.
93. *ague-shake*] shake as in the cold stages of a fever.

2.0.1. Enter DEATH] In Locke's score, a saraband is played before Death's dance.
2. *Quarter*] exemption from death, granted to an enemy who surrenders in battle.
3. *moveable*] a wanderer, a casual worker.
tenement] dwelling, habitation.
7. *cockatrice's eggs*] eggs of a serpent alleged to kill by a glance.
9. *bespoke*] ordered.
10. *physnomy*] physiognomy i.e. face, form.
11. *comfort me*] relieve my fear.
12. *melting downward*] ebbing away.
13.1. *halter*] a form of noose, see Kyd, *The Spanish Tragedy*, 3.12, where Hieronimo enters with a halter.

Despair. A miserable thing.

Chamberlain.   Ay, so thou seem'st.
    Hast not a name?

Despair.   My name, sir, is Despair.   15

Chamberlain. Despair? My time's not come yet: what have I
    To do with thee? What comest thou hither for?

Despair. To find out Death: life is a burden to me;
    I have pursued all paths to find him out,
    And here in the forest had a glimpse on him,   20
    But could not reach him with my feet, or voice.
    I would fain die, but Death flies from me, sir.

Chamberlain. I wonder you should travel in the forest,
    And among so many trees find none convenient,
    Having the tackling ready 'bout your neck too.   25
    Some great affairs take up the devil's time;
    He cannot sure attend these low employments:
    He's busy 'bout Leviathans. I know not,
    There's something in it. You have not made your will, sure.

Despair. Yes, sir, I carry it with me; it wants nothing   30
    But his name, and my subscription.

Chamberlain.   Whose name?

Despair. His name I mean to make my heir.

Chamberlain.   Who's that?

Despair. That charitable man
    Will bring Death to me; there's a blank left for him,
    And if you please to do me, sir, the office,   35
    Even you shall be the man. I have professed
    An usurer these fifty years, and upwards;
    The widows and sad orphans whose estates
    I have devoured are croaking in my conscience.

Chamberlain. And shall he be your heir, that does this feat,   40
    To make you acquainted with this cannibal
    You talk of?

Despair.   O my happiness!

Chamberlain.   I'll do it.
    But I believe you're sorry for your baseness,
    Your rapines and extortion—

Despair.   Mistake not,

---

18. burden] *Q1*; burthen *Q2*.

    25. *tackling*] equipment i.e. rope, noose (for hanging himself).
    28. *Leviathans*] men of formidable power and wealth; probably an allusion to Hobbes's *Leviathan* (1651).
    28–9. *I know . . . it*] i.e. there is some reason why Death is eluding you.
    30. *wants*] lacks.
    31. *subscription*] signature.
    34. *a blank*] a space left for the insertion of the name of the will's beneficiary.
    36. *professed*] led the life of.
    39. *croaking*] groaning, grieving.
    41. *cannibal*] i.e. Death.
    44. *rapines*] acts of plunder or violent robbery.

I am sorry for no mischief I have done;   45
That would come near repentance, which you know
Cures all the achings of the soul. If I
Could but be sorry, Death were of no use to me.
Chamberlain. Keep ye of that mind, you say very right, sir.
I'll try what I can do   50
With Death, to do your conscience a courtesy.
He's now within our house, I'll bring you pen
And ink to write my name too, honest father.
Despair. Thou art my dearest child, take all my blessings.
Chamberlain. [*Aside*] Here's like to be a fortune.   *Exit.*
Despair.   I want strength   55
To climb, I see a very pretty twig else.   *He climbs.*
And space for a most comfortable swing,
'Tis a hard case the devil wo'not help
At a dead lift.   *He falls.*
            O my sciatica!
I have broke my spectacles, and both my hips   60
Are out of joint. Help!—

        Enter CHAMBERLAIN *with a bottle of wine.*

Chamberlain. Death will be with you presently; the last course
Is now on the table. That you may not think
The time long, I have brought you—ha! rise up, sir.
Despair. Alas, I have had a fall: I was endeavouring   65
To do the meritorious work, and hang
Myself, for Death me thought was long a coming,
But my foot slipped.
Chamberlain.   Alas, what pity 'twas!
If I had thought your soul had been in such
Haste, I would have given you a lift before   70
I went.
Despair.   It was my zeal.
Chamberlain.   Alas it seemed so;
You might have took the river with more ease,
The stream would have conveyed you down so gently
You should not feel which way your soul was going.
But against the frights Death might bring with him,   75
I have brought you a bottle of wine. I'll begin, sir.   *He drinks.*
Despair. Would it were poison.
Chamberlain.   So would not I, I thank you,

45–8.] i.e., repentance, an acknowledgement of God's mercy, would negate the desire for suicide.

51. *to . . . courtesy*] i.e. to relieve you of your conscience.

56–7. *I see . . . swing*] Despair spots a branch to bear the noose, with space for the body to drop.

59. *At a dead lift*] in extremity, in a hopeless situation (expression used to describe a horse attempting to pull a weight too heavy for it, see *OED*).

sciatica] painful condition of the back or limbs.

72–4.] i.e., drowning would have been an easy death.

'Tis pure blood of the grape.
Despair.   Wine?
Chamberlain. At my charge. I know you do not use
　　To pay for nectar; I bestow it sir.   80
Despair. That's kindly said, I care not if I taste—
　　　　　　　　　　　　　[*He tastes the wine.*]
Chamberlain. In the meantime please you, I'll peruse the will;
　　I can put in my own name, and make it fit
　　For your subscription. What's here?   [*He*] reads [*aside.*]
　　Ha! A thousand pound in jewels, in ready money   85
　　Ten thousand more, land—ha! Preserve my senses!
　　I'll write my name, and thank heaven afterwards.
　　[*To Despair*] Here sir, before you can subscribe, the gentleman
　　Will come, and kill you to your heart's content.
Despair. Hum! this foolish wine has warmed me. What d'ye   90
　　Call the name on it?
Chamberlain.   Sack.
Despair.   Sack! Why truly, son—
Chamberlain. Nay sir, make haste, for Death will be here instantly.
Despair. At his own leisure, I would not be troublesome;
　　Now I do know his lodging, I can come
　　Another time.
Chamberlain.   But the will, father, you may write now—   95
Despair. Deeds are not vigorous without legal witnesses;
　　My scrivener lives at the next town, and I
　　Do find my body in a disposition
　　To walk a mile or two. Sack, d'ye call it?
　　How strangely it does alter my opinion!   100
Chamberlain. Why, have you no mind to hang yourself?
Despair. I thank you, I find no inclination.
Chamberlain. Shall not I be your heir then?
Despair.   In the humour
　　And spirit I now feel, in brain and body,
　　I may live—to see you hanged; I thank you heartily.   105
Chamberlain. But you will have the conscience, I hope,
　　To pay me for the wine has wrought this miracle.
Despair. Your free gift, I remember; you know, I use not
　　To pay for nectar, as you call it. Yet
　　I am not without purpose to be grateful;   110
　　Some things shall be corrected in my will.
　　In the meantime, if you'll accept of a
　　Small legacy, this hemp is at your service,   *Gives him the halter.*

91. why truly] *Q1*; my truly *Q2*.

79. *charge*] expense.
do not use] are not accustomed.
80. *nectar*] wine.
91. *Sack*] white wine imported from Spain or the Canaries.
96. *vigorous*] valid, enforceable.
97. *scrivener*] notary, lawyer specializing in preparation of deeds, bonds and wills.
113. *hemp*] rope (for hanging).

And it shall cost you nothing, I bestow it.
We men of money, worn with age and cares,   115
Drink in new life from wine that costs us nothing.
Farewell, and learn this lesson from Despair,
Give not your father sack to be his heir.   [*Exit.*]
Chamberlain. Not a tear left! Would's brains were in the bottle.
                                                            Exit.

[*Enter* DEATH.]

Song

Victorious men of Earth, no more   120
Proclaim how wide your empires are;
Though you bind in every shore,
And your triumphs reach as far as night or day,
Yet you proud monarchs must obey,
And mingle with forgotten ashes, when   125
Death calls ye to the crowd of common men.

Devouring famine, plague, and war,
Each able to undo mankind,
Death's servile emissaries are;
Nor to these alone confined,   130
He hath at will
More quaint and subtle ways to kill.
A smile or kiss, as he will use the art,
Shall have the cunning skill to break a heart.

[THIRD ENTRY]

Enter CHAMBERLAIN.

Chamberlain. Ho, master, master!

Enter HOST.

Host.   What's the matter?
Chamberlain. Nothing but to ask you whether you be
    Alive or no, or whether I am not
    My own ghost, that thus walk and haunt your house.
Host. Thou lookest frighted.
Chamberlain.   Death and his train are gone: 5

124. Yet] *Q2;* Tet *Q1.*

---

119. *Not . . . left*] i.e. not a drop of wine left.
119.3. *Song*] Locke's score shows that the song was sung by a soprano, with lines
131–4 repeated as chorus. See Appendix I.
122. *bind*] make captive.
129. *Death's . . . emissaries*] In Ogilby's 'Of Cupid and Death', Plague, War and
Famine are named as Death's companions.
132. *quaint*] ingenious.
133–4.] an allusion to the familiar mythological conjunction of love and death.

3.0.1.] In Locke's score, a galliard was played before the Chamberlain's entry.
5. *his train*] his attendants.

I thank heaven he's departed. I slept not
One wink tonight, nor durst I pray aloud
For fear of waking Death; but he at midnight
Calls for a cup to quench his thirst. A bowl
Of blood I gave him for a morning's draught,   10
And had an ague all the while he drank it.
At parting, in my own defence, and hope
To please him, I desired to kiss his hand,
Which was so cold, o'th'sudden, sir, my mouth
Was frozen up, which, as the case stood   15
Then with my teeth, did me a benefit,
And kept the dancing bones from leaping out.
At length, fearing for ever to be speechless,
I used the strength of both my hands to open
My lips, and now felt every word I spake   20
Drop from it like an icicle.

Host.   This cold
Fit will be over; what said Cupid?

Chamberlain.   He
Was fast asleep.

Host.   The boy went drunk to bed;
Death did not wake him?

Chamberlain. It was not necessary in point of reckoning: 25
Death was as free as any emperor,
And pays all where he comes. Death quits all scores.
I have the *summa totalis* in my pocket;
But he without more ceremony left
The house at morning twilight.   [*A knocking is heard off-stage.*]

Host.   Ha! They knock—   30
Get thee a cup of wine to warm thy entrails.

                              Exit CHAMBERLAIN.

Though Love himself be but a water-drinker,
His train allow themselves rich wines. Your fool
And madman is your only guests to taverns;
And to excess, this licence time affords.   35
When masters pay, their servants drink like lords.

                Enter CHAMBERLAIN.

Chamberlain. Sir, they call for you, Cupid's up and ready,

---

11. drank] Q2; drunk Q1.

11. *ague*] quaking, as in a fever.
14–17.] i.e. kissing Death's cold hand did me good, as it turned out, because my mouth became frozen, preventing my quivering teeth from escaping.
25. *in ... reckoning*] i.e. in terms of preparing their bills.
27. *Death ... scores*] Death settles all bills.
28. summa totalis] sum total, i.e. payment for lodging.
31. *warm thy entrails*] i.e. warm your insides.
35. *this ... affords*] i.e. time affords an excess of opportunities for such licentiousness.

And looks as fresh as if he had known no surfeit
Of virgins' tears, for whose fair satisfaction
He broke his leaden shafts, and vows hereafter   40
To shoot all flames of love into their servants.
There are some music come, to give his godship
Good morrow, so he means to hear one song
And then he takes his progress.
Host.   I attend him.   *Exit.*
Chamberlain. But I have made my own revenge upon him,   45
For the hard-hearted baggage that he sent me;
And Death I have served a trick for all his huffing.
They think not what artillery they carry
Along with them; I have changed their arrows.
How Death will fret to see his fury cozened!   50
But how will Love look pale when he shall find
What a mortality his arrows make
Among the lovers! Let the god look to it,
I have put it past my care, and not expect
To see them again; or should I meet with Death,   55
I shall not fear him now. For Cupid, if
Lovers must only by his arrows fall,
I am safe, for, ladies, I defy you all.   [*Exit.*]

Song

Stay Cupid, whither art thou flying?
Pity the pale lovers dying.   60
They that honoured thee before,
Will no more
At thy altar pay their vows.

Oh, let the weeping virgins strow,
Instead of rose, and myrtle boughs,   65
Sad yew, and funeral cypress now.

Unkind Cupid, leave thy killing,
These are all thy mother's doves;
Oh, do not wound such noble loves,
And make them bleed, that should be billing.   [*Exit.*]   70

---

42. *some music come*] announcing the arrival of a company of musicians.
46. *hard-hearted baggage*] cruel, good-for-nothing woman.
47. *huffing*] arrogance, hectoring behaviour.
50. *cozened*] cheated.
58.1. *Song*] The score shows that the song was sung by a soprano, with lines 64–6 and 67–70 repeated as choral refrains.
64. *strow*] strew.
66. *cypress*] The dense, dark foliage of the cypress was regarded as a symbol of mourning. See Feste's song in *Twelfth Night*, 2.4.
68. *mother's doves*] Venus's innocents. In 'Of Cupid and Death' Cupid 'storms with deadly arrows, myrtle groves / Where perched his mother's doves'.
70. *billing*] kissing.

[FOURTH ENTRY]

The scene is changed into a pleasant garden, a fountain in the midst of it; walks and arbours, delightfully expressed; in diverse places, ladies lamenting over their lovers slain by Cupid, who is discovered flying in the air.

Enter a Lover *playing upon a lute, courting his mistress; they dance.*

Enter NATURE *in a white robe, a chaplet of flowers, a green mantle fringed with gold, her hair loose. They start, and seem troubled at her entrance.*

Nature. Fly, fly my children! Love that should preserve,
    And warm your hearts with kind and active blood,
    Is now become your enemy, a murderer.
    This garden, that was once your entertainment
    With all the beauty of the spring, is now,   5
    By some strange curse upon the shafts of Cupid,
    Designed to be a grave. Look, everywhere
    The noble lovers on the ground lie bleeding,
    By frantic Cupid slain; into whose wounds
    Distracted virgins pour their tears so fast,   10
    That having drained their fountains, they present
    Their own pale monuments. While I but relate
    This story, see, more added to the dead.
    Oh fly and save yourselves! I am your parent,
    Nature, that thus advise you to your safeties.   15

Enter CUPID: *he strikes the* Lover.

    He's come already.
Lover.   Ha! What winter creeps
    Into my heart?
                      [*Exit* CUPID.]
Nature.   He faints; 'tis now too late.
    Some kinder god call back the winged boy,
    And give him eyes to look upon his murders.
    Nature grows stiff with horror of this spectacle;   20
    If it be death to love, what will it be
    When Death itself must act his cruelty?

Enter DEATH.

2. blood] *Q1;* omitted *Q2.*

4.0.3–4. Cupid . . . air] The venue for the masque must have accommodated flying machinery.
0.6. chaplet] garland.
0.7. her hair loose] a sign of grief or distress.
2. *with kind . . . blood*] with gentle, affecting passion.
9. *frantic*] frenzied, mad.
11–12. *they . . . monuments*] i.e. grief causes them to resemble tomb effigies.

And here he comes: what tragedies are next?

Enter [two] old men and women with crutches.

Nature. Two agèd pair; these will be fit for death.
 They can expect but a few minutes more   25
 To wear the heavy burden of their lives,

DEATH *strikes them with his arrow. They, admiring one another, let*
     fall their crutches and embrace. Exit Death.

Nature. Astonishment to Nature! They throw off
 All their infirmities, as young men do
 Their airy upper garments. These were the
 Effects of Cupid's shafts; prodigious change!   30
 I have not patience to behold 'em longer.   *Exit.*

They dance with antic postures, expressing rural courtship. [*Exeunt.*]

Song

 What will it, Death, advance thy name
 Upon cold rocks to waste a flame,
 Or by mistake to throw
 Bright torches into pits of snow?   35
 Thy rage is lost,
 And thy old killing frost.
 With thy arrows thou mayst try
 To make the young or agèd bleed,
 But indeed   40
 Not compel one heart to die.

Chorus

 O Love! O Death! be it your fate
 Before you both repent too late,
 To meet and try
 Upon yourselves your sad artillery.   45
 So Death may make Love kind again,
 Or cruel Death by Love be slain.

---

26. wear] *Q1*; were *Q2*.

---

29. *airy . . . garments*] garments which are thin in texture.
31. *I . . . patience*] i.e. I cannot endure.
31.1. antic] absurd, grotesque.
31.2. *Song*] a song for bass, with lines 42–5 sung in a chorus and lines 46–7 sung
as alto.
32–5.] The suggestion is that Love's arrows (now in the hands of Death) would be
wasted on any but the young.
35. *Bright torches*] an allusion to the torches of Hymen invoked at weddings. Here,
Love's flaming darts.
45. *artillery*] weaponry.
46–7.] Death, having Love's arrows, can rekindle Love's kindness by shooting him.
Love, in turn, can destroy Death with Death's own shaft.

Enter six gentlemen armed as in the field, to fight three against three,
To them DEATH:
he strikes them with his arrow, [he exits] and they, preparing to
charge, meet one another and embrace. They dance.

Song [sung by NATURE]

Change, oh change, your fatal bows,
Since neither knows
The virtue of each other's darts.
Alas, what will become of hearts   50
If it prove
A death to love?
We shall find
Death will be cruel to be kind.   55
For when he shall to armies fly,
Where men think blood too cheap to buy
Themselves a name,
He reconciles them, and deprives
The valiant men of more than lives: 60
A victory, and fame.
Whilst Love, deceived by these cold shafts, instead
Of curing wounded hearts, must kill indeed.

Chorus

Take pity gods! Some ease the world will find,
To give young Cupid eyes, or strike Death blind.   65
Death should not then have his own will
And Love, by seeing men bleed, leave off to kill.
                                    [*Exeunt Omnes.*]

[FIFTH ENTRY]

Enter CHAMBERLAIN *leading two apes.*

Chamberlain. Oh yes, oh yes, oh yes!
    All you that delight to be merry, come see
    My brace of court apes, for a need we be three,

47.4. They dance] In Locke's autograph score for the 1659 production, the dance
is given a specific designation, 'The Hectors' dance'. It was preceded by a suite of airs.
Harris suggests that the dance was given greater prominence in the revival for the
Military Company.

50. *virtue*] power.

55–61.] i.e. Death's arrows will now deprive men on the battlefield of the honour
and renown which they sought to acquire by their death.

5.1–7.] The Chamberlain addresses the audience as though they are at a fair. In
both editions the lines were set in italic type, suggesting that the passage was sung.

3. *court apes*] Apes were fashionable pets at court, as well as providing entertainment at fairs.

for . . . three] i.e. when the need arises (e.g. in a performance) the Chamberlain will
take on the role of a third ape.

I have left my old trade of up and down stairs,
And now live by leading my apes unto fairs.   5
Will you have any sport? Draw your money, be quick, sir,
And then come aloft Jack, they shall show you a trick, sir.
Now am I in my natural condition:
For I was born under a wandering planet,
I durst no longer stay with my old master,   10
For fear Cupid and Death be reconciled
To their own arrows, and so renew with me
Some precious acquaintance.

    Enter DEATH: *he strikes the* CHAMBERLAIN. [*Exit* DEATH.]

                Oh, my heart!
'Twas Death I fear: I am paid then with a vengeance.
My dear apes, do not leave me. Ha! Come near—   15
What goodly shapes they have, what lovely faces!
Ye twins of beauty, where were all those graces
Obscured so long? What cloud did interpose
I could not see before this lip, this nose,
These eyes, that do invite all hearts to woo them,   20
Brighter than stars; ladies' are nothing to them.
O, let me here pay down a lover's duty:
Who is so mad to dote on woman's beauty?
Nature doth here her own complexion spread,
No borrowed ornaments of white and red;   25
These cheeks wear no adulterate mixtures on them
To make them blush as some do: fie upon them!
Look what fair cherries on their lips do grow!
Black cherries, such as none of you can show
That boast your beauties, let me kiss your a—   30

    Enter a Satyr, *that strikes him on the shoulder,*
            and takes away his apes.

What's that? A shot in the shoulder too? Ha!
What will become of me now? O my apes!

30.1. him on the shoulder] Q2; on the him shoulder Q1.

---

   7. *aloft*] up. The Chamberlain alludes to an imaginary wagon or makeshift stage.
   8. *natural condition*] true mode of life.
   9. *born . . . planet*] i.e. born under the influence of a celestial body which creates a disposition to roam widely.
  13. *precious*] costly.
  15–33.] The Chamberlain's absurd passion for his apes recalls Titania's infatuation with Bottom in *A Midsummer Night's Dream.*
  22. *pay down*] perform, discharge.
  26. *adulterate mixtures*] artificial concoctions, i.e. cosmetics.
  30.1. Enter a *Satyr*] It is appropriate that a satyr, a type for lustfulness, should interrupt the Chamberlain in his desire to kiss the ape's arse.

The darlings of my heart are ravished from me.
> *He beckons, and courts them*
> *back with passionate postures.*
No? not yet? nor yet, hard-hearted apes?
I must despair for ever to enjoy them.   35
Despair? That name puts me in mind.
> *He looks in his pocket*
> *and pulls out the halter.*
'Tis here;
Welcome, dear legacy. I see he was
A prophet that bestowed it; how it fits me!
> [*He fits the halter around his neck.*]
As well as if the hangman had took measure.
'Tis honour in some men to fight, and die   40
In their fair ladies' quarrel, and shall I
Be afraid to hang myself in such a cause?
Farewell my pretty apes! When hemp is tied,
Drop tears apace, and I am satisfied.   *Exit.*

> *A dance of the Satyr and apes.*

Upon the sudden a solemn music is heard, and MERCURY *seen descending upon a cloud, at whose approach the others creep in amazed. In a part of the scene, within a bower,* NATURE *discovered sleeping.*

Mercury. Hence ye profane, and take your dwellings up   45
Within some cave that never saw the sun,
Whose beams grow pale and sick to look upon you;
This place be sacred to more noble objects.
> [*Exeunt* Satyr *and apes.*]
And see where Nature, tired with her complaints
To heaven for Death and Cupid's tyranny,   50
Upon a bank of smiling flowers lies sleeping.
Cares, that devour the peace of other bosoms,
Have by an overcharge of sorrow wrought
Her heart into a calm, where every sense
Is bound up in a soft repose and silence;   55
Be her dreams all of me. But to my embassy.   [*Calls to Cupid.*]
Cupid, wheresoe'r thou be,
The gods lay their commands on thee,
In pain of being banished to
The unfrequented shades below   60

44.2. heard] *Q1*; heapd *Q2*.   44.3. others] *This ed.*; other *Q1, Q2*.

33. *ravished*] seized, torn away.
43. *hemp*] rope, i.e. the halter or noose.
44.2. MERCURY] here, messenger of the gods. Cf. Shirley's *Triumph of Beauty*, where Mercury descends to drive away the rowdy shepherds of the anti-masque.
45. *profane*] unholy, sacrilegious beings, i.e. the satyr and apes.
56. *embassy*] mission.
60. *unfrequented shades*] Hades, hell.

At my first summons to appear.
Cupid, Cupid!

Enter CUPID.

Cupid.   I am here.
    What send the gods by Mercury?
Mercury. Thy shame and horror. I remove
    This mist.   *He unblinds him.*
              Now see in every grove   65
    What slaughter thou hast made. All these,
    Fond Cupid, were thy votaries.
    Does not their blood make thine look pale?
    All slain by thee; 'twill not prevail
    To urge mistakes, thy fact appears.   70
    Jove and the gods have bowed their ears
    To groaning Nature, and sent me
    From their high crystal thrones to see
    What blood, like a dire vapour rise,
    Doth spread his wings to blind the eyes   75
    Of heaven and day; and to declare
    Their justice and immortal care
    Over the lower world. But stay—
    Another must his fate obey.   [*Calls to Death.*]
    Death, heretofore the looked for close   80
    To tedious life, the long repose
    To wearied Nature and the gate
    That leads to man's eternal fate:
    I, in the name of every god,
    Command thee from thy dark abode,   85
    As thou wilt fly their wrath, appear
    At my first summons—

Enter DEATH.

Death.   I am here.
Mercury. Nature awake, and with thy sleep
    Shake off the heavy chains that keep
    Thy soul a captive.
Nature.   Mercury?   90
    Or am I still in dreams?
Mercury.   Thy eye

---

69. 'twill not] *This ed.;* 'two'not *Q1, Q2.*   89. off] *Q2;* of *Q1.*

---

65. *unblinds him*] As Harris comments, the previous reference to mist suggests that
Cupid has been blind, not blindfolded.
    67. *Fond*] foolish.
    votaries] devotees.
    69–70. *'twill . . . mistakes*] i.e. it is no excuse to claim it was all a mistake.
    70. *fact*] crime.
    74–6. *What . . . day*] meaning not entirely clear; possibly a pun on blood as sub-
stance and passion: blood, like a deadly vapour, causes havoc.
    89–90. *Shake . . . captive*] i.e. rid yourself of despair.

Take truce with tears. See, much abused
Nature, whom thou hast long accused.
Leave thy wonder, and attend
What the gods by Hermes send.   95
[*To Cupid and Death*] But first I charge you to resign
Your fatal shafts.
Cupid.   Aye, these are mine.   *They change.*
Mercury. Cupid, the gods do banish thee
From every palace. Thou must be
Confined to cottages, to poor   100
And humble cells. Love must no more
Appear in princes' courts; their heart,
Impenetrable by thy dart,
And from softer influence free,
By their own wills must guided be.   105
Cupid. I shall obey.
Mercury.   Death, thou mayst still
Exercise thy power to kill,
With this limit, that thy rage
Presume not henceforth to engage
On persons in whose breast divine   110
Marks of art or honour shine;
Upon these, if thy malice try,
They may bleed, but never die.
These are not to be overcome,
Above the force of age or tomb.   115
Is Nature pleased?
Nature.   The gods are just.
Mercury. To this you both submit?
Cupid and Death.   We must.
Mercury. Ye are dismissed.

                    Exeunt [CUPID and DEATH.]

Nature.   But Mercury,
What satisfaction shall I have
For noble children in the grave,   120
By Cupid slain?
Mercury.   They cannot be
Reduced to live again with thee,

---

92. *Take . . . tears*] make an end of tears.
93. *whom . . . accused*] i.e. Death.
95. *Hermes*] i.e. Mercury. In the *Odyssey*, Hermes is the Guide of Souls.
98–105.] In 'Of Cupid, Death and Reputation', Cupid tells his companions Death and Reputation that he is not to be found 'in prince's courts, nor 'mong the city throngs'; his habitat is a pastoral one amongst shepherds in 'the unfrequented plain'.
115.] i.e. other than by the inevitable consequence of old age.
121–5. *They . . . here*] i.e. as celestial beings they cannot be, nor should they be, recalled to mortal shape.
122. *Reduced*] brought back.

And could thy fancy entertain
In what blest seats they now remain,
Thou wouldst not wish them here.
Nature.   Might I   125
With some knowledge bless my eye,
Nature would put on youth.
Mercury.   Then see
Their blest condition.

The scene is changed into Elysium, where the grand masquers, the slain
lovers, appear in glorious seats and habits.

Nature.   Where am I?
The world no such perfection yields.
Mercury. These are the fair Elysian fields.   130

Song [*Within*]

Open blest Elysian grove,
Where an eternal spring of love
Keeps each beauty fair; these shades
No chill dew or frost invades.
Look how the flowers and every tree   135
Pregnant with ambrosia be;
Near banks of violet, springs appear,
Weeping out nectar every tear;
While the once harmonious spheres,
(turnèd all to ears)   140
Now listen to the birds, whose choir
sing every charming accent higher.

Chorus

If this place be not heaven, one thought can make it;
And gods, by their own wonder led, mistake it.

Nature. Oh, who shall guide me hence? Old Nature's sight   145
Grows feeble at the brightness of this glory.

---

131. Elysian] *This ed.;* Elysium *Q1, Q2.*   141. choir] *This ed.;* quire *Q1, Q2.*

123. *fancy*] imagination.
125–7. *Might . . . youth*] If I could only see a vision of this happiness, I (Nature)
would recover the joys of youth (i.e. be content).
128.1. *Elysium*] the abode of the blessed after death.
128.2. *in glorious seats*] seated in splendour.
130.1. *Song*] The score shows that the song was for soprano and bass; at the top
of the page is a note: 'This song within during which Nature views, listens and admires.'
136. *ambrosia*] food of the gods and immortals.
138. *nectar*] drink of the gods.
139. *once . . . spheres*] a reference to the harmonious sound believed to be produced
by the motion of the spheres, i.e. the concentric heavenly globes thought in the Renaissance to revolve around the earth. Presumably even their harmonies are stilled by the
song of the birds of Elysium.
142. *accent*] melody.

Mercury. I will be Nature's conduct.
Nature. Mercury, be ever honoured.   *Exeunt.*

The grand dance.

Enter MERCURY.

Mercury. Return, return, you happy men,
    To your own blessèd shades again,   150
    Lest staying long, some new desire,
    In your calm bosoms raise a fire.
    Here are some eyes, whose every beam
    May your wandering hearts inflame,
    And make you forfeit your cool groves,   155
    By being false to your first loves.
    Like a perfuming gale o'er flowers,
    Now glide again to your own bowers.

The masquers retreated, the curtain falls.

Finis

158.1. The masquers retreated] *Q1; not in Q2.* the *Q1;* The *Q2.*

---

147. *conduct*] guide.

148.1. The grand dance] i.e. of slain lovers. In the score is the stage direction: 'The slain lovers descend and dance the grand dance following.' Given that this was not a court occasion, it is improbable that members of the audience would have participated in the final dance as was the convention in the earlier masques. It is possible that the grand masquers, the slain lovers, were played by pupils of Luke Channen.

153–6.] i.e. you may be seduced by others ('some eyes') which would cause you to lose your state of eternal happiness in Elysium.

157–8.] According to the 1659 score, these lines were repeated as a grand chorus. The score includes the direction: 'The Grand Chorus with all the voices and instruments during which the slain lovers ascend their thrones and the curtain falls'.

INTRODUCTION

The presentation in May 1656 of William Davenant's quasi-dramatic dialogue *The First Day's Entertainment at Rutland House by Declamations and Music after the Manner of the Ancients* marked a small but significant development in the cultural life of the Republic, in so far as its performance was countenanced by the Council of State. Admittedly, the spectacle was on a small scale, with an attendant audience of little over a hundred at the theatre constructed in the semi-private venue of Davenant's own home, but it served to re-activate public performance. The debate between Diogenes, the cynic, and Aristophanes, the playwright, about the morality and social viability of theatre was an apt beginning for the new drama. At least within the dialogue, the argument for theatrical representation was won or unopposed, and Davenant was able to take the bold step in his next work, *The Siege of Rhodes*, of abandoning debate and re-presenting dramatic narrative in the form of musical theatre.

Considering the limitations of its staging, *The Siege of Rhodes* is indeed an ambitious drama. Davenant integrates two quite different stories and draws on a range of materials. The most famous and last of the sieges of Rhodes by the Turks under Solyman the Magnificent in 1522 had been recounted in considerable military detail by Richard Knolles in *The General History of the Turks*;[1] from this account Davenant focused upon key moments of the Turks' massive assault on the city and its heroic repulse by the international Knights Hospitallers under the Grand Master Philippe Villiers, before the Rhodians were finally forced to surrender.[2] In military terms the siege was represented as the triumph of the Christian few over the overwhelming hordes of Turks: the barracks had been manned by knights who, though grossly outnumbered, managed to hold out against the ferocity of Solyman's forces for a prolonged period. Both Knolles and Davenant emphasize the internecine struggles of the other European powers which distracted them from coming to the Rhodians' aid, a situation which might have carried associations with the failure of the European monarchies to offer military aid to the royalist cause during the civil wars. Davenant, however, departs from his source in exaggerating the tenacity of the English in the defence of their bulwark. In the second entry, Alphonso praises the dauntless courage displayed by the English, whereas in Knolles's account the English bulwark was the first to be undermined by Turkish artillery. Such a celebration of English valour anticipates a similarly dubious glorification of English military exploits figured in *The Cruelty of the Spaniards in Peru* and *The History of Sir Francis Drake*.

With the events of the siege Davenant interweaves the heroic love story of Ianthe and the Sicilian duke Alphonso and, through these protagonists, foregrounds the debate between love and honour which figured so strongly in mid-seventeenth-century drama. When the Turkish fleet is first sighted, Alphonso proclaims that honour will not permit him to leave Rhodes, where he has been temporarily residing in preparation for the annual joust. Ianthe sets out to be reunited with him, but her ship, carrying money and supplies, is intercepted by Solyman's fleet. At this juncture, details are represented from *The Tragedy of Soliman and Perseda*, ascribed to Thomas Kyd, 'wherein is laid open love's constancy, fortune's inconstancy and death's triumph'. When Rhodes is sacked by Solyman's forces in Kyd's play, Perseda is taken prisoner and brought before Solyman. Solyman struggles with his love for Erastus (Davenant's Alphonso), whom he has befriended, and his desire for Perseda. In Davenant's version, there is no display of antipathy toward the 'infidel'; in contrast, the character of Solyman subverts notions of stereotypical alterity. This is not the bloody and uncivil Turk of Elizabethan drama,[3] or the despot who murders his son in Fulke Greville's *Mustapha*. Instead, Solyman, struck by Ianthe's beauty but behaving with perfect honour, offers her and Alphonso safe passage from the siege. Alphonso's jealousy, like that of Othello and Leontes, has no foundation, but can be dispelled only by Ianthe's expressed readiness to die for love. In Kyd's play, on the other hand, Solyman acts the tyrant and, out of lust for Perseda, orders the murder of Erastus, now governor of Rhodes. Davenant, however, is more concerned with moral abstractions and he has shaped the dramatic conflicts in order to figure Neoplatonic ideas of love and beauty and codes of honour which had featured in Caroline drama, particularly in the plays associated with the circle of Henrietta Maria, and which were to predominate in plays by Dryden.

The siege of Rhodes and the romance of Alphonso and Ianthe did not represent purely incidental material for the revival of drama during the Commonwealth: the questions explored in the drama are those which impinged upon post-civil-war mentalities. In the fourth entry Ianthe tries to persuade Alphonso to accept Solyman's offer of safe passage to Sicily, which Alphonso resolutely refuses on the ground that he must participate in the defence of Rhodes. Ianthe argues that they have become embroiled in the affairs of Rhodes through mere chance; Alphonso retorts that their situation has been decreed by providence and so they are 'heaven's prisoners'. The debate remains unresolved, with Alphonso refusing to accept Ianthe's response that Solyman and his proffered protection may equally be part of the providential design. Ideas of providence dominated the language of both Puritans and Royalists during the civil wars and their aftermath.[4] The victory over royalist forces and the establishment of the Commonwealth were seen as divinely ordained, while Cromwell repeatedly insisted that his actions were providentially determined. Equally, a belief that their lost cause and the eventual restoration of the monarchy were part of the divine plan offered consolation to the defeated Royalists. When Ianthe protests, ''Twas fortune that engaged you in this war' and Alphonso replies, ''Twas providence', there are stark reflections of contemporary beliefs and rationalizations concerning the upheavals of the previous decade.

We can assume that there would assuredly have been heightened interest in the dramatic concerns of the first play to be performed officially and publicly in fourteen years. In the action and in the motivations of the central characters—Solyman, Ianthe and Alphonso—we can see obliquely represented various dynamics of the civil wars. The English civil wars had been wars of sieges. The graphic account of the siege of Rhodes, including details of munitions and military strategies, is not so far removed from recent events at the sieges of Colchester, Newark and Bristol. During the first civil war, Davenant had been Lieutenant General of Ordnance under the Earl of Newcastle[5] and his knowledge of military apparatus is conveyed in the language of assault and defence. Certainly, there is a suggestive analogy between the plight of the beleaguered chivalric Knights Hospitaller and that of defeated Royalists. The power of Solyman, who commands the fate of the Rhodians, evokes that of the Cromwell of Marvell's 'Horatian Ode'. Marvell had pronounced of Cromwell in 1651, ''Tis madness to resist or blame / The force of angry heaven's flame.' Davenant has Pirrhus, chief adviser to Solyman, similarly allude to Solyman's irresistible might in providential terms: 'They are not foes, but rebels, who withstand / The power that does their fate command.' As commentators have noted, however, it is in its representation of the romantic love of Alphonso and Ianthe and its figuring of the relationship of Charles I and his Queen, Henrietta Maria, that the work is most closely engaged with recent events. Ianthe's participation in the conflict, and in particular the selling of her jewels in support of the Rhodian cause, evokes quite unambiguously the actions of Henrietta Maria, who in 1642 wrote to Charles that she had pledged, or pawned, jewels which he had given to her and others which she had bought herself in order to raise 'a pretty considerable sum, to commence our design'.[6] When Ianthe arrives at Rhodes, the Admiral praises her loyalty and beneficence, all the more apparent because the Western powers have failed to respond to their plight:

> Look here, ye Western monarchs, look with shame,
> Who fear not a remote, though common, foe;
> The cabinet of one illustrious dame
> Does more than your exchequers joined did do.

> (3.92–5)

The use of the term 'cabinet' to denote the receptacle for Ianthe's jewels evokes the most famous cabinet in the 1650s, that of the executed King, which had been captured by the parliamentarians after the battle of Naseby. This contained letters which had been sent by the Queen in her efforts to solicit foreign aid, together with copies of letters from the

King; the collection of correspondence was published in 1645 with a hostile commentary.[7] As messenger from the Earl of Newcastle to Henrietta Maria during the early stages of the first civil war and, briefly, emissary to the Queen,[8] Davenant was in touch with the emotional dynamics of the relationship between the King and Queen and it might be surmised that these are reflected in the depiction of Ianthe and Alphonso. Ianthe cautions Alphonso (Third Entry) that his extravagant reaction to her conduct in the conflict is jeopardizing her reputation and argues instead her own steadfast loyalty: 'Since I would here before, or with you fall.' In the same way, Henrietta Maria had written to Charles, 'I wish to share all your fortune, and participate in your troubles, as I have done in your happiness, provided it be with honour and in your defence', and chided him for listening to those who would damage her good name: 'I confess that I thought myself the most wretched creature in the world, excepting you, for my reputation will ever remain to me, amongst honest people, and yours would be lost.'[9] The relationship of Alphonso and Ianthe is likewise represented in terms of love, honour and reputation. That such parallels are not coincidental is substantiated by the fact that when Davenant enlarged the play prior to the production of 2 *Siege of Rhodes*,[10] one of the additional scenes depicts Ianthe entering with two women bearing open caskets of jewels. It may be conjectured, however, that in 1656 Davenant would have avoided such explicit figuration of Henrietta Maria in Ianthe's role when theatrical performance awaited sanction.

A persuasive case has been made for Davenant's avoidance of national conflicts in *The Siege of Rhodes* and his other Commonwealth dramas; instead, it is argued, he seeks to explore questions of authority and government by dramatizing international crusades.[11] But the common dramatic strategy of displacement does not necessarily imply avoidance of issues which are relevant to an audience at a particular time. It can be argued that in *The Siege of Rhodes* Davenant is weaving a royalist fantasy narrative. In the stasis of the closure of Part I and the curtailment of the siege, in providing for Ianthe and Alphonso to be reunited and the Rhodians undefeated, Davenant is rewriting history as romance, and with the romance's deferred ending. Davenant rejects both Kyd's tragic closure, which might have made *The Siege of Rhodes* more consistent with the intense finales of continental opera, and Knolles's account of the Rhodians' surrender.

This open-endedness is complemented by multivalency of meaning. Unlike Kyd's sensual and vengeful Turk and Knolles's cruel, exploitative imperialist sultan, Davenant's Solyman is civilised and honourable: 'He seems in civil France,' declares Ianthe of her benefactor. Such an image of Solyman may be a reflection of the availability of more discriminating accounts of the Orient by English travellers of the 1630s,[12] but representation may have been conditioned by the anticipation that the opera's historical setting would be seen as metaphorical. Davenant must surely have been aware that *The Siege of Rhodes* would be eagerly decoded, and the achievement of the piece is that it accommodates a satisfactory decoding on both sides. The English as a military nation are personated as valiant and united in defence of Rhodes against the infidel. Yet there is also a figuring of national self-division through displacement. The chivalric Rhodian knights display fearless tenacity in the face of the military might of their opponent. They are inspired by the active love and honour of the royal Sicilian couple, Alphonso and Ianthe. But this cavalier/royalist idealization is matched by an equivalent idealization of the Turkish foe. Apart from a few lines of jingoistic song, the articulation of religious and racial difference is suppressed, particularly in the representation of Solyman as a man of honour. His military superiority is tacitly acknowledged, while effectively marginalized by the triumph of love and honour to which he contributes. The emotive courtly aesthetic thus sidelines, albeit temporarily, the threat of military power, which is perceived as providential, and hence ultimately irresistible.

The Siege of Rhodes was published prior to performance. This enabled advertisement of the production to circulate, but it was also in line with continental operatic practice that the libretto should already be available to an audience at the first performance. The work was entered in the Stationers' Register on 27 August 1656, where it is, interestingly, designated as a masque. That Davenant may have been nervous about publication is suggested by the fact that he sent a copy of the piece for approval to Bulstrode Whitelocke, a member of the Council of State, and subsequently Cromwell's ambassador to Sweden and occasional Speaker of the House of Commons. Whitelocke's life and career illustrate the argument forcibly made by Margot Heinemann for the Stuart period that parliamentary Puritanism was far from univocal in its opposition to the drama.[13] Whitelocke had been a former Master of the Revels at Middle Temple and a member of the committee responsible for the performance of Shirley's The Triumph of Peace by all four Inns of Court in February 1634.[14] Davenant's approach to Whitelocke, an habitué of the pre-1642 theatre, may be seen as an attempt to gain the active support of moderate Puritans for his reformed theatre. In his note accompanying the newly published entertainment, Davenant evokes Whitelocke's 'ancient relation to the muses', while attesting to the modest character of his composition:

> My Lord, when I consider the nicety of the times, I fear it may draw a curtain between your Lordship and our opera; therefore I have presumed to send your Lordship, hot from the press, what we mean to represent; making your Lordship my supreme judge, though I despair to have the honour of inviting you to be a spectator. I do not conceive the perusal of it worthy of any part of your Lordship's leisure, unless your ancient relation to the muses make you not unwilling to give a little entertainment to poetry; though in so mean a dress as this.[15]

There is no evidence that Whitelocke responded, although he did note the publication and innovative genre of The Siege of Rhodes, recording drily in his journal, 'Sir William Davenant printed his opera; notwithstanding the nicety of the times.'

The performance of *The Siege of Rhodes*, which is believed to have taken place shortly after its publication, has been regarded as a landmark in English theatre for its introduction of operatic features into the drama.[16] In fact, in his *Ariadne Deserted by Theseus*, Richard Flecknoe had already published a drama which was intended to be sung in recitative. In his preface to the work, moreover, Flecknoe claimed that, even before Italian opera had become influential, he had commended the recitative form to Charles I in contrast to the kind of popular drama merely 'patched up with songs of different subjects'. Possibly because he was more of an entrepreneur in his use of domestic space for performance, however, it was Davenant rather than Flecknoe who was able to accomplish the actual production of operatic form.

The score of *The Siege of Rhodes*, a collaboration between a number of composers including Henry Lawes, Henry Cooke and Matthew Locke, has not survived, but from Davenant's address to the reader and the title page we know that when the work was produced, first at Rutland House and later at the Cockpit in Drury Lane, it was performed in the Italian recitative style, with instrumental music between each of the five entries. From the dramatic text it would seem that the piece comprises duets and trios. Ianthe's final speech in the fourth entry was probably sung as a lament and the concluding dialogue between Ianthe and Alphonso approximates to the final love duet which had become a feature of baroque opera. Nevertheless, there is no sustained comparison of stylistic and formal elements, or of subject matter, with Monteverdi's *Orfeo* (1607) or *L'incoronazione di Poppea* (1643), both of which might be considered operatic precedents. The subject matter of Italian opera, imitated by Flecknoe in *Ariadne*, was drawn from familiar myths and later classical history, whereas the roots of *The Siege of Rhodes* are in the Elizabethan drama and the early modern fascination with the Turks and the Ottoman empire.[17] There is nothing in Davenant's text to evoke the great arias or voluptuous finales of the Monteverdi opera. It is notable that *The Siege of Rhodes* seems always to have been associated with its librettist and not, as with Monteverdi's operas, primarily with the composer. Clearly, the musical element was subordinate to the drama, a point which appears to be borne out by the fact that, when the entertainment was revived at the Restoration, Davenant reverted to the spoken text, retaining only the *entr'acte* instrumental music, already a familiar feature of Jacobean and Caroline private theatre performance.

While the element of sung drama was undoubtedly innovatory in England in 1656, many of the stylistic elements of *The Siege of Rhodes* derive from the court masque. In the masque, music was already an expressive as well as an incidental medium. It was Davenant who had composed *Salmacida Spolia* for the Caroline court, a work devised by Inigo Jones and the last masque performed before the civil wars.[18] The text of *The Siege of Rhodes* which Davenant prepared for publication in 1656, with its scenic descriptions and division into entries rather than acts, typographically resembles a pared-down version of a printed masque text. This affiliation with an aesthetic form favoured by the Stuart court was not, of course, one which Davenant would have wished to pursue. In his address to the reader, Davenant instead draws attention to his innovatory use of recitative, hitherto 'unpractised' in England, but 'of great reputation amongst other nations'. The implication is that, under the auspices of the new regime, Davenant is attempting to ensure that theatrical representation is no longer perceived as reflecting the tastes of an insular clientele.

The identification with continental operatic practice might, however, have been enhanced by the presence of the proscenium arch and by the use of changing scenes. The advertisement of the play as a 'representation by the art of perspective in scenes' indicates the importance which Davenant attached to scenery as a medium for the drama. This was, of course, a familiar feature in the production of court masques, although not in the public theatres. Scenes for *The Siege of Rhodes* were designed by John Webb, who was the nephew and pupil of Inigo Jones, Surveyor of the Works to James I and Charles I. Webb claimed that, through Jones's tutelage, he had been raised 'on the study of architecture, as well that which relates to building as for masques, triumphs and the like'.[19] He had worked with Jones on scenic devices for performances at the Cockpit in Drury Lane and at court, and he was thus well equipped to design shutters and relieve scenes[20] for the small stage at Rutland House, which were later transferred to the Cockpit. Webb's drawings have survived and, together with Davenant's detailed descriptions of the scene at the opening of each entry, they enable us to reconstruct technically and pictorially the visual dimension of *The Siege of Rhodes*.

The set comprised a frontispiece six inches back from the front of the stage, consisting of columns and a decorated frieze (figure 4). This accommodated a curtain which, since the stage action was continuous, was raised and dropped only at the beginning and end of the performance. In comparison with the elaborate and sumptuous scene changes and machinery of the masque, the scenic devices for *The Siege of Rhodes* were simple. The three pairs of flat wings depicting a rocky coast remained fixed throughout the performance; only the back shutters, which ran on grooves, facilitated changes of scene. Three pictorial representations are described by Davenant and sketched by Webb (figures 5–7): Rhodes in prosperity (First Entry); Rhodes under siege (Second, Third and Fourth Entries); and an assault on the town at the English bulwark (Fifth Entry). In addition, when the back shutters were opened, two relieve scenes depicting Solyman's pavilion and the building of the castle on Mount Philermus were displayed during the third and fourth entries respectively (figures 8 and 9).

As Richard Southern has stated, Webb was not attempting a naturalistic setting, but furnishing Davenant with generalized pictorial back-

4   Frontispiece and wings, *The Siege of Rhodes* (design by John Webb).

5   'Scene Rhodes: a shutter' (design by John Webb).

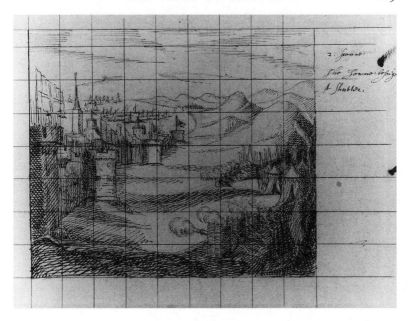

6 'The town beseiged: a shutter' (design by John Webb).

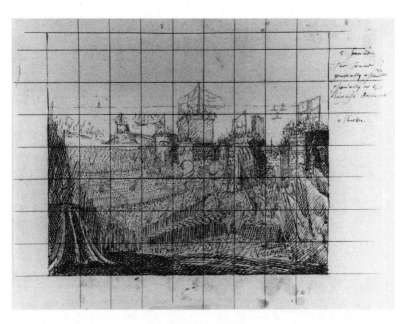

7 'The town generally assaulted, especially in the English bulwark: a shutter' (design by John Webb).

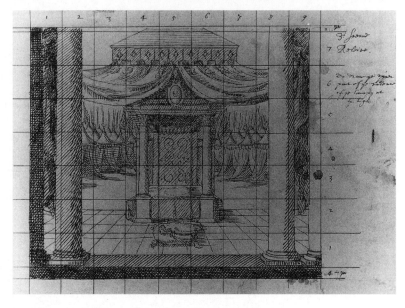

8   Solyman's pavilion: a relieve (design by John Webb).

9   Building of the castle on Mount Philermus: a relieve (design by John Webb).

grounds.[21] The scenery served as a counterpoint to the plot, its purpose decorative rather than illusionistic. Davenant had defended the use of scenes in *The First Day's Entertainment* against Diogenes's claim that they were only 'useless visions of imagination' by arguing that, in functional terms, they provided the quickest route to an audience's understanding and that, aesthetically, they provided 'some variety of experience by a short journey of the sight'.[22] The pictorial setting was thus a significant element in a drama which, in its concentration on moments of heroic crisis, could not afford to be rhetorically descriptive. Webb's scenes, apart from their aesthetic value, were important in conveying to the audience the quick turn of event and location.

The evident practical constraints on the first production of *The Siege of Rhodes* would have made it a kind of chamber work not unlike the early intimate performance of Monteverdi's *Orfeo*. Davenant ruefully acknowledges in his address to the reader that, because of the small cast and confines of space, he has been obliged to compress the drama 'to a small narration'. The strains of presenting so much narrative material in short compass are apparent at one moment at least in the drama. In the final entry, the Admiral refers to a letter written by Ianthe which has evoked feelings of deep remorse in Alphonso. This dramatic incident appears only in this one reference and its brief inclusion indicates a tension between the imperatives of a compressed plot and the narrative demands of the unfolding drama. When Davenant enlarged the text for the 1663 version he not only introduced additional scenes and characters but expanded by several speeches the final exchange between Ianthe and Alphonso leading to their reconciliation (see Appendix 2). The addition enhances the emotional experience of the scene, which was so compressed in the earlier productions as to obscure meaning.

A NOTE ON THE TEXT

I Siege of Rhodes was first published in 1656 (Q1). Another issue appeared in the same year (Q1a), printed in part from the same setting of type, but with additional paratextual material containing names of musicians. A second edition appeared in 1659 (Q2), with the detail on the title page that the work had been performed at the Cockpit in Drury Lane. In 1663, an enlarged version, reusing sheets printed in 1659 and inserting three half-sheets and one single leaf into Q2, was published. This was reprinted in the same year (Q3).[23] With the expanded version was published a 'second part'. Both parts were included in the *Works* (F) of 1673. *1 and 2 Siege of Rhodes* were edited by Ann-Marie Hedbäck (Studia Anglistica Upsaliensia, 14, Uppsala, 1973). Hedbäck's text is a composite one based on Q1, but incorporating the additions of Q3.

This edition has as copy text the quarto of 1656, which was almost certainly set up from Davenant's manuscript and is the text which is closest to the performance at Rutland House. It has been collated with

Q3, F and Hedbäck's edition. Substantive changes in Q2 noted by Hedbäck are recorded in the collation. The additions to the entertainment when *The Siege of Rhodes* became a spoken text and closer to rhetorical drama appear separately in Appendix 2.

NOTES

1 Richard Knolles, *The General History of the Turks*, fourth edition (1631), pp. 580–93.
2 See H. J. A. Sire, *The Knights of Malta* (New Haven and London, 1994), pp. 57–8.
3 See Nabil Matar, *Islam in Britain 1558–1685* (Cambridge, 1998), pp. 50–63.
4 See Blair Worden, 'Providence and Politics in Cromwellian England', *Past and Present*, 108 (1985), 55–99.
5 For these details of Davenant's career, see Alfred Harbage, *Sir William Davenant: Poet Venturer, 1606–1668* (Philadelphia, 1935), p. 89.
6 See *Letters of Queen Henrietta Maria*, edited by M. A. E. Green (London, 1857), pp. 112–13.
7 See Lois Potter, *Secret Rites and Secret Writing: Royalist Literature 1641–1660* (Cambridge, 1989), pp. 58–62.
8 See Mary Edmond, *Rare Sir William Davenant* (Manchester, 1987), pp. 99–100.
9 *Letters*, p. 118.
10 The enlarged *1 Siege of Rhodes*, with *2 Siege of Rhodes*, was not published until 1663, although *2 Siege of Rhodes* was entered in the Stationers' Register on 30 May 1659. W. W. Greg has claimed that unsold stock of the 1659 edition was brought into agreement with the new enlarged text incorporated in the joint edition of 1663. See *Bibliography of English Drama* (Oxford, 1951; reprinted 1970), 4 vols, 4, p. 870.
11 See S. J. Wiseman, 'History Digested: Opera and Colonialism in the 1650s' in *Literature and the English Civil War*, edited by Thomas Healy and Jonathan Sawday (Cambridge, 1990), pp. 189–204.
12 See Samuel C. Chew, *The Crescent and the Rose: Islam and England during the Renaissance* (1937; reprinted New York, 1965), p. 43. Henry Blount described the 'incredible civility' of Turks to foreign visitors in *Voyage into the Levant* (1636), p. 75.
13 Margot Heinemann, *Puritanism and Theatre: Thomas Middleton and Opposition Drama under the Early Stuarts* (Cambridge, 1980), pp. 18–26.
14 Martin Butler, *Theatre and Crisis* (Cambridge, 1984), pp. 134–5.
15 *The Diary of Bulstrode Whitelocke, 1605–1675*, edited by Ruth Spalding (Oxford, 1990), p. 449.
16 See, for example, Eric White, *A History of English Opera* (London, 1983), pp. 65–6.
17 See Matar, *Islam in Britain*, pp. 11–16.
18 See Martin Butler, 'Politics and the Masque: *Salmacida Spolia*', in *Literature and the English Civil War*, pp. 59–75.
19 See John Orrell, *The Theatres of Inigo Jones and John Webb* (Cambridge, 1985), p. 15.
20 Webb labelled two of his drawings as 'relieve' scenes, that is, scenes which were flat and cut out round the edge. See Richard Southern, *Changeable Scenery: Its Origin and Development in the British Theatre* (London, 1952), p. 63.
21 Southern, *Changeable Scenery*, p. 114.
22 *The First Day's Entertainment at Rutland House* (1656), p. 37.
23 For details of the printing history of *The Siege of Rhodes* see Ann-Marie Hedbäck, 'The Printing of *The Siege of Rhodes*', *Studia Neophilologica* 45(1973), 68–79.

THE SIEGE OF RHODES

Made a Representation by the Art of Perspective in Scenes,
And the story sung in Recitative Music

At the back part of Rutland House in the upper end of
Aldergate Street, London.

Printed by J. M. for Henry Herringman, and are to be sold at his shop, at the sign of
the Anchor, on the Lower-Walk in the New-Exchange, 1656.

I may receive disadvantage by this address designed for excuses for it will too hastily put you in mind that errors are not far off when excuses are at hand. This refers to our Representation and some may be willing to be led to find the blemishes of it; but would be left to their own conduct to discover the beauties, if there be any. Yet I may forewarn you that the defects which I intend to excuse are chiefly such as you cannot reform but only with your purse: that is, by building us a larger room, a design which we began and shall not be left for you to finish, because we have observed that many who are liberal of their understanding when they would issue it out towards discovery of imperfections, have not always money to expend in things necessary towards the making up of perfection. 5

It has been often wished that our scenes (we have obliged ourselves to the variety of five changes according to the ancient dramatic distinctions made for time) had not been confined to eleven foot in height, and about fifteen in depth, including the places of passage reserved for the music. This is so narrow an allowance for the fleet of Solyman the Magnificent, his army, the island of Rhodes and the varieties attending the siege of the city that I fear you will think we invite you to such a contracted trifle as that of the Caesars carved upon a nut. 10 15 20

As these limits have hindered the splendour of our scene, so we are like to give no great satisfaction in the quantity of our argument, which is in story very copious; but shrinks to a small narration here, because

TO THE READER] Q_1, Q_2; To the Right Honourable the Earl of Clarendon Q_3, F.

---

3. *Representation*] from the Italian *rappresentazione* meaning performance. See Nash, 'For coming from Venice . . . it was my happe . . . to light in fellowship with that famous Francatrip' Harlicken, who, perceiving me to be an English man by my habit and speech, asked me many particulars of the order and manner of our plays, which he termed by the name of representations.' Nash, *An Almond for a Parrot*, McKerrow, III. 342.

13. *scenes*] slides painted in perspective at the back and sides of the stage as a decorative adjunct and to note progress of mood and some change of location in the play.

14–15. *five changes . . . time*] an allusion to Horace's five-act division, 'Let no play be either shorter or longer than five acts' (*Ars poetica*, 189).

16–17. *places . . . music*] The position of the musicians depended upon the venue. In the Cockpit, the musicians could have been in a temporarily constructed room above the stage, supported by a horizontal grid from which were suspended cloud borders. The domestic setting of Rutland House did not allow for such a construction, hence Davenant's complaint that the stage area was limited—the musicians would necessarily have occupied some of the stage, though screened from the audience by the standing scene which allowed a passage at the rear of the stage.

20. *contracted trifle*] miniscule morsel.

19–21. *we invite . . . nut*] Davenant compares the compression of the historical events in the drama to the task of recording the exploits of the early Roman emperors on a nut shell.

we could not convey it by more than seven persons, being constrained 25
to prevent the length of recitative music as well as to conserve, without
incumbrance, the narrowness of the place. Therefore you cannot expect
the chief ornaments belonging to a history dramatically digested into
turns and counter-turns, to double walks and interweavings of design.

This is expressed to forbid your excess of expectation; but we must 30
take care not to deter you from the hope of some satisfaction, for that
were not only to hang out no bush, but likewise to shut up our doors.
Therefore, as you have heard what kind of excellencies you should not
expect, so I will in brief (I hope without vanity) give you encouragement
by telling you there are some things at least excusable which you may 35
resolve to meet.

We conceive it will not be unacceptable to you if we recompense the
narrowness of the room by containing in it so much as could be
conveniently accomplished by art and industry, which will not be
doubted in the scenes by those who can judge that kind of illustration 40
and know the excellency of Mr John Webb, who designed and ordered
it. The music was composed, and both the vocal and instrumental is
exercised, by the most transcendent of England in that Art, and perhaps
not unequal to the best masters abroad; but being recitative, and
therefore unpractised here, though of great reputation amongst other 45
nations, the very attempt of it is an obligation to our own. The story
represented (which will not require much apology because it expects
but little praise) is heroical, and notwithstanding the continual hurry
and busy agitations of a hot siege, is (I hope) intelligibly conveyed to
advance the characters of virtue in the shapes of valour and conjugal 50
love. And though the main argument hath but a single walk, yet perhaps
the movings of it will not seem unpleasant. You may inquire, being a
reader, why in an heroic argument my numbers are so often diversified

---

25. *more . . . persons*] This means that soloists in the cast at the end of the text
would have doubled as the chorus.

25-6. *being . . . music*] Because of the restrictions on the scale of the production, the
recitative cannot be expanded.

26. *recitative music*] declamatory speech-like singing, free in rhythm, serving for dialogue and as exposition in opera. As in early opera, the solo voice would have been
accompanied by a simple chordal accompaniment improvised above a single bass line
by one or more instruments.

27-9. *Therefore . . . design*] see Richard Flecknoe, 'For the plot, I have taken a middle
way betwixt the French and the English, the one making it too plain, and the other too
confused and intrigued. I imagining one of these pieces . . . as a pleasant garden composed
of diverse walks, with variety and uniformity so mixt.' *Love's Dominion* (1654), A7r.

28. *chief ornaments*] embellishments, full grandeur of events.

29. *turns . . . design*] complications of plot and double plot structure.

32. *bush*] the sign-board of a tavern.

41. *Mr John Webb*] nephew and pupil of Inigo Jones who had been Surveyor of the
Works to James I and Charles I.

43. *transcendent*] pre-eminent.

46. *obligation . . . own*] i.e. a service for which our nation owes gratitude.

51. *single walk*] having no sub-plot.

53. *numbers . . . diversified*] parts or divisions of the work are metrically varied.

and fall into short fractions, considering that a continuation of the usual
length of English verse would appear more heroical in reading. But   55
when you are an auditor you will find that in this, I rather deserve
approbation than need excuse: for frequent alterations of measure
(which cannot be so unpleasant to him that reads as troublesome to
him that writes) are necessary to recitative music for variation of airs.
If what I have said be taken for excuses, I have my intent, because   60
excuses are not always signs of error, but are often modest explanations
of things that might otherwise be mistaken. But I have said so much to
vindicate myself from having occasion to be excused for the poem that
it brings me, at last, to ask pardon for the length of the epistle.

August 17   William Davenant
1656

---

54. *fractions*] fragments.

54–5. *usual . . . reading*] i.e. blank verse, characteristic of English heroic and tragic
drama, might seem to the reader a more appropriate medium.

55–9. *But . . . airs*] Changes in metrical period are essential for the variations in
melody of recitative music.

63. *poem*] applied to any composition which has the qualities of poetry.

THE PERSONS REPRESENTED

SOLYMAN, *the Magnificent*
VILLERIUS, *Grand Master of Rhodes*
ALPHONSO, *a Sicilian Duke*
IANTHE, *Wife to Alphonso*
ADMIRAL, *of Rhodes*   5
PIRRHUS, *Bassa*
MUSTAPHA, *Bassa*
[Soldiers of several nations
Chorus of women
Chorus of men and women   10
Chorus of wives
Two mutes (attendants)]

The Scene: Rhodes

The Persons Represented] *Other characters included* in *Q3 and* F: Rustan, Bassa; Haly, Eunuch Bassa; High Marshal of Rhodes; Roxolana, wife to Solyman; women, attendants to Roxolana; women, attendants to Ianthe; four pages, attendants to Roxolana.

THE PERSONS REPRESENTED] In *Q3* and *F* the additional characters above appear in the First, Third, Fourth and Fifth Entries. See Appendix 2.

1. *SOLYMAN*] Fourth Emperor of the Turks, 1520–66.

2. *VILLERIUS*] Philippe Villiers de l'Isle Adam, elected Grand Master of the Knights of Rhodes, 1521.

6. *PIRRHUS*] chief counsellor to Solyman.

Bassa] bashaw, earliest form of pasha, a military commander and officer of high rank, also provincial governor.

7. *MUSTAPHA*] instigated with Solyman the expedition against Rhodes.

8. *Soldiers of several nations . . . Chorus of wives*] Since Davenant refers in the address 'To the Reader' to the narration being conveyed by no more than seven people, the cast members must have doubled as the various choruses who sing at the end of each entry.

The ornament which encompassed the scene consisted of several columns of gross rustic work, which bore up a large frieze. In the middle of the frieze was a compartment, wherein was written Rhodes. The compartment was supported by diverse habiliments of war intermixed with the military ensigns of those several nations who were famous for 5
defence of that island, which were the French, Germans and Spaniards, the Italians, Avergnois and English. The renown of the English valour made the grand master Villerius to select their station to be most frequently commanded by himself. The principal enrichment of the frieze was a crimson drapery, whereon several trophies of arms were 10
fixed: those on the right hand representing such as are chiefly in use amongst the western nations, together with the proper cognisance of the order of the Rhodian knights; and on the left, such as are most esteemed in the eastern countries; and on an antique shield, the crescent of the Ottomans. 15

The Scene Before the First Entry

The curtain being drawn up, a lightsome sky appeared, discovering a maritime coast full of craggy rocks and high cliffs, with several verdures naturally growing upon such situations; and, afar off, the true prospect of the city Rhodes, when it was in prosperous estate, with so much view of the gardens and hills about it as the narrowness of the room could 5
allow the scene. In that part of the horizon, terminated by the sea, was represented the Turkish fleet making towards a promontory some few miles distant from the town.

The entry is prepared by instrumental music.

---

4. city] *Q1, Q2*; city of *Q3, F*.

1. ornament . . . scene] embellishment framing the scenic stage.
2. rustic] rough-hewn.
   frieze] horizontal sculptured band between the columns.
3. compartment] a separate section of the design.
4. habiliments] accoutrements.
5. ensigns] standard, emblem.
7. Avergnois] The nobility of the Auvergne, in central France, were prominent amongst the Knights Hospitaller.
12–13. proper . . . knights] distinguishing emblem of the order.
14–15. *crescent . . . Ottomans*] crescent moon, military symbol of the Turkish empire. In the popular imagination of the Renaissance, it often symbolized Islam in general (see Chew, p. 149).

1.2.2. verdures] plants or trees in a green and flourishing state.

FIRST ENTRY

Enter ADMIRAL.

Admiral. Arm, arm, Villerius, arm!   10
    Thou hast no leisure to grow old;
    Those now must feel thy courage warm,
    Who think thy blood is cold.

Enter VILLERIUS.

Villerius. Our admiral from sea?
    What storm transported thee?   15
    Or bringst thou storms that can do more
    Than drive an admiral on shore?
Admiral. Arm, arm, the Bassa's fleet appears.
    To Rhodes his course from Chios steers.
    Her shady wings to distant sight   20
    Spread like the curtains of the night.
    Each squadron thicker and still darker grows;
    The fleet like many floating forests shows.
Villerius. Arm, arm! Let our drums beat
    To all our out-guards, a retreat;   25
    And to our main-guards add
    Files double lined from the parade.
    Send horse to drive the fields;
    Prevent what ripening summer yields.
    To all the foe would save   30
    Set fire, or give a secret grave.
Admiral. I'll to our galleys haste,
    Untackle every mast;
    Hale them within the pier,
    To range and chain them there,   35
    And then behind St Nicholas cliffs
    Shelter our brigants, land our skiffs.

---

15. transported] *Q1*; transporteth, *Q2, Q3, F.*

18. *Bassa's fleet*] the fleet of one of Solyman's provincial governors, probably Mustapha or Pirrhus.

19. *Chios*] an island in the Aegean sea, off the coast of Turkey.

20. *Shady wings*] sails.

22. *squadron*] detachment of warships.

25. *out-guards*] guards at the outpost.

26. *main-guards*] guards within the fortress.

26–7.] i.e. strengthen the principal guard of the city by calling up troops from the general muster.

27. *Files*] columns (of soldiers).

28–30. *Send . . . grave*] i.e. destroy the harvest to deprive the enemy of food and forage.

33. *Untackle*] let loose the ropes.

34. *hale*] fetch.

36. *St Nicholas cliffs*] a haven defended by the Tower of St Nicholas, built on a promontory where once had stood the great Colossus of Rhodes.

37. *brigants*] probably an abbreviation of brigantine, meaning a small boat used for reconnoitring and protecting larger vessels.

    skiffs] small light boats.

Villerius. Our field and bulwark-cannon mount with haste.
 Fix to their blocks their brazen bodies fast,
 Whilst to the foe their iron entrails fly.   40
 Display our colours, raise our standard high!

            Exit ADMIRAL.

      Enter ALPHONSO.

Alphonso. What various noises do mine ears invade
 And have a consort of confusion made?
 The shriller trumpet, and tempestuous drum,
 The deafening clamour from the canon's womb,   45
 Which through the air like sudden thunder breaks,
 Seems calm to soldiers' shouts and women's shrieks.
 What danger, reverend lord, does this portend?
Villerius. Danger begins what must in honour end.
Alphonso. What vizards does it wear?
Villerius.   Such, gentle prince,   50
 As cannot fright, but yet must warn you hence.
 What can to Rhodes more fatally appear
 Than the bright crescents which those ensigns wear?
 Wise emblems that increasing empire show,
 Which must be still in nonage and still grow.   55
 All these are yet but the forerunning van
 Of the prodigious gross of Solyman.
Alphonso. Pale show those crescents to our bloody cross.
 Sink not the western kingdoms in our loss?
 Will not the Austrian Eagle moult her wings,   60
 That long hath hovered o'er the Gallic kings,
 Whose lilies too will wither when we fade,
 And the English lion shrink into a shade?
Villerius. Thou seest not, whilst so young and guiltless too,
 That kings mean seldom what their statesmen do   65

---

38. *bulwark-cannon*] cannon to be fired from the ramparts of the city.
mount] raise.
39. *blocks*] supports for elevating cannon.
40. *iron entrails*] cannon balls.
43. *consort*] miscellany of jarring sounds.
47. *to*] in comparison with.
50. *vizards*] outward appearance.
54. *Wise emblems*] i.e. as if aware of their imperial destiny.
55. *nonage*] early stages of growth.
56. *van*] the foremost detachment of land or naval force.
57. *prodigious gross*] enormous, full fleet.
58. *bloody cross*] emblem of Christendom.
60. *Austrian Eagle*] the eagle, emblem of the Holy Roman Empire and of the Hapsburg Empire.
61.] a reference to the rivalry between the Valois Francis I and the Habsburg Charles V for the title of Holy Roman Emperor.
62.] The French, represented by their heraldic lily, fleur-de-lis, would also be dishonoured by the triumph of the Turks.

Who measure not the compass of a crown
To fit the head that wears it but their own,
Still hindering peace because they stewards are,
Without account, to that wild spender, war.
Still Christian wars they will pursue, and boast   70
Unjust successes gained, whilst Rhodes is lost;
Whilst we build monuments of death to shame
Those who forsook us in the chase of Fame.
Alphonso. We will endure the colds of court delays;
Honour grows warm in airy vests of praise.   75
On rocky Rhodes we will like rocks abide.
Villerius. Away, away, and hasten to thy bride!
'Tis scarce a month since thy nuptial rites
Thou camest to honour here our Rhodian knights,
To dignify our sacred annual feast: 80
We love to lodge, not to entomb a guest.
Honour must yield where reason should prevail.
Aboard, aboard, and hoise up every sail
That gathers any wind for Sicily!
Men lose their virtue's pattern losing thee.   85
Thy bride doth yield her sex no less a light;
But, thy life gone, will set in endless night.
Ye must like stars shine long ere ye expire!
Alphonso. Honour is colder virtue set on fire;
My honour lost, her love would soon decay,   90
Here for my tomb or triumph I will stay.
My sword against proud Solyman I draw,

69.1. *additional s.d., Enter* HIGH MARSHAL OF RHODES *Q3, F.*   70–3. *Still . . .*
Fame] lines attributed to High Marshal, Q3, F.   81. to entomb] *Q1, Q3;*
entomb *F.*   84. That] *Q1, Q3, F;* what *Q2.*   85. virtue's] vertu's *Q1;* virtu's *Q3,*
F.

68–73.] Knolles comments that the Grand Master sent letters to Spain, Rome and
France 'craving the aid of these Christian princes, for relief of the City, by sea and land
besieged. But all in vain, for they, carried away with the endless grudge of one against
another, or respecting only their own states, returned the ambassadors with good words,
but no relief' (Knolles, p. 581).

68–73.] i.e. Kings will pursue wars out of self-interest, regardless of their cost, while
they ignore the pleas of Rhodes.

74. *court delays*] prevarications of potential royal allies.

75.] i.e. honour will flourish when clothed in praise.

80. *our sacred annual feast*] an annual joust of chivalry attended by knights from
across Europe. In *Soliman and Perseda*, the knights are assembled on Rhodes 'to try
their force in arms' in honour of the marriage of the Prince of Cyprus to the daughter
of the governor of Rhodes (*Soliman and Perseda*, A3r–v).

83. *hoise*] hoist, raise aloft.

85. *virtue's pattern*] conveying the sense of the Italian *virtù*, valour, courage as well
as virtue.

85–7.] While Ianthe is an exemplum to women, Alphonso's glorious renown means
that his death would be totally devastating.

89–90.] i.e. honour is the one virtue which is allied to passion. Alphonso would lose
Ianthe's love if he lost his honour.

His cursèd prophet and his sensual law.
Chorus. [Alphonso and Villerius]
    Our swords against the proud Solyman we draw,
    His cursèd prophet and his sensual law.   *Exeunt.*   95

[*Enter*] Chorus.
By Soldiers of Several Nations

I

Come ye termagant Turks,
If your Bassa dare land ye,
Whilst the wine bravely works
That was brought us from Candy.

2

Wealth the least of our care is,   100
For the poor ne'er are undone;
A vous, Monsieur of Paris,
To the back-swords of London.

3

Diego, thou in a trice
Shalt advance thy lean belly.   105
For their hens and their rice
Make pilau like a jelly.

4

Let 'em land fine and free;
For my cap, though an old one,
Such a turban shall be,   110
Thou wilt think it a gold one.

5

It is seven to one odds,
They had safer sailed by us:

95.1. *Enter* IANTHE, MELOSILE, MADINA *(her two women) bearing two open caskets with jewels* Q3, F. (See Appendix 2.)   97. dare] *Q1,* dares *Q3, F.*   99. That] *Q1,* Which *Q3, F.*

---

93. *His cursèd prophet*] Muhammad.
sensual] secular, irreligious.
94. *Chorus* [Alphonso and Villerius]] In early opera it was the custom for soloists to form a chorus.
96. *termagant*] savage, violent; name of the imaginary deity held by medieval Christians to be worshipped by Muhammadans (*OED*).
99. *Candy*] Crete.
102. *A vous . . . Paris*] probably a toast to French comrades, also a colloquial term, meaning 'certainly', 'assuredly' (*OED*, vous).
103. *back-swords*] fencers with swords of only one cutting edge.
104-5.] i.e. the Spaniard will fatten himself on the dishes of the Turks.
107. *pilau*] oriental dish of rice boiled with fowl, meat or fish; the most common dish to be associated with the Turks in the seventeenth century.
109-11.] i.e. my old or worn cap will be a match for their gleaming turbans.

Whilst our wine lasts in Rhodes
They shall water at Chios.   *Exeunt.*   115

End of the First Entry

The scene is changed, and the city, Rhodes, appears beleaguered at sea and land. The entry is again prepared by instrumental music.

SECOND ENTRY

Enter VILLERIUS *and* ADMIRAL.

Admiral. The blood of Rhodes grows cold! Life must expire!
Villerius. The Duke still warms it with his valour's fire!
Admiral. If he has much in honour's presence done,   5
    Has saved our ensigns or has others won,
    Then he but well by your example wrought
    Who well in honour's school his childhood taught.
Villerius. The foe three moons tempestuously has spent
    Where we will never yield, nor he relent.   10
    Still we but raise what must be beaten down
    Defending walls, yet cannot keep the town;
    Venturing last stakes where we can nothing win,
    And, shutting slaughter out, keep famine in.
Admiral. How oft and vainly Rhodes for succour waits   15
    From triple diadems and scarlet hats:
    Rome keeps her gold, cheaply her warriors pays,
    At first with blessings and at last with praise.
Villerius. By armies stowed in fleets, exhausted Spain
    Leaves half her land unploughed, to plough the main;   20
    And still would more of the old world subdue,
    As if unsatisfied with all the new.
Admiral. France strives to have her lilies grow as fair
    In others' realms as where they native are.
Villerius. The English lion ever loves to change   25
    His walks, and in remoter forests range.
Chorus. [*Admiral and Villerius*]
    All gaining vainly from each other's loss;
    Whilst still the crescent drives away the Cross.

2.3. *blood . . . cold*] The Rhodians are losing heart.

6. *ensigns*] emblems of the knights hospitaller.

7–8.] Alphonso, as a former pupil of Villerius, is only emulating the honourable conduct of the master.

9–10.] an indication that the siege has been taking place for three months.

13. *Venturing last stakes*] placing our last bets.

16. *triple . . . hats*] probably a reference to the Pope and the cardinals of Rome.

19–26. *stowed . . . range*] references to Spanish expansionism and to colonization of the New World by the European powers.

20. *the main*] the Spanish main, i.e. mainland of America adjacent to the Caribbean Sea.

27–8.] The Turkish empire is expanding while Christian powers fight amongst themselves.

Enter ALPHONSO.

Alphonso.   *1*

    How bravely fought the fiery French,
    Their bulwark being stormed.   30
    The colder Almans kept their trench,
    By more than valour warmed.

2

    The grave Italians paused and fought,
    The solemn Spaniards too;
    Studying more deaths than could be wrought   35
    By what the rash could do.

3

    The Avergnian colours high were raised;
    Twice ta'en, and twice relieved.
    Our foes, like friends to valour, praised
    The mischiefs they received.   40

4

    The cheerful English got renown,
    Fought merrily and fast;
    'Tis time, they cried, to mow them down,
    War's harvest cannot last.

5

    If Death be rest, here let us die.   45
    Where weariness is all
    We daily get by victory,
    Who must by famine fall.

6

    Great Solyman is landed now.
    All fate he seems to be,   50

---

38. ta'en] tane *Q1–Q3, F.*

---

    30. *bulwark*] fortification. The city was defended by 'five mighty bulwarks', garrisoned by the French, the English, the Germans, the French Avergnians and the Spanish (Knolles, p. 581).

    31. *Almans*] Germans.

    35. *Studying*] meditating upon.

    36. *rash*] plague.

    39–40.] The Turks are forced to admire the courage and tenacity of the Rhodian defeat.

    41–4.] In fact, the English bulwark was the first to be undermined as the English forces were overwhelmed (see Knolles, p. 584).

    49.] Knolles describes how Solyman on arriving at the Turkish camp and addressing the soldiers from his royal seat broke out into a 'choleric speech' at the soldiers' reluctance to attack the city (Knolles, p. 583).

    50. *All . . . be*] He seems to be Destiny itself.

And brings those tempests in his brow
Which he deserved at sea.

Villerius. He can at most but once prevail,
    Though armed with nations that were brought by more
    Gross galleys than would serve to hale   55
    This island to the Lycian shore.
Admiral. Let us apace do worthily and give
    Our story length, though long we cannot live.
Chorus. [*Villerius, Admiral and Alphonso*]
    So greatly do, that being dead,
    Brave wonders may be wrought   60
    By such as shall our story read
    And study how we fought.   *Exeunt.*

         Enter SOLYMAN *and* PIRRHUS.

Solyman. What sudden halt hath stayed thy swift renown,
    O'er-running kingdoms, stopping at a town?
    He that will win the prize in honour's race   65
    Must nearer to the goal still mend his pace.
    If age thou feelest, the active camp forbear;
    In sleepy cities rest, the caves of fear.
    Thy mind was never valiant if, when old,
    Thy courage cools because thy blood is cold.   70
Pirrhus. How can ambitious manhood be expressed
    More than by marks of our disdain of rest?
    What less than toils incessant can, despite
    Of canon, raise these mounts to castle-height?

---

62. we] *Q1, Q2, F;* me *Q3.*

---

54. *Though . . . nations*] i.e. despite being supported by the military might of tributary nations.
   55. *Gross*] massive.
galleys] vessels with one deck, sails and banks of oars, often used as warships.
hale] pull, drag, haul.
56. *Lycian shore*] region of the Mediterranean coast of Turkey.
57. *apace*] at once.
57–8. *give . . . length*] i.e. let our bravery enhance the telling of events.
60–2.] The history of our valorous deeds may inspire future emulation.
63. *stayed*] impeded.
66. *mend*] increase.
67. *active camp forbear*] i.e. withdraw from active service.
68. *the caves of fear*] i.e. the cities as places of refuge.
73–4.] Fifty thousand pioneers did 'with incredible celerity bring that to pass, which was thought impossible. They cut ways through the most hard stony rocks, raising the plains as high as mountains, with earth brought two miles off, and laying the mountains even with the plains, and yet they never wrought in safety, but were miserably rent in sunder with the great ordnance out of the town' (Knolles, p. 582).
despite / Of canon] in spite of cannon fire from the city while elevating the plain.
   74. *mounts*] mounds of earth, earthworks.

Or less than utmost of unwearied strength   75
Can draw these lines of battery to that length?
Solyman. The toils of ants, and molehills raised in scorn
Of labour, to be levelled with a spurn:
These are the pyramids that show your pains.
But of your armies' valour, where remains   80
One trophy to excuse a Bassa's boast?
Pirrhus. Valour may reckon what she bravely lost;
Not from successes all her count does raise.
By life well lost we gain a share of praise.
If we in danger's glass all valour see,   85
And death the farthest step of danger be,
Behold our mount of bodies made a grave;
And prize our loss by what we scorned to save.
Solyman. Away! range all the camp for an assault!
Tell them, they tread in graves who make a halt.   90
Fat slaves, who have been lulled to a disease,
Crammed out of breath, and crippled by their ease!
Whose active fathers leapt o'er walls too high
For them to climb. Hence, from my anger fly:
Which is too worthy for thee, being mine,   95
And must be quenched by Rhodian blood or thine.

               Exit PIRRHUS, *bowing.*

In honour's orb the Christians shine.
Their light in war does still increase,
Though oft misled by mists of wine,
Or blinder love the crime of peace;   100
Bold in adultery's frequent change
And every loud expensive vice;
Ebbing out wealth by ways as strange
As it flowed in by avarice.
Thus vilely they dare live, and yet dare die.   105
If courage be a virtue, 'tis allowed

75. Or] Q3, F; of Q1.

75–6.] i.e. what other than inexhaustible reserves of strength can deploy these lines of artillery across that distance?
78. *spurn*] kick (of the foot).
80–1. *where ... boast*] i.e. what has been captured to justify such claims?
85. *glass*] mirror, reflection.
87. *mount*] mound, heap.
88.] i.e. judge (in terms of valour) our (apparent) failure by the courage with which we sacrificed our lives.
91. *lulled ... disease*] i.e. soothed into the sickness of lethargy.
92. *Crammed*] over-fed.
97. *orb*] sphere of action.
97–105.] Solyman appears to veer between apparently conflicting impressions, i.e. admiration for the honourable conduct of the Christians when engaged in war and disdain for their perceived general vices.
100.] possibly a faint allusion to the non-aggressive foreign policy of the Stuarts.
101.] i.e. guilty of serial infidelity.
106–8.] Courage is regarded as the prerogative of the nobility who support the crown, yet is feared in the populace. The speech implicitly contrasts the Christians with

But to those few on whom our crowns rely,
And is condemned as madness in the crowd.

Enter MUSTAPHA, IANTHE *veiled.*

Mustapha. Great sultan, hail! though here at land
   Lost fools in opposition stand,   110
   Yet thou at sea dost all command.
Solyman. What is it thou wouldst show, and yet dost shroud?
Mustapha. I bring the morning pictured in a cloud,
   A wealth more worth than all the sea does hide
   Or courts display in their triumphant pride.   115
Solyman. Thou seemest to bring the daughter of the night
   And givest her many stars to make her bright.
   Dispatch my wonder and relate her story.
Mustapha. 'Tis full of fate, and yet has much of glory.
   A squadron of our galleys that did ply   120
   West from this coast met two of Sicily,
   Both fraught to furnish Rhodes. We gave them chase
   And had, but for our number, met disgrace;
   For, grappling, they maintained a bloody fight,
   Which did begin with day and end with night.   125
   And though this bashful lady then did wear
   Her face still veiled, her valour did appear.
   She urged their courage when they boldly fought;
   And many shunned the dangers which she sought.
Solyman. Where are the limits thou wouldst set for praise 130
   Or to what height wilt thou my wonder raise?
Mustapha. This is Ianthe, the Sicilian flower,
   Sweeter than buds unfolded in a shower,
   Bride to Alphonso, who in Rhodes so long
   The theme has been of each heroic song;   135
   And she for his relief those galleys fraught,
   Both stowed with what her dower and jewels bought.
Solyman. O wonderous virtue of a Christian wife!
   Adventuring life's support and then her life

---

131. my wonder] *Q1*; thy wonder *Q3, F.*

---

the Turks, who had a reputation for harsh military discipline and incorruptibility, redoubtable courage, and abstinence from wine and other 'European vanities' (see Chew, pp. 110, 120–1).

108.1.] Davenant took the image from *Soliman and Perseda*. When Soliman is brought the captive Perseda, he orders her face to be covered, fearing the effects of her beauty (*Soliman and Perseda*, F2r).

110.] i.e. the Rhodians are foolishly defending a hopeless cause.

116. *daughter . . . night*] a reference to the fact that Ianthe is veiled, her beauty hidden.

118. *Dispatch my wonder*] i.e. rid me of my astonishment and perplexity.

120. *ply*] work windward.

122. *fraught*] laden.

136–7.] See introduction to text, pp. 183–4.

138.] Solyman expresses admiration at Ianthe's active virtue.

139. *Adventuring*] risking.

To save her ruined lord! Bid her unveil!   140

IANTHE steps back.

Ianthe. It were more honour, Sultan, to assail
    A public strength against thy forces bent
    Than to unwall this private tenement,
    To which no monarch but my lord has right;
    Nor will it yield to treaty or to might,   145
    Where heaven's great law defends him from surprise.
    This curtain only opens to his eyes.
Solyman. If beauty veiled so virtuous be,
    'Tis more than Christian husbands know
    Whose ladies wear their faces free;   150
    Which they to more than husband show.
Ianthe. Your Bassa swore, and by his dreadful law,
    None but my lord's dear hand this veil should draw;
    And that to Rhodes I should conducted be
    To take my share of all his destiny;   155
    Else I had quickly found
    Sure means to get some wound,
    Which would in death's cold arms
    My honour instant safety give
    From all those rude alarms   160
    Which keep it waking whilst I live.
Solyman. Hast thou engaged our prophet's plight
    To keep her beauty from my sight
    And to conduct her person free
    To harbour with mine enemy?   165
Mustapha. Virtue constrained the privilege I gave:
    Shall I for sacred virtue pardon crave?
Solyman. I envy not the conquests of thy sword:
    Thrive still in wicked war.
    But, slave, how didst thou dare,   170
    In virtuous love, thus to transcend thy lord?
    Thou didst thy utmost virtue show;
    Yet somewhat more does rest,
    Not yet by thee expressed,

---

141. *to assail*] to attack.

141–2.] i.e. it would be more honourable to attack your opponents by force of arms than to make me defenceless by unveiling.

143. *tenement*] the body (as abode of the soul).

146. *heaven's . . . law*] i.e. the Ten Commandments given by God to Moses, especially the sixth against adultery.

defends . . . surprise] protects him from the shock of betrayal.

152. *Your Bassa*] i.e. Mustapha.

dreadful] inspiring reverence (i.e. the law of Muhammad).

158–61.] i.e. while I am alive, my honour must be constantly alert to threats.

162–3.] i.e. have you entered into the Islamic pledge [not to uncover a woman's face] to prevent my having sight of her beauty?

166. *constrained*] compelled.

171.] i.e. to exceed me in displays of chaste love.

Which virtue left for me to do.   175
Thou great example of a Christian wife,
Enjoy thy lord and give him happy life.
Thy galleys with their freight,
For which the hungry wait,
Shall straight to Rhodes conducted be;   180
And as thy passage to him shall be free,
So both may safe return to Sicily.

Ianthe. May Solyman be ever far
From impious honours of the war;
Since worthy to receive renown   185
From things repaired, not overthrown.
And when in peace his virtue thrives,
Let all the race of loyal wives
Sing this his bounty to his glory
And teach their princes by his story: 190
Of which, if any victors be,
Let them, because he conquered me,
Strip cheerfully each other's brow,
And at his feet their laurel throw.

Solyman. Straight to the port her galleys steer;   195
Then hale the sentry at the pier.
And though our flags ne'er used to bow,
They shall do virtue homage now.
Give fire still as she passes by,
And let our streamers lower fly.   *Exeunt several ways.*   200

               [*Enter*] Chorus *of women.*

                          I

Let us live, live! for being dead,
The pretty spots,
Ribbons and knots,
And the fine French dress for the head,
No lady wears upon her   205
In the cold, cold bed of honour.
Beat down our grottoes, and hew down our bowers,

---

182. may] *Q3, F;* my *Q1.*

183–4.] i.e. let Solyman be ever associated with reverent, honourable conduct in war.
184. *repaired*] restored.
189. *bounty*] benevolence.
192–4.] i.e. let all princes who have earned glory pay homage to Solyman by casting their own laurels at his feet.
196. *hale*] fetch, hail.
199. *Give fire*] salute by firing canon.
200. *streamers*] flags.
200.1. several ways] in different directions.
200.2. *Chorus* of women] There was only one female actor/singer who must have been joined by male altos in female attire.
202. *pretty spots*] beauty spots.

Dig up our arbours, and root up our flowers.
Our gardens are bulwarks and bastions become.
Then hang up our lutes; we must sing to the drum.   210

2

Our patches and curls
(So exact in each station),
Our powders and our pearls
Are now out of fashion.
Hence with our needles, and give us your spades;   215
We that were ladies grow coarse as our maids.
Our coaches have drove us to balls at the court;
We now must drive barrows to earth up the port.   [*Exeunt.*]

End of the Second Entry

The further part of the scene is opened, and a royal pavilion appears displayed, representing Solyman's imperial throne; and about it are discerned the quarters of his Bassas and inferior officers.

The entry is again prepared by instrumental music.

THIRD ENTRY

Enter SOLYMAN, PIRRHUS, MUSTAPHA.

Solyman. Pirrhus, draw up our army wide!   5
Then from the gross two strong reserves divide,
And spread the wings,
As if we were to fight
In the lost Rhodians sight,
With all the Western kings!   10
Each wing with Janizaries line;
The right and left to Haly's sons assign;
The gross to Zangiban.

End of] The end of *Q1*.   12. Haly's] *F*; Hally's *Q1–Q3*. *Spelt* Haly *in* The Persons Represented, *Q3*.

208–10.] The women must renounce their refined leisures and defend the city.
212. *station*] position; perhaps also a pun on station as a military port.
218. *earth … port*] i.e. build earthworks around the walls to strengthen fortification.

3.6. *the gross*] the main body.
reserves] troops held back behind the front line attackers to act as reinforcements.
7. *wings*] two divisions on each side of the main body of the army.
11. *Janizaries*] the Sultan's guard, and the main part of the standing army. The body, first organized in the fourteenth century, was composed mainly of children of tributary Christians (*OED*).
12. *Haly's sons*] presumably commanders of the army, not mentioned by Knolles. Haly is amongst the persons represented in *Q3* and *F*.
13. *Zangiban*] captain or commander of the army, not mentioned by Knolles.

The main artillery
With Mustapha shall be.   15
Bring thou the rear, we lead the van.
Pirrhus. It shall be done as early as the dawn;
    As if the figure by thy hand were drawn.
Mustapha. We wish that we, to ease thee, could prevent
    All thy commands, by guessing thy intent.   20
Solyman. These Rhodians who of honour boast,
    A loss excuse, when bravely lost:
    Now they may bravely lose their Rhodes,
    Which never played against such odds.
    Tomorrow let them see our strength, and weep   25
    Whilst they their want of losing blame;
    Their valiant folly strives too long to keep
    What might be rendered without shame.
Pirrhus. 'Tis well our valiant prophet did
    In us not only loss forbid,   30
    But has enjoined us still to get.
    Empire must move apace
    When she begins the race,
    And apter is for wings than feet.
Mustapha. They vainly interrupt our speed   35
    And civil reason lack,
    To know they should go back
    When we determine to proceed.
Pirrhus. When to all Rhodes our army does appear,
    Shall we then make a sudden halt   40
    And give a general assault?
Solyman. Pirrhus, not yet; Ianthe being there.
    Let them our valour by our mercy prize.
    The respite of this day
    To virtuous love shall pay   45
    A debt long due for all my victories.
Mustapha. If virtuous beauty can attain such grace
    Whilst she a captive was, and hid,
    What wisdom can his love forbid
    When virtue's free and beauty shows her face?   50
Solyman. Dispatch a trumpet to the town;

---

31. enjoined] *Q1;* conjoyn'd *Q3, F.*

---

15. *Mustapha*] The bassa Mustapha, married to Solyman's natural sister, was condemned to death by the Emperor for drawing the Turks into such a dangerous expedition, but was pardoned following the intercession of other counsellors.
    18. *figure*] shape, configuration.
    19. *prevent*] forestall.
    26. *Whilst . . . blame*] blame their history of resisting aggressors; blame their need
to lose with honour (rather than capitulate).
    31. *enjoined*] commanded; imposed as duty.
    34.] Empires must expand rapidly, not by degrees.
    36. *civil reason*] good sense.
    49–50.] i.e. what judgement can restrain his love?

Summon Ianthe to be gone
Safe with her lord. When both are free
And in their course to Sicily,
Then Rhodes shall for that valour mourn   55
Which stops the haste of our return.
Pirrhus. Those that in Grecian quarries wrought,
And pioneers from Lycia brought,
Who like a nation in a throng appear,
So great their number is, are landed here: 60
Where shall they work?
Solyman.   Upon Philermus hill.
There, ere this moon her circle fills with days,
They shall, by punished sloth and cherished skill,
A spacious palace in a castle raise:
A neighbourhood within the Rhodians' view,   65
Where, if my anger cannot them subdue,
My patience shall out-wait them, whilst they long
Attend to see weak princes make them strong.
There I'll grow old, and die too, if they have
The secret art to fast me to my grave.   *Exeunt.*   70

The scene is changed to that of the town beseiged.

        Enter VILLERIUS, ADMIRAL, ALPHONSO, IANTHE.

Villerius. When we, Ianthe, would this act commend,
We know no more how to begin
Than we should do, if we were in,
How suddenly to make an end.   75
Admiral. What love was yours which these strong bars of Fate
Were all too weak to separate?
Which seas and storms could not divide,
Nor all the dreadful Turkish pride,
Which passed secure, though not unseen,   80
Even double guards of death that lay between.
Villerius. What more could honour for fair virtue do?
What could Alphonso venture more for you?

---

58. *pioneers*] foot soldiers who march in advance of the army to dig trenches; the
Turks brought fifty thousand, 'men better acquainted with country labour and keeping
of cattle, than with wars' (Knolles, p. 582).
   Lycia] see Second Entry, l. 56.
   61. *Philermus hill*] Following the Rhodians' repulsion of Turkish assaults, Solyman
ordered the building of a sumptuous castle upon the top of Mount Philermus 'to show
unto the Rhodians that he purposed not to depart' (Knolles, p. 589).
   62. *ere . . . days*] i.e. one calendar month.
   67–8. *long . . . strong*] wait indefinitely for aid from weak foreign powers to build
up their strength.
   70. *fast me*] speed me.
   74–5. *if . . . end*] i.e. if we had started [to praise Ianthe's actions] how would we con-
clude our acclamation?
   81. *double . . . death*] i.e. the fearful power of Solyman's forces.

Admiral. With wonder and with shame we must confess,
    All we ourselves can do for Rhodes is less.   85
Villerius. Nor did your love and courage act alone,
    Your bounty too has no less wonders done.
    And for our guard you have brought wisely down
    A troop of virtues to defend the town:
    The only troop that can a town defend,   90
    Which heaven before for ruin did intend.
Admiral. Look here, ye Western monarchs, look with shame,
    Who fear not a remote, though common, foe:
    The cabinet of one illustrious dame
    Does more than your exchequers joined did do.   95
Alphonso. Indeed I think, Ianthe, few
    So young and flourishing as you,
    Whose beauties might so well adorn
    The jewels which by them are worn,
    Did ever muskets for them take,   100
    Nor of their pearls did bullets make.
Ianthe. When you, my lord, are shut up here,
    Expense of treasure must appear
    So far from bounty that, alas,
    It covetous advantage was;   105
    For with small cost I sought to save
    Even all the treasure that I have.
    Who would not all her trifling jewels give,
    Which but from number can their worth derive,
    If she could purchase or redeem with them   110
    One great inestimable gem?
Admiral. Oh, ripe perfection in a breast so young!
Villerius. Virtue has tuned her heart and wit her tongue.
Admiral. Though Rhodes no pleasure can allow,
    I dare secure the safety of it now.   115
    All will so labour to save you
    As that will save the city too.
Ianthe. Alas, the utmost I have done
    More than a just reward has won,
    If by my lord and you it be but thought   120
    I had the care to serve him as I ought.
Villerius. Brave Duke, farewell, the scouts for orders wait,
    And the parade does fill.

113. tuned] tun'd *Q1, F*; turn'd *Q3.*

---

87. *bounty*] the wealth and relief Ianthe has brought to Rhodes.
94. *cabinet*] a case for the safe custody of jewels, valuable letters or documents. See Introduction to the text, pp. 183–4.
94–5.] Alphonso's subsequent lines reveal that Ianthe's jewels have been pawned to provide weapons.
103. *Expense*] outlay, using up.
105. *covetous advantage*] gain of what was desired, i.e. Alphonso.
121. *care*] love.
123. *parade*] level space forming the interior of the fortification.

Alphonso. Great master, I'll attend your pleasure straight,
    And strive to serve your will.   125
Exeunt VILLERIUS, ADMIRAL.

    Ianthe, after all this praise
    Which fame so fully to you pays,
    For that which all the world beside
    Admires you, I alone must chide.
    Are you that kind and virtuous wife,   130
    Who thus expose your husband's life?
    The hazards, both at land and sea,
    Through which so boldly thou hast run
    Did more assault and threaten me
    Than all the Sultan could have done.   135
    Thy dangers, could I them have seen,
    Would not to me have dangers been,
    But certain death: now thou art here,
    A danger worse than death I fear.
    Thou hast, Ianthe, honour won,   140
    But mine, alas, will be undone:
    For as thou valiant wert for me,
    I shall a coward grow for thee.
Ianthe. Take heed, Alphonso, for this care of me
    Will to my fame injurious be: 145
    Your love will brighter by it shine,
    But it eclipses mine.
    Since I would here before or with you fall,
    Death needs but beckon when he means to call.
Alphonso. Ianthe, even in this you shall command,   150
    And this my strongest passion guide;
    Your virtue will not be denied.
    It could even Solyman himself withstand;
    To whom it did so beauteous show
    It seemed to civilize a barbarous foe.   155
    Of this your strange escape, Ianthe, say
    Briefly the motive and the way.
Ianthe. Did I not tell you how we fought,
    How I was taken, and how brought
    Before great Solyman? but there   160
    I think we interrupted were.
Alphonso. Yes, but we will not be so here,
    Should Solyman himself appear.
Ianthe. It seems that what the Bassa of me said,

    130–43.] Alphonso complains that Ianthe's courageous exploits, though celebrated by everyone else, have actually put him at risk: at first, he implies that he would have been destroyed by his fears of Ianthe's likely fate; but then his grievance appears to be resentment that the praise won by Ianthe will overshadow anything he can achieve.

    145. *my fame injurious*] damage my honour.

    157. *motive*] reason.

Had some respect and admiration bred   165
In Solyman; and this to me increased
The jealousies which honour did suggest.
All that of Turks and tyrants I had heard,
But that I feared not death, I should have feared.
I, to excuse my voyage, urged my love   170
To your high worth; which did such pity move
That straight his usage did reclaim my fear.
He seemed in civil France, and monarch there:
For soon my person, galleys, freight, were free
By his command.
Alphonso.   O wondrous enemy!   175
Ianthe. These are the smallest gifts his bounty knew.
Alphonso. What could he give you more?
Ianthe.   He gave me you;
And you may homewards now securely go
Through all his fleet.
Alphonso.   But honour says not so.
Ianthe. If that forbid it, you shall never see   180
That I and that will disagree:
Honour will speak the same to me.
Alphonso. This Christian Turk amazes me, my dear!
How long, Ianthe, stayed you there?
Ianthe. Two days with Mustapha.
Alphonso.   How do you say?   185
Two days, and two whole nights? alas!
Ianthe. That it, my lord, no longer was,
Is such a mercy, as too long I stay
Ere at the altar thanks to heaven I pay.
Alphonso. (*Aside*) To heaven confession should prepare the way. 190
                                    Exit IANTHE.

She is all harmony and fair as light;
But brings me discord and the clouds of night.
And Solyman does think heaven's joys to be
In women not so fair as she.
'Tis strange! Dismiss so fair an enemy?   195
She was his own by right of war.
We are his dogs, and such as she, his angels are.

166–9. *this to me . . . feared*] i.e. Solyman displayed greater vigilance in protecting
Ianthe than honour impelled. Ianthe acknowledges that, had she feared death, the reputation of the Turks would have made her fearful.

167. *jealousies*] vigilance in protecting a person from danger; zeal.

172. *usage*] conduct.

173. *in civil France*] Ianthe attributes to Solyman the alleged honourable conduct
of a Western monarch.

reclaim] quell.

187–9.] i.e. it is merciful that I was detained no longer as I have yet to offer thanks
for my release.

190. *To heaven . . . way*] Alphonso implies that before she can hope for salvation
Ianthe has sins which must be confessed.

O wondrous Turkish chastity!
Her galleys, freight, and those to send
Into a town which he would take!   200
Are we beseiged then by a friend?
Could honour such a present make,
Then when his honour is at stake?
Against itself, does honour booty play?
We have the liberty to go away!   205
Strange above miracle! But who can say,
If in his hands we once should be,
What would become of her? For what of me,
Though love is blind, even love may see.
Come back my thoughts, you must not rove!   210
For sure Ianthe does Alphonso love.
O Solyman, this mystic act of thine
Does all my quiet undermine:
But on thy troops, if not on thee,
This sword my cure and my revenge shall be.   *Exit.*   215

           [*Enter*] Chorus *of men and women.*

Men. Ye wives all that are, and wives that would be,
        Unlearn all ye learnt here of one another,
        And all ye have learnt of an aunt or a mother.
        Then straight hither come, a new pattern to see,
        Which in a good humour kind fortune did send: 220
        A glass for your minds as well as your faces.
        Make haste then, and break your own looking-glasses:
        If you see but yourselves, you'll never amend.
Women. You that would teach us what your wives ought to do,
        Take heed: there's a pattern in town too for you.   225
        Be you but Alphonsos, and we
        Perhaps Ianthes will be.
Men. Be you but Ianthes, and we
        Alphonsos a while will be.
Both. Let both sides begin then, rather than neither;   230
        Let's both join our hands, and both mend together.

                 End of the Third Entry

215.1.] *Additional stage direction: Enter* ROXOLANA, PIRRHUS, RUSTAN *Q3.   The scene changes to Solyman's camp. Enter* ROXOLANA, PIRRHUS, RUSTAN *F. See Appendix 2.   216.* that would] *Q1;* would *Q3, F.   224.* would] *Q1;* will *Q3, F.*

204. *does . . . play*] i.e. does honour offer itself as spoils of war?
208–9. *For . . . see*] The paradox captures Alphonso's sudden jealousy and suspicions of Solyman's motives. Love (Cupid) may be conventionally blind, but it is not deceived.
209. *love is blind*] proverbial, Tilley, L506.
212. *mystic*] mysterious, of hidden meaning.
223. *If you . . . amend*] i.e. if you fail to emulate Ianthe's virtue, you will never improve your moral condition.

*The scene is varied to the prospect of Mount Philermus: artificers
appearing at work about that castle which was there, with wonderful
expedition, erected by Solyman. His great army is discovered in the
plain below, drawn up in battalia, as if it were prepared for a general
assault.*   5

The Entry is again prepared by instrumental music.

FOURTH ENTRY

Enter SOLYMAN, PIRRHUS, MUSTAPHA.

Solyman. Refuse my passport, and resolve to die
    Only for fashion's sake, for company?
    O costly scruples! But I'll try to be,
    Thou stubborn honour, obstinate as thee.   10
    My power thou shalt not vanquish by thy will;
    I will enforce to live whom thou wouldst kill.
Pirrhus. They in tomorrow's storm will change their mind;
    Then, though too late instructed, they shall find
    That those who your protection dare reject   15
    No human power dares venture to protect.
    They are not foes, but rebels, who withstand
    The power that does their fate command.
Solyman. O Mustapha, our strength we measure ill.
    We want the half of what we think we have;   20
    For we enjoy the beastlike power to kill,
    But not the godlike power to save.
    Who laughs at death, laughs at our highest power:
    The valiant man is his own emperor.
Mustapha. Your power to save, you have to them made known,   25
    Who scorned it with ingrateful pride.
    Now, how you can destroy must next be shown;
    And that the Christian world has tried.
Solyman. 'Tis such a single pair
    As only equal are   30
    Unto themselves; but many steps above
    All others who attempt to make up love.

16. human] humane *Q1, Q3, F.*

4.1. artificers] soldier mechanics (*OED*).
4. battalia] order of battle, battle array.
7. *passport*] authorization of safe passage.
8.] i.e. just to share the fate of the Rhodians.
19. *ill*] badly, improperly.
20. *want*] lack.
24.] i.e. the man who scorns death fears nobody.
28. *tried*] put to the proof.
29. *single*] singular, special.
32. *make up love*] represent themselves as lovers.

Their lives will noble history afford
And must adorn my sceptre, not my sword.
My strength in vain has with their virtue strove;   35
In vain their hate would overcome my love.
My favours I'll compel them to receive.
Go Mustapha, and strictest orders give
Through all the camp, that in assault they spare
(And in the sack of this presumptuous town)   40
The lives of these two strangers, with a care
Above the preservation of their own.
Alphonso has so oft his courage shown,
That he to all but cowards must be known.
Ianthe is so fair, that none can be   45
Mistaken, amongst thousands, which is she.   *Exeunt.*

The scene returns to that of the town besieged.

Enter ALPHONSO, IANTHE.

Ianthe. Alphonso, now the danger grows so near,
    Give her that loves you leave to fear.
    Nor do I blush this passion to confess,   50
    Since it for object has no less
    Than even your liberty, or life;
    I fear not as a woman, but a wife.
    We were too proud no use to make
    Of Solyman's obliging proffer;   55
    For why should honour scorn to take
    What honour's self does to it offer?
Alphonso. To be o'ercome by his victorious sword
    Will comfort to our fall afford.
    Our strength may yield to his; but 'tis not fit   60
    Our virtue should to his submit.
    In that, Ianthe, I must be
    Advanced, and greater far than he.
Ianthe. Fighting with him who strives to be your friend,
    You not with virtue, but with power contend.   65
Alphnso. Forbid it, heaven, our friends should think that we
    Did merit friendship from an enemy.
Ianthe. He is a foe to Rhodes, and not to you.
Alphonso. In Rhodes besieged, we must be Rhodians too.
Ianthe. 'Twas fortune that engaged you in this war.   70
Alphonso. 'Twas providence! Heaven's prisoners here we are.

34.] i.e. Ianthe and Alphonso must pay tribute to Solyman rather than die at his hands.

40. *sack*] ransacking, occupation.

63. *Advanced*] superior.

70–1.] Ianthe claims that Alphonso has been caught up in the siege through chance alone whereas Alphonso attributes the cause of events to the role of divine providence in their affairs. See Introduction to the text, pp. 182–3; the lines also recall the debates of

Ianthe. That providence our freedom does restore;
    The hand that shut, now opens us the door.
Alphonso. Had heaven that passport for our freedom sent,
    It would have chose some better instrument   75
    Than faithless Solyman.
Ianthe.   Oh, say not so!
    To strike and wound the virtue of your foe
    Is cruelty, which war does not allow:
    Sure he has better words deserved from you.
Alphonso. From me, Ianthe? No!   80
    What he deserves from you, you best must know.
Ianthe. What means my lord?
Alphonso.   For I confess, I must
    The poisoned bounties of a foe mistrust:
    And when upon the bait I look,
    Though all seem fair, suspect the hook.   85
Ianthe. He, though a foe, is generous and true:
    What he hath done declares what he will do.
Alphonso. He in two days your high esteem has won.
    What he would do I know; who knows what he has done?
    (*Aside*) Done? Wicked tongue, what hast thou said?   90
    What horrid falsehood from thee fled?
    O jealousy (if jealousy it be),
    Would I had here an asp instead of thee.
Ianthe. Sure you are sick; your words, alas,
    Gestures and looks distempers show.   95
Alphonso. Ianthe, you may safely pass;
    The pass, no doubt, was meant to you.
Ianthe. [*Aside*] He's jealous, sure; oh, virtue, can it be?
    Have I for this served virtue faithfully?
    Alphonso—
Alphonso.   Speak, Ianthe, and be free.   100
Ianthe. Have I deserved this change?
Alphonso.   Thou dost deserve
    So much that emperors are proud to serve
    The fair Ianthe; and not dare
    To hurt a land whilst she is there.
    Return (renowned Ianthe) safely home,   105
    And force thy passage with thine eyes;
    To conquer Rhodes will be a prize
    Less glorious than by thee to be o'ercome.
    But since he longs (it seems) so much to see

---

the chorus in *Soliman and Perseda*, where Love, Death and Fortune, prefacing each act, claim a part in the drama.

    86–7.] Ianthe still does not recognize the drift of Alphonso's suspicions.

    93. *asp*] a small viper; a possible allusion to Cleopatra's suicide by applying an asp to her breast, *Antony and Cleopatra*, 5.2.

    95. *distempers*] derangement.

    105–6.] i.e use your bewitching eyes to secure a safe voyage.

And be possessed of me,   110
Tell him I shall not fly beyond his reach:
Would he could dare to meet me in the breach.
                                        [*Exit* ALPHONSO.]
Ianthe. Tell him! Tell him? Oh, no, Alphonso, no;
   Let never man thy weakness know.
   Thy sudden fall will be a shame   115
   To man's and virtue's name.
   Alphonso's false! for what can falser be
   Than to suspect that falsehood dwells in me?
   Could Solyman both life and honour give?
   And can Alphonso me of both deprive?   120
   Of both, Alphonso; for believe
   Ianthe will disdain to live
   So long as to let others see
   Thy true, and her imputed, infamy.
   No more let lovers think they can possess   125
   More than a month of happiness.
   We thought our hold of it was strong,
   We thought our lease of it was long:
   But now, that all may ever happy prove,
   Let never any love.   130
   And yet these troubles of my love to me
   Shall shorter than the pleasures be.
   I'll till tomorrow last; then the assault
   Shall finish my misfortune and his fault.
   I to my enemies shall doubly owe,   135
   For saving me before, for killing now.   *Exit.*

                Enter VILLERIUS, ADMIRAL.

Admiral. From out the camp a valiant Christian slave
   Escaped, and to our knights assurance gave
   That at the break of day
   Their mine will play.   140
Villerius. Oft Martiningus struck and tried the ground,
   And counter-dug, and has the hollows found:
   We shall prevent
   Their dire intent.

112. meet me in the breach] *Q2, Q3, F;* meet in a breach *Q1.*   142. counter-dug]
counter-digged *Q1, Q3, F.*

───────────────────────────

   112. *breach*] gap in the fortification, i.e. open combat.
   124. *imputed infamy*] alleged shame.
   140. *mine will play*] A mine will be blown to undermine the city.
   141. *Martiningus*] the Venetian Gabriele Tadini da Martinengo, employed by
Rhodes. He was one of the most famous military engineers of his day: 'by whose industry and cunning, fifty five mines which the Turks did with infinite labour and charge
make (by reason of the springing of the water, and hardness of the rocks) during the
siege, were all by countermines disappointed and defeated' (Knolles, p. 581).
   142. *counter-dug*] dug an excavation in order to interrupt a mine laid by the Turks.
hollows] ditch where mine is laid.

Where is the duke, whose valour strives to keep   145
Rhodes still awake, which else would dully sleep?
Admiral. His courage and his reason is o'erthrown.
Villerius. Thou singest the sad destruction of our town!
Admiral. I met him wild as all the winds,
    When in the ocean they contest: 150
    And diligent suspicion finds
    He is with jealousy possessed.
Villerius. That arrow, once misdrawn, must ever rove.
    O weakness sprung from mightiness of love!
    O pitied crime!   155
    Alphonso will be overthrown
    Unless we take this ladder down,
    Where, though the rounds are broke,
    He does himself provoke
    Too hastily to climb.   160
Admiral. Invisibly, as dreams, fame's wings
    Fly everywhere,
    Hovering all day o'er palaces of kings.
    At night she lodges in the people's ear:
    Already they perceive Alphonso wild,   165
    And the beloved Ianthe grieved.
Villerius. Let us no more by honour be beguiled.
    This town can never be relieved;
    Alphonso and Ianthe being lost,
    Rhodes, thou dost cherish life with too much cost!   170
Chorus. [*Villerius and Admiral*]
    Away, unchain the streets, unearth the ports:
    Pull down each barricade
    Which women's fears have made,
    And bravely sally out from all the forts!
    Drive back the Crescents, and advance the Cross,   175
    Or sink all human empires in our loss!   *Exeunt.*

---

176. human] *Q3*; humane *Q1, F.*

145–6. *the duke . . . sleep*] i.e. Alphonso's courage inspires the Rhodians.
151. *diligent suspicion*] careful observation.
153.] i.e. love once damaged by jealousy will ever be restless.
156–9.] Alphonso has allowed his passions an uncontrolled ascent which will be self–destructive.
158. *though . . . broke*] i.e. though there is no foundation for his jealousy.
rounds] rungs.
161. *fame's wings*] i.e. rumour.
167.] i.e. we must no longer be deceived by talk of honour.
171. *unchain the streets*] remove the blockade.
172. *unearth the ports*] pull down the earthworks from the gateways of the city.
172–3] See Second Entry, lines. 205–16.
174. *sally out*] venture forth.
176.] i.e. or else the Turkish supremacy will destroy the Christian world.

[*Enter*] Chorus *of wives.*

I

[*Woman*] 1. This cursed jealousy, what is it?
[*Woman*] 2. 'Tis love that has lost itself in a mist.
[*Woman*] 3. 'Tis love being frighted out of his wits.
[*Woman*] 4. 'Tis love that has a fever got;   180
               Love that is violently hot,
               But troubled with cold and trembling fits.
               'Tis yet a more unnatural evil.
Chorus.   'Tis the god of love, 'tis the god of love, possessed with
               a devil.

2

[*Woman*] 1. 'Tis rich corrupted wine of love,   185
               Which sharpest vinegar does prove.
[*Woman*] 2. From all the sweet flowers which might honey make,
               It does a deadly poison bring.
[*Woman*] 3. Strange serpent which itself does sting!
[*Woman*] 4. It never can sleep, and dreams still awake.   190
[*Woman*] 1. It stuffs up the marriage bed with thorns!
Chorus.   It gores itself, it gores itself, with imagined horns.
                          [*Exeunt.*]

End of the Fourth Entry

The scene is changed into a representation of a general assault given to the town; the greatest fury of the army being discerned at the English station.

The entry is again prepared by instrumental music.

FIFTH ENTRY

Enter PIRRHUS.

Pirrhus. Traverse the canon! Mount the batteries higher!   5
      More gabions, and renew the blinds!
      Like dust they powder spend,
      And to our faces send

176.1. *Enter* ROXOLANA, PIRRHUS, RUSTAN, *and two of her women* Q3, F. See Appendix 2.   191. 1] Q1; 5 Q3, F.   192.1. End of] The end of] Q, F.

---

192. *gores*] pierces.
imagined horns] i.e. thinking itself cuckolded.

5.5. *Traverse*] move, turn.
6. *gabions*] wicker baskets intended to be filled with earth (*OED*).
blinds] screens erected to protect combatants.
7.] i.e. they use gunpowder as freely as if it were dust.
8–9.] The Rhodians threw down fire, scalding oil and burning pitch upon the Turks (Knolles, p. 586).

The heat of all the element of fire;
And to their backs have all the winds!   10

Enter MUSTAPHA.

Mustapha. More ladders, and reliefs to scale!
  The fire-crooks are too short! Help, help to hale!
  The battlement is loose, and straight will down.
  Point well the canon, and play fast!
  Their fury is too hot to last.   15
  That rampire shakes! They fly into the town!
Pirrhus. March up with those reserves to that redout!
  Faint slaves! the Janizaries reel!
  They bend, they bend! and seem to feel
  The terrors of a rout.   20
Mustapha. Old Zangar halts, and reinforcement lacks!
Pirrhus. March on!
Mustapha.   Advance those pikes, and charge their backs.

Enter SOLYMAN.

Solyman. Those platforms are too low to reach!
  Haste, haste! call Haly to the breach!
  Can my domestic Janizaries fly,   25
  And not adventure life for victory!
  Whose childhood with my palace milk I fed;
  Their youth, as if I were their parent, bred.
  What is this monster death, that our poor slaves,
  Still vexed with toil, are loath to rest in graves?   30
Mustapha. If life so precious be, why do not they,
  Who in war's trade can only live by prey,
  Their own afflicted lives expose

---

30. loath] loth *Q1, Q3, F.*

10.] The Turks feel the blast of the Rhodian barrage, while the smoke and heat drift away from the defenders who have the wind at their backs.

 11. *reliefs*] height of battlements; the relief was the difference in level between the crest of the parapet and the bottom of the ditch (*OED*).

 12. *fire-crooks*] large hooks for pulling down burning buildings (*OED*).

help to hale] help to pull.

 14. *play fast*] fire rapidly.

 16. *rampire*] rampart.

 17. *redout*] bulwark.

 18. *Janizaries*] see Third Entry, line 11 and note.

 20. *rout*] complete overthrow.

 21. *Zangar*] presumably Zangibar referred to earlier by Solyman (3.13).

 22. *Advance . . . backs*] Mustapha orders the line of pikemen to push up behind the main body of the army.

pikes] long spears with pointed heads of iron or steel. The pike was the main weapon of the footsoldier.

 23. *platforms*] level structures on which cannons are mounted.

 25. *domestic*] of Solyman's household.

 31-4. *why . . . foes*] i.e. why are the Janizaries, who can survive only by killing their opponents, so reluctant to take the lives of their more fortunate enemies?

To take the happier from their foes?
Pirrhus. Our troops renew the fight!   35
    And those that sallied out
    To give the rout,
    Are now returned in flight!
Solyman. Follow, follow, follow! make good the line!
    In Pirrhus, in! look, we have sprung the mine!   40

                                              Exit PIRRHUS.

Mustapha. Those desperate English n'er will fly!
    Their firmness still does hinder others' flight,
    As if their mistresses were by
    To see and praise them whilst they fight!
Solyman. That flame of valour in Alphonso's eyes   45
    Outshines the light of all my victories!
    Those who were slain when they his bulwark stormed,
    Contented fell,
    As vanquished well.
    Those who were left alive may now,   50
    Because their valour is by his reformed,
    Hope to make others bow.
Mustapha. Ere while I in the English station saw
    Beauty, that did my wonder forward draw,
    Whose valour did my forces back disperse;   55
    Fairer than woman, and than man more fierce,
    It showed such courage as disdained to yield,
    And yet seemed willing to be killed.
Solyman. This vision did to me appear,
    Which moved my pity and my fear: 60
    It had a dress much like the imagery
    For heroes drawn, and may Ianthe be.

                Enter PIRRHUS.

Pirrhus. Fall on! the English stoop when they give fire!
    They seem to furl their colours and retire!
Solyman. Advance! I only would the honour have   65
    To conquer two whom I by force would save.   *Exeunt.*

       Enter ALPHONSO *with his sword drawn.*

Alphonso. My reason by my courage is misled!
    Why chase I those who would from dying fly,
    Enforcing them to sleep amongst the dead,

---

66. *Exeunt*] *Q1; not in Q3, F.*

39. *make . . . line*] reform the line of assault.
40. *sprung*] exploded.
51. *reformed*] renewed.
54. *did . . . draw*] i.e. drew forth my amazement.
63. *Fall on*] advance.
    stoop . . . fire] i.e. betray signs of weariness.
64. *to furl*] to roll up.

Yet keep myself unslain, that fain would die?   70
Do not the prisoners whom we take declare
How Solyman proclaimed through all his host,
That they Ianthe's life and mine should spare?
Life ill preserved is worse than basely lost.
Mine by dispatch of war he will not take,   75
But means to leave it lingering on the rack;
That in his palace I might live, and know
Her shame, and be afraid to call it so.
Tyrants and devils think all pleasures vain
But what are still derived from others' pain.   80

Enter ADMIRAL.

Admiral. Renowned Alphonso, thou hast fought today
    As if all Asia were thy valour's prey.
    But now thou must do more
    Than thou hast done before;
    Else the important life of Rhodes is gone.   85
Alphonso. Why from the peaceful grave
    Should I still strive to save
    The lives of others, that would lose mine own?
Admiral. The soldiers call, Alphonso! thou hast taught
    The way to all the wonders they have wrought;   90
    Who now refuse to fight
    But in thy valour's sight.
Alphonso. I would to none example be to fly;
    But fain would teach all humankind to die.
Admiral. Haste, haste! Ianthe in disguise   95
    At the English bulwark wounded lies;
    And in the French, our old great master strives
    From many hands to rescue many lives.
Alphonso. Ianthe wounded? Where, alas,
    Has mourning pity hid her face?   100
    Let pity fly, fly far from the oppressed,
    Since she removes her lodging from my breast!
Admiral. You have but two great cruelties to choose.
    By staying here, you must Ianthe lose,
    Who ventured life and fame for you,   105
    Or your great master quite forsake,
    Who to your childhood first did show
    The ways you did to honour take.
Alphonso. Ianthe cannot be
    In safer company: 110

---

72. *host*] army.
    95–6. *Ianthe . . . lies*] Davenant may have taken this image from *Soliman and Perseda* where, in defending Rhodes, 'Perseda comes upon the walls in man's apparel' (H3r).
    103–42.] The choice between love and duty, honour and pity, is imposed on many protagonists in the heroic drama of the late seventeenth century.

For what will not the valiant English do
When beauty is distressed, and virtue too?
Admiral. Dispatch your choice, if you will either save.
    Occasion bids you run:
    You must redeem the one   115
    And I the other from a common grave.
    Alphonso, haste!
Alphonso. Thou urgest me too fast!
    This riddle is too sad and intricate;
    The hardest that was e'er proposed by fate.   120
    Honour and pity have
    Of both too short a time to choose:
    Honour the one would save,
    Pity would not the other lose.
Admiral. Away, brave duke, away!   125
    Both perish by our stay.
Alphonso. I to my noble master owe
    All that my youth did nobly do.
    He in war's school my master was,
    The ruler of my life;   130
    She my loved mistress, but, alas,
    My now suspected wife.
Admiral. By this delay we both of them forsake!
    Which of their rescues wilt thou undertake?
Alphonso. Hence Admiral, and to my master hy!   135
    I will as swiftly to my mistress fly,
    Through ambush, fire and all impediments
    The witty cruelty of war invents.
    For there does yet some taste of kindness last,
    Still relishing the virtue that is past.   140
    But how, Ianthe, can my sword successful prove,
    Where honour stops, and only pity leads my love.
        Exeunt several ways.

Enter PIRRHUS.

Pirrhus. O sudden change! repulsed in all the heat
    Of victory, and forced to loose retreat!
    Seven crescents, fixed on their redouts, are gone!   145
    Horse, horse! we fly
    From victory!
    Wheel, wheel from their reserves, and charge our own!

135. my] *Q1;* thy *Q3, F.*

---

113. *Dispatch*] hasten.
114. *Occasion*] urgent necessity.
118. *riddle*] question.
135. *hy*] hie, go swiftly.
138. *witty*] skilful in contriving evil (*OED*).
144. *loose retreat*] ragged, undisciplined retreat.
145. *redouts*] bulwarks.
148. *wheel*] turn around.

Divide that wing!
More succours bring!   150
Rally the fled,
And quit our dead!
Rescue that ensign and that drum!
Bold slaves! they to our trenches come,
Though still our army does in posture stay   155
Drawn up to judge, not act, the business of the day,
As Rome, in theatres, saw fencers play.

Enter MUSTAPHA.

Mustapha. Who can be loud enough to give command?
Stand, Haly, make a stand!
Those horses to that carriage span! Drive, drive!   160
Zangar is shot again, yet still alive!
Coyns for the culverin, then give fire
To clear the turnpikes and let Zangar in!
Look Pirrhus, look, they all begin
To alter their bold countenance, and retire!   165

The scene returns to that of the castle on the Mount Philermus.

Enter SOLYMAN.

Solyman. How cowardly my numerous slaves fall back.
Slow to assault, but dextrous when they sack.
Wild wolves in times of peace they are;
Tame sheep and harmless in the war.   170
Crowds fit to stop up breaches and prevail,
But so as shoals of herrings choke a whale.
This dragon-duke so nimbly fought today,
As if he wings had got to stoop at prey.
Ianthe is triumphant, but not gone;   175
And sees Rhodes still beleaguered, though not won.

150. succours] *Q1, Q3;* succour *F.*   166. the Mount] *Q1;* Mount *Q3, F.*

149. *wing*] division of the army on each side of the main body.
150. *succours*] support, reinforcement.
155. *posture*] position.
155–7.] i.e. instead of taking part in the action, our army watches as if it were entertainment.
160. *span*] harness.
162. *Coyns*] wedges used for raising and lowering mounted guns.
culverin] cannon.
163. *turnpikes*] spiked banners (placed across a road to obstruct an enemy's passage).
168. *dextrous . . . sack*] nimble at claiming the spoils of war when towns are sacked.
171. *Crowds . . . breaches*] Knolles comments on the miserable state of the common
soldiers whose bodies were used to fill up town ditches (Knolles, p. 591).
171–2. *prevail . . . whale*] i.e. they prevail by force of numbers, just as a multitude
of fish might choke a whale.
174. *stoop*] swoop, pounce.
176. *beleaguered*] besieged.

Audacious town! thou keepest thy station still,
And so my castle tarries on that hill;
Where I will dwell till famine enter thee,
And prove more fatal than my sword could be.   180
Nor shall Ianthe from my favours run,
But stay to meet and praise what she did shun.

The scene is changed to that of the town besieged.

Enter VILLERIUS, ADMIRAL, IANTHE.
She in a nightgown and a chair is brought in.

Villerius. Fair virtue, we have found
    No danger in your wound.   185
    Securely live,
    And credit give
    To us, and to the surgeon's art.
Ianthe. Alas, my wound is in the heart;
    Or else, where e'er it be,   190
    Imprisoned life it comes to free,
    By seconding a worser wound that hid doth lie.
    What practice can assure
    That patient of a cure,
    Whose kind of grief still makes her doubt the remedy?   195
Admiral. The wounded that would soon be eased
    Should keep their spirits tuned and pleased.
    No discord should their minds subdue:
    And who, in such distress
    As this, ought to express   200
    More joyful harmony than you?
    'Tis not alone that we assure
    Your certain cure;
    But pray remember that your blood's expense
    Was in defence   205
    Of Rhodes, which gained today a most important victory.
    For our success, repelling this assault,
    Has taught the Ottomans to halt;
    Who may, wasting their heavy body, learn to fly.
Villerius. Not only this should hasten your content,   210
    But you shall joy to know the instrument
    That wrought the triumph of this day:
    Alphonso did the sally sway,
    To whom our Rhodes all that she is does owe,

---

198. discord] *Q1;* discords *Q3, F.* minds] mind *Q1–Q3, F.*   210. Villerius] *F;*
Admiral *Q1–Q3.*

---

   192. *seconding*] adding to.
   198. *tuned*] contented.
   209.] i.e. the Turks may flee in spite of their weight of numbers (or possibly because
of the wastage of life).
   213. *Alphonso . . . sway*] i.e. Alphonso inspired and led the rush of the Rhodians
upon the Turks.

And all that from her root of hope can grow.   215
Ianthe. Has he so greatly done?
     Indeed he used to run
     As swift in honour's race as any he
     Who thinks he merits wreaths for victory.
     This is to all a comfort, and should be,   220
     If he were kind, the greatest joy to me.
     Where is my altered lord? I cannot tell
     If I may ask, if he be safe and well?
     For whilst all strangers may his actions boast,
     Who in their songs repeat   225
     The triumphs he does get,
     I only must lament his favours lost.
Villerius. Some wounds he has; none dangerous but yours
     Ianthe cured, his own he quickly cures.
Ianthe. If his be little, mine will soon grow less.   230
     Ay me! What sword
     Durst give my lord
     Those wounds which now Ianthe cannot dress.
Admiral. Ianthe will rejoice when she does hear
     How greater than himself he did appear   235
     In rescue of her life; all acts were slight
     And cold, even in our hottest fight,
     Compared to what he did,
     When with death's vizard she her beauty hid.
Villerius. Love urged his anger, till it made such haste   240
     And rushed so swiftly in,
     That scarce he did begin
     'Ere we could say the mighty work was passed.
Ianthe. All this for me? Something he did for you:
     But when his sword begun,   245
     Much more it would have done
     If he, alas, had thought Ianthe true.
Admiral. Be kind Ianthe, and be well!
     It is too pitiful to tell
     What way of dying he expressed   250
     When he that letter read
     You wrote before your wounds were dressed,
     When you and we despaired you could recover:
     Then he was more than dead,
     And much out-wept a husband and a lover.   255

          Enter ALPHONSO *wounded, led in by two mutes.*

228. dangerous] *Q1;* desperate *Q2, Q3, F.*   234. does hear] *Q1;* did hear *Q2, Q3,*
F.   235. did appear] *Q1;* does appear *Q2, Q3, F.*   240. haste] *Q3, F;* hast *Q1.*
250. he] *Q1;* is *Q3, F.*

239.] i.e. when Ianthe was believed to be near death.
251–2. *that . . . dressed*] the first allusion to any letter from Ianthe to Alphonso, an
example of Davenant's difficulty in compressing narrative details.
255.1. led in by two mutes] presumably a reference to silent performance (as in a
dumb show).

Alphonso. Tear up my wounds! I had a passion, coarse
　　　And rude enough to strengthen jealousy;
　　　But want that more refined and quicker force
　　　Which does outwrestle nature when we die.
　　　Turn to a tempest all my inward strife:　　　　　　　　　　260
　　　Let it not last,
　　　But in a blast
　　　Spend this infectious vapour, life!
Ianthe. It is my lord! Enough of strength I feel
　　　To bear me to him, or but let me kneel.　　　　　　　　265
　　　[*To Admiral*] He bled for me when he achieved for you
　　　This day's success; and much from me is due.
　　　Let me but bless him for his victory,
　　　And hasten to forgive him ere I die.　　　[*She approaches Alphonso,*
　　　　　　　　　　　　　　　　　who starts back in amazement.]
Alphonso. Keep back Ianthe, for my strength will fail　　　270
　　　If on thy cheeks I see thy roses pale.
　　　Draw all the curtains, and then lead her in;
　　　Let me in darkness mourn away my sin.　　　　　*Exeunt.*

　　　　　　　　[*Enter*] Chorus *of soldiers.*

　　　　　　　　　　　　1

　　　With a fine merry gale,
　　　Fit to fill every sail,　　　　　　　　　　　　　　275
　　　They did cut the smooth sea
　　　That our skins they might flea.
　　　Still as they landed, we firked them with sallies;
　　　We did bang their silk sashes,
　　　Through sands and through plashes,　　　　　　　280
　　　Till amain they did run to their galleys.

　　　　　　　　　　　　2

　　　They first were so mad
　　　As they jealousies had

270. will fail] *Q1*; does fail *Q3, F.*　　　271. If] *Q1*; When *Q3, F.*　　　269.1. *See Appendix*
2.　　　273.1. Enter [SOLYMAN] ROXOLANA, and women attendants *Q3, F. See Appendix* 2.

256. *Tear up my wounds*] a powerful image of self-mutilation.
256–9. *I had . . . die*] i.e although Alphonso had a fierce rage which served to increase his (unwarranted) jealousy, he has not sufficient mental strength to overcome the grief and remorse he feels at Ianthe's apparent death.
260–63.] Alphonso wishes his inner turmoil could consume his entire being, i.e. believing Ianthe to be dead, he desires death.
263. *Spend*] use up, terminate.
277. *flea*] flay.
278. *firked*] thrashed, beat.
sallies] sudden attacks, sorties.
279.] We rained blows on them (literally, on their silk turbans).
280. *plashes*] shallow pools.
281. *amain*] at full speed; in full force of numbers.
283–9.] i.e. their zeal deluded them into thinking that we would offer no resistance.

That our isle durst not stay,
But would float straight away,   285
For they landed still faster and faster.
And their old Bassa Pirrhus
Did think he could fear us;
But himself sooner feared our Grand Master.

3

Then the hugeous great Turk   290
Came to make us more work,
With enough men to eat
All he meant to defeat;
Whose wonderful worship did confirm us
In the fear he would bide here   295
So long till he died here,
By the castle he built on Philermus.

4

You began the assault
With a very long hault;
And, as haulting ye came,   300
So ye went off as lame,
And have left our Alphonso to scoff ye.
To himself, as a dainty,
He keeps his Ianthe;
Whilst we drink good wine, and you drink but coffee. 305

End of the Fifth Entry

The curtain is let fall.

Finis

292. enough] enow *Q1, Q3, F.*

---

288. *fear us*] make us fearful.
290. *hugeous great Turk*] i.e. Solyman; 'hugeous' may refer to the size of his fleet.
294. *worship*] devotion, i.e. of the Turks to Solyman.
299. *hault*] wait, delay.
300. *haulting*] limping, hobbling.
302. *scoff*] mock.
303. *dainty*] delight, a glorious person.

The story personated

SOLYMAN	Capt. Henry Cook.	
VILLERIUS	Mr Gregory Thorndell.	
ALPHONSO	Mr Edward Coleman.	
ADMIRAL	Mr Matthew Locke.	5
PIRRHUS	Mr John Harding.	
MUSTAPHA	Mr Henry Purcell.	
IANTHE	Mrs Coleman, wife to Mr Edward Coleman.	

The Composition of Vocal Music was performed by

First Entry	Mr Henry Lawes.	10
Second Entry	Capt. Henry Cook.	
Third Entry	Capt. Henry Cook.	
Fourth Entry	Mr Matthew Locke.	
Fifth Entry	Mr Henry Lawes.	

The Instrumental Music was composed by Dr Charles Coleman and   15
Mr George Hudson.

The Instrumental Music is performed by

1. The story personated] In *QIa* two actors are assigned to some of the characters, distinguished as 'Double parted'. The additional names are Dubartus Hunt (Villerius), Roger Hill (Alphonso), Peter Rymon (Admiral), Alphonso March (Pirrhus), Thomas Blagrave (Mustapha).　5. ADMIRAL Mr Matthew Locke] *This ed.*; Admiral by Mr Matthew Lock *QIa*.　Locke] Lock *Q1, QIa*.　7. Purcell] Persill *QIa*.　9. was performed by] was performed *Q1, QIa*.　12. Third Entry Capt. Henry Cook] The Third Entry by Capt. Henry Cook *Q1 QIa*.　15–23. The Instrumental Music... Banister] *QIa, Hedbäck; not in Q1, Q2*.　17. is performed by] *This ed.*; is performed *QIa*, where 'by' appears between Humphrey Madge and Thomas Balser.

2. *Capt. Henry Cook*] musician and royalist captain. At the Restoration, he wrote the music for the coronation of Charles II and was appointed master of the children of the Chapel Royal.

4. *Edward Coleman*] teacher of the viol, lute and singing and celebrated during the Restoration for his singing. Composed for Shirley's Masque 'Contention of Ajax and Ulysses' (1633).

5. *Matthew Locke*] later composer-in-ordinary to Charles II. He wrote the music with Christopher Gibbons for the 1659 production of Shirley's *Cupid and Death* and the instrumental music for the adaptation of *The Tempest* by Dryden and Davenant.

7. *Henry Purcell*] Gentleman of Charles I's Chapel Royal and 'master of the children' of Westminster Abbey where he was also music copyist. Father of the composer Henry Purcell.

8. *Mrs Coleman*] Catherine Coleman, a singer rather than an actress. Probably she was the first woman to perform professionally on the stage in England.

10. *Henry Lawes*] Gentleman of Charles I's Chapel Royal. He wrote the music for Milton's masques *Arcades* (1633) and *Comus* (1634). He also composed a recitative scene, a solo lament to be sung by a woman, *Ariadne Deserted by Theseus*, published by John Playford in 1653.

15. *Dr Charles Coleman*] member of Charles I's private band. Contributed music to Davenant's *First Day's Entertainment*. In 1662 appointed composer to the King.

Mr William Webb.
Mr Christopher Gibons.
Mr Humphrey Madge.   20
Mr Thomas Balser, *A German.*
Mr Thomas Baites.
Mr John Banister.

---

19. *Christopher Gibbons*] son of Orlando Gibbons, composer and organist. Probably the major composer of the 1653 production of Shirley's *Cupid and Death*.

INTRODUCTION

The re-staging of *The Siege of Rhodes* in the public space of the Cockpit seems to have paved the way for the performance in the same theatre of *The Cruelty of the Spaniards in Peru* in 1658. In following the success of *The Siege of Rhodes*, Davenant did not, however, imitate its production style within a new narrative but composed a novel form of dramatic entertainment. There is no indication that *The Cruelty of the Spaniards* was sung in the recitative which had characterized *Rhodes*, and it has been conjectured that Davenant reverted to the declamatory style of *The First Day's Entertainment*.[1] It is in its formal, not dramatic, structure that *The Cruelty of the Spaniards* resembles that of *Rhodes*. There are six entries which advance the narrative, each of which comprises a declamation by the Inca Priest of the Sun detailing the decline of the rule of the Incas as a result of both civil dissent and the invasion of the Spanish. This is followed in turn by an acrobatic display by the Priest's attendant and a song commenting on the action. The piece ends with the fortuitous arrival of the English, who save Peru from further colonial depredations at the hands of the Spanish.

The idea for *The Cruelty of the Spaniards in Peru* had been broached by Davenant in a letter of 1656 to John Thurloe, Secretary of State. Davenant advanced economic and pragmatic reasons for the official sanction of a dramatic revival; but it would seem that the political utility of the proposal carried the most weight. In the final paragraph of the letter Davenant proposes his subject: 'If moral representation be allowed . . . the first arguments may consist of the Spaniards' barbarous conquests in the West Indies and of their several cruelties there exercised upon the subjects of this nation: of which some use may be made.'[2] At the time of his approach to Thurloe, Davenant's proposal for a moral entertainment was firmly rooted in, and designed to appeal to, the anti-Habsburg colonialist policy of the Republic. With the signing of a peace between England and the Netherlands in April 1654, there was to be a new development in foreign policy. Reviving the anti-Spanish rhetoric last promulgated under Elizabeth, Cromwell had in December 1654 despatched an expedition under Admiral William Penn and General George Venables with the intention of launching a surprise attack on the Spanish West Indies, the source of Habsburg wealth. Cromwell defended his action in a Declaration of 1656, accusing the Spanish of violating the rights of Englishmen and the native Indians, 'in whose blood [the Spanish] have founded their empire'.[3] Pamphlets fuelled anti-Spanish antagonism. John Milton, as Cromwell's Latin secretary, had produced in 1655 a manifesto for the Protector, 'wherein is shown the reasonableness of the cause of this Republic against the depredations of the Spaniards'. Milton justified the attack on certain islands in the West Indies, 'for some time in the hands of the Spaniards', on the grounds that the Spanish had long been hostile to England in the colonies, and that 'their having so often robbed and murdered our own countrymen was cause sufficient of itself for having undertaken that late expedition, and has given us abundant reason to avenge ourselves on that People'.[4] The alleged victimization of the English settlers also provides the occasion for an attack on the Stuarts for a failure to espouse their cause in a 'manner suitable to the ancient glory of the English nation'.

This recovery of Elizabethan rhetoric of nationhood is again present in a publication to which *The Cruelty of the Spaniards in Peru* is indebted: the translation by Milton's nephew, John Phillips, of Fr Bartolomé de Las Casas's *Brevissima relación de la destrucción de las Indias* (1652). Phillips presented Las Casas's first-hand account of Spanish colonization and brutalities in the Americas under the more emotive title *The Tears of the Indians* and dedicated the work to Cromwell. Deploying biblical imagery, he calls upon the Protector to avenge the atrocities of the Spanish colonizers:

> I have laid prostrate before the throne of your justice above twenty mil-
> lions of the souls of the slaughtered Indians . . . Yet methinks I hear a
> sudden stillness among them; the cry of blood ceasing at the noise of your
> great transactions, while you arm for their revenge . . . crowning you like
> his holy warrior, David, with the highest degree of earthly fame. There-
> fore hath he inspired your Highness with a proudness like that of Joshua,
> to lead his armies forth to battle . . . your just anger against the bloody and
> popish nation of the Spaniard.[5]

Clearly, Phillips appropriates Las Casas's text in the cause of anti-Hispanism, as it had earlier been appropriated in 1583,[6] and in order to cite Cromwell as Protestant saviour. Davenant's proposal to Thurloe for an entertainment dramatizing Spanish atrocities in the Caribbean would seem to be capitalizing on a venture which, according to one popular pamphlet, was 'the discourse of the Nation'.[7] There is no record of Thurloe's response to Davenant's specific plan for the revival of drama, but it may be assumed that, since the production did not take place until 1658, there was some reservation about its putative subject. While Da-venant's plans for the production of drama underwriting the so-called Western design may have espoused its objectives, in 1656 they could only throw into relief its abject failure. The quest for colonial domination, economic and Protestant, began with the failure to take San Domingo in Hispaniola; it ended in May 1655 with the inglorious occupation of Jamaica, which became a possession constantly threatened by the resist-ance of Spanish guerillas as well as counter attacks from Cuba.[8] On their return to England Penn and Venables were imprisoned for deserting their posts.

That *The Cruelty of the Spaniards in Peru* was not staged immediate to Davenant's proposal to Thurloe was probably related to the outcome

of the West Indies expedition. The incongruity of an entertainment celebrating a colonial venture which had largely been a failure would account
for Davenant's shift to the dramatic preoccupations of *The First Day's
Entertainment* and *The Siege of Rhodes*. The drama which Davenant had
implied would serve the propaganda war against Spain was eventually
produced during the last months of the Protectorate. By 1658 it was
possible to set the failure in the Spanish Indies against a more glorious
perception of Cromwell's imperial design. Writing in praise of Cromwell
immediate to his death Richard Flecknoe had commented: 'Though in the
Spanish Indies we failed of that success we hoped for, what praises does
he deserve of England who intended the erecting of the whole Indies into
one entire trophy of our victory, to show the mightiness of the English
nation.'[9]

Davenant drew not only from the corpus of literature describing
Spanish atrocities in the New World, subsequently known to the Spanish
as the Black Legend,[10] but also to a greater extent from Peruvian history
and mythology, as recounted by Garcilaso de la Vega in *The Royal Commentaries of Peru*.[11] In each entry of the entertainment, the royal Priest
of the Sun narrates those events in Peruvian history, culminating in the
fatal civil war between the Inca brothers, which facilitated a successful
Spanish invasion and colonization. In the first entry, the Sun Priest's declamation, describing a way of life before the Inca conquest, heightens the
anti-colonial celebration of primitive man, unaffected by civil codes and
martial conflicts and governed by a social hierarchy according to natural
law. This primitivism is echoed in the song, which evokes nostalgically a
time of lost political innocence when the Indians, ignorant of both city
life and war, 'feared the weather more than power'.

Throughout the text the language works metaphorically to move the
lament from the particular disruption of the native Peruvian civilization
through civil war and foreign invasion to grief for the displacement of a
society characterized by peace and sportive pleasures. In the third entry,
the imagery advances the masque beyond the immediate context of the
Inca war by alluding to general causes of civil strife engendered by the
intrusion of domestic concerns in State affairs. The twelfth Inca had defied
the tradition of marrying one of his sisters by choosing as one of his wives
a woman not of Inca blood. The third song concludes with an explicit
critique of this impingement of private familial interests on public action:
'But Kings who move / Within a lowly sphere of private love / Are too
domestic for a throne.' This would seem to be more than an endorsement
of the Inca belief in their own divinity and of the necessity of keeping 'the
royal blood entire' and carries possible allusions to the fate of Charles I.
It seems quite possible that an audience would have decoded the dramatic
situation as an image of the King's reputed subservience to the advice of
his Queen, Henrietta Maria, reflecting a view of the marriage which had
become common currency since the publication of the King's private correspondence in 1645.[12] The Sun Priest's pronouncement on civil war and

the song which follows move the text beyond colonialist politics to more explicitly national concerns.

The Inca text controls *The Cruelty of the Spaniards in Peru* until the fourth entry, when the Spanish invasion becomes the dramatic focus. At first, as in the various accounts of the arrival of the Spanish in the New World recounted by Las Casas, the Spanish are sighted and received with both foreboding and the belief that they are angels from heaven.[13] The song of the fourth entry expresses wonder at the arrival of the colonizers, which abruptly changes to fear in the fifth entry when Spanish brutalities are exposed. Visual and verbal effects contribute to images of Spanish atrocities, which Las Casas had described as more excessive than were to be found anywhere else in the New World. The fifth declamation by the Sun Priest evokes the cynicism with which the Spanish proselytize. The colonizers present themselves as providentially sent 'as just destroyers of idolatry', yet, since under Christian law conversion brings with it freedom from slavery, they do not encourage the Indians to abandon their idols. The Indians thus remain open to legitimate exploitation and abuse, graphically illustrated in the final stage direction of the fifth entry when three Peruvians enter 'limping in silver fetters' and, having been driven into the woods, reappear 'loaden with Indian baskets full of gold ingots and silver wedges'. The image is culled from Garcilaso's account of Spanish colonization as recounted by Purchas: 'The Spanish forced them by tortures to bring them gold; if any having it fled those torturers into the woods, the Spaniards hunted them with dogs.'[14] A stark scene of torture in the previous entry, depicting an Indian prince being basted upon a spit, was later to be reused as part of the scenic design of another drama dealing in atrocity, Dryden's *Amboyna or the Cruelties of the Dutch to the English Merchants* (1672).[15] The latter, based on the brutal massacre of English merchants by the Dutch in 1623 at Amboyna in the East Indies, served a similar ideological purpose to that of *The Cruelty of the Spaniards in Peru* in fuelling a specific nationalist sentiment and was no doubt influenced by it.

In the arrival of the English, Davenant represents a fantastic colonial encounter. Through the vision of the Sun Priest and the visual effect of the scene in the sixth entry, Davenant predicates the scattering of the Spanish forces by English soldiers in red coats, the uniform of the infantry of Cromwell's New Model Army.[16] The song further predicts the subordination of the Spanish conquerors and, in the symbol of the emblematic lion, their supersession by the English as colonizers of the New World. In the final ritualistic dance, recalling the triumphant and harmonic endings of the masque, we are left with images of submissive foes and victorious celebration: the Spanish are forced to pay homage to the English, while the response of the Indians to the English suggests an idealized harmony of colonizer and colonized. The entertainment thus looks both ways. In its appeal to English military strength and colonial expansionism, it celebrates the Republic, while in its nostalgic evocation of life before the

Inca civil war *The Cruelty of the Spaniards in Peru* is redolent of royalist reminiscences of an age of ease and recreation before the advent of
war.

As do *The Siege of Rhodes* and *Sir Francis Drake*, *The Cruelty of the
Spaniards* serves national self-interest; but it is much less a dramatic text
than are Davenant's other Commonwealth dramas. Narrative commentary comprises much of the libretto which circulated prior to performance, while the central figure, the Inca Priest of the Sun, who is confined
to a role of narrative and exposition, is hardly a character, as even Drake
can claim to be. Yet the piece has notable theatrical qualities. With its use
of evocative scenic images, symphonic music, song, adaptation of popular
dance tunes, rope dancing and, particularly, the spectacular acrobatic
turns of the attendant to the Priest of the Sun, *The Cruelty of the
Spaniards in Peru* represents innovative and hybrid theatre practice.
Antecedents as aesthetically distanced as court opera and rope dancing
at country fairs all contribute to its particular form and design. While
the ostensible purpose of the piece is far removed from the reification of
Stuart monarchy in the court masque, Davenant nevertheless appropriates the form in the service of the Republic. This is particularly apparent
in the symbolic dance closing the final entry. Instead of exalting and
mystifying royal authority as in the masque, the dance of *The Cruelty
of the Spaniards* envisions, in the figures of the red-coated soldiers,
the dominance of British military power and the defeat of Spanish
imperialism.

A NOTE ON THE TEXT

The Cruelty of the Spaniards in Peru, based on the performance at the
Cockpit in Drury Lane, was published in 1658. The piece was later incorporated, as the fourth act, into Davenant's Restoration miscellany, *A Playhouse to be Let*, included in the Folio edition of Davenant's *Works* (1673).
The Folio version is prefaced by a dialogue between a player and the
'house-keeper' of the playhouse, which creates a comic nuance entirely
absent in the 1658 text. Commenting on the appearance of the Priest of
the Sun, the house-keeper asks the player, 'What's he? a human bird?'
This edition has as copy text the 1658 Quarto (Q) collated with the Folio
text.

NOTES

1 See Eric Walter White, *A History of English Opera* (London, 1983), p. 75.
2 See C. H. Firth, 'Sir William Davenant and the Revival of the Drama during the
Protectorate', *English Historical Review*, 18 (1903), 319–21.
3 *Declaration of his Highness, by the advice of his council; setting forth . . . the justice
of their cause against Spain*, 26 October 1656, p. 138.

4 See *A Manifesto of the Lord Protector . . . Wherein is shown the reasonableness of the cause of the Republic against the depredations of the Spaniards. Written in Latin by John Milton and First Printed in 1655, now translated into English* (1738), p. 6.

5 John Phillips, *The Tears of the Indians* (1656), A3v.

6 *The Spanish Colony: or, brief chronicle of the acts and gestes of the Spaniards in the West Indies* (1583). It was exploited by Richard Hakluyt in his *Discourse concerning Western Planting* (1584).

7 *A dialogue containing a compendious discourse concerning the present design in the West-Indies*, 20 September 1655, p. 2.

8 See G. M. D. Howat, *Stuart and Cromwellian Foreign Policy* (London, 1974), pp. 86–90. Misinformation about the expedition meant that news of its failure was slow to circulate. Cromwell was unable to reconcile defeat with his belief in his providential role. See David Armitage, 'The Cromwellian Protectorate and the Language of Empire', *The Historical Journal*, 35:3 (1992), 531–55, p. 540.

9 Richard Flecknoe, *The Idea of his Highness Oliver, late Lord Protector, with certain brief reflections on his life* (1659), pp. 41–2.

10 See William S. Maltby, *The Black Legend in England: The Development of Anti-Spanish Sentiment, 1558–1660* (Durham, NC, 1971), pp. 13–15.

11 This was popularized by Samuel Purchas in the Fourth Part of *Purchas His Pilgrims* (1625). Purchas summarizes *The Royal Commentaries* as 'the History of things done by the Incas, before the Spanish Conquest', Purchas, chapter 13, p. 1454.

12 See Lois Potter, *Secret Rites and Secret Writing: Royalist Literature 1641–1660* (Cambridge, 1989), pp. 58–62.

13 See Las Casas, pp. 112–13.

14 Purchas, p. 1454.

15 See Winn, p. 219. Dryden dramatized the story of Dutch sadism, adding scenes of rape and torture. The King's Company had inherited the old scenery from Davenant's company, the Duke's Company.

16 The New Model Army wore red coats from the beginning. *Perfect Passages* notes 'The Men are Redcoats all, the whole army only are distinguished by several facings of their coats', 7 May 1645.

The Cruelty of the Spaniards in Peru

Expressed by instrumental and vocal music, and by art of perspectives in scenes, &c. Represented daily at the Cockpit in Drury Lane, at three after noon punctually.

London

Printed for Henry Herringman, and are to be sold at his shop at the Anchor in the Lower Walk in the New Exchange.

1658

DRAMATIS PERSONAE

[PRIEST OF THE SUN
His attendant
[CHORUS of] Peruvians
Spaniards
English soldiers
Two apes in costume]

5

1. *PRIEST OF THE SUN*] High Priest of the Incas; of royal blood.

THE CRUELTY
OF THE SPANIARDS IN PERU

The Description of the Frontispiece

An arch is discerned raised upon stone of rustic work; upon the top of
which is written, in an antique shield, Peru; and two antique shields
are fixed a little lower on the sides, the one bearing the figure of the
sun, which was the scutcheon of the Incas, who were Emperors of Peru:
the other did bear the spread-eagle, in signification of the Austrian   5
family. The design of the frontispiece is, by way of preparation, to give
some notice of that argument which is pursued in the scene.

The Argument of the Whole Design, Consisting of Six Entries

The design is first to represent the happy condition of the people of
Peru anciently when their inclinations were governed by Nature; and
then it makes some discovery of their establishment under the twelve   10
Incas, and of the dissensions of the two sons of the last Inca. Then
proceeds to the discovery of that new western world by the Spaniard,
which happened to be during the dissension of the two royal brethren.
It likewise proceeds to the Spaniards' conquest of that Incan empire,
and then discovers the cruelty of the Spaniards over the Indians, and   15
over all Christians (excepting those of their own nations) who, landing
in those parts, came unhappily into their power. And towards the
conclusion, it infers the voyages of the English thither, and the amity
of the natives towards them, under whose ensigns (encouraged by a
prophecy of their chief priest) they hope to be made victorious, and to   20
be freed from the yoke of the Spaniard.

0.1–7. The description . . . scene] *not in* F.   0.8. The Cruelty of the Spaniards in Peru] F.

   0.1. frontispiece] emblematic decoration at the front of the stage, framing the stage picture.
   1. rustic] rough-hewn.
   4. scutcheon] escutcheon, badge.
   5. spread-eagle] The representation of an eagle with body and wings displayed was an emblem of the Habsburgs and formerly symbolic of the Holy Roman Empire. When Francisco Pizarro conquered Peru 1531–33 under the Inca emperor Atahualpa he did so in the name of the Habsburg Empire.
   7. *argument*] subject matter.
   7.1. *entries*] Davenant continues the masque-like practice, adopted in *The Siege of Rhodes*, of employing the term 'entry' instead of 'act'. Unlike in the masque, however, each entry is clearly defined as advancing the dramatic narrative.
   11. dissensions . . . Inca] a reference to the rivalry between Huáscar, the direct heir of the Inca Huayna Capac, and the Inca's favourite son Atahualpa.
   18. infers] leads to, projects to.
   19. ensigns] military or naval banners.

The curtain is drawn up.

FIRST ENTRY

The audience are entertained by instrumental music and a symphony
(being a wild air suitable to the region); which having prepared the
scene, a landscape of the West Indies is discerned; distinguished from
other regions by the parched and bare tops of distant hills, by sands
shining on the shore of rivers, and the natives, in feathered habits and   5
bonnets carrying, in Indian baskets, ingots of gold and wedges of silver.
Some of the natives being likewise discerned in their natural sports of
hunting and fishing. This prospect is made through a wood, differing
from those of European climates by representing of coco trees, pines
and palmitos; and on the boughs of other trees are seen monkeys, apes   10
and parrots; and at farther distance, valleys of sugarcanes.
   The symphony being ended, the chief priest of Peru enters with his
attendant after him. The priest is clothed in a garment of feathers longer
than any of those that are worn by other natives, with a bonnet whose
ornament of plumes does likewise give him a distinction from the rest,   15
and carries in his hand a gilded verge. He likewise, because the
Peruvians were worshippers of the sun, carries the figure of the sun on
his bonnet and breast.

The First Speech

Spoken by the Priest of the Sun: taking a short view of their condition,
before the royal family of the Incas taught them to live together in   20
multitudes under laws and made them by arms reduce many other
nations.

Priest. Thus fresh did Nature in our world appear,
         When first her roses did their leaves unfold:
         Ere she did use Art's colours, and ere fear   25
         Had made her pale, or she with cares looked old.
         Parents and age first taught the laws of sway.

0.1. The curtain . . . drawn up] *not in* F.

   1.1. symphony] piece of music played in concert.
   2. wild] fast, exuberant.
   3. a landscape . . . discerned] Beyond the arch would have been a curtain, drawn up
at the beginning of the performance to reveal a scenic stage.
   10. palmitos] diminutive species of palm.
   coco] coconut.
   16. verge] a rod or ward carried as an emblem of authority (*OED*).
   17. figure] emblem.
   19. Priest of the Sun] According to Purchas, the Priest of the Sun was of royal blood.
The speech which follows is an idealized version of Purchas's account of the primitive
life of the Indians before the Incas taught them the use of arts and arms (Purchas, pp.
1456–62).
   21. reduce] conquer.
   27.] i.e. conduct was directed by reverence for age and parents.
   sway] authority

When yet we no just motive had to fear
Our bolder Incas would by arms be raised;
When, temperately, they still contented were,   30
As great examples, to be only praised.
When none for being strong did seek reward,
Nor any for the space of empire strove:
When valour courted peace and never cared
For any recompense, but public love.   35
We fettered none, nor were by any bound;
None followed gold through labyrinths of the mine:
And that which we on strands of rivers found,
Did only on our priests in temples shine.
Then with his verge, each priest   40
Could, like an exorcist,
The coldest of his students warm,
And thus provoke them with a charm.

The speech being ended, the priest waves his verge, and his attendant,
with extraordinary activity, performs the Somerset: and afterwards,   45
waving his verge towards the room where the music are placed behind
the curtain, this song is sung.

> [*Exit* PRIEST *and* attendant.]

> [*Enter* CHORUS of Peruvians.]

The First Song

In pursuance of the manner of their life, before their Incas brought them
to live in cities, and to build forts.

1

Whilst yet our world was new,   50
When not discovered by the old,
Ere beggared slaves we grew,
For having silver hills, and strands of gold.

44–7.] *not in* F.

30. *temperately*] with moderation, showing self-restraint.
38. *strands*] banks.
40–3. *each priest . . . charm*] i.e. the early Inca priests employed rituals which
allowed the people to express their natural vigour. This is represented in the physical
prowess of the attendant's acrobatic turns.
43. *provoke*] spur on, rouse.
charm] incantation.
45. Somerset] somersault. The first of a number of lively acrobatic tricks performed
by the priest's attendant.
46. the music] i.e. the musicians, who were probably placed in a curtained 'room'
constructed on a grid or roof set at a level with the frontispiece border. See *Rhodes*, p.
194 nn. 16–17, and Orrell, p. 74.
47.3. the First Song] The songs at the end of each entry would seem to be sung by
a soloist and a chorus of Peruvians.
50–1.] i.e. before colonization.

Chorus

We danced and we sung,
And looked ever young,   55
And from restraints were free,
As waves and winds at sea.

2

When wildly we did live,
Ere crafty cities made us tame:
When each his whole would give   60
To all, and none peculiar right did claim.

Chorus

We danced and we sung, &c.

3

When none did riches wish,
And none were rich by business made;
When all did hunt or fish,   65
And sport was all our labour and our trade.

Chorus

We danced and we sung, &c.

4

When forts were not devised,
Nor citadels did towns devour:
When lowly sheds sufficed,   70
Because we feared the weather more than power.

Chorus

We danced and we sung, &c.

5

When garments were not worn,
Nor shame did nakedness resent:

53.1. Chorus] i.e. refrain.
58. *wildly*] freely.
59. *crafty*] strong, powerful, mighty (*OED*).
61. *none . . . claim*] no claims were made for private property.
68–71.] Purchas's account of native Peruvian culture contains a description of how under the Incas cities were built and men were trained to arms (Purchas, p. 1456).
69. *citadels*] fortresses commanding cities, serving both to protect and to keep them in subjection.
70. *sheds*] huts.
73–5.] 'The Queen . . . taught the women to work in cotton and wool, and to make garments for their husbands and children, with other household offices' (Purchas, p. 1456).
74.] i.e. we felt no shame at our nakedness.

Nor poverty bred scorn,   75
When none could want, and all were innocent.

Chorus

We danced and we sung, &c.   [*Exit* CHORUS.]

After this song, a rope descends out of the clouds, and is stretched to
a stiffness by an engine while a rustic air is played, to which two apes
from opposite sides of the wood come out, listen, return; and, coming   80
out again, begin to dance. Then, after a while, one of them leaps up
to the rope, and there dances to the same air, whilst the other moves
to his measures below. Then both retire into the wood. The rope
ascends.

SECOND ENTRY

An almain and coranto are played: after which a trumpet air changes
the scene; where a fleet is discerned at distance, with a prospect of the
sea and Indian coast; the ships bearing in their flags the spread-eagle,
to denote the Austrian family; and on the right side are seen some
natives of Peru, pointing with amazement to the fleet (as never having   5
had the view of ships before), and in a mourning condition take their
leaves of their wives and children because of an ancient prophecy
amongst them, which did signify that a bearded people (those of Peru
having ever held it uncomely to wear beards) should spring out of the
sea and conquer them. The object having remained a while, the Priest   10
of the Sun enters with his attendant.

The Second Speech

Describing briefly the pleasant lives of the Incas till this season of
fulfilling that prophecy, when a bearded people should come from the

78–84. After this song ... ascends] *not in F.*   1. coranto] *This ed. (throughout);*
corante *Q and F.*   11. with his attendant] *not in F.*

78–9. a rope descends ... engine] the first indication that the refurbished *Cockpit*
contained some machinery for spectacular events. The dances evidently took place on
the scenic stage.
   79. two apes] Although trained monkeys did appear on stage, here they are clearly
actors in costume (see Feinberg, 'Like Demie Gods the Apes Began to Move', p. 2).
   83. measures] dance steps.

   2.1. almain] dance music in slow time.
   coranto] a tune in triple time accompanying a dance. But neither tune is accompanied here by dancing.
   1–2. after ... scene] i.e. the music is played while the new scene is slid into place.
   7. an ancient prophecy ... conquer them] In Purchas, the twelfth Inca, Huayna Capac,
relates the prophecy of the Spanish conquest as a dying address to his servants. In contrast
to Davenant's redaction, the King represents the Spanish as a valiant nation exceeding in
every way the Incas, and commands his people to obey and serve them (see Purchas, p. 1482).
   8. bearded people] i.e. the Spaniards.
   10. object] spectacle.

sea to destroy them and two of the Incan family ruin that empire which
twelve of the emperors had erected.   15

Priest. In all the soft delights of sleep and ease,
  Secure from war, in peaceful palaces,
  Our Incas lived: but now I see their doom.
  Guided by winds, the bearded people come!
  And that dire prophecy must be fulfilled,   20
  When two shall ruin what our twelve did build.
  'Tis long since first the sun's chief priest foretold,
  That cruel men, idolators of gold,
  Should pass vast seas to seek their harbour here.
  Behold, in floating castles they appear!   25
  Mine eyes are struck! Away, away
  With gentle love's delicious sway!
  The Incas from their wives must fly!
  And ours may soon believe
  We mourn to see them grieve,   30
  But shall rejoice to see them die.
  For they by dying safety gain:
  And when they quit,
  In death's cold fit,
  Love's pleasure, they shall lose life's pain.   35

The priest having waved his verge, his attendant performs the trick of
activity called the sea horse.
          [*Exit* PRIEST *and attendant.*]

     [*Enter* CHORUS.]

     The Second Song

Intimating their sorrow for their future condition (according to the
prophecy) under their new masters, the Spaniards.

        I

    No more, no more,   40
    Shall we drag to the shore
    Our nets at the ebb of the flood;
    Nor after we lay
    The toils for our prey,
    Shall we meet to compass the wood.   45

36–7.] *not in* F.

---

 25. *floating castles*] galleons, large vessels of both war and trade.
 29. *ours*] i.e. our eyes.
 29–30.] It is better for Peruvian wives to die than endure Spanish cruelty.
 36–7. *trick . . . sea horse*] another acrobatic turn (as with the attendant's subsequent actions, it is not recorded in *OED*).
 37.3. The Second Song] The first two stanzas are sung by a soloist and the third in chorus.
 44. *toils*] traps, snares (for wild animals).
 45. *compass*] surround.

Nor with our arrows e'er delight
To get renown
By taking down
The soaring eagle in his flight.

2

Make haste! make haste!   50
You delights that are past!
And do not to our thoughts appear:
Lest vainly we boast
Of joys we have lost,
And grieve to reckon what we were.   55
The Incas' glory now is gone!
Dark grows that light
Which cheered our sight;
Set is their deity, the sun.

Chorus

All creatures when they breed   60
May then with safety feed.
All shall have times for liberty but we:
We, who their masters were,
Must now such masters fear,
As will no season give us to be free.   [*Exit* CHORUS.]   65

*This song being ended, a doleful air is heard which prepares the
entrance of two Indians, in their feathered habits of Peru; they enter
severally from the opposite sides of the wood, and, gazing on the face
of the scene, fall into a mimic dance, in which they express the argument
of the prospect by their admiration at the sight of the ships (which was   70
to those of Peru a new and wonderful object) and their lamentation at
beholding their countrymen in deep affliction and taking their leaves of
their wives and children. [They exit.]*

THIRD ENTRY

*A symphony consisting of four tunes prepares the change of the scene:
the prospect consisting of a plain Indian country, in which are discerned*

48–9. *By . . . flight*] by killing at great distance the eagle, a bird of prey; possibly
also an allusion to the eagle as emblem of the Habsburgs, thus of the Spanish.

59. *their deity, the sun*] The Incas' rule is over; the Incas believed that they derived
their pedigree from the Sun, to whom Death returned them.

65.] i.e. unlike animals, who have seasons (times) when they can be free from preda-
tors in order to breed, the Indians will be continually consigned to Spanish slavery.

66. doleful] sorrowful.

67–8. they . . . wood] This suggests that as part of the scenic stage there were fixed
wings depicting wooded scenes.

69–70. fall . . . prospect] The Indians mime the events depicted on the scene, i.e.
their amazement at the sighting of the Spanish followed by the expression of grief at
their fate.

3.2. plain] flat, level.

at distance two Peruvian armies marching and ready to give battle,
being led by the two royal brethren, sons of the last Inca, armed with
bows, glaves and spears, and wearing quivers on their backs. The object   5
having continued a while, the Priest of the Sun enters with his attendant.

The Third Speech

Intimating the unhappy event of the love of the last Inca; for he
(contrary to the custom of all his royal ancestors, who always married
their own sisters) had chosen to his second wife the beautiful daughter
of an inferior prince: his priests and people having always believed no   10
blood less distant than that of his sisters worthy to mingle with his own
for propagation of the imperial race. This foreign beauty so far
prevailed on his passion that she made him in his age assign a
considerable part of his dominion to a younger son, his ancestors never
having, during eleven generations, divided their Empire. This youth,   15
growing ambitious after his father's death, invaded his elder brother at
that unfortunate time when the Spaniards, pursuing their second
discovery of the Peruvian coast, landed and made a prodigious use of
the division of the two brethren, by proving successful in giving their
assistance to the unjust cause of the younger.   20

Priest. How fatal did our Inca's passion prove,
    Whilst long made subject to a foreign love.
    Poor lovers, who from empire's arts are free,
    By nature may entirely guided be.

---

6. with his attendant] *Q; not in* F.

3–4. two . . . last Inca] armies led by Huáscar, the lawful heir, and by Atahualpa, also son of Huayna Capac, but by a secondary wife.

5. glaves] glaive, a weapon consisting of a blade fastened to a long handle; a kind of halbert (*OED*).

8–9. always married their own sisters] The Inca emperors married within the family to prevent the royal blood—and what they believed to be their divine origins—from being tainted. The Inca Sinchi Roca, for example, according the Purchas, 'married with his eldest sister, after the manner of his parents, and of the Sun and Moon, thinking the Moon to be sister and wife to the Sun' (Purchas, p. 1458).

9–10. daughter . . . prince] the daughter of King Quitu, vassal to Huayna Capac.

13. in his age] i.e. in his old age.

17–19. second . . . brethren] The supposed events of Davenant's entertainment took place in 1530 when Francisco Pizarro made his second expedition to Peru during the Inca civil war. The first expedition had been in 1524.

20. younger] i.e. Atahualpa.

21–34. our Inca's . . . heart] Huayna Capac married two of his sisters, but, having no children with them, he married his cousin and had a son, Huáscar. According to Purchas, Huayna Capac had over two hundred children, but he favoured particularly Atahualpa, son of the daughter of King Quitu: 'finding his son Atahualpa witty, wise, warlike and comely of personage, he much affected him, and still would have him about him, and so handled the matter that with the consent of his brother Huáscar he set him in possession of the Kingdom of Quintu and other provinces' (Purchas, p. 1481).

23. empire's arts] the responsibilities of government.

They may retire to shady cottages,	25
And study there only themselves to please:
For few consider what they mean or do;
But nations are concerned when monarchs woo.
And though our Inca by no law was tied
To love but one, yet could he not divide	30
His public empire as his private bed;
In thrones each is to whole dominion bred.
He blindly prized his younger son's desert,
Dividing empire as he did his heart.
And since his death, this made the younger dare	35
To affront the elder's sovereignty with war.
Ambition's monstrous stomach does increase
By eating, and it fears to starve, unless
It still may feed, and all it sees devour.
Ambition is not tired with toil, nor cloyed with power.	40

*This speech being ended, the priest waves his verge, and his attendant
very actively performs the spring; and they departing, this third song
is sung.*

[*Enter* CHORUS.]

The Third Song

*Which pursues the argument of the speech, and farther illustrates the
many miseries which the civil war between the two royal brothers	45
produced.*

I

Twelve Incas have successively
Our spacious empire swayed;
Whose power whilst we obeyed,
We lived so happy and so free,	50
As if we were not kept in awe
By any law,
Which martial king aloud proclaim.
Soft conscience, Nature's whisp'ring orator,

41–3.] *Q; not in F.*

32.] i.e. Kings are born to preserve the integrity of their kingdoms.
33. *desert*] merits.
37–9.] i.e. ambition is never satiated; it will not rest, in the knowledge that there is
more to conquer.
40. *nor cloyed*] never satisfied.
42. the spring] another energetic dance, perhaps representing the ambitious energy
of Atahualpa.
48. *swayed*] ruled.
49–57.] Even if laws were in effect backed by military power, they did not need to
be enforced as the Peruvians were happy to obey them. They were guided by conscience
('Nature's whisp'ring orator') which divined the natural law.

Did teach us what to love or to abhor;   55
And all our punishment was shame.

2

Our late great Inca fatally
Did by a second wife
Eclipse his shining life,
Whilst reason did on love rely.   60
Those rays she often turned and checked,
Which with direct
Full beams should have adorned his known
And first authorisèd race: but kings who move
Within a lowly sphere of private love   65
Are too domestic for a throne.

Chorus

Now rigid war is come, and peace is gone,
Fear governs us, and jealousy the throne.
Ambition hath our chiefs possessed.
All now are waked, all are alarmed.   70
The weary know not where to rest,
Nor dare the harmless be unarmed.   [*Exit.*]

*After this song a warlike air is played, to which succeeds a martial dance
performed by four Peruvians armed with glaves, who enter severally
from opposite sides of the wood, and express by their motions and   75
gestures the fury of that civil war which, by the ambition of the younger
brother, has engaged their country; and then depart in pursuit of each
other.*

[*Enter* CHORUS.]

FOURTH ENTRY

*A symphony consisting of four tunes prepares the change of scene,
which represents a great Peruvian army put to flight by a small body
of Spaniards. This object is produced in pursuance of the main
argument, for the Spaniards, having first bred an amazement in
the natives by the noise and fire of their guns, and having afterwards   5
subverted the elder Inca by assisting the younger, did in a short*

---

58. *second wife*] actually, one of a number of wives. Davenant reduces the com-
plexity of the Incan domestic arrangements.
58–64. *Did . . . race*] The suggestion is not only that Huayna Capac's infatuation
clouded his judgement but that his 'second' wife deliberately diverted his affections
away from his more direct heirs and towards her son.
67. *rigid*] harsh, severe.
68. *jealousy*] i.e. rivalry, resentment.
70. *waked*] watchful, abstaining from sleep.
73. martial dance] warlike dance.

4.6–7. subverted . . . conquest] Purchas's account emphasizes the tyranny of Atahualpa rather than his complicity with the Spaniards.

time attain the dominion over both by conquest. The object of this
scene having remained awhile, the Priest of the Sun enters with his
attendant.

The Fourth Speech

Intimating the amazement of the Peruvians at the sight of the Spaniards   10
in arms; the consideration of the great distance of the region from
whence they came, of the ill effects of armour worn by a people whom
they never had offended, and of the security of innocence.

Priest. What dark and distant region bred
    For war that bearded race,   15
    Whose every uncouth face
    We more than death's cold visage dread?
    They could not still be guided by the sun,
    Nor had they every night
    The moon to inform their sight,   20
    How durst they seek those dangers which we shun?
    Sure they must more than mortal be,
    That did so little care
    For life, or else they are
    Surer of future life than we.   25
    But how they reason's laws in life fulfil
    We know not; yet we know,
    That scorn of life is low,
    Compared to the disdain of living ill.
    And we may judge that all they do   30
    In life's whole scene is bad,
    Since they with arms are clad,
    Defensive and offensive too.
    In nature it is fear that makes us arm,
    And fear by guilt is bred.   35
    The guiltless nothing dread,
    Defence not seeking, nor designing harm.

8–9. with his attendant] *Q; not in* F.

---

12. *ill*] harmful.
16. *uncouth*] alien, foreign; strange and unpleasant.
17. *visage*] face.
18. *still*] constantly, unchangingly.
18–20.] i.e. the Priest suggests that the Spaniards must be deprived of the constant light of the sun and the moon, and that the lack of those guiding influences leads them to embark on long voyages of conquest.
19. *had they*] could they have had.
21. *durst*] dare.
26.] how they reconcile their acts with the natural law.
28–9.] The Spaniards' disregard for the lives of the Peruvians is a base trait especially when compared with (the Peruvians') distaste for dishonourable ways of life.
32–3.] i.e. they wield weapons ('offensive' arms), as well as wearing armour and carrying shields ('defensive' arms).
37.] In their natural state the Peruvians do not need any form of defence since they neither cause nor intend harm to anyone.

*The Priest of the Sun waves his verge, and his attendant performs the
self-spring.*

> [*Exit* PRIEST *and* attendant.]

> [*Enter* CHORUS.]

The Fourth Song

Pursuing the argument of the amazement and fear of the natives,   40
*occasioned by the consideration of the long voyage of the Spaniards to
invade them.*

I

> Those foreign shapes so strange appear,
> That wonderful they seem;
> And strangeness breeds esteem,   45
> And wonder doth engender fear,
> And from our fear does adoration rise.
> Else why do we incline
> To think them powers divine,
> And that we are ordained their sacrifice?   50

Chorus

[*Chorus Member*] 1. When we our arrows draw,
> It is with dreadful awe:
[*Chorus Member*] 2. Moving towards them whom we are loath to
> meet,
[*Chorus Member*] 3. As if we marched to face our destiny;
[*Chorus Member*] 4. Not trusting to our arrows but our feet,   55
> As if our business were to fly, to fly!

2

All in Chorus.   We thought them more than human kind,
> That durst adventure life
> Through the tempestuous strife
> Of seas, and every raging wind.   60
> Through seas so wide, and for their depth so
> feared,
> That we by leaps as soon
> May reach the ascended moon,

38–9.] Q; *not in* F.

39. self-spring] possibly a backwards somersault, suggesting the Peruvians' alarm at
the arrival of the Spaniards.

43–50.] The oft-repeated Inca prophecy, mediated through Purchas and Garcilaso
de la Vega, was that the Spanish would bring better law and customs (Purchas, p. 1486).
Las Casas records that on the island of Puna (off modern Ecuador) 'the Spaniards were
welcomed by the ruler and his people as if they were angels from heaven' (Las Casas,
p. 113).

52. *dreadful*] fearful.

55–7.] i.e. anticipating that the only means of survival is through flight.

> As guess through what vast dangers they have
> steered.

Chorus

[*Chorus Member*] 1. When we our arrows draw, &c. [*Exit.*] 65

This song being ended, a saraband is played, whilst two Spaniards enter from the opposite sides of the scene, exactly clothed and armed according to the custom of their nation and, to express their triumph after the victory over the natives, they solemnly uncloak and unarm themselves to the tune and afterwards dance with castanets. [Spaniards 70 exit.]

FIFTH ENTRY

A doleful pavane is played to prepare the change of scene, which represents a dark prison at great distance; and farther to the view are discerned racks and other engines of torment, with which the Spaniards are tormenting the natives and English mariners, which may be supposed to be lately landed there to discover the coast. Two Spaniards 5 are likewise discovered, sitting in their cloaks and appearing more solemn in ruffs, with rapiers and daggers by their sides; the one turning a spit, whilst the other is basting an Indian prince, which is roasted at an artificial fire. This object having remained a while, the Priest of the Sun enters with his attendant. 10

The Fifth Speech

The horror of the natives, bred by the object of the diversity of new torments devised by the Spaniards.

---

70. castanets] castanietos *Q, F.*   10. with his attendant] *Q; not in F.*

66. saraband] a country dance.
66–70. two Spaniards . . . castanets] There is a similar stage direction in Dryden's *Indian Emperor*, 4.2. See also *Drake*, Fifth Entry, lines 172–3.

5.1. pavane] music for a dance in simple duple time and of stately character.
2–9. represents . . . fire] a perspective scene later reused in Dryden's *Amboyna or The Cruelty of the Dutch to the English Merchants* (1672).
3–4. racks . . . mariners] In Purchas's account, the *mestizos*, born of Peruvian mothers and Spanish fathers, were particularly subjected to torture by the Spaniards.
5. discover] explore.
5–9. Two Spaniards . . . fire] The reference to an 'artificial fire' makes clear that the representation of Spanish torture was not part of the scenic stage. See Winn, p. 239.
8. an Indian prince] Atahualpa. Las Casas records, amongst the Spaniards' many atrocities in Peru, the fate of Atahualpa. The Spanish bargained with him for his ransom but, once the gold was paid, they betrayed their promise and Atahualpa was condemned to be burned alive. See Las Casas, pp. 114–15. His sentence was in fact commuted to strangling.
9. artificial] pictured, imitation, i.e. not real.

Priest. These study arts of lengthening languishment,
 And strengthening those for pains whom pain hath spent.
 They make the cramp, by waters drilled, to seize   15
 Men ready to expire,
 Baste them with drops of fire,
 And then they lay them on the rack for ease.
 What race is this, who for our punishment
 Pretend that they in haste from heaven were sent,   20
 As just destroyers of idolatry?
 Yet will they not permit
 We should our idols quit,
 Because the Christian law makes converts free.

 Or if, to please their priests, some chief permits   25
 A few of us to be their proselytes;
 Yet all our freedom then is but deceit.
 They ease us from our chains
 To make us take more pains,
 Lightening our legs to give our shoulders weight.   30

 And other Christian strangers landing here,
 Straight, to their jealous sight, as spies appear:
 And those, they so much worse than heathens deem,
 That they must tortured die.
 The world still waste must lie,   35
 Or else a prison be to all but them.

---

13. *languishment*] suffering.

14. *strengthening . . . spent*] i.e. revive those who have already been tortured for further torments.

15. *cramp*] vice-like instrument (of torture).

by waters drilled] i.e. bored through so that the hot water runs in a kind of channel through the apparatus.

seize] hold fast.

17.] i.e. pour hot water on to the victims.

20–4.] i.e. the Spaniards justify their invasion and the torture of the Peruvians in the cause of converting the Indians to Christianity. To gratify the Church, a few conversions are allowed; but the majority are not permitted to give up their own gods, because, once converted to Christianity, they could no longer be treated as slaves.

22–4.] This is not in Purchas, who recounts the Incas' offer to promote the Gospel 'as a better law', and the enforced conversion of Prince Tupac (brother of Huáscar) before his execution (Purchas, pp. 1486–8). Las Casas also comments on the brutal methods of conversion on the Spanish main (pp. 48–9).

25. *chief*] i.e. some Spanish captain.

26. *proselytes*] Christian converts.

28–30.] i.e. even the few who are allowed to convert (see n. 20–4 above), though released from torture, are still enslaved and made to perform arduous tasks.

32. *jealous sight*] The Spaniards are suspicious, fearing that all other Christian colonizers or adventurers will reconquer the occupied territory.

35–6. *the world . . . them*] The world must be left in utter devastation or become a place of enslavement.

His speech being ended, he waves his verge, and his attendant performs
the porpoise.

[*Exit* PRIEST *and* attendant.]

[*Enter* CHORUS.]

The Fifth Song

Pursuing the argument of the speech, by a further detestation of that
cruelty which the ambition of the Spaniards made them exercise in Peru.   40

1

If man from sovereign reason does derive
O'er beasts a high prerogative,
Why does he so himself behave
That beasts appear to be
More rational than he   45
Who has deserved to be their slave.

2

How comes wild cruelty in human breasts?
Proud man more cruel is than beasts.
When beasts by hunger are enraged,
They no long pains devise   50
For dying enemies,
But kill, and eat, and are assuaged.

3

So much is man refined in cruelty
As not to make men quickly die.
He knows by death all pains are passed.   55
But as he hath the skill
A thousand ways to kill,
So hath he more to make pains last.

Chorus

When beasts each other chase and then devour,
'Tis nature's law, necessity,   60
Which makes them hunt for food, and not for power.
Men for dominion, Art's chief vanity,
Contrive to make men die;
Whose blood through wantonness they spill,
Not having use of what they kill.   [*Exit.*]   65

37–8.] *Q; not in F.*

---

38. porpoise] another acrobatic turn, imitating the leaping movement of the porpoise.
40. ambition] lust for power.
42. *prerogative*] a natural privilege or advantage.
62. *dominion*] conquest.
vanity] worthless indulgence.
64. *wantonness*] uncontrolled brutality.

This song being ended, a mournful air is played, preparing the entrance
of three Peruvians, limping in silver fetters. They are driven into the
wood by an insulting Spaniard with a truncheon; then enter again
loaden with Indian baskets full of golden ingots and silver wedges and,
lying down with the weight of their burdens, are raised by the blows   70
of the Spaniard and fall into a halting dance, till the Spaniard, reviving
their weariness with his truncheon, drives them again into the wood.

SIXTH ENTRY

A symphony prepares the last change of the scene, and an army is
discerned at distance, consisting of English and Peruvians; the van is
led by the English, who are distinguished by the ensigns of England and
their red coats. The rear is brought up by Peruvians, who are known
by their feathered habits, glaves and spears. There is likewise discerned   5
a body of armed Spaniards, their backs turned and their rear scattered,
as if put to flight. These imaginary English forces may seem improper,
because the English had made no discovery of Peru in the time of the
Spaniards' first invasion there; but yet in poetical representations of this
nature, it may pass as a vision discerned by the Priest of the Sun before   10
the matter was extant, in order to his prophecy. This object having
remained a while, the Priest of the Sun enters with his attendant.

The Sixth Speech

Intimating their first adoration of the Spaniards when they landed, the
behaviour of the Spaniards towards them and a prophecy that they shall
be relieved by the English.   15

Priest. We on our knees these Spaniards did receive
    As gods, when first they taught us to believe.
    They came from heaven, and us o'er heights would lead,
    Higher than e'er our sinful fathers fled.
    Experience now (by whose true eyes, though slow,   20
    We find at last what oft too late we know)
    Has all their cozening miracles discerned:
    'Tis she that makes unlettered mankind learned.

---

12. with his attendant] *Q; not in F.*

---

68. truncheon] a club, cudgel.
71. halting dance] limping dance.

6.2. van] vanguard, foremost division of a military force.
4. red-coats] uniform of Cromwell's New Model Army, which wore red from its
beginnings in 1645.
10–11. before . . . extant] before events came to pass.
11. in order . . . prophecy] i.e. to fulfil his prophecy.
17–24.] The Spanish would have the Peruvians believe that they are heavenly beings
and claim that they can save the Peruvians. But experience has slowly made the Peruvians
wise and disclosed the cheating nature of the supposed Spanish miracles and prophecies.
19. *our sinful fathers*] i.e. our ancestors.
22. *cozening*] cheating.
23. *she*] i.e. Experience.

She has unmasked these Spanish dark divines.
Perhaps they upward go;   25
But hasten us below,
Where we, through dismal depths, must dig in mines.
When first the valiant English landed here,
Our reason then no more was ruled by fear:
They straight the Spaniards' riddle did unfold,   30
Whose heaven in caverns lies, of others' gold.
Our griefs are past, and we shall cease to mourn
For those whom the insulting Spaniards scorn,
And slaves esteem,
The English soon shall free;   35
Whilst we the Spaniards see
Digging for them.

The priest having ended his speech, waves his verge, and his attendant
performs the double somerset.
                              [*Exit* PRIEST *and* attendant.]

The priest being gone, a wild air is played (differing from that in the   40
first entry), which prepares the coming in of a Spaniard out of the wood,
loaden with ingots of gold and wedges of silver. He makes his footing
to the tune of the instruments; and after a while he discovers a weariness
and inclination to sleep, to which purpose he lies down, with his basket
for his pillow. Two apes come in from opposite sides of the wood, and   45
dance to the air. After a while, a great baboon enters and joins with
them in the dance. They wake the Spaniard, and end the antique
measures with driving him into the wood.

                      [*Enter* CHORUS.]

                  The Sixth Song

Pursuing the argument of that prophecy which foretells the subversion
of the Spaniards by the English.   50

              We shall no longer fear
              The Spanish eagle darkly hovering here;
              For though from farthest climes he hither fled,
              And spaciously his wings has spread,

38–9.] *Q; not in F.*

---

24. *divines*] preachers.
25–7.] i.e. perhaps they will go to paradise, while they damn us to hell and to the
slavery of the mines.
30–1.] i.e. they exposed the Spaniards' duplicity by revealing that their true desire
was Peruvian gold.
42. makes his footing] steps in time to the music.
45–6. Two apes . . . baboon enters] again, as in the first entry, actors in costume.
46. to the air] i.e. to the music.
47–8. antique measures] antiquated or bizarre, grotesque dance steps.
49. subversion] overthrow.

Yet the English lion now   55
Does still victorious grow,
And does delight
To make his walks as far
As the other e'er did dare
To make his flight.   60

Chorus

[*Chorus Member*] 1. High,
[*Chorus Member*] 2. High,
[*Chorus Member*] 3. And high
[*Chorus Member*] 4. Our arrows shall fly,
And reach the wingèd for our prey.   65
Our nets we'll cast, and springes lay:
The air, the river and the wood
Shall yield us sport and change of food.

All in Chorus.   After all our disasters,
The proud Spaniards our masters,
When we extol our liberty by feasts,   70
At table shall serve,
Or else they shall starve;
Whilst the English shall sit and rule as our
    guests.

[*Exit* CHORUS.]

This song being ended, an air consisting of three tunes prepares the   75
grand dance, three Indians entering first, afterwards to them three
English soldiers, distinguished by their red coats; and to them a
Spaniard, who, mingling in the measures with the rest, does in his
gestures express pride and sullenness towards the Indians, and pays a
lowly homage to the English, who often salute him with their feet,   80
which salutation he returns with a more lowly gravity; whilst the
English and the Indians, as they encounter, salute and shake hands,
in sign of their future amity. This dance being performed, the
entertainment ends, and

The curtain falls

Finis

---

66. springes] sprindges, F.   83–7. This dance . . . after noon] Q; *not in* F.

55. *English lion*] From 1603, the English lion and the Scottish unicorn comprised
the royal arms. The lion was an heraldic emblem, along with the Irish harp and the
cross of St George. See *Drake*, 4.72–3, note.
    64–8.] The words of the chorus here suggest a return to the idealized life, the passing
of which is mourned in the Second Song.
    66. *springes*] snares.
    80. salute him . . . feet] probably a kick as a gesture indicating the Spaniard's
subordination.
    81. with . . . gravity] i.e. with a low bow.

Notwithstanding the great expense necessary to scenes and other   85
ornaments in this entertainment, there is a good provision made of
places for a shilling. And it shall [   ] after noon.

87. [   ] after noon] *page cropped.*

85–7.] This suggests, as does the title page, that the published text is circulating as
a form of advertisement for the production.

INTRODUCTION

Davenant's final Commonwealth drama, *The History of Sir Francis Drake*, was written and performed in 1659,[1] after the death of Cromwell the preceding September, under the short Protectorate of Richard Cromwell. Both aesthetically and ideologically, the work continued to reflect the practices of *The Siege of Rhodes* and *The Cruelty of the Spaniards in Peru*. Like the earlier works, it is divided into masque-like entries, comprised, as in *Rhodes*, of recitative and choral singing, and it was performed on the scenic stage of the Cockpit in Drury Lane. Self-evidently, the entertainment is more dramatic than *Peru*. Events are represented through character and interaction rather than by non-dramatic exposition, as in the monologues of the Priest of the Sun in *Peru*. But, that aside, Davenant draws on the same elements of song, scenic representation and dance to promulgate national self-interest.

The continuity with *The Cruelty of the Spaniards* is immediately evident in the opening description of the text when Davenant refers to the reuse of the frontispiece, claiming that it was 'convenient to continue it, our argument being in the same country'. For 'country' we have to read the Spanish Indies, for only three entries appear to be set in Peru, while others are located near Panama. Although new back shutters must have been devised to convey the different subjects, there is some similarity in the scenic stages as they are described in the two texts. It can be deduced that in *Sir Francis Drake* Davenant re-employed the fixed wing scenes from *The Cruelty of the Spaniards*. In the description of the scene which prefaces the first entry of both pieces, for example, Davenant alludes to 'the prospect' as revealed through a wood represented by 'coco trees, pines and palmitos'. The exotic and arcadian existence of the Peruvians before the advent of Spanish imperialism is thus part of the visual aspect of both dramas.

The two texts are evidently supportive of Cromwell's 'western design', the policy of striking against Spain through its American colonies,[2] although the intention is less overt in *Drake*. We have seen how Davenant dramatized the English invasion in *The Cruelty of the Spaniards*, symbolically representing Cromwell's hope for a providential defeat of Spain which would enable England to become overlord in the Indies. By the time *Drake* was composed, a direct appeal to such a policy would have been anachronistic, and in its place Davenant configures notions of the superiority of English honour. In both dramas history is reinvented so that the English take up the cause of, or identify with, the peoples oppressed by the Spanish: the Peruvians in *The Cruelty of the Spaniards* and the escaped negro slaves, the Symerons,[3] in *Drake*. In the latter text Davenant reconstructs the past to turn what was essentially a raid on the Spanish

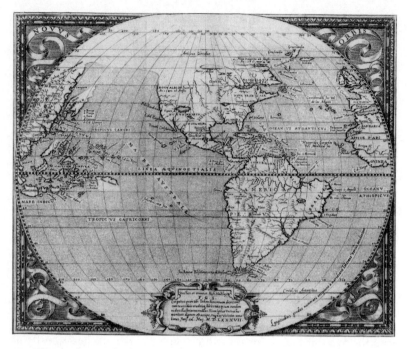

10   *De orbe novo* (1581).

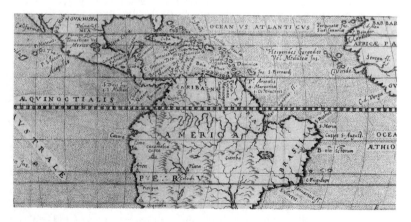

11   Detail from *De orbe novo*: Panama Isthmus and Peru.

main, motivated by financial gain and fuelled by a bitter hatred of the Spaniards, into an heroic venture in which gold is subservient to national honour.[4]

The principal source for the piece was the account of Drake's voyage to the Indies in 1572–73, *Sir Francis Drake Revived*, compiled by Philip Nichols and written at Drake's instigation in order to appeal to Elizabeth I and to recover her good favour.[5] The objective did not fully materialize, and the work was first published in 1628 by Drake's nephew, Francis Drake. Nichols's account focuses on Drake's voyage to the Panama isthmus, in which he hoped to intercept the Spanish mule trains bearing the wealth of Peru in gold and silver bars from Panama on the Pacific to Nombre de Dios on the Atlantic (figure 11). Drake had sailed with only two small ships, the *Pascha*, containing forty-seven men, and the *Swan*, captained by his brother John, and carrying twenty-six men. Although the numbers at his disposal were so limited, Drake launched an assault on the treasure stores of Nombre de Dios, which was to miscarry when his men saw that he had been wounded in an earlier skirmish with armed civilians, and subsequently an attack on the *recuas*, the mule trains from Panama. With such a small crew, the aid that Drake received from the Symerons was indispensable. Being familiar with the dense tropical territory, the Symerons acted as guides, as well as hunting and providing shelter for Drake and his men. Such a force of banditry and piracy employing guerilla tactics was a real threat to the Spanish.[6] But Davenant makes a point of humanizing the relationship between the two groups. This is notable in the encounter between Drake and the 'king of the Symerons' in the second entry, in which they exchange lavish compliments, and in Drake's befriending of Pedro, his Symeron guide. In the fourth entry, it is Pedro who urges Drake to climb an immensely tall tree, from which he sees both the Pacific and the Atlantic oceans. This act foreshadows Drake's circumnavigation both in *The History of Sir Francis Drake* and in the play's source.

When Francis Drake, Drake's nephew, published *Sir Francis Drake Revived*, he did so with the admonition to 'this dull and effeminate age' to emulate Drake's enterprises. In his heroic representation of Drake, Davenant was evidently motivated by similar objectives. To this end, he presents a very different version of events even from that of Nichols's hagiographic account. There is no mention, for example, of James Ranse's withdrawal from the enterprise following a disagreement with Drake: instead, the two are seen only as expressing mutual admiration. Davenant omits the death of Drake's brother, John Drake, following an assault on a passing frigate, and the death of his other brother, Joseph, from yellow fever. The muddy soldiering in the jungle heat which was the reality of the expedition is barely touched upon and the drama closes with a successful attack on the mule train, when in actuality the ambush was thwarted by the noise of a drunken soldier. Instead, Davenant reconstructs a mythical Drake of courteous and honourable dealing whose rhetoric evokes that of the Elizabethan adventurer. This image is strongly represented in the fictive events of the Fifth Entry, when the Symerons take hostage members of a Spanish wedding party and the safety of the bride is threatened. Drake and his companion Ranse see this as an affront to national honour and hasten to free the bride and reprimand the Symerons. Pedro attempts to rationalize the Symerons' behaviour on the grounds that they have long been oppressed by Spanish brutality, but for the stern, moralistic Drake this will not do. Similarly, in the final moments of the drama, Drake urges his men not to attack for plunder, but solely for national pride:

> All I would speak, should tell you, I despise
> That treasure which I now would make your prize:
> Unworthy 'tis to be your chiefest aim.
> For this attempt is not for gold, but fame;
> Which is not got when we the reco get,
> But by subduing those who rescue it.
>
> (Sixth Entry, 24–9)

Considering the historical reality of Drake's massive raids on the Spanish Indies and his repeated pillaging of Spanish vessels off the coasts of Peru and Chile, *The History of Sir Francis Drake* presents an altogether distorted account of that history.

The choice of a sanitized Drake for the drama of the Republic was, of course, not simply fortuitous. After his fall from grace under Elizabeth and his comparative neglect under the early Stuarts, Drake's reinstatement by Davenant was a belated gesture to the Republic's colonizing, imperial agenda. Drake was the ideal figure to embody prevalent anti-Spanish sentiments and to represent the past success of English seafaring and naval power. Thomas Gage, a former Dominican who had proselytized in the Indies, had, in *The English American* (1648), produced arguments for an invasion of the Spanish Americas and in justification of Cromwell's designs against the Spanish. In the book's preface, Thomas Chaloner, an MP with classical republican sympathies, had advocated a return to the days of 'worthy Hawkins and the famous Drake'.[7] Moreover, Drake was a figure who could appeal to both sides of the ideological divide. In his ode 'Sitting and drinking in the chair made out of the relics of Sir Francis Drake's ship', the 'Cavalier' poet Abraham Cowley had reminisced on the 'good pirate' and his quest for Peruvian gold and, when drunk, imagined himself sailing 'round the ocean in this chair'.[8] Drake was also the subject of an anonymous epigram 'On Francis Drake'[9] in which he is lauded as a fellow traveller of the sun in terms similar to the praise heaped upon him by the king of the Symerons. *The History of Sir Francis Drake* is more than hagiography, however. The drama helps to promote the idea of a continuity of British sea domination and colonization from the 1580s to the 1650s. A revival of interest in Elizabethan and Jacobean political literature also took place in the early 1650s.[10] Davenant's hybrid drama

on the most famous Elizabethan seafarer of his age represents a late intervention in that neo-Elizabethan movement. From the title page advertisement it would seem that Davenant planned a second part to Drake's
'heroic' ventures. That a sequel did not materialize in the Anglican
Royalist context of the Restoration[11] is not surprising, since under
the new dispensation Francis Drake had outstayed his usefulness as a
unifying national hero.

A NOTE ON THE TEXT

The History of Sir Francis Drake was revived as the third act in Davenant's Restoration miscellany *A Playhouse to Be Let*, included in the
Works published in 1673. In the dialogue between the house-keeper and
the player preceding the act, there is a self-conscious allusion to the
drama's semi-operatic form and the more elitist connotations of that
form. The house-keeper comments: 'Now we shall be in stilo recitativo.
I'm in a trance when I hear vocal music'; to which the player makes the
riposte: 'Thou understand'st recitative music as much as a dray horse does
Greek.'

This edition has as its copy text the 1659 quarto, which has been
collated with the text of *A Playhouse to Be Let*.

NOTES

1 *The History of Sir Francis Drake* was entered into the Stationers' Register on 20
January 1659.
2 For a discussion of the imperial dimension of Cromwell's 'western design' against
the Spanish, see David Armitage, 'The Cromwellian Protectorate and the Language
of Empire', *The Historical Journal*, 35:3 (1992), 531–55.
3 I have retained Davenant's spelling of 'Symerons' rather than the modern Spanish
cimarrónes. See textual note, p. 270.
4 The best evaluation of Drake's voyage to the Indies in 1672–73 is that of John
Cummins, *Francis Drake: The Lives of a Hero* (London, 1995), pp. 44–64. See also
Harry Kelsey, *Sir Francis Drake: The Queen's Pirate* (New Haven and London,
1998), pp. 40–67.
5 See David B. Quinn, 'Early Accounts of the Famous Voyage' in *Sir Francis Drake
and the Famous Voyage, 1577–1580*, edited by Norman J. W. Thrower (Berkeley
and Los Angeles, 1984), pp. 33–49.
6 See K. R. Andrews, 'The English in the Caribbean 1560–1620' in *The Western
Enterprise: English Activities in Ireland, the Atlantic, and America 1480–1650*,
edited by K. R. Andrews, N. P. Canny and P. E. Hair (Liverpool, 1979), p.
113.
7 Thomas Gage, *The English American*, A5v.
8 'Verses written on several occasions' in *The Works of Mr Abraham Cowley* (1668).
9 *Wits Recreations. Selected from the finest fancies of modern muses* (1640), D7r–v.
The epigram appears in *The Penguin Book of Renaissance Verse 1509–1659*,
selected by David Norbrook, edited by H. R. Woudhuysen (Harmondsworth,
1992), p. 437.

10 Blair Worden, 'Classical Republicanism and the Puritan Revolution' in *History and Imagination: Essays in Honour of H. R. Trevor-Roper*, edited by Hugh Lloyd-Jones, Valerie Pearl and Blair Worden (London, 1981), p. 190.

11 In June 1664 Charles II ordered the Governor of Jamaica to prevent all attacks on Spanish shipping. See Steven C. A. Pincus, *Protestantism and Patriotism: Ideologies and the Making of English Foreign Policy, 1650–1668* (Cambridge, 1996), p. 254.

The History of Sir Francis Drake

Expressed by Instrumental and Vocal Music
and by art of perspective in scenes

The First Part
Represented daily at the Cockpit in Drury Lane at
three after noon punctually.

London.

Printed for Henry Herringman, and are to be sold at his shop at the
Anchor in the Lower Walk in the New Exchange.

1659.

DRAMATIS PERSONAE

[SIR FRANCIS DRAKE
DRAKE JUNIOR
CAPTAIN ROUSE
BOATSWAIN
STEERSMAN   5
KING OF THE SYMERONS
PEDRO, *a Symeron*
Page
Peruvians
Mariners   10
Soldiers
Seaman
Father of the bride
Bridegroom
Symerons]   15

---

1. *SIR FRANCIS DRAKE*] Elizabethan seafarer, noted for his challenges to Spain's power in South America and his circumnavigation of the globe in 1577–80.

2. *DRAKE JUNIOR*] John Drake, the brother of Francis Drake, captain of the *Swan*. In contrast to Davenant's version of events, in actuality he died on the expedition.

3. *CAPTAIN ROUSE*] a misnomer for Captain James Ranse who had accompanied Drake and Hawkins on earlier expeditions.

6. *KING OF THE SYMERONS*] In Nichols, there is a reference to the 'chiefest of the Symerons', who advises Drake as to what provisions he should take on the expedition to Venta Cruz. The King of the Symerons is alluded to only as living in a city sixteen leagues south-east of Panama (probably Ronconcholon).

15. *Symerons*] from the Spanish *cimmarónes*, formerly a word used to describe escaped black slaves, hence Davenant's reference in the Second Entry to their Moorish origins. The Spanish *cimarrón* is used to denote a wild or untamed person; when combined with *negro* or *esclavo* the meaning is a runaway or fugitive slave. Such associations are not appropriate in this dramatic context. Since the modern English word cimarron (or cimmaron) denotes only a type of Rocky Mountain sheep or bighorn (*OED*), Davenant's original spelling has been retained.

The Description of the Frontispiece

An arch is discovered, raised upon stone of rustic work; upon the top
of which is written, in an antique shield, Peru; and two antique shields
are fixed a little lower on the sides, the one bearing the figure of the
Sun, which was the scutcheon of the Incas, who were emperors of Peru:
the other did bear the spread-eagle, in signification of the Austrian　　5
family. This frontispiece was the same which belonged to the late
representation; and it was convenient to continue it, our argument being
in the same country.

FIRST ENTRY

The preparation of the opening of the scene is by a prelude and coranto.
Afterwards the curtain rises by degrees to an ascending air, and a　　10
harbour is discerned (which was first discovered by Sir Francis Drake,
and called by him Port Pheasant) where two ships are moored, and sea
carpenters are erecting a pinnace, whilst others are felling trees to build
a fort. The narrowness to the entrance of the harbour may be observed,
with rocks on either side; and out at sea a ship towing a prize. And　　15
likewise on the top of a high tree, a mariner making his ken. This
prospect is made through a wood, differing from those of European

---

0.1–8. This frontispiece . . . country] *not in* F. 2. antique] antick Q.　　9. coranto]
This ed. (throughout); corante Q, F.

0.1. Frontispiece] emblematic decoration at the front of the stage, framing the stage
picture.

1. rustic] rough-hewn.

4. scutcheon] (e)scutcheon: emblem, armorial design (on a shield).

5. spread-eagle] the representation of an eagle with body and wings displayed; an
emblem of the Habsburgs and formerly symbolic of the Holy Roman Empire.

6–7. late representation] i.e. *The Cruelty of the Spaniards in Peru.*

7–8. our argument . . . country] Three entries are set in Peru, and three near
Panama.

7. argument] story.

1.9. prelude] musical introduction.
coranto] a dance tune in triple time.

10. ascending air] tune rising in pitch.

12. Port Pheasant] 'our Captain had so named it in his former voyage, by reason of
the great store of those goodly fowls which he and his company did then daily kill, and
feed on in that place' (Nichols, p. 255). The port, on the coast of Nombre de Dios,
towards Acla, was where Drake established headquarters.

13. pinnace] a small light boat accompanying a larger vessel.

15. towing a prize] see First Entry, p. 273 n. 50.

16. making his ken] keeping watch.

climates by representing of coco-trees, pines and palmitos. And on the
boughs of other trees are seen monkeys, apes and parrots.

> *The Introduction of the Entry is by a Martial Saraband.*

> *The Saraband being ended, enter* DRAKE JUNIOR *and* Boatswain.

Drake Junior. Climb, Boatswain, climb! and from the height   20
   Of that steep rock inform thy sight!
   From yonder point our master call.
   I'll here attend our Admiral.

> *Exit* Boatswain.

   The mist ascends, and south'rd it grows clear!
   Methinks at distance somewhat does appear   25
   Which wakens us with hope.
Boatswain. [*within*]   A sail! a sail!
Drake Junior. 'Tis English built, or else my sight does fail.
Boatswain. (*within*) Oho! oho! another ship I spy,
   And by their course both to this harbour ply.
Drake Junior. She lowers her main sail, the wind does rise!   30
Boatswain. (*within*) She now bears in, and she does tow a prize.

> *Enter* DRAKE SENIOR.

Drake Senior. To sea, to sea! Man out the boat!
Drake Junior. It has not tide enough to float.
Drake Senior. Stir, mates! stir! stir! and bring more hands;
   Shove, shove, and roll her o'er the sands!   35
   Launch forth, and make your ken!
   Both by her rigging and her mould
   She brings our countrymen,
   And has a rich and heavy hold.   *Exeunt.*

> *Enter* First Mariner.

First Mariner. Ho, mate! ho, ho! what canst thou see   40
   From the top-gallant of that tree?

39.1. *Enter* First Mariner] Enter a Mariner *Q*, *F.*

---

  18. coco-trees] coconut trees.
palmitos] (palmetto) diminutive species of palm.
  19.1. Saraband] a slow and stately dance tune in triple time.
  19.2. DRAKE JUNIOR] John Drake, the brother of Francis Drake.
Boatswain] ship's officer in charge of sails.
  22. *master*] master of the ship.
  23. *Admiral*] Drake Senior.
  29. *ply*] make their way.
  36. *make your ken*] i.e. cover the distance (to the ship).
  37. *mould*] ship's hull; here referring to the ship's low position in the water due to
its heavy load.
  38.] Probably a rendezvous at Port Pheasant with James Ranse (known in the text
as 'Rouse') had been arranged.
  41. *top-gallant*] the highest of the mizen masts.

Mariner. (*Within*) The ship does anchor cast;
    And now her boat does haste
    To reach the shore.
First Mariner. What seest thou more?   45
Mariner. (*Within*) Enough to make me hasten down:
    For, if my eyes prove true,
    The bowels of Peru
    Shall be ripped up and be our own.
    The lion Rouse is landed here.   50
First Mariner. I'll run to meet him at the pier.
    A ton of yellow gold
    Concealed within our hold,
    For half my share I scorn to take
    When he is joined with Dragon Drake.   *Exit.* 55

*Two mariners, having met with another newly landed, dance to a
rustic air. The dance being ended, [they exit.] Enter* DRAKE SENIOR,
CAPTAIN ROUSE, DRAKE JUNIOR *and* Page.

Drake Senior. Welcome to land, my brother of the sea!
    From childhood rocked by winds and waves like me.
    Who never canst a danger dread,
    Since still in dangerous tempests bred;
    Yet still art safe and calm within thy breast,   60
    As lovers who in shady coverts rest.
    Thy fame about the world does make her flight,
    And flies as swiftly as the wings of light.
Rouse. My fame does lay her trumpet down,
    When yours does publish your renown.   65
Drake Senior. What is your prize?
Rouse. 'Tis fraught with spies:
    A carvel rigged at Seville for this coast,
    To fetch from hence
    Intelligence;   70
    But, meeting me, she has her voyage lost.
Drake Senior. Brave friend, wilt thou now guided be

---

68. Seville] Sivell *Q, F.*

---

42. *cast*] drop.
48–9.] i.e. we shall claim the riches from the mines of Peru.
50. *the lion Rouse*] Ranse. He brought with him on this occasion two prizes, a carvel
(a small, light Spanish ship) carrying dispatches and an oared shallop (a light open boat).
54–5.] i.e. I disdain sharing in the spoils when Rouse and the fierce Drake are united.
55. *Dragon Drake*] a pun on Drake's name in Spanish, *El Draque* or *El Draco.*
55.2. *rustic air*] simple country melody.
59. *still*] ever, always.
61. *coverts*] concealed places.
64–5.] i.e. my fame is overshadowed by yours. 'This Captain Rouse [*sic*], understanding our captain's purpose, was desirous to join in consort with him, and was
received upon conditions agreed on between them' (Nichols, p. 258).
67. *spies*] Spanish crew who had been dispatched to gain intelligence of the
Caribbean coast.

By that bright star which ushers me?
Rouse. What man is that, loved Admiral,
    Who does not hasten at your call?   75
    He must be either deaf, or ever lame,
    Who follows not your loud and leading fame.
Drake Senior. My course must now not be
    Upon the open sea:
    Our country's foes we must invade   80
    Through woods, and seek them in the shade;
    And follow them where Phoebus never shines,
    Through depths as dark and winding as their mines.
Chorus of all. That which enlightens, and does lead
    The world, and all our victories breed,   85
    We in those caverns shall behold,
    In seeing man's bright mistress, gold.
Drake Senior. Boat all our guns! haste, haste aboard!
    Unlade! then let our ships be moored!
    To raise our fort, some hew down trees!   90
    Whilst other rig our pinnaces.
    Their watchful guards let every sentry keep,
    That, after labour, all may safely sleep.
    Some o'er remoter grounds
    Walk, and relieve their rounds: 95
    Whilst some secure each post
    On outlets of the coast.
    That, after wandering long to trace
    Wild rivers, we may find this place
    For our embarkment free,   100
    To wander more at sea.
Drake Junior. The jealous Spaniards long have understood
    The danger of this harbour's neighbourhood.
    'Tis therefore fit
    That thou shouldst leave behind,   105
    To govern it,
    A great experienced mind.

---

73. *that bright star*] probably the North Star, used in navigation.
  ushers] leads.
  80–3.] Drake plans to journey inland to intercept the Spanish mule trains making their way from Panama on the Pacific coast of the isthmus through heavily wooded terrain to Nombre de Dios.
  82. *Phoebus*] the sun.
  84. Chorus of all] i.e. Drake Senior, Drake Junior and Rouse.
  88. *Boat . . . guns*] i.e. return all our guns to the ship.
  89. *Unlade*] unload (the ship's cargo).
  91. *rig*] make ready for the sea.
  94. *remoter grounds*] more secluded parts.
  95. *relieve their rounds*] i.e. take the place of those on watch.
  98–100.] i.e. we may return to the fort once we have journeyed inland.
  102. *jealous*] suspicious, distrustful, especially towards other colonizers and adventurers.
  103.] i.e. the harbour's vulnerability to invasion.

Drake Senior. I know it is of high import.
    My second thoughts conclude, thou Rouse shalt stay,
    To finish and secure the fort;   110
    Whilst we to Venta Cruz enforce our way.
Chorus of all. We must the main forbear,
    And now a coasting go,
    Then up with rivers steer,
    To watch how far they flow.   115
    But if landing we pass
    Where recoes through fords are long wading,
    Then we in pity, alas,
    Their mules must ease of their lading.   *Exeunt omnes.*

SECOND ENTRY

A symphony variously humoured prepares the change of the scene.

The scene is changed.

*In which is discerned a rocky country of the Symerons, who were a
Moorish people, brought formerly to Peru by the Spaniards as their
slaves, to dig in mines; and, having lately revolted from them, did live*   5
*under the government of a king of their own election. A sea is
discovered, and ships at distance, with boats rowing to the shore and
Symerons upon the rocks.*

    The prospect having continued a while, this song is sung by a
    Steersman *in the foremost boat, and the chorus by mariners*
                rowing in it.

          I

Steersman. Aloof! and aloof! and steady I steer!
    'Tis a boat to our wish,   10
    And she slides like a fish,
    When cheerily stemmed, and when you row clear.

---

    109. *Rouse shalt stay*] Ranse was left in charge of larger vessels at Port Plenty, the
name given by the English to the main anchorage on the Isle of Pines.
    111. *Venta-Cruz*] Venta Cruz was inland, west of Panama, and was one of the prin-
cipal links with the Caribbean for the mule trains carrying plate from Panama to
Nombre de Dios.
    112. *the main*] the high seas.
    117. *recoes*] *recuas*, mule-trains.
    118–19.] i.e. we must capture the treasure load carried by the mules.

    2.1. symphony] instrumental interlude, probably comprising three sections in
quick–slow-quick form.
    variously humoured] comprising a variety of tunes of contrasting tone and mood.
    3. a rocky country] probably the coastal region to the east of Nombre de Dios.
    8.2. the foremost boat] probably a relieve shutter with the steersman and mariners
positioned behind it. See Introduction to *Rhodes*, p. 192 n. 19.
    9. *Aloof*] away to windward.
    12. *stemmed*] keeping course.
    clear] smoothly.

She now has her trim!
Away let her swim.
Mackerels are swift in the shine of the moon,   15
And herrings in gales when they wind us;
But, timing our oars, so smoothly we run
That we leave them in shoals behind us.

Chorus. Then cry, one and all!
        Amain! for Whitehall!   20
        The Diegos we'll board to rummage their hold;
        And drawing our steel, they must draw out their gold.

2

Steersman. Our master and his mate, with bacon and peas,
        In cabins keep aboard,
        Each as warm as a lord: 25
No queen, lying in, lies more at her ease.
        Whilst we lie in wait
        For reals of eight,
And for some gold quoits, which fortune must send:
But, alas, how their ears will tingle,   30
When finding, though still like Hectors we spend,
        Yet still all our pockets shall jingle.

Chorus. Then cry, one and all!
        Amain, *etc.*

3

Steersman. But oh, how the Purser shortly will wonder,   35
        When he sums in his book
        All the wealth we have took,
And finds that we'll give him none of the plunder.

---

13. *trim*] the most favourable position of a ship on the water.

16. *wind us*] i.e. haul us along.

20. *Amain for Whitehall*] i.e. full speed ahead for Whitehall (the former royal palace, outside the City of London, where Cromwell had resided).

21. *Diegos*] the Spaniards. *Diego* is the Spanish equivalent of 'James', the name of the patron saint of Spain. The term was applied, often disparagingly, as a generic proper name to Spaniards.

rummage] pillage.

22. *drawing our steel*] drawing our swords.

23. *with bacon and peas*] suggesting that the master and mate enjoy luxurious fare.

28. *reals of eight*] denomination of Spanish silver coin; pieces of eight.

29. *quoits*] disks, i.e. coins.

31. *Hectors*] i.e. London revellers: the term 'Hectors' was applied in the second half of the seventeenth century to gangs of roisterous young men and to a particular band who frequented the streets and taverns of London (*OED*).

35-44.] The crew has ensured that the purser does not come into possession of the money. The purser would have pilfered much of the booty instead of paying over the tax due to the state and the commission due to the owners.

35. *Purser*] officer on board ship who keeps accounts.

36. *sums*] makes an account.

He means to abate
The tithe for the state.   40
Then for our owners some part he'll discount:
But his fingers are pitched together,
Where so much will stick, that little will mount
When he reckons the shares of either.

Chorus. Then cry, one and all!   45
   Amain, *etc.*

                         4

Steersman. At sight of our gold, the boatswain will bristle,
   But not finding his part,
   He will break his proud heart,
And hang himself straight in the chain of his whistle.   50
Abast and afore!
Make way to the shore!
Softly as fishes which slip through the stream,
   That we may catch their sentries napping.
Poor little Diegos, they now little dream   55
Of us, the brave warriors of Wapping.

Chorus. Then cry, one and all!
   Amain, *etc.*

      This song being sung, [*exit* Steersman *and* Mariners.]

Enter the KING OF THE SYMERONS, DRAKE SENIOR, PEDRO *and* Page.

King. Great wand'rer of the sea,
   Thy walks still pathless be.   60
   The races thou dost run
   Are known but to the sun.
   And as the walk above,
   Where he does yearly move,
   We only guess, though him we know   65
   By great effects below:
   So, though thy courses traceless are,

39–40. *abate / The tythe*] deduct tax.
   42. *pitched together*] covered in tar so that the coins stick to his fingers.
   48.] but not receiving his share.
   50. *hang . . . whistle*] i.e. use the chain around his neck to hang himself.
   51. *Abast and afore*] i.e. fore and aft.
   56. *brave . . . Wapping*] Wapping, on the embankment of the Thames in East London, was a popular resort of seamen.
   58.2. Enter . . . *SYMERONS*] The meeting between Drake and the King allowing such elaborate compliments to Drake is apocryphal.
   59–62.] Cf. the short anonymous epigram 'On Francis Drake', which concludes 'The Sun himself cannot forget / His fellow traveller.' *Wit's Recreations* (1640), D7r-v.
   60.] i.e. you journey through uncharted territory.
   63–6.] On the pre-Copernican assumption that the sun moves round the earth, the King compares Drake's expedition with the unknown orbit of the sun, perceived only by its effects on the natural world.

As if conducted by a wandering star,
Yet by thy deeds all climes acknowledge thee;
And thou art known and felt as much as he.   70
Drake Senior. So narrow is my merit wrought
That when such breadth you thus allow my fame,
I stand corrected, and am taught
To hide my story, and to show my shame.
King. As tireless as thy body is thy mind: 75
No adverse current can thy progress stop.
Thy forward courage leaves all doubts behind.
And when thy anchor's lost, thou keepest thy hope.
Welcome! and in my land be free,
And powerful as thou art at sea.   80
Drake Senior. Monarch of much! and still deserving more
Than I have coasted on the Western shore!
Slave to my Queen! to whom thy virtue shows
How low thou canst to virtue be;
And, since declared a foe to all her foes,   85
Thou makest them lower bow to thee.
King. Instruct me how my Symerons and I
May help thee to afflict the enemy.
Drake Senior. Afford me guides to lead my bold
Victorious seamen to their gold: 90
For nothing can afflict them more,
Than to deprive them of that store
With which from hence they furnished are
To afflict the peaceful world with war.
King. Here from my bosom Pedro take,   95
And him thy chief conductor make;
Who once was an unhappy slave to them,
But now is free by my deserved esteem.
He is as watchful as the Eye

---

69. *climes*] countries, realms.
70. *felt*] i.e. your achievements have as great an effect as the sun.
71. *wrought*] created, shaped.
73–4.] i.e. I do not deserve such extravagant praise.
77. *doubts*] fears.
78.] i.e. when drifting, of uncertain destination, you maintain your spirit.
81–2. *still . . . shore*] i.e. you deserve to rule over even more territory than the Spanish West Indies.
82. *coasted*] explored, traversed.
83–6.] i.e. the King of the Symerons honourably humbles himself in submitting to the virtuous authority of the Queen; and he will in turn require their joint enemy [the Spanish] to abase themselves before him.
88. *afflict the enemy*] Drake and the Symerons made common cause against the Spaniards.
95. *Pedro*] Pedro is referred to in Nichols as the 'chief Symeron' (p. 297). He became the leader on the advance to Panama to intercept the mule trains.
96. *conductor*] guide.
98. *esteem*] good favour.
99–100.] i.e. he is as vigilant as an aged husband towards a young wife; the common trope of *Senex Amans*.

Of Age still waked with jealousy;   100
And like experienced lovers wisely true,
Who after long suspicion find
They had no cause to be unkind,
And then with second vows their loves renew.
Drake Senior. He is, since so deservingly expressed,   105
    Removed but from thy bosom to my breast.
King. All other aids required to thy design,
    Choose and receive: for all my strengths are thine.   *Exeunt.*

Enter four Symerons, who dance a Morisco for joy of the arrival of
SIR FRANCIS DRAKE *and depart. Then this song is sung by a* Chorus
of Mariners *within.*

Chorus of Mariners within.
    Winds now may whistle, and waves may dance to 'em,
    Whilst merchants cry out, such sport will undo 'em.   110
    And the master aloud bids, lee the helm, lee!
    But we now shall fear nor the rocks nor the sand,
    Whilst calmly we follow our plunder at land,
    When others in storms seek prizes at sea.

THIRD ENTRY

*The change of the scene is prepared by a symphony, consisting of a
martial air; which having continued a while, the scene changes and
represents a Peruvian town, pleasantly situated with palmeto trees,
guavas and cypresses growing about it, whilst English land soldiers and
seamen seem to be drawn up towards the west end; whilst the Peruvians   5
are feasting their guests, and two of their boys bearing fruit towards
the strangers.*

    This object having continued a while, enter DRAKE SENIOR,
        DRAKE JUNIOR, PEDRO, Page.

Drake Senior. March! march! wheel to the right hand still,
    To shun loose footing on that hill.
    From thy meridian run,   10

---

100. *waked*] alert, sharp-eyed.

108.1. Morisco] a Moorish dance. The name, common from the fifteenth to seventeenth centuries, denoted no fixed rules as to rhythm or style. It was often applied to
any crude or grotesque dance, featuring dancers with blackened faces or in animal
costume. For a description of the dance, see Thoinot Arbeau, *Orchesographic* (1589),
pp. 94–5.

111. *lee*] leeward; the sheltered side, opposite of windward.

3.3. Peruvian town] This part of the drama is apocryphal, recalling the Arcadian
existence of the Peruvians in *Peru*. In fact, Drake's assault on the Spanish-occupied
Nombre de Dios miscarried.

10. *meridian*] highest point (midday).

10–11.] As his men are marching uphill under the midday sun, Drake longs for its
decline.

O thou inflaming sun!
The air above us else to fire will turn,
And all this sand beneath like cinders burn.
Now give the word!
Drake Junior. Stand! 15
(*Within*) *First Soldier.* Stand.
(*Within*) *Second Soldier.* Stand.
(*Within*) *Third Soldier.* Stand.
Drake Senior. All firm and sudden to command!
Halt for our rear awhile, and then 20
West from that wood draw up our men.
Stand to your arms till we send out
Our trusty Symerons to scout.
Pedro. Scouts I have chosen who can trace
All the retreats, which in the chase 25
The hunted seek; all shades to which they run
When strength leaves them, and they the hunters shun.
Drake Senior. Are these Peruvians friends, or by surprise
Must we secure them as our enemies?
Pedro. Great chief, they reverence thy renown, 30
And thou mayst quarter in their town.
Yet so advance with care,
In all the shapes of war;
That when the Spaniards know
How well they treat their foe, 35
The entertainment may appear
Not the effect of love, but fear.
Drake Junior. Their dwelling seems so fresh and flourishing,
As if it still the nursery were
Of all the seeds that furnish out the spring 40
For ev'ry clime, and all the year.
Drake Senior. Here nature to her summer court retires:
Our northern region is the shade,
Where she grows cold and looks decayed,
And seems to sit by artificial fires. 45

---

16. First Soldier] 1. Q.   17. Second Soldier] 2. Q.   18. Third Soldier] 3. Q.

19. *sudden*] prompt, quick.

23. *trusty . . . scout*] The Symerons' main contribution to the expedition was their knowledge of the country, but they also carried provisions and hunted for food.

28–9.] Drake questions the support of the townspeople and considers the option of forced occupation.

31. *quarter*] lodge.

36–7.] i.e. to deceive the Spaniards, Drake must create the impression of an assault, so that his hospitable reception by the townspeople will appear to be the result of fear of his power, rather than their respect for his reputation.

38–45.] Davenant draws a conspicuous comparison between English and Spanish attitudes towards the New World by introducing this incongruous appreciation of the region's natural beauty during the planning of a military advance.

39. *nursery*] plot of ground in which young plants are reared, i.e. nursery garden.

Drake Junior. Advance, advance,
　　And in the rear,
　　To make our number more appear,
　　Let all our trusty Symerons spread
　　Their ranks, and be by Pedro led.   50
Chorus of all. All order with such clemency preserve,
　　That such as to our power submit
　　May take delight to cherish it,
　　And seem as free as those whom they shall serve.   *Exeunt.*

Peruvians *enter, and dance to a rustic air, after which this song is*
sung by a Peruvian, *and the chorus to it by his countrymen, whilst*
they dance again in a round.

1

Peruvian. With boughs and with branches trim up our bowers,   55
　　And strew them with flowers:
　　To receive such a guest
　　As deserves for a feast
　　All that the forest, or the field,
　　Or deeper lakes and rivers yield.   60

Chorus. Still round, and round, and round,
　　Let us compass the ground.
　　What man is he who feels
　　Any weight at his heels?
　　Since our hearts are so light, that all weighed together   65
　　Agree to a grain, and they weigh not a feather.

2

Peruvian. The lord of the sea is welcome to land,
　　And here shall command
　　All our wealth and our arms,
　　For his name more alarms   70
　　The Spaniards than trumpets or drums:
　　Hark how they cry, Drake comes, Drake comes!

Chorus. Still round, and round, and round,
　　Let *etc.*

54.1. Peruvians *enter*] *Q;* Five Peruvians enter *F.*

51–4.] another demonstration of the supposed beneficence of the English in their
treatment of the Peruvians.
　54.3. round] ring dance.
　55. *trim up*] decorate.
　62. *compass*] traverse (in a circle).
　65–6.] i.e. all are equally light at heart.
　68–9.] 'They all entreated our captain very earnestly to make his abode with them
some two or three days, promising that by that time they would double his strength if
he thought good' (Nichols, p. 299).
　70–1.] i.e. Drake's name arouses more fear in the Spaniards than the sounds of war
itself.

3

Peruvian. Though to his foes like those winds he is rough,   75
    That meet in a huff:
    Yet that storm quickly ends,
    When embraced by his friends.
    Then he is calm and gentle made
    As love's soft whispers in a shade.   80

Chorus. Still round, and round, and round,
    Let *etc.*

FOURTH ENTRY

*A wild air, by way of symphony, prepares the change of the scene: which
having continued a while, the scene is changed; wherein is discerned
upon a hill, a wood, and in it a tree which was famous in those times
for extraordinary compass and height; on the top of which, Pedro
(formerly a slave to the Spaniards, but now employed by the Moorish*   5
*king to conduct Sir Francis Drake towards Panama) had promised Sir
Francis Drake to show him both the North and the South Atlantic seas.
English soldiers and mariners are reposing themselves under it. At
distance the natives are discerned in their hunting of boars; and at
nearer view, two Peruvians are killing a stag. This object having*   10
remained a while,

        Enter DRAKE SENIOR, DRAKE JUNIOR, Page.

Drake Senior. A boar so fierce and large,
    No hunter e'er did charge.
    Advance thy spear,
    And turn him there.   15
Drake Junior. This last encounter he has bravely stood;
    But now has lost his courage with his blood.
Drake Senior. He foams, and still his tusks does whet,
    As if he still disdained retreat.
Drake Junior. The wound you gave him makes him turn his head   20
    To seek the darker shades, where he was bred.
Page. Follow, follow!

---

   76. *huff*] storm.

   4.4. compass] span, circumference.

   4–7. Pedro . . . seas] A famous episode, in which Drake climbed the lofty tree to see
the Pacific and the Atlantic oceans and 'besought Almighty God of his goodness to give
him life and leave to sail once in an English ship in that sea' (Nichols, p. 300). Drake's
venture into the Pacific led to his circumnavigation from November 1577 to September 1580.

   9. natives] i.e. Peruvians.

   14. *advance*] thrust.

   15. *turn him*] force the boar to turn aside from its assault.

   18. *tusks does whet*] sharpens its tusks (for an attack).

   21. *darker shades*] i.e. the depths of the forest.

Drake Senior. Stay, my victorious boy!
  When a courageous beast does bleed,
  Then learn how far you should proceed   25
  To use advantage where you may destroy.
  To courage even of beasts some pity is due;
  And where resistance fails, cease to pursue.

Enter PEDRO.

Pedro. Our men have firmly stood and swiftly run:
  The game was plenteous and the chase is done.   30
Drake Junior. Pedro in several forms has all
  That everywhere we merit call.
Drake Senior. Wary in war as chiefs grown old;
  And yet in sudden dangers bold.
  Civil and real too in courts;   35
  Painful in business and in sports.
Pedro. Behold that tree which much superior grows
  To all that in this wood
  Have many ages stood:
  Beneath whose shade your warriors may repose.   40
Drake Junior. There let us stay
  And turn our prey
  Into a feast
  Till in the west
  The cypress curtain of the night is drawn;   45
  Then forward march as early as the dawn.
Drake Senior. Is this that most renowned of western trees
  On whose main top
  Thou gavest me hope
  To view the North and South Atlantic seas?   50
Pedro. It is, therefore with speed
  Thither, my chief, proceed:
  And, when your climbing have attained the height,
  Report will grow authentic by your sight.
Drake Senior. When from those lofty branches I   55
  The South Atlantic spy,
  My vows shall higher fly,
  Till they with highest heav'n prevail
  That, as I see it, I may on it sail.

53. your] you *Q, F.*

25–6.] i.e. understand that you should sometimes restrain yourself from killing, although you have the power to do so.
31–2.] i.e. Pedro has all the best human qualities.
35. *Civil*] decent, honourable.
real] honest, loyal.
36. *Painful*] diligent, painstaking.
45. *cypress*] cypress-like; dark, gloomy.
48. *main top*] highest branch.
54. *grow authentic*] be verified.
57. *vows*] prayers.

Drake Junior. No English keel hath yet that ocean ploughed.   60
Pedro. If prophecy from me may be allowed,
    Renownèd Drake, heaven does decree
    That happy enterprise to thee.
    For thou of all the Britons art the first
    That boldly durst   65
    This western world invade;
    And as thou now art made
    The first to whom that ocean will be shown,
    So to thy isle thou first shalt make it known.
Chorus of all. This prophecy will rise   70
    To higher enterprise.
    The English lion's walk shall reach as far
    As prosperous valour dares adventure war;
    As winds can drive, or waves can bear
    Those ships which boldest pilots steer.   *Exeunt.*   75

      [*Enter two* Soldiers *and two* Seamen.]

    This song is sung by two Land Soldiers *and two* Seamen.

           The Song

Seamen. How comes it you landmen, and we of the sea,
    Though oft mixed together, yet seldom agree?

Landmen. A riddle, which we can find out no more
    Than you can, why seas contest with the shore.

Seamen. We give a shrewd guess how our quarrels have grown;   80
    For still when at land we are jointly designed
    To the dainty delight of storming a town,
    You run to the plunder and leave us behind.

Landmen. Alas, our dear brothers! How can we forbear?
    But aboard when you have us, where wonderful gold   85
    Is shovelled like ballast, you are even with us there:
    We fight on the decks, whilst you rummage the hold.

Seamen. But now we shall march where the Diegos (though loath
    To part with it civilly) may soon oblige both.

---

60. *keel*] ridge-like timber at base of ship; here meaning the ship itself.
61–9.] Pedro predicts Drake's circumnavigation.
72–3. *The English . . . war*] i.e. the adventuring of the English shall extend as far as their valour will take them. While a direct reference to Drake's circumnavigation, the line also suggests the Cromwellian policy of overseas expansionism. The lion, representing the British nation, was also an emblem of Oliver Cromwell, as engraved on the arms of the Commonwealth together with the personal motto, 'Peace is sought by war' (see *Peru*, 6.55, note).
81. *designed*] applied, engaged.
82. *dainty*] rare; valuable.
86. *ballast*] heavy material such as gravel, sand or stones placed in the hold of a ship so as to prevent it capsizing.
87. *rummage*] to ransack, search thoroughly the ship's hold.

Landmen. They so much are scared from their wits with their
    dangers   90
    That now they want wit to be civil to strangers.

Chorus of all. Come let us join hands then, and ne'er part asunder,
    But, like the true sons of trusty old mothers,
    Make equally haste to a snap of the plunder,
    Then justly divide and spend it like brothers.   95

    This song being ended, the two land soldiers and the two seamen
        dance a jig, to intimate their future agreement.
                                        [Exit Seamen *and* Soldiers.]

FIFTH ENTRY

*This entry is prepared by an air and coranto; and then the scene is
changed: in which is discovered the rising of the sun through a thick
wood, and Venta-Cruz at great distance on the south side. Which being
discerned a while,*

          Enter DRAKE SENIOR, DRAKE JUNIOR, Page, Soldier.

Drake Junior. Bold Rouse, doubting our safety by our stay,   5
    Thinking his patience longer than our way,
    And having well secured our port,
    Our trenches digged, and raised our fort,
    Is here arrived, resolving still to be
    A sharer in your worser destiny.   10
    He was conducted by a Symeron;
    And bows for what his rasher love has done.
Drake Senior. I shall be very slow
    When I must backward go,
    With punishment to overtake   15
    The errors which my friend did make.

95.2. agreement] *Q*; amity *F.*

90–1.] They are so far out of their minds with terror that they have lost the good
sense to treat foreigners with courtesy (ironic, i.e. 'they are so frightened that they don't
realize it is in their best interests to hand over the gold with good grace').
    94. *to a snap . . . plunder*] i.e. to snatch a share of the booty.
    95.2. jig] a lively country dance in compound duple or triple time.

    5.1. coranto] a tune in triple time, usually accompanying a dance, but here there is
no dancing.
    5. *Bold Rouse*] Davenant represents Ranse in an heroic light and as loyal to Drake.
Ranse had in fact withdrawn earlier from the expedition when it lay at Port Plenty, Isle
of Pines. 'Captain Ranse forecasting diverse doubts of our safe continuance upon that
coast, being now discovered, was willing to depart; and our captain no less willing to
dismiss him' (Nichols, p. 270).
    12. *bows . . . done*] i.e. submits himself to your mercy for his reckless actions which
were inspired by his love for you.
    13–20.] i.e. Drake is unwilling to punish his friend for his mistaken judgement when
it cannnot be remedied and is ready to greet him with affection despite his error.

Tell him I know his fault is past;
And now I cannot but go fast
When I shall forward move
To meet approaching love.   20

Exit Soldier.

The morn begins her glory in the east;
And now the world prepares
To entertain new cares,
Though the old sufficed to hinder all our rest.
Drake Junior. Benighted seamen now their course reform   25
Who, coasting, were misguided by a storm.
Now merchants to imported stowage haste,
Whilst ploughmen drive from cottages their teams.
The poor in cities rise to toil and fast;
And lovers grieve to leave their pleasant dreams.   30
Drake Senior. Be careful not to let
The camp's reveille beat
To make our warriors rise and move:
But as heaven's traveller above
Unheard begins, and silently his way   35
Does still continue 'til he perfects day,
So all this progress must be calmly made.
The winds, which still unseen
Have in their motion been,
Oft pass without a whisper through the shade.   40
Drake Junior. Each, duteous as your slave,
Does to your orders grow;
And all, as in the grave,
Are hushed and private now.
Drake Senior. Ere we begin to march, send out   45
The Symerons again to scout.
Let not our wings be loosely spread;
The van I'll at some distance lead.
Those who the baggage bear
Let Pedro still relieve, and close   50
Secure their haltings in our gross.
You shall command the rear.

Enter ROUSE.

Rouse. Arm, arm! make haste, and bring me to my chief!
Drake Senior. What great distress does hasten for relief?

---

25. *Benighted*] overtaken by the darkness.
26. *misguided*] driven off-course.
27. *stowage*] cargo goods stored in a warehouse.
28. *teams*] i.e. of oxen.
32. *reveille*] military waking signal.
34. *heaven's traveller*] i.e. the sun.
47.] i.e. the flanks of soldiers should remain close to the main body of the force.
48. *van*] foremost division of a military force.
50–1. *close . . . gross*] i.e. protect [the baggage carriers] by stationing them within the main body of the army.

Rouse. I come not now thy pardon to receive,   55
  Because my rasher love without thy leave
  Durst venture for a share
  Of thy mishaps in war.
Drake Senior. What wildness more
  Than I have seen before   60
  In deserts openly exposed,
  Or woods with ancient growth of shades enclosed,
  Or seas, when nought but lightning has appeared
  And only thunder and the winds were heard,
  Does now thy wondering looks possess?   65
Drake Junior. What more than yet thou canst express?
Rouse. Drake, thy beloved renown is lost,
  Of which thy nation used to boast:
  Since now, where thou a sword dost wear,
  And many marks of power dost bear,   70
  The worst of licence does best laws invade.
  For beauty is an abject captive made;
  Even whilst those flowery ornaments are worn
  Which should the bridal dignity adorn.
  If thus the crowd be suffered to deride   75
  The sacred rites and honours of a bride,
  Let savage war devour all civil peace,
  Love fly from courts to camps, and sexes cease.
Drake Senior. Thy mystic meaning thou dost less
  By words than by thy looks express.   80
Drake Junior. That we may better know
  Thy thoughts, make haste to show
  The object of our wonder, and thy fear.
Rouse. Turn your unhappy eyes, and see it there.

The scene is suddenly changed into the former prospect of the rising of   85
the morning, and Venta Cruz; but, about the middle, it is varied with
the discovery of a beautiful lady tied to a tree, adorned with the
ornaments of a bride, with her hair dishevelled, and complaining with
her hands towards heaven: near her are likewise discerned the Symerons
who took her prisoner.   90

---

89. near her] *Q*; about her *F*.

---

 58. *mishaps*] misfortunes.
 59–60. *more . . . before*] i.e. more than I have ever seen.
 65. *wondering*] astonished, appalled.
 66.] i.e. what more (than your looks have already expressed) can you tell us?
 69–71. *where . . . invade*] Despite the presence of Drake and the might of his army (i.e.
as upholders of the rule of law), the greatest abuse of good governance has taken place.
 75. *suffered*] allowed.
 78. *sexes*] i.e. affections.
 79. *mystic*] concealed.
 85–90.] This scene has no basis in fact. Although the father and the groom do appear
on stage, the lady is part of the scenic representation.
 86–90. but, about . . . prisoner] presumably a relieve design, as used in the Second
Entry and in *The Siege of Rhodes*, p. 192 n. 19. See Orrell, p. 76.

Drake Senior. What dismal beauty does amaze my sight,
    Which from black sorrow breaks like morn from night?
    And though it sweetest beauty be,
    Does seem more terrible to me
    Than all the sudden and the various forms   95
    Which death does wear in battles and in storms.
Rouse. A party of your Symerons (whose eyes
    Pierce through the darkness which does night disguise,
    Whom weary toils might sleepy make,
    But that revenge keeps them awake)   100
    Did ere the early dawning rise,
    And close by Venta Cruz surprise
    A bride and bridegroom at their nuptial feast,
    To whom the Symerons now
    Much more than fury show;   105
    For they have all those cruelties expressed
    That Spanish pride could e'er provoke from them
    Or Moorish malice can revenge esteem.
Drake Senior. Arm! arm! the honour of my nation turns
    To shame, when an afflicted beauty mourns.   110
    Though here these cruel Symerons exceed
    Our number, yet they are too few to bleed
    When honour must revengeful be
    For this affront to love and me.
Drake Junior. Our forces of the land,   115
    Brave chief, let me command.
Drake Senior. March on! whilst with my seamen I advance,
    Let none, before the dice are cast, despair,
    Nor after they are thrown, dislike the chance;
    For honour throws at all, and still plays fair.   120
Rouse. In beauty's noble cause no seaman doubt,
    If poets may authentic be.
    For sea-born Venus' sake, let them march out:
    She leads them both at land and sea.
Drake Senior. Long yet ere night   125
    I shall in fight

---

98. the darkness] *Q;* that darkness *F.*

---

91. *dismal*] miserable, doleful.
    amaze] overwhelm with wonder.
    106–8.] i.e. for they have treated [the wedding party] with a barbarity such as they would only ever inflict upon Spaniards, or such as their hatred [malice] could inflict upon the pride of their enemies. As is later evident (line 170), the wedding party is Spanish.
    106. *expressed*] manifested, revealed.
    118. *before . . . cast*] i.e. before we act.
    120.] i.e. honour affords everyone the same chance to succeed.
    122. *authentic*] truthful.
    123. *sea-born Venus*] Venus, goddess of love, alleged by Hesiod to have sprung from the foam of the sea.
    124.] The sailors are inspired by love (Venus), both when at sea and on dry land.

Their stormy courage prove.
Each seaman hath his mermaid too;
And by instinct must love,
Though he were never taught to woo.   130

Enter PEDRO.

Pedro. Stay! stay! successful chief! my heart as low
As the foundation where thou treadst does bow.
But 'tis not for my own offence;
For if I should offend
My king, in thee his friend,   135
I would not with my self dispense.
Thy mercy shall our pattern be.
Behold, the afflicted bride is free.

*The scene is suddenly changed again, where the lady is vanished, and
nothing appears but that prospect which was in the beginning of the*   140
Entry.

She is as free and as unblemished too
As if she had a prisoner been to you.
Drake Senior. What are they who, disguised in night's dark shade,
Unlicensed, from our camp this sally made?   145
Straight to the stroke of justice bring me those!
Pedro. They thought their duties were to take their foes.
Be merciful, and censure the offence
To be but their mistaken diligence.
Drake Junior. Suspect not Pedro in this crime, who still   150
Has shown exact obedience to thy will.
Pedro. And noble chief, the cruelties which they
Have often felt beneath the Spaniards' sway
(Who, midst the triumphs of our nuptial feasts,
Have forced our brides and slaughtered all our guests)   155
May some excuse even from your reason draw:
Revenge does all the fetters break of law.
Drake Senior. The future guidance and the care
Of their demeanour in this war

147. were] was *Q, F.*

---

127. *prove*] put to the test.
128.] The sailors have their lovers, the mythical mermaids or sirens.
132. *foundation*] ground.
136–7.] i.e. I would not seek to excuse myself, but depend on you for mercy.
142. *unblemished*] unharmed.
145. *sally*] sortie, assault.
147. *their foes*] i.e. the Spanish.
149. *mistaken diligence*] over-zealousness.
155. *forced*] taken forcibly, raped.
156. *reason*] judgement.
157.] i.e. revenge ignores the constraints of the law.
159. *demeanour*] behaviour.

Is strictly, Pedro, left to thee: 160
The gentle sex must still be free.
No length of studied torments shall suffice
To punish all unmanly cruelties.
March on! they may ere night redeem
By virtuous valour my esteem.
    Exeunt DRAKE SENIOR, DRAKE JUNIOR, ROUSE *and* Page. 165
Pedro. Ho! ho! the prisoners straight unbind,
 And let the bride all homage find;
 The father and the bridegroom hither bring.
 Ere yet our van shall far advance,
 Know, Diegos, you must dance.   170
 Strike up, strike up! in honour of my king.

*Enter the father of the bride and her bridegroom; the bridegroom
dancing with castanets to express the joy he receives for his liberty,
whilst the father moves to his measures, denoting the fright he had
received from the Symerons, when he was surprised at his nuptial* 175
entertainment.
   [*Exit* PEDRO, *the father of the bride and the bridegroom.*]

SIXTH ENTRY

*This entry is prepared with a martial air, and presently the scene is
changed; wherein is discovered the prospect of a hilly country, with the
town Panama at a distance, and recoes of mules in a long train, loaden
with wedges of silver and ingots of gold and travelling in several roads
down a mountain. There likewise may be discerned their drivers and* 5
guards.

   Enter DRAKE SENIOR, DRAKE JUNIOR, Page.

Drake Junior. The reco is not yet within our ken.
Drake Senior. It will be straight. Draw up our men,
 And in low whispers give our orders out.
Drake Junior. Where's Pedro now?   10
Drake Senior. Upon the brow
 Of that high hill: I sent him there to scout.

---

173. *castanets*] *This ed.;* castanietos *Q, F.*

---

 164. *redeem*] recover.
 170. *Diegos*] confirmation that the wedding party was Spanish.
 174. *measures*] dance steps.

 6.1–6. *the scene . . . guards*] The final entry depicts an apocryphal ambush of a mule
train travelling from Panama. In fact, the plan failed when one of the English soldiers
mistakenly attempted to capture a mule train travelling *to* Panama (i.e. one which had
not yet collected the gold or silver from Peru).
 7. *ken*] range of sight.
 8. *straight*] immediately, without delay.

Enter ROUSE.

Rouse. Chief, we are all into a body drawn,
    And now an hour is wasted since the dawn.
Drake Senior. The time will yet suffice. We halted here   15
    To stay for our tired baggage in the rear.
Rouse. If aught from new resolves thou wilt command,
    Speak, chief, we now in expectation stand.
Drake Senior. If English courage could at all be raised
    By being well persuaded, or much praised,   20
    Speech were of use: but valour born, not bred,
    Cannot by art (since being so,
    It does as far as Nature go)
    Be higher lifted, or be farther led.
    All I would speak, should tell you, I despise   25
    That treasure which I now would make your prize:
    Unworthy 'tis to be your chiefest aim.
    For this attempt is not for gold, but fame;
    Which is not got when we the reco get,
    But by subduing those who rescue it.   30

Enter a Soldier.

Soldier. Pedro descends the hill, and does desire
    That from this open plain you would retire,
    And wheel behind that wood a little space.
Drake Senior. Divide our forces to secure the pass.   *Exeunt.*

Enter DRAKE JUNIOR, *a* Soldier, ROUSE *and a* Mariner, *the soldier
and mariner being brought to be placed as sentries.*

Drake Junior. This must your station be;   35
    Stand steadfast as that tree!
Rouse. Bravely alive upon this ground,
    Or greater else in death be found.
                Exeunt DRAKE JUNIOR *and* ROUSE.
        The bells of the mules are heard from within.

Mariner. Mules! mules! I hear their walking chime, ting, ting!
    They love sad tunes, how dolefully they ring.   40
Soldier. This sound seems single, and from far does come.
    Would I were leading one rich mule at home.

---

17. aught] ought *Q, F.*

    14. *is wasted*] has been lost.
    16.] i.e. to wait until those carrying the baggage had caught up.
    17–18] i.e. if you want to change any of your plans, we are ready to receive your command.
    29–30.] i.e. there is glory not in capturing the mule train, but in defeating the Spanish when they try to recover it.
    33. *wheel*] move, turn (in curving or circular motion).
    41. *single*] solitary.

Mariner. Still one and all I cry.
Soldier. The rest are passing by.
    Hark! hark! this mournful tolling does foretell   45
    Some Diego's death, it is his passing bell.

    Enter PEDRO, *leading a* Symeron *to be placed as a sentry.*

Pedro. Here Symeron, you must bold and watchful be.
    Two foes resist, but if oppressed by three,
    Then straight fall back to that next sentry there:
    Or if in gross the enemy does appear,   50
    Both to the third retirement make,
    Till we the alarm, advancing, take.
Mariner. Friend Pedro, friend! Is it one and all?
Pedro. Speak softly, sentry, dost thou call?
Mariner. How many golden recoes didst thou spy?   55
Pedro. But two in which I guess,
    By distant view, no less
    Than ninety loaden mules are passing by.
Mariner. What number is their guard who march before?
Pedro. Five hundred foot, their horse may seem threescore.
                                    Exit [PEDRO].   60
Soldier. Friend of the sea, their number is not small.
Mariner. I will serve our turn, they crying one and all!
    But brother of the land,
    We now must understand
    That 'Basta' is the word!   65
Soldier. Would thou were safe aboard.
Mariner. Asleep under deck, and danced on a billow
    With two silver wedges, each for my pillow.
                      [*A volley of shots is heard.*]

    Enter DRAKE SENIOR, *with his sword drawn.*

Drake Senior. That volley was well fired!
    Our outguards are retired.   70
    Draw all our sentries in!
    The skirmish does begin.   *Exit.*
          Clashing of arms is heard afar off.

    Enter DRAKE JUNIOR.

---

  43. *one and all*] all together, each and everyone.
  45–6. *does . . . bell*] i.e. anticipates the murder of a Spaniard.
  50. *in gross*] in a mass.
  51. *retirement*] stage in retreat.
  52. *the alarm . . . take*] take warning of the danger ahead.
  62. *I will . . . turn*] i.e. I will play my part.
  64–5.] i.e. this is all we came for.
  65. *Basta*] 'Enough!', referring to the plunder to be taken.
  67. *billow*] wave, swell.
  68. *wedges*] ingots.
  70. *outguards*] advance guards.

Drake Junior. More pikes! More pikes to reinforce
    That squadron, and repulse the horse.

Enter ROUSE.

Rouse. The foe does make his first bold countenance good.   75
    Our charge was bravely made, and well withstood.

Enter PEDRO.

Rouse. Your Symerons, valiant Pedro, seem to reel.
Pedro. Suspect your rocks at sea. They do but wheel.
    Haste! haste! brave Symerons, haste to gain that bank,
    And with your arrows gall them in the flank.   *Exeunt.*   80
Clashing of arms within again.

Enter DRAKE SENIOR, Page.

Drake Senior. How warmly was this strife
    Maintained 'twixt death and life,
    Till blood had quenched the flame of valour's fire.
    Death seeming to advance in haste,
    Whilst life, though weary, yet stood fast;   85
    For life is still unwilling to retire.
    My landmen bravely fought
    And high renown have got,
    For twice my seamen they from death relieved.
    As oft my seamen have   90
    Preserved them from the grave,
    And did requite the rescue they received.

Enter DRAKE JUNIOR.

Drake Junior. They fly! they fly! yet now they seem to face
    All those who them pursue,
    And would the fight renew.   95

Enter ROUSE and PEDRO.

Rouse. They fly, they fly!
Drake Senior. Away, make good the chase.
Exeunt omnes.
Chorus of all within. Follow, follow, follow!

Enter DRAKE SENIOR, DRAKE JUNIOR, ROUSE, PEDRO, Page.

---

   73. *pikes*] the soldiers' main weapon, a long wooden shaft with a pointed head of iron.
   74. *squadron*] small detachment [of soldiers].
   75. *make . . . good*] i.e. make an impressive show of courage.
   77. *reel*] waver.
   78. *suspect . . . sea*] i.e. you would sooner believe that rocks might move than that the Symerons would retreat.
   80. *gall*] assault, attack.
   flank] side, i.e. the wing of the Spanish formation.
   81. *warmly*] fiercely, vigorously.

Pedro. The mules are seized, and in our power remain.
Drake Senior. Draw out new guards, and range them in the plain.   100
　　Those who hereafter on our legend look
　　And value us by that which we have took
　　May over-reckon it, and us misprise.
　　Our dangerous course through storms and raging floods,
　　And painful march through unfrequented woods,   105
　　Will make those wings by which our fame shall rise.
　　Your glory, valiant English, must be known,
　　When men shall read how you did dare
　　To sail so long and march so far,
　　To tempt a strength much greater than your own.   110
Drake Junior. And now by making our retreat
　　We shall new wreaths and statues get.

　　　　　The grand chorus, first sung by DRAKE SENIOR.

Drake Senior. Our course let's to victorious England steer!
　　Where, when our sails shall on the coast appear,
　　Those who from rocks and steeples spy   115
　　Our streamers out, and colours fly,
　　Will cause the bells to ring,
　　Whilst cheerfully they sing
　　Our story, which shall their example be
　　And make succession cry, to sea, to sea.   120
　　　　　[The song is repeated by Chorus of all.]
　　　　　　　　　　　　Exeunt omnes.

*The grand dance begins, consisting of two land soldiers, two seamen,
two Symerons and a Peruvian; intimating, by their several interchange
of salutations, their mutual desires of amity. The dance being ended,*

　　　　　　　　The curtain falls.

　　　　　　　　　　Finis

113. Drake Senior] Chorus of all *Q and F.*   123. The dance being ended ... Finis]
Q; not in F.

―――――――――――――――――――――――――――――――――――

　99. *The mules ... seized*] The mule train with its riches has been captured.
　101. *legend*] story (of our exploits).
　103. *May ... misprise*] i.e. our achievement is not to be measured only by the value
of the plunder.
　over-reckon] over-estimate.
　us misprise] under-estimate us (i.e. the nature of our achievement).
　110. *tempt*] test.
　111. *retreat*] withdrawal (to return to England).
　116. *colours*] the flag or standard of the ship.
　120. *succession*] posterity.
　121. grand dance] The term is reminiscent of the final dance of the masque, although
here it is evident that there was no audience participation.

APPENDIX 1
Song from the Second Entry of *Cupid and Death*

This setting for the song at the close of the Second Entry of *Cupid and Death*, 'Victorious Men of Earth', was written by Christopher Gibbons for the production of the masque in 1653 and printed separately in the same year. Reprinted from *Musica Britannica*, Volume II. Copyright The Musica Britannica Trust. Reproduced by kind permission of Stainer & Bell Ltd., London, England.

Sop.

Vic - to - rious men of Earth, no more Pro - claim how wide your em - pires

are; Though you bind in ev -'ry shore, And your tri - umphs reach as

far As night or day, Yet you proud mon - archs must o - bey, And min - gle with for - got - ten

ash - es, when Death calls ye to the crowd of com - mon men. De - vour - ing

fa - mine, plague, and war, Each a - ble to un - do man - kind,

Death's ser - vile e - mis - sa - ries are; Nor____ to these a - lone con - fin'd.

He hath at will more quaint and sub - tle ways to kill; A smile, or kiss, as he will

use____ the Art, Shall have the cun - ning____ skill to____ break____ a heart.

APPENDIX 2
Additional passages from the enlarged version of *The Siege of Rhodes* (1663)

The positions of these additional passages from Q3 and F of *Siege of Rhodes* are indicated in the collation notes.

FIRST ENTRY, line 95.1]

          Enter IANTHE, MELOSILE, MADINA
     (her two women) bearing two open caskets with jewels.

Ianthe. To Rhodes this fatal fleet her course does bear.
    Can I have love, and not discover fear?
    When he, in whom my plighted heart doth live
    (Whom Hymen gave me in reward
    Of vows, which he with favour heard, 5
    And is the greatest gift he e'er can give)
    Shall in a cruel siege imprisoned be,
    And I, whom love has bound, have liberty!
    Away! Let's leave our flourishing abodes
    In Sicily, and fly to with'ring Rhodes. 10
Melosile. Will you convert to instruments of war,
    To things which to our sex so dreadful are,
    Which terror add to Death's detested face,
    These ornaments which should your beauty grace?
Madina. Beauty laments! and this exchange abhors! 15
    Shall all these gems in arms be spent
    Which were by bounteous princes sent
    To pay the valour of your ancestors?
Ianthe. If by their sale my Lord may be redeemed,
    Why should they more than trifles be esteemed, 20
    Vainly secured with iron bars and locks?
    They are the spawn of shells and warts of rocks.
Madina. All Madam, all? Will you from all depart?
Ianthe. Love a consumption learns from chemists' art.
    Sapphires, and harder diamonds must be sold 25
    And turned to softer and more current gold.
    With gold we cursèd powder may prepare
    Which must consume in smoke and thinner air.
Melosile. Thou idol-Love, I'll worship thee no more
    Since thou dost make us sorrowful and poor. 30
Ianthe. Go seek out cradles and with childhood dwell;
    Where you may still be free
    From love's self-flattery,
    And never hear mistaken lovers tell

Of blessings and of joys in such extremes   35
As never are possessed but in our dreams.
They woo apace, and hasten to be sped,
And praise the quiet of the marriage-bed;
But mention not the storms of grief and care
When love does them surprise   40
With sudden jealousies,
Or they are sever'd by ambitious war.
Madina. Love may perhaps the foolish please:
But he shall quickly leave my heart
When he persuades me to depart   45
From such a hoard of precious things as these.
Ianthe. Send out to watch the wind! With the first gale
I'll leave thee Sicily and, hoisting sail,
Steer straight to Rhodes. For love and I must be
Preserved (Alphonso!), or else lost with thee.   *Exeunt.*   50

THIRD ENTRY, 215.1]

Enter ROXOLANA, PIRRHUS, RUSTAN.

Rustan. You come from sea as Venus came before;
And seem that goddess, but mistake her shore.
Pirrhus. Her temple did in fruitful Cyprus stand;
The Sultan wonders why in Rhodes you land.
Rustan. And by your sudden voyage he doth fear   5
The tempest of your passion drove you here.
Roxolana. Rustan, I bring you more wonder than I find;
And it is more than humour bred that wind
Which with a forward gale
Did make me hither sail.   10
Rustan. He does your forward jealousy reprove.
Roxolana. Yet jealousy does spring from too much love;
If mine be guilty of excess,
I dare pronounce it shall grow less.
Pirrhus. You boldly threaten more than we dare hear.   15
Roxolana. That which you call your duty is your fear.
Rustan. We have some valour or our wounds are feigned.
Roxolana. What has your valour from the Rhodians gained?
Unless Ianthe, as a prize, you boast;
Who now has got that heart which I have lost.   20
Brave conquest where the taker's self is taken!
And, as a present, I
Bring vainly ere I die
That heart to him which he has now forsaken.
Rustan. Whispers of eunuchs, and by pages brought   25
To Licia, you have up to story wrought.
Roxolana. Lead to the Sultan's tent! Pirrhus, away!
For I dare hear what he himself dares say.   *Exeunt.*

FOURTH ENTRY, 176.1]

Enter ROXOLANA, PIRRHUS, RUSTAN, *and two of her women.*

Roxolana. Not come to see me ere th'assault be past?
Pirrhus. He spoke it not in anger but in haste.
Rustan. If mighty Solyman be angry grown,
    It is not with his empress but the town.
Roxolana. When stubborn Rhodes does to him anger move,   5
    'Tis by detaining there what he does love.
Pirrhus. He is resolved the city to destroy.
Roxolana. But more resolv'd Ianthe to enjoy.
Rustan. T'avoid your danger, cease your jealousy.
Roxolana. Tell them of danger who do fear to die.   10
Pirrhus. None but yourself dares threaten you with death.
1. Woman. Do not your beauty blast with your own breath.
2. Woman. You lessen't in your own esteem
    When of his love you jealous seem.
1. Woman. And but a faded beauty make it   15
    When you suspect he can forsake it.
2. Woman. Believe not, Empress, that you are decay'd,
    For so you'll seem by jealous passion sway'd.
Roxolana. He follows passion, I pursue my reason:
    He loves the traitor, and I hate the treason.   20

Enter HALY.

Haly. Our foes appear! Th'assault will straight begin.
Pirrhus, Rustan (in chorus). They sally out where we must enter in.
Roxolana. Let Solyman forget his way to glory;
    Increase in conquest and grow less in story.   25
    That honour which in vain
    His valour shrinks to gain,
    When from the Rhodians he Ianthe takes,
    Is lost in losing me whom he forsakes.   *Exeunt several ways.*

FIFTH ENTRY, 269.1]

Alphonso. Be not too rash, Ianthe, to forgive.
    Who knows but I ill use may make
    Of pardons which I could not take
    For they may move me to desire to live.
Ianthe. If ought can make Ianthe worthy grow   5
    Of having power of pardoning you
    It is because she perfectly doth know
    That no such power to her is due
    Who never can forget herself, since she
    Unkindly did resent your jealousy.   10
    A passion against which you nobly strove.
    I know it was but over-cautious love.
Alphonso. Accursed crime! Oh! let it have no name
    Till I recover blood to show my shame.

Ianthe. Why stay we at such distance when we treat?   15
    As monarchs' children, making love
    By proxy, to each other move,
    And by advice of tedious councils meet.

FIFTH ENTRY, 273.1]

    Enter [SOLYMAN,] ROXOLANA *and women attendants.*

Solyman. Your looks express a triumph at our loss.
Roxolana. Can I forsake the Crescent for the Cross?
Solyman. You wish my spreading Crescent shrunk to less.
Roxolana. Sultan, I would not lose by your success.
Solyman. You are a friend to the besiegers grown?   5
Roxolana. I wish your sword may thrive,
    Yet would not have you strive
    To take Ianthe rather than the town.
Solyman. Too much on wand'ring Rumour you rely;
    Your foolish women teach you jealousy.   10
1. Woman. We should too blindly confident appear,
    If, when the Empress fears, we should not fear.
2. Woman. The camp does breed that loud report
    Which wakens Echo in the Court.
1. Woman. The world our duty will approve,   15
    If, for our mistress' sake,
    We ever are awake
    To watch the wand'rings of your love.
Solyman. My war with Rhodes will never have success
    Till I at home, Roxana, make my peace.   20
    I will be kind if you'll grow wise;
    Go, chide your whisp'rers and your spies.
    Be satisfied with liberty to think;
    And, when you should not see me, learn to wink.   [*Exeunt.*]

INDEX

The Index lists subjects and topics which are referred to in the General Introduction and the specific Introductions to the texts, or which receive particular attention in the Commentary.

Note: 'n' after a page reference indicates the line number of an annotation on that page. Where an annotation relates to a number of lines (e.g. lines 9–12 on page 148), the reference is to the first of those lines (i.e. 148n.9). Page numbers in *italic* refer to illustrations.

Channen, Luke 155, 156, 160n.4,
180n.148.1
Chapman, George, *Bussy
d'Ambois* 44
Charing Cross, performance at 22
Charles I, King of England 17,
20, 24, 27, 46, 183–4,
186, 237
execution of 19–20, 35
Charles Stuart (Charles II, King of
England) 21, 23, 27, 46,
47, 268n.11
Cicero, Marcus Tullius 28, 41–6
background 42, 52n.2, 57n.13,
113n.24, 148n.9
death of 148n.5.10.2
De Finibus 59n.69, 133n.90
De Natura Deorum 45
De Officiis 28
First Catilinarian 63n.166
misjudgement of Octavius 42–4
parens patriae 113n.24
Philippics 42–3, 58n.16,
88n.2.3.1, 98n.3.3.4,
148n.9
and *pietas* 45–6
proscription of 46
Tusculan Disputations 28,
122n.4.5.1
Works (edited by Dionysius
Lambinus) 42
see also *Tragedy of That
Famous Orator Marcus
Tullius Cicero, The*
Cicero, Quintus (the elder) 44,
52n.3, 140n.11
Cicero, Quintus (the younger) 45,
58n.35, 140n.11
Claypole, Lady Elizabeth 29, 48
closet drama 18–21
Cockpit theatre 3, 4, 6, 186, 187,
191, 194n.16, 235, 239,
247n.78, 263
Coleman, Catherine 35
Coleman, Charles 232n.15
Coleman, Edward 232n.4

commonwealth
denoting State 65n.222,
146n.132
model represented in *Oceana*
47–9
Commonwealth 154, 182
contested meaning 25–6
context of *Siege of Rhodes* 184
Council of State 7, 29, 155,
163n.42
creation of, in *The Famous
Tragedy of King Charles I*
17–18
drolls and interludes 21–3
expansionist policies 32–3,
284n.72
dramatic innovation during 35
pamphlet plays 17
restriction of drama 1–7
revival of theatre 29–35, 153
royalist drama 23–4, 26–9
warnings in *Cicero* 24, 47, 49
see also Republic, English
Concealed Fancies, The 7
Consort of Musicke 156, 157n.4
Cooke, Henry 186, 232n.2
Cooke, William 4
Corneille, Pierre
Horatius 19
Polyeuctes 19, 20
Cowley, Abraham 266
Cox, Robert, *John Swabber the
Seaman* 22
Crafty Cromwell 10, 11–12
Crassus, Marcus Licinius 119n.17
Cromwell, Oliver 10, 17, 27, 29,
46, 47–9, 153, 182, 183,
263
character in *Crafty Cromwell*
12
character in *Newmarket Fair*
12–13
colonial policy 235–7, 263,
266, 284n.72
comparisons with Julius Caesar
27–8, 47, 49